STEPHEN COLE

HOCKEY NIGHT FEVER

MULLETS, MAYHEM AND THE GAME'S COMING OF AGE IN THE 1970S

**Doubleday
Canada**

Doubleday Canada and colophon are registered trademarks of Random House of Canada Limited

Library and Archives Canada Cataloguing in Publication

Cole, Stephen, author
    Hockey night fever : mullets, mayhem and the game's coming of age / Stephen Cole.

Issued in print and electronic formats.
ISBN 978-0-385-68212-1 (bound).—ISBN 978-0-385-68213-8 (epub)

    1. Hockey--History. I. Title.

GV846.5.C63 2015   796.96209   C2015-901975-3
                                                       C2015-901976-1

Cover and text design: Andrew Roberts
Cover images: (Bobby Clarke and Ken Dryden) Bruce Bennett Studios; (Phil Esposito) Tony Triolo / *Sports Illustrated*; (game) Melchior DiGiacomo. All from Getty Images. Printed and bound in the USA

Published in Canada by Doubleday Canada,
a division of Random House of Canada Limited,
a Penguin Random House Company

www.penguinrandomhouse.ca

10 9 8 7 6 5 4 3 2 1

Penguin
Random House
DOUBLEDAY CANADA

To Frank and Frances

Contents

PART TWO: CLOCKWORK ORANGE
Philadelphia Flyers (1969–76)

PART THREE: *LES GLORIEUX*
Montreal Canadiens (1932–79)

FOREWORD

OBJECTS IN THE REAR-VIEW MIRROR

I f you were there at the time, a bell-bottomed kid living and dying with a favourite National Hockey League team, you'll know why a return ticket to the 1970s might be a welcome, thrilling journey. Like, oh boy, turning back the clock and reuniting with your first girlfriend, if only for a little while. Hockey at the time was an astonishing, decade-long surprise party. Bobby Orr, a teenager, one of our tribe, had taken over what was North America's most conservative, stodgy sport in 1966, changing everything. Soon, a series of big-haired baby boomers, from Brad Park to Guy Lafleur to some kid named Wayne Gretzky, would follow in his jet stream.

And talk about *boom!* Hockey in the 1970s was as passionate and violent as the music, movies and politics that define the era.

Oh no, more punishing geezer nostalgia, you may be thinking. Some old fart saying everything was better *once upon a time*. Why should anyone under 40 care about games now decades old? Because it says here that if you truly want to understand and appreciate modern hockey, which I would argue is better—faster, smarter and more competitive—than ever, you need to understand the sport's wild, formative years. If the child is father to the man, the wilful, hungry adolescent is the barely supressed self who still calls the shots when duty calls.

NHL expansion was first contemplated in 1963. The league doubled in size (to 12 teams) in 1967. In coming years, hockey would experience a crazy, difficult-to-predict—or fathom—growth spurt. All the major characteristics of the modern game—the calculated aggression, furious pace, preoccupation with size and reliance on analytics—arrived in the turbulent, pell-mell '70s.

That's why it's important to understand what happened to hockey at the time, to feel or re-experience the cold-shower shock of all the surprises. The perpetually last-place, presumably doomed Boston Bruins, led by the aforementioned Orr, winning the Stanley Cup in 1970! Two years later, a Russian hockey team—mere amateurs, it was said—clobbering NHL all-stars in Montreal. And then, a month later, those same professionals, chastened, bent on revenge, accomplishing something Napoleon never managed: capturing Moscow.

Yes, international hockey, our intermittent obsession, began with a clash of cymbals in the '70s. With a clash of symbols, too—Team Canada vs. the Soviet Union was advertised as a contest between good and evil. It goes without saying that both sides figured their opponents were the bad guys. Another surprise, although it wouldn't sink in for a while: the country that would benefit most from the collision of hockey-playing nations would be Bobby Orr's adopted homeland, the United States, now the sport's youngest superpower.*

The good-vs.-evil stuff didn't end with international hockey. Making the battle for NHL supremacy—the playoffs—an even more potent adventure, two very different NHL superpowers emerged in the mid-'70s. Incredibly, the Philadelphia Flyers, a seven-year-old expansion team full of agitated, twitchy bruisers—the Dirty Two Dozen, if you will—won the Stanley Cup in consecutive years before facing the

---

* The biggest ever American TV audience for a hockey game remains the evening rerun of the 1980 Winter Games upset of the Soviet Uniion national team by the United States, represented by an unlikely, overachieving group of collegians. The Miracle on Ice attracted 34.2 million viewers.

Montreal Canadiens in the 1976 playoff finals. The Habs were seen as standard bearers for "old-fashioned" hockey—the heroic, gallant Flying Frenchmen. In truth, they too were something new. The Broad Street Bullies, as the Flyers were then and are still known, won by bending the rules and changing how the game was played—being more aggressive, playing faster, turning lines over more quickly, than opponents. The Canadiens would succeed by mounting a carefully plotted counter-insurgency, compiling a bigger, faster, younger team than the Flyers.

They turned the game up another notch.

Both teams practised harder than anyone else (except maybe the luckless New York Rangers). Under coach Freddy Shero, the Flyers were the first NHL team to build a weight room and to perform calisthenics on ice. They worked endlessly on a defensive system, memorizing breakout patterns and plays that would become ingrained, automatic. Montreal's coach, Scotty Bowman, an obsessive strategist so familiar with performance numbers—who did what against certain lines—that he would be nicknamed "Rain Man," attacked the Flyers by mixing and matching lines on the fly.

It could be argued that every modern Stanley Cup final is a return to the 1976 Habs–Flyers confrontation—chess played with explosives.

Seventies hockey remains with us in practice and in spirit. Every January, there is a nationally televised all-star prospects game held in Canada. The country's best teenagers play for scouts, fans and fun. The coaches are always the same: the True North's patron saints of shinny, Bobby Orr and Don Cherry—both '70s hockey guys forever. Scotty Bowman remains an advisor to what is the NHL's most successful team, the Chicago Blackhawks. Son Stan Bowman is the general manager.

In some essential ways, '70s hockey never ended. That is why games and players from so long ago remain relevant. Yes, objects in the rear-view mirror are often closer than they seem.

PROLOGUE

LADY BYNG DIED IN BOSTON

Everyone stared. Why was he coming to class with an overripe plum spilling from his eye?

Oh no, that *was* his eye!

He was an Ottawa 67. I forget his name. It was the spring of 1971. Other junior hockey players went to Glebe Collegiate in Ottawa. Wayne Merrick, later a star with the New York Islanders, was in science class with me. Mr. Plum hardly ever made it to art class—maybe because it was first period, too early for a kid getting home late from games in Sudbury or Windsor. Days earlier, he evidently showed up for a match with the London Knights. Ottawa–London playoffs were wars—fights, stick-swinging out of Robin Hood, young blood everywhere. A reporter even then, I pressed for details.

"Aw, two guys got me in a corner."

"Going to play tonight?"

"Don't know. My mom says I shunt play anymore."

Derek Sanderson became a National Hockey League player because his dad was impressed by a *Maclean's* magazine article declaring hockey to be Canada's most admired profession. That was back when Louis St. Laurent was prime minister. The '50s. Twenty years later, it was a different story: the '70s saw 16 NHL players arrested for on-ice mayhem. Later in the decade, Ontario's attorney general held a formal investigation into hockey violence. To this day, many believe the *Clockwork Orange*

Philadelphia Flyers mugged Lord Stanley's Cup. (In the 1954–55 season, hockey's toughest team, the Detroit Red Wings, engaged in 22 fights. By comparison, the Flyers' Dave "The Hammer" Schultz had 37 brawls all on his own in 1974–75.)

Mom says I shunt play anymore. How did hockey, Canada's great character builder, suddenly become bad for you? NHL president Clarence Campbell was once asked this very question. "I consider [the violence] part of a worldwide phenomenon," Campbell responded. "We're all aware of the breakdown in respect for constituted authority. I believe this is reflected in sports."

So it was society's fault. Interesting theory—one at odds with the standard explanation of how hockey went "bad" in the '70s, a story that goes something like this . . .

The NHL was an eastern, six-team, train-travel league in 1967. The '70s sports boom proved to be too much. On the skate heels of expansion in '67, the World Hockey Association arrived in 1972—a shifting confederacy that saw a dozen teams hopscotch North America. Who can forget the Miami Screaming Eagles? Or remember the Dayton Arrows? The NHL grew, too, with teams arriving in pairs, like animals boarding Noah's Ark, in 1970, 1972 and 1974. What with franchises skipping town to beat rent, big-league hockey became attached to nearly 40 locations in the '70s. There wasn't enough talent. Suddenly, minor-league outlaws made it big.

Goodbye, Lady Byng, hockey's great patroness; hello, Ogie Ogilthorpe, lead villain from the movie *Slap Shot.*

The only problem with the theory that expansion coarsened hockey is that it ignores history. Like how Edmonton police quelled an on-ice riot during the 1965 Memorial Cup. Indeed, the crucial moment when tactical violence came to the NHL probably occurred while JFK was in the White House: on October 8, 1963, when the Montreal Canadiens and the Boston Bruins took the ice at the Boston Garden. Twelve seconds in, rookie John Ferguson whaled the piss out of Boston's Ted Green. *What could Terrible Teddy have possibly done to irk Ferguson?* Nothing. Tired of having their wings clipped by Anglo ruffians, the Flying Frenchmen had signed the first of a new breed—the hired gun who shot first.

Maybe Clarence Campbell was right. It wasn't expansion. A fever had swept the planet—riots in the United States, revolution in the air in Paris and Montreal. What to make of the lady streaker who in 1973 turned L.A.'s Fabulous Forum into the Folies Bergère? Or the race riot in Quebec City during the 1971 Memorial Cup? (One spectator threw a knife at Marcel Dionne, the Drummondville "traitor" who had "defected" to Ontario to play hockey.) What about other sports? There was Disco Demolition Night, held during a 1979 Chicago–Detroit baseball double-header at Comiskey Park. Fans invaded the field after 20,000 albums were blown sky high, stealing bats and gloves while eluding incoming missiles from the stands (albums by Kid Creole and the Coconuts). The second game was cancelled.

Could all this have been the Philadelphia Flyers' fault?

No. For some reason, blood boiled at a lower temperature in the '70s. A college memory: it's November 1976, days after René Lévesque's Parti Québécois was elected, scaring the hell out of English Canada. I'm sitting in a Montreal movie theatre on a Friday night in Westmount, the prosperous English side of town. Ladies shake off their furs, reaching for creamy toffees in their purses. Husbands settle in, hoping not to snore. And then "our" national anthem comes on—it played before movies then—and seconds later, this reserved crowd, most of them strangers, join as one, on their feet, singing:

> *With glowing hearts, we see thee rise*
> *The true north strong and free . . .*

Patriotism was a growth industry in those days. The 3,000 Canadians who flew to Moscow to watch "our boys" take on Russia in the 1972 Summit Series were given two maple leaf banners, one for each hand, as they boarded planes—gifts from a new corporate body, Hockey Canada (it was official: we were now a nation-sport). Some NHL teams became religious cults. In Philadelphia, Kate Smith showed up to sing "God Bless America" before big games. Bobby Orr's teammates called him God. In Montreal, Guy Lafleur was sometimes confused with King Louis XIV. "Do you like Guy?" folk-rocker Robert Charlebois asked a 1976 Montreal crowd. Screams shook Stade Olympique. "I like him too," said Charlebois. "In the winter, he replaces the sun."

Delirium spilled into violence when cults collided. Three great teams— the Boston Bruins, the Philadelphia Flyers and the Montreal Canadiens— dominated the NHL in the 1970s, winning every Stanley Cup. Their fans may not have been ready to die for their team, but they were prepared to kill. Boston supporters frequently intruded on storylines, not just by cheering on the home side, but by offering to personally "handle" things, sometimes even pulling a Jack Ruby, jumping out of a crowd to harm a hated opponent.

Protestors and supporters began showing up at games, bearing signs. This was new. Except for the Richard Riot on St. Patrick's Day, 1955, when placard-bearing demonstrators ("*Pas de Richard, pas de Coupe*") arrived at the Montreal Forum to challenge Campbell's suspension of Rocket Richard, fans would never picket, let alone call for murder en masse. They did now. Cut to Boston Garden, April 2, 1969, minutes after Toronto's Saint Paddy's Day float, Pat Quinn, knocked out God. What was it that the crowd was shouting?

"Get Quinn! Get Quinn! Get Quinn!"

In 1970, Bruins fans swarmed the ice when their guys won the Cup. First time that ever happened. "We won" clearly meant something more than it once had—the distinction between my team and myself had become blurred. And not just among beer-blind fans in the cheap seats. In the Summit Series, Team Canada organizer Alan Eagleson, executive director of the NHL Players' Association and president of the Conservative Party of Ontario, decided a goal light hadn't come on fast enough in Moscow and took matters into his own clenched fists, wading through the Russian army in a bid to switch the damn goal light on himself.

While 3,000 Canadians, guests of the Union of Soviet Socialist Republics, chanted, *"Da da Canada; nyet, nyet Soviet."*

Yes, it was a different time . . . not more exciting, but certainly more excited. And it all began in Boston, where the signs first showed up. "The Garden is festooned with banners," the great *Hockey Night in Canada* play-by-play man Danny Gallivan told us one night. JESUS SAVES, BUT ESPOSITO SCORES ON THE REBOUND, read bumper stickers throughout New England. The Boston Garden was also where the idea of sportsmanship in hockey was put away, mothballed like an old-fashioned sweater. Once upon a time, in 1925, Marie Evelyn Moreton, Lady Byng, wife of Canada's governor general, invited her favourite Ottawa Senator, Frank Nighbor, to Rideau Hall, offering him tea and a trophy to be donated to hockey players who, like the "Pembroke Peach," combined sportsmanship with hockey excellence.

Though up for the occasional tea party, Boston didn't take its hockey with peaches or cream. One night, as the *HNIC* camera panned the Garden, you could read a sign that said all you need to know about professional hockey in the 1970s:

LADY BYNG DIED IN BOSTON

PART 1

THE BOSTON BRUINS
Two-Drink Minimum
(1965–76)

SON OF A GUN

So this kid walked into the Boston Bruins' dressing room. Strolled right in like he owned the place. Most likely the interloper was working a chaw of Dubble Bubble; indeed, five years later, he'd be chewing gum on Johnny Carson's *Tonight Show*, slouched in the guest chair, explaining to the king of American late-night TV that the only good-looking chick in Niagara Falls had dumped him, so he split. Polished brass and a sprouting fountain of raven-black hair would one day put him on *GQ* magazine's list of the 25 Coolest Athletes of All time.* But we're getting ahead of ourselves. On December 11, 1965, Derek "Turk" Sanderson was just another 19-year-old who had seen too many Steve McQueen movies.

---

* *GQ*'s 25 coolest athletes of all time: Muhammad Ali, Mario Andretti, Arthur Ashe, George Best, Bjorn Borg, Tom Brady, Jim Brown, Julius Erving, Tim Lincecum, Walt Frazier, Bob Gibson, Allen Iverson, Bo Jackson, Michael Jordan, Jean-Claude Killy, Evel Knievel, Pete Maravich, Joe Namath, Arnold Palmer, Pelé, Gary Player, Derek Sanderson, Kelly Slater, Ken Stabler, and Ted Turner.

As for Turk's new teammates, they were a weary, gallant lot—NHLers in a six-team league, among the top 120 hockey players in the word. *Pros!* Still, Boston had lost to Montreal, 8–3, just a couple nights earlier. Before that, Chicago had pushed them around like mops, winning 10–1. (Stan Mikita had a hat trick; Phil Esposito, a galling 23-year-old loudmouth, two goals and an assist.) Tonight, even with future Hall of Famer Bernie Parent in net, Boston would be shredded, losing 8–3 to Toronto in Maple Leaf Gardens. Mired in a month-long winless streak that would see them outscored 65–25, the beleaguered Bruins had come to process defeat with elaborate tomfoolery—RCAF flyboys prior to a skirmish early on in the Battle of Britain, laughing hard to numb the sense of impending doom.

Sanderson's studied nonchalance was too much for some. One NHL veteran, 33-year-old journeyman Ron Stewart, fell to his knees, giving Sanderson the Allah-be-praised treatment: "Are we supposed to bow down to you, great stranger?"

"The fuck you talking about?"

The kid had everyone's attention now. Like children at an adult gathering, NHL rookies were supposed to be seen, not heard. "You're going to take us by the hand and lead us out of the woods so that we have a winning season," Stewart continued, his smile tightening.

"Somebody's going to have to," Turk snorted. "You haven't made the playoffs in six years, so it may as well be me. Get up off your knees, asshole." Suddenly, the Bruins dressing room was library quiet. A junior dripping wet behind the ears had just kneecapped a roomful of NHLers.

First minute he met them.

While chewing gum.

Ladies and gentlemen, we give you Turk Sanderson—born to raise eyebrows. To celebrate his 17th birthday, Turk swilled 30 draft beers in as many minutes to impress junior teammates. Or maybe he invented the story years later to win a reporter's attention. Turk liked to be noticed. And the quickest routes to notoriety in the mid-'60s involved sex and violence. At first, Derek concentrated on the latter. His first mention in the New England sporting press had come months earlier, when the *Boston Globe* printed the following summary of a game from the Canadian junior championship, the 1965 Memorial Cup final: "The [Edmonton] Oil Kings beat [Niagara] Falls, 5–1, in a game that had to be called three minutes before the end because of fighting on the ice and in stands . . . police reserves halted the brutality . . . three Edmonton fans dragged Derek Sanderson into a room under the stands and beat him up."

What had happened was, with the game lost, Niagara Falls initiated a Wild West saloon brawl. Fights broke out, 20 or so arms windmilling en masse. All that was missing was a guy with garters on his shirtsleeves playing honky-tonk piano. Gum-chewing Sanderson and Oil King Bob Falkenberg were conspicuous wallflowers at the beginning, watching little Fran Huck of Edmonton take a beating from bruiser Guy Allen. When Falkenberg relaxed, looking down to sweep a fallen stick from his feet, Turk came alive, unveiling a looping sucker punch that caught his opponent flush in the jaw. Falkenberg was out cold, still holding his stick, upon hitting the ice. Sanderson then leapt upon his prey, landing seven rights to Falkenberg's twitching face before a game official (with a cast on his hand) yanked him away. A minute later, cops boot-skated onto the ice, twirling batons. And the Edmonton Gardens' real-life organist broke into "God Save the Queen" to remind players who and where they were.

> . . . *And let our Empire be*
> *Loyal, united, free*
> *True to herself and Theeee*
> *God save the Queen.*

Sanderson's savagery did not go unnoticed by Oil Kings alumni, who formed a grumbling posse, intercepting Turk before he made the dressing room. Tossing him into darkened first-aid quarters, the trio bludgeoned the Ontario junior, throwing his slack, bloodied body into the hallway. Sanderson would later say that Glen Sather, former Oil King and future GM/coach of the Edmonton Oilers and New York Rangers, was one of the vigilantes. But let's not let that fascinating tidbit distract us from the greater question: What was up with Derek Sanderson?

In a sport where interns traditionally observe a variation of *omertà*—the Sicilian code of silence—how to explain a purposefully violent motormouth who put on a show as easily as others slip on a shirt? Well, it was complicated. On one hand, Sanderson so infuriated Niagara Falls Flyers GM Hap Emms that Emms had the centre wear a puck—dangling from a skate lace—around his neck, forcing Turk to go two weeks at school with a scarlet letter bouncing atop his chest—*Puck hog!* At the same time, Sanderson was painfully shy growing up. He cried the first time a referee gave him a penalty in peewee. At a Grade 9 YMCA mixer, Derek asked a girl to dance. She said yes, but then exploded into laughter when the hockey player tried to bust a move. Turk never, ever danced again.

Later, in high school, at Niagara Falls Collegiate Institute, in public speaking class, Derek was asked to deliver an address to his school. The petrified teenager was given 12 days to prepare for the speech.

He quit high school on the 11th day.

Show business is crowded with insecure show-offs who need the love of millions to validate their self-worth. Or as Beatle John summed it up it in his 1970 confessional, "I Found Out": *I heard something 'bout my ma and my pa / They didn't want me so they made me a star.* Derek was well loved by parents Harold and Caroline. Still, family history helps explain why Turk was bound for glory. Dumped by his girlfriend at age 17, Derek's dad quit high school and joined the Scottish Foreign Legion, enlisting in the Cameron Highlanders. Just so he could strut past his ex's, resplendent in tartan. *Take that!* Seven weeks later, Harold Sanderson was in Britain, operational, First Battalion out of Ottawa, one of 800 marching soldiers. That number was whittled down by D-Day. There were so many battles—Caen, Carpiquet, the Orne, Bourguébus Ridge. It went on: Faubourg de Vaucelles, Falaise, Quesnay Wood, the Liaison, Boulogne, the Scheldt, Breskens Pocket, the Rhineland, Waal Flats, the Hochwald, the Rhine, Zutphen, Deventer, Leer, the Battle of Northwest Europe. Two hundred of Harold's fellow Highlanders were killed.

Derek's dad was wounded twice, collecting five medals and a lifetime of supressed nightmares.

He recuperated from his first war wound in Kircaldy, Scotland. The weekend before he returned to the front, he went to a movie, wearing his dress kilt to impress the natives. Once inside, he only had eyes for a busy, attractive usherette. Harold stayed for five showings, coming alive whenever the dark-haired beauty passed, waving her torch. *Hey there, I'm a . . .* No response. Undaunted, Harold returned to the same theatre the next day, hours before shipping out—five more screenings of the same bloody movie. When the cinema finally closed, he pursued the petrified usherette out the door, sitting behind her on the bus, babbling like a fool.

Yep, sure rains a lot in Scotland . . .

Not even a smile.

Still yakking, Harold followed the girl home. Eventually, she escaped, running up stairs and disappearing into her home. Moments later, her father materialized, staring down at a skinny Canadian teenager drowning in a baggy tartan skirt.

"How is the war going, son?"

"Fine, sir."

Harold talked his way inside. Addresses were exchanged. Letters flew. *Dear Caroline . . . Dearest Harold.* When Harold was wounded a second time, he asked to return to Kircaldy.

He and Caroline spent their wedding night in a grandfather's home—a building that was bombed weeks later. Derek's older sister Karen was born while Harold was fighting in Germany; Derek himself was conceived in Kircaldy before the newlyweds returned to Niagara Falls, where Harold quickly found a job at Kimberly-Clark, helping in the manufacture of feminine hygiene products.

What is it that Oscar Wilde called Niagara Falls—"The second great disappointment for a woman on her honeymoon"? Could a sparky daredevil like Harold Sanderson find happiness pushing Kotex past the finish line in sleepy postwar Ontario? What to do with all that restless energy? He was reading at home one day after work, nursing a beer probably, when—*eureka!*—an idea hit him: "Listen to this, Caroline. *Maclean's* has a story here that ranks the most respected professions in Canada. What do you think is the most respected profession?"

"Doctor?"

"You'd think so, wouldn't you? They say playing hockey is Canada's most respected profession. I'll be damned." A few seconds later: "My boy is going to be a hockey player."

And so Turk Sanderson's apprenticeship began. Harold fixed butter knives to the bottom of Derek's first shoes. Later, he spread linoleum on the driveway, building a practice net from abandoned (?) pipes at Kimberly-Clark. After work, Harold swung by the Niagara Falls Memorial Coliseum, searching for pucks lost under seats. Thirsty for knowledge, Harold attended *CBC's Sports College,** a Saturday morning radio show hosted by hockey guru Lloyd Percival. Derek learned hockey the new-fashioned way. The way Russian coaches, who memorized pirated editions of Percival's slim volume, *The Hockey Handbook,* taught the game back in Moscow and Minsk—skating first. To ensure that Derek could turn and push off both skates, Harold adopted one of Percival's drills, insisting that his son carry the puck around a backyard rink 200 times in one direction, then 200 times in the opposite direction.

And what a rink! Like many Canadian baby boomers, Derek grew up in virgin suburbs—Popsicle-stick trees stabbed into freshly sodded emerald lawns; three bedrooms and a bath, plus a finished basement that had anyone over six feet doing the limbo. The $4,000 bungalows came with modest backyards perfect for smoky barbecues and, in

---

*   At one point, almost three-quarters of a million listeners were registered as *CBC's Sports College* fans. Percival's book, *The Hockey Handbook,* would become more influential in the Soviet Union than in his native country. "I have read [it] like a schoolboy," Anatoli Tarasov, the godfather of Soviet hockey, once told Percival.

winter, two-on-two hockey, if Dad was willing to stand outside in his pyjamas and duffle coat before going to bed, smoking a cigarette down to the filter, laying down a fresh layer of ice with a gurgling garden hose.

But why stop at a regulation backyard rink? The neighbour behind Harold Sanderson, an Italian fellow, enjoyed gardening. Harold approached him with an idea. *You scratch my back* . . . Mr. Sanderson supersized Derek's rink, joining two backyards into a vast frozen oval. In return, the neighbour was allowed to convert the joint properties into a lush, steaming tomato orchard in the summer.

Derek played organized youth hockey (United Electrical, Local 53), plus all the unorganized versions—on the street, on the driveway and on his deluxe, personalized backyard arena. Weekends were all hockey. Saturday night was spent watching *Hockey Night in Canada*; plopped on the chesterfield next to Dad, who supplemented Bill Hewitt's play-by-play of Leafs games with his own running commentary.

See the way Davey Keon drops his stick at the last second for a sweep check? . . . *Beautiful.*

Hockey, hockey, hockey. It never stopped. "Don't forget to brush your teeth," Caroline Sanderson shouted to Derek at bedtime. "Why bother?" Dad chuckled from the couch, lost in a magazine. "He's going to be a hockey player—won't have any teeth." Even sleep gave way to shinny. Derek received free ice time for working as an ice scraper at Flyers games. The arena was his after midnight on Sundays. There was a catch. Memorial Coliseum didn't leave the lights on. Who cared? Turk and his pals chased about like phantoms, intuiting each other's positions from the scratch of skates.

Still, it wasn't butter knives on baby shoes or playing hockey in the dark that made young Derek Sanderson into the combustible package that exploded onto the NHL in 1967. The player everyone called Turk emerged from one-on-ones with Dad—interludes where Lloyd Percival's name seldom came up. His second practice in peewee, minutes into his hockey career, Derek took an errant puck to his naked head. Minutes later, he reached up and felt a wet knot on his skull. "Holy cow, I'm bleeding," the seven-year old cried. "Dad, Dad, look at this."

Coach Sanderson skated over. "Only 20 minutes left in practice . . . you won't bleed to death," Harold told his boy before turning to the team. "Line up, stops and starts."

Let's go, I'm running a steamship here, not a mission.

Derek continued, blood raining from his head. Teammates and parents hanging over the boards stared in wonder. For a tyke who wasn't sure he could measure up to his war hero dad, the outpouring of respect felt like a warm-spreading drug. Derek was to have other hockey instructors in Niagara Falls. Harold, though, remained his head coach. A few winters later, Derek scored four goals in a game but backed away from a donnybrook, wanting to stay on the ice. Afterwards, Harold was fuming. Never back away from a fight, he told his son. *Never!* Hit first and hit hard, and then watch how the world gets out of your way. Harold learned that during the war.

Next game, during the warm-up, the same teams performed lazy circles in their own ends, getting loose. Derek timed his next lap, arriving at centre ice the same time as the guy he'd refused to fight in the game previous. *Ka-pow*—the old Pearl Harbor move. The other player crumpled to the ice, with Derek on top of him, pounding away. As Derek would remember in *Crossing the Line*, his as-told-to autobiography with Kevin Shea, "I got kicked out of the game, but there was never a happier guy on the planet than my dad! My teammates gave me more respect, and the word went out: 'Don't hit Sanderson—he's crazy!' Once that message started circulating, it was amazing the respect I got. I liked that."

Soon as Derek joined the hometown Flyers, GM Emms made it clear to the youngster that his father was no longer coach. Still, Harold had the last word. In late 1965, the Boston Bruins had their two Ontario junior teams, the Niagara Falls Flyers and apprentice saviour Bobby Orr's Oshawa Generals, square off in the Boston Garden. All in an effort to convince Hub fans that help was on the way. Harold provided

Derek with a game plan: "There are only two guys everyone is going to notice in Boston," he advised his boy, "Bobby Orr and the player who fights Bobby Orr."

They noticed Turk, all right, when he made his first trip to Boston. It was the Monday after Christmas, and only 5,778 fans turned up at the Garden. Other stuff was happening: *Thunderball*, the underwater Bond, had just opened. Besides, kids were still spinning Christmas gifts—The Beatles' *Rubber Soul*, along with The Rolling Stones' *December's Children*, the Byrds' *Turn! Turn! Turn!* and The Who's *My Generation* had all been released within a magical 48 hours a few weeks before. Nevertheless, hockey loyalists who made the trek to the "Gah-den" were glad they did. Orr was fantastic, collecting a goal and two assists in the first period. Sanderson was held scoreless, but had fans' heads turn-turn-turning anyway.

All he did, according to the *Boston Globe*, was incite a riot.

It happened in the middle of Orr's spectacular opening 20 minutes. Number Two in the black Oshawa jersey (Bruins legend Eddie Shore's old number!) was minding his own budding-superstar business, slipping and sliding past opponents like a downhill skier eluding stationary markers in an obstacle course. Then one of the obstacles turned into a locked turnstile, throwing out a stick. *I'm here, too, buddy-boy.* Turk Sanderson, number 17 on the bumble-bee outfitted (white-yellow-black) Niagara Falls Flyers, low-bridged Orr with his Northland. Orr responded with an elbow. And they were off—two Celt teenagers screaming and swearing at each other. Soon, both Boston junior farm teams were at war; there were 17 penalties, including lots of fights, in the very first period.

Emms stormed into the junior teams' dressing rooms during the first intermission and gave everyone hell.

We're not looking for the next Sonny Liston here, boys—play hockey!

The most telling moment in the exhibition match probably came after the game, when a *Globe* reporter sought Sanderson out in the dressing room. "Why'd you fight Orr?" he asked. Turk shrugged. "Would you be talking to me if I didn't?"

Derek Sanderson led the Ontario Hockey Association Junior A league in scoring (101 points) and came second in penalties (193 minutes) in 1966–67, his final junior season.* He was also tops in quotable quotes. A good hockey player, Turks was better copy. The high school dropout instinctively understood celebrity. (*Who's got the microphone? Where's the camera?*) He claimed never to read the stories he created, but he remained locked in public attention–seeking mode. That's the way the pros did it. ("Don't read your reviews, weigh them," the era's premier artist on the make, Andy Warhol, once said.) Turk figured out the hustle early on, becoming hockey's first sports celebrity.

"Hockey players in the old days were 20 London Fog trench coats; nobody spoke out of turn," Sanderson would later tell TV interviewer Mike Anscombe. In the fall of 1967, when Derek broke into the NHL, "old days" was a pejorative. Before Derek, hockey players, even young-sters like Ron Ellis and Paul Henderson, dressed like your uncle Hughie. Or worse still, a nark. They were also unfailingly quiet. Not Derek. By decade's end he was wearing flared trousers, a *Sgt. Pepper* haircut and walrus moustache—hockey's first soup strainer since the Leafs' Garth Boesch back in the '40s. And Turk talked and talked . . . as if he had been vaccinated with a phonograph needle.

"Why didn't you win the MVP of the Ontario junior league?" the *Boston Globe* asked him at the Bruins' 1967 training camp in London, Ontario. "They give a thing up there, but it's for the most impressive and most gentlemanly player," Turk laughed. "You know I was out on that gentlemanly thing."

Derek appeared on *Hockey Night in Canada* for the first time on January 6, 1968. Disappointing parents and high school teachers every-where, he chewed gum throughout the interview. Bemused host Ward

---

* The OHA Junior A penalty leaders in 1966–67: Jim Dorey, London Nationals, 196 minutes; Derek Sanderson, Niagara Falls Flyers, 193; John Schella, Peterborough Petes, 182; Steve Hunt, Peterborough Petes, 179; Mike Pelyk, Toronto Marlboros, 146.

Cornell closed off their chat with, "And Derek, you're still a bachelor?"

"Oh yeah," Turk grinned.

Women were suddenly part of the image. Radio station WBZ 1030 in Boston held a "Win a Date with Derek" contest—103 girls won a night out with Turk, all at the same time. Soon, he was an expert on the subject. "There are no better women in North America than in Montreal," he confided to one interviewer, and then he threw in a scouting tip: "Pittsburgh is terrible."

"What's your pre-game meal?"

"A steak and a blonde."

The TV appearances piled up. He soon had his own half-hour show in Boston—*Everybody's Talkin' at Me: The Derek Sanderson Show.* Linda Ronstadt was a guest. There was a tribute single—"Ballad of Derek the Turk" backed with "Score One More." He wrote a book with Stan Fischler, *I've Got to Be Me,* and showed up on *The Dick Cavett Show* and Johnny Carson's *Tonight Show* (twice). "Derek, you've got a pretty good career going for yourself," said Johnny, "but what are you going to do when it's over?"

Two beats. "Your seat doesn't look too bad," Derek said, eliciting big laughs. Johnny's chortling sidekick, Ed McMahon, looked ready to explode. Sanderson was great at playing puck's bad boy. Once, in Vegas, Muhammad Ali spotted Derek at a table and approached him, smiling. "I'm a big fan," he said.

Thanks, Champ. Y'mind? I'm trying to play some cards here.

Turk let the good times roll all over him. He opened a nightclub with the National Football League's (NFL) reigning superstar, Broadway Joe Namath, and then a saloon of his own, Daisy Buchanan's, at the corner of Newbury and Fairfield, in the heart of Boston. Suddenly he was Rick in *Casablanca.* There was a Playboy club just down the street and Derek could write off any tab. Bunnies drank free.

At first even the hangovers worked out all right. *Boston* magazine wanted to do a cover story on Derek for its January 1971 issue. A photographer, John van-Schalkwyk, summoned the hockey player to his studio. Turk showed up drunk and was sent home. Next day, they shot for two unproductive hours. Derek was a mess. In withdrawal from a two-pack-a-day Export "A" habit (he puffed two cigarettes between periods every game), the hockey player begged for a smoke break. He put his hands together as if in prayer. *Pretty please.* Grabbing quickly for his Hasselbad 500, van-Schalkwyk snapped Turk's happy response to finally being allowed to spark up.

The resulting photograph came with the cover line "The Beatification of Derek Sanderson." Perfect—Turk Sanderson, hoodlum saint. Derek was suddenly the hippest athlete-celebrity in the world.

Actually, the rebel-angel stuff was a crock. Derek wore a moustache not because he wanted to be a walrus like Beatle Paul, but because his dad wore one. He flashed a peace sign after fights not out of solidarity with 1968 Paris student protesters, but because Winston Churchill, the original V-for-victory guy, was Harold Sanderson's hero. Throw away the fighting and yapping, and Derek Sanderson was maybe the most conservative 20-something hockey player around. His signature play—the sweep check—was almost extinct by the time he arrived in the NHL. And Derek had veteran, old-pro skills. He was excellent at faceoffs, responsible defensively, good at killing penalties.

He was Davey Keon with a harem and rock-star wig.

But how were millions of impressionable young hockey fans, boomers in search of a hockey protagonist who resembled their guitar heroes, to know that? To us, he looked like a character right out of the Rolling Stones' "Street Fighting Man." He sure skated the skate. Once, in Montreal, during a nationally televised *Hockey Night in Canada* game, Turk responded to a debris-throwing heckler by chasing the fan out the corridor of the Forum, down a ramp, and through two separate doorways out onto the street. Then he gave chase—on chopping skates—down a busy boulevard, losing the perp at the corner of Lambert-Closse and Ste-Catherine.

The assumption that Derek Sanderson was an angry child of the '60s, a rabble-rouser in search of establishment scalps, was understandable. But really, Derek and his war-hero dad had the '40s and '70s transposed. In 1963, when Derek took his first seven stitches in a peewee game, Harold Sanderson pulled the sutures out with pliers and then carefully tucked away the brittle tracks of thread in a grey velvet watch box. He would preserve each of Derek's subsequent 400 stitches. They were Turk's World War II medals. Blood-red badges of courage. Reminders of what it cost to survive.

Derek was a very good hockey player. He would do a lot to make the Bruins world champions. Still, he did more to make them famous. Other teammates, particularly Terrible Teddy Green, Boston's stick-swinging Paul Bunyan, and unlicensed surgeon Wayne Cashman, were far tougher. But Turk was maybe the active ingredient that made the Big Bad Bruins seem like plundering, recklessly thrilling pirates. All those sudden, dramatic mood swings. The kamikaze attacks. Once, in Toronto, he leapt over a net to get at a defender playing cat and mouse with the puck behind the goalie.

He could be dramatically unpredictable—irrational, even. Where did it come from? One explanation—Harold Sanderson's boy was a sleeper agent from World War II . . . a bomb lit in 1944 that finally went off a quarter century later.

Frequently, the explosions came in newspapers: "The [Montreal] Canadiens don't have the team, the defence, the talent or the guts," Derek told reporters prior to the 1969 playoffs. "We have tougher workouts in practice than we've had in our games with the [St. Louis] Blues," he informed scribes a winter later.

Derek Sanderson had a need to impress everyone (and maybe convince himself) that he was a big deal, tougher than the rest. The kid who cried over his first penalty in peewee hockey wanted to measure up to his charismatic war-hero dad. Occasionally, the desperation showed. One spring, after the playoffs, Derek found himself in Mexico, severely under the volcano. His companion from the night previous was gone. The Bruins star was alone with his thoughts—too much to bear. So, out of the blue, he phoned a reporter at the *Boston Globe*, making up a story about saving a damsel in distress, some actress, getting into a horrible fight over her honour.

All lies. Who knows why he told them? Maybe because life was sometimes was too difficult for Derek Sanderson. That was when Turk took over.

PETER PUCK

The key to kick-starting a business is uncovering a fresh audience. So when commissioner David Stern arrived at the floundering National Basketball Association in the late '70s, he turned the game into a college kegger, with loot-tossing cheerleaders and wall-to-wall party music. The NFL and baseball owned dads and moms, a settled, loyal demographic. The NBA went after undeclared spenders: bell-bottomed kids soon to collect their first paycheques.

NBC tried the same trick with hockey. In the winter of 1972, the US network launched a weekly NHL game. Instead of throbbing disco, NBC tempted young Americans with an inexplicably cheerful cartoon figure, "Your ol' pokecheck perfesser," Peter Puck. Young Canadians hated Peter worse than geometry class, but they endured his squeaky intermission lectures ("Now we come to icing the puck—*brrr-rrrr*") for a chance to watch Sunday afternoon games on cable—more hockey! There were two prime-time contests on NBC's 1972–73 lineup; both featured the Boston Bruins. The NHL's schedule was also rejigged to maximize

Bruins appearances north of the border. Five of Boston's six visits to Toronto and Montreal this season were on Saturdays, for *Hockey Night in Canada.*

The Bruins were popular on radio, too. By 1970, Bruins games on WBZ, with Fred Cusick and Johnny Peirson, were picked up in 38 states and much of the Great White North.

What gives? How could the locked-in-the-basement Bruins, the woeful pity party Turk Sanderson crashed in 1965, have become so popular?

Bobby Orr, that's how. Bobby was the *real* Peter Puck, hockey's first child star. Because of injuries (Achilles knees), Bobby was maybe more Peter Pan than Peter Puck; still, in nine miraculous seasons, from 1966–67 through 1974–75, the Hockey Star Who Was Never Allowed to Grow Up converted a generation of New Englanders to his sport, while convincing many English-Canadian kids to switch brand loyalties.

So long, Maple Leafs. See you later, Red Wings.

It was love at first sight—teenage love, and you know how that works. Really, it may be impossible for fans who grew up watching Bobby Orr not to become foolish talking about him. He seemed made up—preposterously, storybook good; a figment of our imagination, maybe. He was an NHL rookie at age 18, just out of Grade 11. At the time, though, Bobby looked five years younger, with a nervously bobbing Adam's apple and ghastly, my-dad-made-me crew cut. In other words, he looked just like awkward, adolescent us. We watched him and felt ourselves soar. It would happen two or three times a period: the most modest of stars, Bobby would try to fit in for a shift or two, headmanning the puck to forwards. But every now and then, the thrill of his talent overwhelmed him; the teenager spotted an opening and took off like a paper scrap in the wind.

New England fell for Bobby particularly hard. That his family was from the old sod helped. Grandfather Robert Orr was a soccer star in Ballymena, Northern Ireland, before immigrating to the port of Parry Sound, three hours up Highway 400 from Toronto. Bobby's dad, Doug, was a gifted hockey player who could've turned pro with the Eastern

This Topps hockey card booklet from 1971, The Bobby Orr Story—*thanks, Mom, for not throwing it out—captures our fantasy hero's voyage of discovery pretty well exactly as we imagined it. See photo insert for more . . .*

Hockey League Atlantic City Seagulls, but instead joined the Royal Canadian Navy in 1942. After the war, Dougie played sports, drank beer and worked intermittently in a dynamite factory. *Talk about Irish!* That the Orrs hailed from the Emerald Isle helped Bobby in the most Irish city in America.* Boston's Murphys and O'Tooles loved shinny. Mayor John "Honey Fitz" Fitzgerald and his daughter Rose—President John Fitzgerald Kennedy's mother—attended the city's first big hockey game: a boisterous,

---

* Even today, Boston is the most Irish of all American cities: 20.4 per cent of all Bostonians are descendants of Irish immigrants. Overall, 11.1 per cent of Americans claim an Irish heritage . . . except on St. Patrick's Day, of course. Source: Sarah Kliff, "The Irish-American population is seven times larger than Ireland," *Washington Post,* March 17, 2013.

packed 1910 exhibition match between Toronto's St. Michael's College and the Boston Hockey Club. (Canadian Micks won, 5–3.)

Journalist Peter Gzowski once elaborated on Boston's hardscrabble, Fenian ways in *Maclean's*: "There are really two cities in Boston. On the one hand there is the old, puritanistic headquarters of the Cabots and the Lowells, the Boston of Beacon Hill, Black Bay and John Phillips Marquand, of Harvard Yard and bone china and the Isabella Stewart Garner Museum. On the other hand, there is the lusty, saloon-tough seaport of the Shanty Irish . . . There is no confusion about which Boston is reflected by the Boston Bruins . . . they are delicate as stevedores . . . The Bruins have played the game with a joy-through-brawling that is Boston Irish as a last hurrah."

There was, however, a catch as big as Moby Dick when it came to Boston hockey. Before Bobby, the Bruins always seemed to be in last place. The basketball Boston Celtics, meanwhile, won an incredible ten NBA championships between 1957 and 1969. Didn't matter; Boston was a hockey town. Even in the bad old days, Bruins games sold out. Attendance was always the same—13,909—whereas the Celtics reached an average of 10,000 fans only once in their championship run. Part of the reason—there is no getting around it—was racism. Blacks played basketball; whites, hockey. And prejudice was alive and well on the Boston sports scene at the time. The Red Sox were the last team in Major League Baseball to employ a black player, Pumpsie Green, in 1959, a dozen seasons after Jackie Robinson integrated baseball. And Pumpsie was a pinch runner, reserve infielder, not even a starter.

Still, it should be made clear that the Bruins outdrew the Celtics even before the National Basketball Association integrated in the '50s. "You go anywhere in America and say 'Bruins,' people think of UCLA [college basketball] Bruins," Celtics GM Red Auerbach would say, growing hot as his cigar. "You say 'Bruins' in New England, they think hockey." Boston sports fans of the era liked rough-and-tumble entertainment, bodychecks, a fight or two—made the beer taste better. Class solidarity was also a factor. The Celtics were college men: Bob Cousy attended

Holy Cross; Bill Russell, the University of San Francisco. The year Bobby Orr turned pro (1966–67), only 17 per cent of NHL players had completed high school.* The Boston fans' favourite Bruins always had names that sounded like the guy who worked on the next machine over down at the factory—Eddie Shore, Dit Clapper, Milt Schmidt, Leo Boivin, Bronco Horvath and Jerry Toppazzini.

If the Bruins were popular before Bobby, they'd become a near obsession afterwards. In 1964, there were nine full-sized arenas and 288 registered youth hockey leagues in Maine, Massachusetts, New Hampshire, Vermont, Rhode Island and Connecticut. Ten years later, the totals had jumped to 30 arenas and 2,100 leagues. The real Peter Puck somehow turned New England into Canada's 11th province.

It worked the other way, too: Boston rubbed off on Bobby. There was no tougher sporting venue than the Boston Garden, a yellow-brick heap on top of the city's North Station and a labyrinth of screeching trains. If the Bruins and Celtics weren't playing, the only thing open on Causeway Street was the Hayes-Bickford cafeteria. Stepping into the Bick felt like walking into an Edward Hopper painting—five guys sitting alone, staring into their coffee, wondering how their lives went so wrong. Visiting teams stayed at a dilapidated hotel nearby, the Manger. Famed boxing trainer Ray Arcel was beaten with a lead pipe in front of the Manger in 1953. A mob hit, everyone figured.

Everything in the Garden was shoved together and on the cheap: the Celtics' famed parquet floor, introduced in 1946, was the result of a cost-cutting move. Before the Second World War, the arena had no skate-sharpening equipment. Players hung their uniforms on nails in a dressing room that boasted two washroom stalls. Showers didn't always work, especially in the officials' change room when the home team lost. NHL refs got around that hazard by changing at the Manger. "We'd leave

---

* From a great treasure trove of Boston sports history, *The Rock, the Curse and the Hub,* edited by Randy Roberts and published in 2005 by the Harvard University Press.

beer cooling on ice in the bathtub and hurry across the street in our uniforms with our skates over our shoulders," referee Bruce Hood told me.

And then—*sniff*—there was the arena's ever-present aroma. The "Garden" was anything but. The place reeked of spilled beer and used straw from circus elephants. There were also rats, "so tough they wear leather jackets," Grateful Dead guitarist Jerry Garcia claimed. Fans were pretty scary too. Every section featured one or two beer-breathed assassins, guys who chewed on cigars and unwanted Bruins. Since the Garden was the smallest rink in the NHL, with a protruding balcony that hung over the ice, players—coaches, too—heard about it when they did something wrong. In 1974, coach Don Cherry turned away from the ice after losing his first home game. Just then, a fan called directly into his ear, "Hey Chair-eee, there's a bus for Providence in five minutes—be under it."

The Gah-den became Bobby Orr's winter home, and he was more than eager to fit in. When statistics are cited to measure Bobby's legacy, goals and assists are most often used. Like the 120 points he scored in 1969–70, making him the first defenceman to lead the NHL in scoring. He would exceed that total three times, topping out at 139 points in 1970–71. But there are other numbers that define Bobby's years in Boston. Peter Puck was Boston's Joe Louis—hockey's fighting champion. Most hockey fans assume Gordie Howe is the sport's all-time tough-guy superstar. Hardly. According to the website DropYourGloves.com, Old Man Winter had 31 fights in 2,186 games. Orr accumulated 51 punch-ups in 659 matches.

Bobby's on-ice adversaries included all the heavyweight contenders of the day: Vic Hadfield, Reggie Fleming, Ted Harris, Dennis Hextall, Keith Magnuson, Gary Dornhoefer, Pat Quinn, Rosaire Paiement, Bugsy Watson, Jim Schoenfeld and Moose Dupont. But it was more than just one-on-one battles—Bobby also led the NHL in being an accessory after the fact. Hockey's best player, Orr played 35 minutes a game, so he was around for a lot of Bruins fighting. Turk Sanderson, Terrible Teddy Green, Wayne Cashman, Ken Hodge and Boston's all-weather spark plug, Johnny "Pie" McKenzie, liked to go at it. When they did, Bobby always heard a cavalry trumpet sound in his head. If Bobby was in 51 one-on-one fights, he participated in at least three times as many brawls.

Orr would frequently be described in supernatural terms. Other Bruins called him God when he wasn't around—*Is God here yet? What did God do last night?* Soon after the young defenceman conquered Boston, a joke spread through New England tap rooms:

This guy dies and goes to heaven, right? Gets there, he's sailing around, all lovey-dovey and everything, flies over this little frozen pond. It's winter and there's this old guy dressed in robes, halo around his head, pushing a puck around. New guy sees all this and asks a passing angel, he goes, "Hey, who's the guy in the robe there playing hockey?"

"Oh that's God," the angel laughs. "He thinks he's Bobby Orr."

Yes, Orr's talents were otherworldly. Still, there was menace as well as miracles in Bobby's game. Bruins coach Harry Sinden liked to call Orr "The Godfather." Nevertheless, the stained-glass window of Bobby as a shepherd with a hockey stick that graces John Harvard's brew house in Harvard Square—you can still see it there today—is somehow appropriate. Orr would attract devotees that numbered in the millions. At the same time, the fantastic, hot-tempered hockey star was very much a saint in the city. Lots of athletes visit kids hospitals and show up at charity events; for Bobby, though, doing the right thing, helping those less fortunate, would become almost a physical need. After every game, he shared a heartfelt ritual with a young Bruins fan, Deanna Deleidi, who would wait for him in a wheelchair outside the Garden.

"How's your love life?"

"I'm waiting for you," Bobby said, kissing Deanna on the cheek.

"Watch out—I'll jump right out of this chair!"

At the time, Bobby was chairman of the Muscular Dystrophy Association of Canada and the United Fund of Boston. He also did work for the March of Dimes and showed up regularly at hospitals and orphanages. Priests, even other players, pulled Bobby aside, asking for charity. Every pub crawl the Bruins made was interrupted by a waiter with a hard-luck story. *My nephew, poor little guy . . . My friend's kid, geez, she ain't doing too well, Bobby.* "Yeah, yeah," the Bruins muttered, some rolling their eyes. Next time the team hit the bar, though, sure enough, Bobby had a signed stick or a Bruins uniform—literally the shirt off his back—for the waiter's ailing ward.

It was all too much, friends worried. "He's been too damn good and he better cut it out," a Bruins teammate told Jack Olson of *Sports Illustrated* for a cover story on Orr in 1970. "All this running around to mental hospitals and V.A. hospitals and poor people's parishes—it's gonna start showing up on the ice, in his play. This is his big problem, the way other people have problems with liquor or dope or women." Orr's good pal, roommate and Bruins trainer, Frosty Forristall, more or less agreed. "Every time I turn around in the apartment, there's five kids from Cerebral Palsy and a photographer, and it's time to go to the game and Bobby's saying, 'No, no hurry. This is more important.'"

In retrospect, Alan Eagleson's comment to *Sports Illustrated* is chilling: "He's a bleeding heart and a do-gooder, that's all," Bobby's "older brother"/agent complained. "And most of it is private. He doesn't even tell me about it. He doesn't get receipts and we lose all kinds of tax deductions . . . He'll get $500 for an appearance somewhere, and he'll give it to the first charity worker he sees. I asked him what happened to his bonus check last year. He says, 'Oh, I remember, I endorsed it over to Father Chase.'"

"No man is a hero to his valet," said Montaigne. In the same way, maybe no sporting hero is god to his agent. *He's a bleeding heart and do-gooder.* You can almost hear the Eagle, a cynical, tough-guy lawyer, spitting those words out. *All right, if he's just going to give it away . . .*

Why was Bobby such a brawler? How to explain his empathy? Probably the impulses were related. It was natural for Bobby to feel for the wounded. Deep down, he must've always known he was playing hockey on borrowed time. On December 4, 1966, just 20 games into his pro career, Orr tried to bend around Marcel Pronovost of the Maple Leafs. The old war-horse threw out a concrete hip and mangled the teenager's left knee. The following summer, Bobby hurt the other knee during a charity hockey game in Winnipeg—bad ice. His second pro season was worse: operations on both knees, along with a fractured cheekbone and separated shoulder. His nose was broken twice. A *Boston Globe* report from February 18, 1968, was grim: "The All-Star defenseman, who faces possible knee surgery, got off the plane and didn't look up once as he made his way through the airport." A reporter approached. "I just don't know," Bobby said. "Please, I just don't want to talk about it."

Please . . .

So much was expected of Childe Bobby, as the *Globe* sometimes called him. Decades later, the Dropkick Murphys' lead singer, Ken Casey, would remember that the first words his union-worker grandfather taught him were "Bobby Oah." Bruins play-by-play man Fred Cusick once reported that fans told him their parakeets could replicate the broadcaster's signature cry: "Score, Bobby Orr . . . Score, Bobby Orr."

Yes, the prince of the parish was revered in Boston. But what would be left of Peter Puck when the Puck disappeared? It's important to remember that Bobby was only a kid, barely 100 pounds, when he was first swallowed up like Jonah by the great whale, Fame. In his biography *Searching for Bobby Orr,* author Stephen Brunt rescued some wonderful snapshots of the Parry Sound prodigy that help explain his sensitivity and abiding need for hockey. When Bobby moved from home to play for the Oshawa Generals at age 14, he billeted with a nice family, the Wilds. Mom Cora Wild quickly took to Bobby, treating him like one of her own. Once, she ironed Bobby's jeans, leaving a sharp crease.

I pressed your slacks all nice for school, Robert.

Ah gee, thanks, Mrs. Wild, you shunta.

Who wants a sharp crease in their dungarees? That morning Bobby went to school with a bag under his arm, changing before class into a second pair of pants so as not to hurt Mrs. Wild's feelings. Another time, Bobby got home late from an out-of-town game. When he woke late next morning, Mrs. Wild told him some kids had dropped by earlier, asking if he wanted to play ball hockey. Mrs. Wild had shooed them away.

You got in so late, honey. You need your rest.

Hearing the story, Bobby smiled, but made one thing clear: *Next time the kids call, wake me up, OK?*

Bobby Orr craved hockey the way Popeye needed spinach. One time, the Oshawa Generals were playing the St. Catharines Black Hawks, and Bobby found himself sized up and smashed against the boards by the Hawks' biggest player (and Bobby's future teammate), Kenny Hodge. Orr collapsed in evident distress, but got up and managed to play the rest of the game. Afterwards, GM Wren Blair raced to the dressing room. "You OK?" Blair asked Orr. Bobby stared ahead, letting the words settle. "What do you mean?" he suddenly shouted.

"I saw you get hit. I wanted to know if you were all right."

Sensing he had somehow intruded, Blair tiptoed away. Bobby wasn't finished, however. Picking up his skates, he sent two weighted tomahawks whizzing past Blair. "Don't you ever ask me that again," Bobby said, pronouncing every word with fury. "If I'm hurt, I'll come and tell you. You don't come and ask me."

Bobby Orr was hockey. God help anyone who tried to split them up. Bruce Hood was sometimes that someone. Predictably, he and Orr didn't always get along. "I never thought Bobby gave officials any respect," Hood comments today. "We were a necessary evil. And he had a temper. Great player, but he could be a real jerk sometimes."

Not all referees had problems with Bobby. A contemporary of Hood's, Ron Wicks, dropped the right name to placate the great, sometimes-angry Bruin. "I used to take a bus up to Sudbury from Parry Sound to see my girlfriend," Wicks told me in a 2014 interview. "We dressed in a suit in those days, for some reason, and I had a skate for a tie clip. Anyways, I'm in a Parry Sound coffee shop and this waitress—lovely lady—sees my tie and says, 'Are you a hockey player?' I go, 'No, I'm a referee.' And she says, 'Well, my son is a hockey player: Robert Orr. Keep an eye on him for me.' Well, first game I referee Bobby, he starts giving me shit. I go, 'Bobby, I'm surprised. Arva always told me you were respectful of officials.' His head kind of snapped back. After that, I never had a problem with Bobby."

Wicks and Hood agree that Bobby could be a handful when his Irish was up. "When Bobby got into a fight, boy, that was something," Hood says, offering a low whistle. "You almost didn't want to get involved. Have you ever seen a trapped, caged animal—that look it gets in its eyes, fighting? That was Bobby when he was throwing punches. Kill or be killed. It was scary to see. That was the funny thing about Bobby. He was far and away the best player in the league, but . . . I don't know, it was funny, like he was always trying to prove himself. *Am I that good?* He never took a shift off. I mean *never.* He'd race up the ice, make a play— defencemen didn't do that then—and then he'd put his head down and kill himself to be the first back. He pushed himself incredibly hard. His intensity, that's what I remember."

Am I that good?

Once, in his rookie year, Bobby led a rush into the Rangers' zone and heard a stick slapping the ice behind him. "Pass, pass." Without looking, Bobby dropped the puck to the Rangers' Vic Hadfield, who sped the other way, scoring. The kid had fallen for the oldest trick in the book. Afterwards, he skated off, head down, finding a perch at the end of the Bruins bench, where he turned away from teammates and cried.

Another story from *Searching for Bobby Orr*: after his first NHL season, Bobby returned to Parry Sound to get away from it all. One day, the young Bruin and a friend from minor hockey, Bob Cardy, went on an overnight fishing trip to Bobby's favourite spot, the secluded channels of nearby Moon River. The boys stayed up late, fishing, watching the reds and silvers drain from a dying sunset, talking quietly, checking occasionally on the health of barbed minnows or trolling deep and slow with crank baits, hoping for leaping largemouth bass or walleye—"eyes," as they're known around Georgian Bay. When the conversation died, all you could hear was the plucked-banjo bleating of frogs from the nearby shore. Bobby was quiet for a while, and then it all came pouring out: *I wasn't that good this year, Bob. I made so many mistakes. Injuries, I got hurt a couple times. And we didn't make the playoffs. Cripes, we finished in last place. Maybe I'm not as good as everyone says . . .*

As they were reeling in to call it quits for the night, one of the boys turned on the boat radio to hear what was happening in the world. And that was when Bobby discovered he'd been named the NHL's rookie of the year.

The awards piled up. In his too-brief career, Bobby was named top defenceman eight seasons, league MVP three times, playoff MVP twice. Still, the young superstar never had it made. For every conquered summit, there was a dark, scary valley—hospitals, scalpels . . . legs that stopped working. So many expectations, so much pressure; no wonder he sometimes exploded, fists flying. *No, you can't take hockey away!* And don't forget, he was a small-town kid. Bobby conquered the world, but for the longest while he never really left Parry Sound.

Parry Sound.

"A sad, friendly little place," Frank DeFord called Bobby's birthplace in *Sports Illustrated*. "The kind of town where the men stop to peer carefully into hardware store windows and where pretty girls turn fat before they grow old." That was Parry Sound to a big-time New York sportswriter, maybe, but not to Bobby. As a youngster, he thrived in the town of 6,000 on Lake Ontario. The Orrs were a close, loving family. Phoning home in junior, Bobby hoped sister Pat didn't answer if teammates were around. That was because, as soon as he heard his older sister's voice, Bobby started blubbering. Then Patricia would blow.

Not only did Orr come from a little town, but for the longest time he was too small himself. One summer, Bobby worked at the Brunswick Hotel as a bellhop. Frustrating work, it turned out, because patrons refused to give him their luggage, fearing that a packed suitcase might bowl the little guy over.

I gotta carry your bags, sir.

No, I got them.

Please, I'll get in trouble.

The following year, Bobby began playing against 200-pound juniors. He must have wondered if he'd ever be big or good enough. The Orrs lived right next to a railway track on Great North Road in Parry Sound. Bobby went to sleep every night to the sound of fellow citizens departing town. However, his family didn't have a car. Leaving a small town wasn't always easy. His dad, who won a Parry Sound track meet in 1939 and was the best hockey player in the area, never did.

Maybe leaving was dangerous. Parry Sound has the world's deepest freshwater port. Take a step or two from shore and you were in way over your head.

When Bobby scored in the NHL, he almost always caught himself before celebrating. Lowering his head, he'd coast by teammates, nodding, embarrassed almost, aware of 15,000 fans in the rink watching him, along with all the cameras, millions of television eyes. Bobby moved slowly back to the blue line and would stare down at the ice, waiting for the crowd to settle and the ensuing centre-ice faceoff . . .

Come on, let's just play hockey again . . .

That wary uncertainty was Bobby's public persona. Unless he was with kids or teammates or was engaged in the game he played better than anyone else, Orr was uncomfortable in the public arena. "Many a time, Bobby and I would be out somewhere eating," Orr's first roommate, Johnny Bucyk, told a TV interviewer at the time, "and people would start looking at Bobby. 'C'mon let's eat in our room,' Bobby would say. And we'd leave, go order room service and play euchre."

Increasingly, hockey rinks became his refuge and the Bruins his close, volatile family. Unless he had a charity event, Bobby would be the first Bruin at the rink, arriving at 2:30 for a 7 o'clock game. Dressed to the waist in his uniform—a hockey centaur—he'd sort through sticks, weighing them for heft and balance, looking for a Victoriaville with a goal or two in it. Other than fixing his blade with a few strands of black cotton tape, Bobby had one other ritual that set him apart. He didn't wear socks. Once, in junior, Bobby forgot to pack a pair and liked the way it felt—his feet closer to the ice. Eventually, he didn't bother with tape on the blade of his stick, either. It was as if he wanted nothing between himself and hockey. That and for games to go on forever. He was the last Bruin out of the shower, waiting for reporters to leave. After he'd been with the Bruins a season, the real Peter Puck struck upon an idea that might allow hockey games to go all night. And so the young superstar made his first public policy statement, asserting himself in the dressing room.

Every Bruin, he decreed, had to go to the bar after the game. For at least two drinks.

All for one and at least two for all . . .

Since games weren't over until 10 o'clock, Bobby's "two-drink minimum" effectively meant the Bruins hung out at bars until closing time. Sure, NHL teams had gone out drinking before—but not every player, after every game. Boston was closer than most other teams and increasingly militant. Hockey had always been a rough sport, but in the late '60s the game coarsened considerably (even as it became, with Orr playing, more beautiful and thrilling). "The ethic of hockey is solidarity and revenge," American journalist Tom Dowling wrote, contemplating what was happening in Boston. Football teams boasted of "giving it the old college try." Hockey's credo, he said, seemed to be "We'll get the bastards."

The Bruins had last won the Stanley Cup when Cooney Weiland (great Bruins name!) was coach, way back in 1941. They had finished out of the playoffs eight straight years from 1959 through 1967. Enough already. After games, Bobby and the Bruins hit bars like they meant it, raising hell and contemplating payback. Yes, the Big Bad Bruins were on their way. The team's rough-hewn constituency was ecstatic. On the other hand, referees and visiting teams looked forward to games in Boston like they did to a trip to the dentist. With every passing game, it got—depending on your perspective—better or worse.

"If you fight one Bruin, you have to fight 18 of us," their coach, Harry Sinden, told a reporter. And so Boston's fights sometimes seemed to go on forever. Not that hockey brawls were anything new. No one outside of a maximum-security facility could have been any tougher or more ready to go than the sport's early bad men, guys like Sprague Cleghorn, Eddie Shore and Ted Lindsay. But a whole team dead-set on vengeance, fighting for each other, sometimes just for the hell of it—that was new.

The Big Bad Bruins were devoted to good times and turning their franchise around. Inevitably, happiness, staying healthy and winning came down to making sure Bobby Orr was OK. Anyone on the other team lifted as much as an eyebrow at Bobby, another Bruin knocked him on his rear end. Since Orr was always mixing it up himself and held simmering feuds with any number of enemy players, looking after Bobby required adopting a militant, aggressive posture. The *New York Times* noticed the Bruins' latent hostility in 1968. "They seem to think they're always going to be hit by somebody, so they hit first," Gerald Eskenazi observed.

A *Toronto Star* headline in 1969 called the Bruins "Bobby and the Animals," a reference to the then popular rock band Eric Burdon and the Animals, as well as a comment on the league-record 1,291 penalty minutes Boston accumulated in the 1968–69 season. Increasingly, that's how the Bruins were defined by the hockey world. There was Bobby, the greatest star in the game, surrounded by a rough, tough supporting cast. But make no mistake, despite his peerless on-ice brilliance, admirable charity and aw-shucks demeanour, Bobby was always the Bruin with the thorn in his paw.

The young defender's brilliance and vulnerability, not to mention his quick-fire Irish temper, turned the Boston Garden into a seething partisan environment. Only Rocket Richard, another superstar who fought for team and tribe, was as beloved (and watched over) by fans. If anyone touched either star, the public would rise up together, demanding vengeance. Bobby could do no wrong in Boston. The story that best demonstrates the devotion of local fans to their long-promised saviour involved a rare on-ice blunder. During a wild goalmouth scramble in Boston's end, Bobby attempted to clear the puck, accidentally shooting it into his own net.

There was an astonished pause in the Garden as everyone blinked to make sure they weren't having a bad dream. Then, suddenly, a fan in the balcony shouted, loud enough for everyone to hear, "That's OK, Bobby, goalie should have had it."

PAINT IT BLACK

After wearing Tweety Bird yellow for years, the Boston Bruins broke out pirate-black uniforms in the fall of 1967 as part of an overall get-tough campaign. The Bruins had been *trying* to improve and beef up for . . . well, it seemed like forever. Saviour Bobby Orr may have won the NHL's rookie of the year award in 1966–67, piling up more than 100 penalty minutes, but the Bruins finished last again. There was just no saving some hockey teams, it seemed.

At least the farm system was improving. Millionaire owner Weston Adams, a grocery store heir who once played goal for Harvard, had successfully invested in Canadian junior teams—Turk Sanderson's 1965 Memorial Cup champions, the Niagara Falls Flyers, Orr's Oshawa Generals and, out west, the Estevan Bruins. Years earlier, Adams himself traversed the vast pink dominion in a car, scouting juveniles. Like many bluebloods sensitive to the perception of a pampered upbringing, Weston favoured rugged, forthright employees—insisting, for example, that Sanderson make the Niagara Falls team over GM Hap Emms's protests.

Can't skate, plus he's a bit of a jerk. The Bruins' top minor-league farm team, the Oklahoma City Blazers of the Central Hockey League (CHL), also won league championships in 1966 and 1967—with a coach who could swear and swill rum with the worst pirates.

"I remember refereeing the CHL when Harry Sinden was coach of Oklahoma City," Bruce Hood told me, reeling in the years. "They had those black sweaters Boston would soon be wearing, and they were the tough guys in the league. [The Boston franchise] was obviously up to something. Harry—well, Harry was Harry. Let me go back a few years, when he was playing coach for the Minnesota Bruins. I was a young official. My boss, Carl Voss, was in watching a game and I told the captain of Minnesota, 'Hey, my boss is here, so tell Harry, let's play a good game.' You know, like a heads-up I'd be calling it close. Anyway, the captain skates back a minute later with a message: 'Harry says, "Just call the fucking game and don't worry about him."'"

A playmaking defenceman who captained the Whitby Dunlops to a world championship over Russia in 1958, Sinden had undeniable swagger. Still, it was Harry who went down with the Boston ship in 1966–67. What was wrong with the Bruins? Assistant GM Milt Schmidt figured he knew. "We [have] too many little guys," Schmidt told writer Stan Fischler at the time. "I got to thinking of the guys who played for the Bruins in the days we were winning. I thought of Dit Clapper, Eddie Shore, Johnny Crawford and Ray Getliffe. At one point, you know, they used to say if you could get through the door, you couldn't play for the Bruins."

In the late '60s, the Bruins' top centres, will-o'-the-wisps Hubert "Pit" Martin and Murray Oliver, were generously listed at 170 pounds. Big for accountants, maybe, but Montreal's top pivot, *Le Gros Bill,* Jean Béliveau, was six feet, three inches, and 205 pounds. And the kid who helped Toronto to a Stanley Cup in May 1967, Pete Stemkowski, was a monster. The NHL was getting bigger. And other than Sanderson, the Bruins had no physical centres coming up the pipe. What to do? It wasn't like NHL teams were throwing away 200-pound playmakers.

Or were they? On Monday, May 15, 1967, Schmidt got a call from

Florida. "Milt, let's make a deal," Chicago GM Tommy Ivan shouted over the phone. "Tommy," Schmidt sighed, "we've been talking and talking [all year] and you don't want to do anything." Schmidt was in no mood to kibitz because he was working on a deal to land hockey's bounding, in-your-face Marmaduke, Eddie Shack, from Toronto. The NHL's grand expansion draft was coming up. The league would soon be doubling to 12 teams, and the "Original Six" clubs were fussing over which players to protect, or withhold, from the draft. Schmidt needn't have worried about Ivan wasting his time, though. The Chicago GM was still fuming from the first-place Blackhawks' playoff upset at the hands of the Toronto Maple Leafs. Tommy was ready—anxious, in fact—to trade name players. Specifically, he wanted to get rid of the guy he felt most responsible for his team's most recent playoff disappointment.

That Italian loafer Phil Esposito.

Twice a top-ten NHL scorer and still just 25, the six-foot, one-inch, 205-pound centre had been held scoreless in the most recent postseason. Esposito also had a rap sheet going back to junior. With St. Catharines, he'd been nabbed breaking curfew, caught swan-diving into a hotel window in the wee hours. More recently, he'd gone on a toot with linemate Bobby Hull in Hollywood. The Golden Jet had parlayed his status as a celebrity pitchman into a visit to the set of *Bewitched*. Bobby and Phil were rendered starry-eyed by the sight of the TV show's star, Elizabeth Montgomery, floating about in a gauzy negligee—a condition made worse by a prolonged stay on various Los Angeles bar stools. Esposito was also suffering from a charley horse. What with his wounded heart and hip, the young centre wondered if he could play the Hawks' upcoming game.

"Phone Billy," Hull commanded, referring to coach Billy "The Tulip" Reay.

"I dunno."

"PHONE BILLY!"

Esposito did as he was told, dialling the coach's number. But the bar was loud and the young hockey player's head spinning. "Hey Bill, Phil Esposito," Esposito shouted into the din. "I got a pretty bad fucking leg here." Hearing this, Hull broke out laughing. Did the coach hear him? Maybe Espo should try again, louder.

HEY BILL—PHIL. I GOT . . . I GOT A LEG PRETTY FUCKING BAD . . . BILL?

Hull was crying now, and Esposito still wasn't sure his coach had heard him. The Tulip grasped what was going on, though. "You guys are drunk!" Reay properly concluded.

Esposito's stock took another hit after the Blackhawks clinched first place in the 1966–67 season with a 5–0 whitewashing of Toronto in March. Chicago's big line of Hull, Esposito and Kenny Hodge scored three goals in the first period. Days later, the Hawks had an official team celebration—champagne, beer, plenty of food. An overgrown boy from the Soo, Esposito was a bad judge of sparkling wines. By the time GM Tommy Ivan entered the celebration, the big centre was flush, over-flowing with opinions. "They're going to fuck it up," Esposito snorted, gesturing to Ivan.

"Why don't you go over there and tell him?" the always-helpful Hull suggested.

"I think I will."

Seconds later, Esposito was breathing kerosene in his boss's face. "We've got a dynasty here," Esposito told Ivan. "Don't screw it up." But then the playoffs arrived and Esposito was shut out. Hodge, too. And so Ivan was now on the phone with Milt Schmidt, ready to deal. "Ah, Esposito can't get along with Billy Reay," he volunteered. "He's causing a little problem there."

"I think I can put up with that problem," Schmidt offered, coaxing saliva into a parched throat. *Holy smokes, Esposito . . .* An old centre him-self, Schmidt knew Phil had everything—size, soft hands, decent speed once he got his big legs untangled. And the kid seemed to just be coming into his own. Espo finished number two in second-half scoring in 1966–67. Not bad for a guy who didn't get much power-play time. Ivan was also offering Hodge—younger and bigger than Esposito, built like a phone booth, 63 goals his last year in junior. Oh, and it got better: Chicago was also willing to throw in Fred Stanfield, another good-sized centre. As it happened, Freddy had worked in Schmidt's summer hockey camp back in Fenelon Falls, Ontario. Schmidt loved the way the kid handled the puck and wondered why Chicago had never given him a chance.

In return, Chicago wanted Pit Martin, Gilles Marotte and a backup goalie, Jack Norris. What's the catch? Schmidt wondered. Martin was a nice little centre. As for Marotte, well, he was a promising, hard-hitting defender, but he was coming off a lousy year. Besides, Boston had Orr, Ted Green and a bunch of young rearguards in Oklahoma. Defencemen, they had. Big, skilled forwards, they needed. "I think we can do this," Schmidt told Ivan, trying not to sound overexcited. "But I have to check a few things."

What he had to do was vet the trade with departing GM Hap Emms. Hap had one month left on his contract with Boston before returning to Niagara Falls and junior hockey. "You can't trade Marotte," Emms quickly told Schmidt.

"Hap, we have to make this trade."

"Well, you can't trade Marotte."

Panicking, Schmidt climbed over Emms's head, phoning owner Weston Adams, who was sick in bed at home. "Milt, if you think this is going to help our hockey club, go ahead and do it," Adams advised. Schmidt was about to pull the trigger, but paused . . . *What if something's wrong with Esposito?* He shared his concerns with colleague Tom Johnson, the great old Canadiens defencemen. Johnson said he'd phone Red Fisher at the *Montreal Star*.

"Everything about the deal is too good to be true," Johnson told the reporter, wondering if Esposito had a drinking problem, maybe something worse. After some grumbling (what a good reporter would do to maintain a source), Fisher agreed he'd look into it and gave Stan Mikita, Chicago's star centre, a call. "Here's the story, Stan," Fisher advised Mikita. "The Bruins have been offered Esposito. The deal is so one-sided, they figure there's something wrong with Espo. They asked me to check him out with one of the Chicago players, which is why I'm calling you."

"Give me that again?" Mikita moaned. "The management guys here are ready to give up Esposito?" Long pause. "Okay, here it is. Tell the Bruins this, and tell 'em exactly the way I'm telling it to you. Tell the fuckers there's nothing wrong with Espo. Like the rest of us, he takes a beer after a game, but that's it. Got that?"

One beer? Cripes, Marotte's nickname on the Bruins was "Six-Pack Marotte." Minutes later, Esposito, Hodge and Stanfield were Boston Bruins. Announcing the Bruins' big pre-expansion trade haul to TV cameras that week, Schmidt sounded like a rancher discussing prize stock. "Here we've got Stanfield, who looks small, but goes 185," Milt told a reporter from WSBK, channel 38. "We got Hodge and Esposito, who goes 200. And Eddie Shack [secured from Toronto], he's no lightweight . . ."

Of course, Esposito didn't want to go to Boston, to go from first to worst, from Bobby Hull to . . . *Eddie Shack?* He complained to wife Linda all summer in Sault Ste. Marie. Eventually, he told Schmidt he wasn't going to report for $8,000, his current salary. "I want $12,000," he said.

"Phil, we can't do that."

"OK, give me a $1,000 bonus for 25 goals."

"For 25 goals?"

"And another $1,000 if I get 35 . . ."

"For 35?"

"And another for 40 and another thou for 50 goals."

"Fifty goals?" Only three players in NHL history—Hull, Rocket Richard and Boom Boom Geoffrion—had ever reached that figure. Schmidt must have been wondering by now if all the stories about Esposito were true. How he talked more than six barbers and always, always had the needle out. Upset that Esposito imitated him behind his back, Billy Reay once approached the big centre in the dressing room and said, "You know your problem?"

"What?"

"You're aloof."

When Reay disappeared, Esposito turned to Hull. "What's 'aloof'?" he asked.

You know, a Loof—like Tim Horton or Allan Stanley.

"Why don't we just stay at home?" wife Linda asked Esposito after his talk with Schmidt. "You can go to work in the steel plant and forget about hockey."

Made sense. Phil had seniority at Algoma Steel. That meant the day shift—seven until three—driving a truck. He'd be foreman in seven years, with a left-arm tan and a good pension. Hell, Boston was only going to pay him $8,000. A little overtime, he could make that at the plant. Longer career, too. And he could still play baseball and hockey with his *paesanos* after work—Pat Nardini, Clem Giovanatti, Chubby Sanko, Fuzzy Pezzuto . . .

Still, Phil's dream had always been the NHL. His welder father, Pasquale Esposito, had bought Phil and brother Tony twin-blade skates as Christmas presents in 1945. Phil was four at the time; Tony, two. After Mass that Christmas, Dad got his little guys all decked out in scarves and toques and gave them a little push on the frozen pond behind the house. Pasquale—everyone called him Pat or Bushel (he weighed 260 pounds)— played hockey himself once, but that ship sank when he punched out a referee. Yeah, the old man had a temper. Once, Tony looked at his dinner and complained, "Aw, spaghetti again!" Pat fired the fork he was hold-ing—*fwwt!*—right into the future NHL goalie's forehead, tines sticking in and everything.

Usually, though, Pasquale Esposito was a sweetheart. Made pizza and popcorn to go with *Hockey Night in Canada* on Saturdays; handed Phil a salmon-coloured two-dollar bill while he was working the stove—*Be a good boy and run down the store there and gimme six Pepsi-Cola . . . away you go.* The Espositos watched hockey games between mouthfuls of food, rooting for the Detroit Red Wings because of Alex Delvecchio. The Canadiens had Lou Fontinato. The Leafs? Everyone knew they were prejudiced against Italians.

Once, young Phil got up in the middle of the night and found his dad outside, watering the backyard rink. Three in the morning, freezing out, and the old man's shift at Algoma started in a couple hours. Pat Esposito also protected his eldest from teachers who complained he was only interested in hockey. "Let the boy follow his dream," he told them. Defending Phil turned into a second job. The teenager was kicked out of Sault Collegiate. Hit a basketball coach in the head with a ball, the school said. *Hey, it slipped, honest to God.* Then there were complaints from senior girls. For fun, Phil would sneak up and pop open the backs of their bras—undid the clasp just by snapping his fingers. (Milt Schmidt was right. The kid had soft hands.) Eventually, Espo was sent to an all-boys' Catholic school. In Grade 12, he fell asleep during an exam. A nun whacked him awake. Phil scrawled "I don't know nothing" on a piece of paper and quit school forever.

"You plant potatoes, you grow potatoes," Pasquale Esposito always said. Son Phil worked summers at Algoma until he was 30—but *just* summers. When Labour Day 1967 rolled around, the hockey player loaded up his car and drove 14 hours straight to the Bruins' training camp in London, Ontario. He must've figured he'd landed in heaven upon arriving. First thing Coach Sinden told him was, "Phil, I want you to learn how to play the slot." The Bruins intended to run their offence through Esposito.

For his part, Harry heard about the Esposito trade while at an event at Royal Military College in Kingston, Ontario, his hometown. As well as coaching hockey, Sinden was a military buff and a foodie. His favourite meal was Napoleon's victory banquet—chicken Marengo, a diced bird sautéed in oil, garlic and tomato, garnished with fried eggs and crayfish. Alas, he seldom dined on chicken Marengo during hockey season. There were too few victories worth celebrating. And Sinden knew why: the Bruins' power play stank—34 goals in 250 chances the year previous. If the Bruins played football, they would have been better off declining penalties. With the speedy Orr, Murray Oliver and Pit Martin, the Bruins had a decent fast break, but no half-court game; they couldn't slow things down and work the puck to the net. But with Esposito . . .

Phil, I want you to learn how to play the slot. Until now, NHL centres were playmakers. Wingers inevitably led the league in scoring—Hull,

Howe, the Rocket, Boom Boom Geoffrion, Doug Bentley. *But Esposito is our best scorer,* Sinden reasoned. Wouldn't it make more sense for wingers to feed him? And so, before he had even slipped into the Bruins' new Jolly Roger–black jersey, Espo was anointed *the man.*

Finally! As a kid, Phil hadn't made bantam or midget teams on his first try. At 18, he'd failed to land a spot on the St. Catharines Teepees, Chicago's junior affiliate. Too fat, slow and loud, coaches complained. Hey, the Espositos were emotional and loved to eat. Phil's old man hid salami and pepperoni in the chesterfield. ("If you squeal, you're in trouble," he would tell the boys.) Despite carrying a spare tire and talking too much, Phil could score. After being cut by the Teepees, he played for the Junior B Sarnia Legionnaires, collecting 12 points in one game. At 19, he finally made St. Catharines—as a backup! When a regular centre, Ray Cullen, was hurt, the Teepees finally gave Espo a regular shift.

He popped four goals in his first game.

He would also score in Chicago—over 20 goals in three straight seasons. But the Blackhawks figured anyone could knock in 20 rebounds playing on Hull's line. They didn't appreciate him at all. When Phil waltzed into GM Tommy Ivan's office to collect on his breakthrough rookie year, the executive pulled a scam that would have made Ebenezer Scrooge blush.

"Phil, come on in, sit down. Now about your salary . . ."

"That's right, Mr. Ivan. Well, I scored 23 goals last year. That's pretty good . . ."

Ivan's phone rang on cue. "He wants *how* much?" the GM yelled into the receiver. "That's ridiculous. Does he think we're made out of money? Tell him I'll send him to the minors before I pay that kind of dough . . ." After hanging up, he turned to Esposito and purred, "Now, Phil, about your contract . . ."

"Whatever you think is fair, Mr. Ivan," Esposito found himself saying. That ended up being the minimum—$6,500.

Like the popular comedian Rodney Dangerfield, Phil Esposito never got any respect. Even when he was named grand marshal of a parade one summer in the Soo, he ended up humiliated. Bobby Hull came up for the event. Canada's Country Gentleman, singer Tommy Hunter, performed. And if you believe Phil's autobiography, *Thunder and Lightning,* Phil's wife drank too much and spent all her time dancing with the octopi Hull and Hunter.

I tell you, I don't get any respect. Last week I bought a used car and found my wife's clothes in the back seat.

But now, Phil was in Boston, the centre on the Bruins' number one line. *Phil, I want you to learn how to play the slot.* Respect at last. After practice, Espo stayed out on the ice and submitted to a unique drill, standing in front of the net with another player or rink worker draped over him. Another Bruin—sometimes trainer Frosty Forristall—stood in the corner and fired pucks to the beleaguered slot man, who wrestled free of grabbing arms to deflect and tip pucks into corner slivers of the net.

It was worse in real games, of course. Enemy defencemen came at Phil like strike-breaking Pinkertons, chopping at the backs of his legs. But you couldn't destroy Esposito's focus. Or crush his resolve. Once, at age ten, playing ball hockey on his street in the Soo, Phil fought through a stomach ache—net-hanging, probably, tormenting Tony in goal, snapping furless tennis balls past his little brother's outstretched baseball mitt. After a while, though, Phil felt really sick. Still, he continued. The pain worsened. Phil hung in there. *Hey, I'm open. Pass . . . pass.* Eventually, he threw up. Kept on on arguing and scoring, though. Right up until he turned whiter than the nearby snowbanks and collapsed. Only then was he rushed to the hospital, where doctors removed a swelling appendix.

Sinden realized he was right about Esposito's scoring potential after Phil's second game as a Bruin. Boston beat Montreal 6–2 that night. Phil scored four goals, three with a man advantage. And every goal came from the slot, with Phil wearing a Habs defender. Next game, Boston beat Chicago, 7–1. Stanfield had two goals and assists. Hodge also scored.

Where's that cookbook? Time to whip up some chicken Marengo!

But it was a preseason game at home in 1967 that Harry would later identify as the moment when New England's hockey team finally came

together, earning the quadruple-B brand—Boston's Big Bad Bruins—
that made them famous. Montreal was in town, finishing off the exhibition schedule. Midway through the first period, Orr and Ted Harris
collided along the boards. Orr surprised the bigger Canadien with a fast
flurry of punches. (No one could get mad faster than Bobby.) When referee Art Skov separated the combatants, Sanderson was now in Harris's
face. "Try *me*," he said.

"I'm going to take care of you," a winded Harris promised.

"What are you going to do?" Bruins defenceman Ted Green countered.

"I've got no problem with you, Teddy."

"If you want *him,* you do."

Too late. Sanderson and Harris were at it. The benches cleared. It took
over an hour to play the first period. Thirty-four penalties were called
in the game—20 to Boston. After fighting Orr and Sanderson, Harris
wobbled to the penalty box with an ice pack covering his face. Boston
fans hammered the glass along the railings, happy and hungry for more.
They'd get it, too. Orr was ejected in the third period for getting into
a second fight, with Bugsy Watson. Another Montreal defender, Terry
Harper, was injured in a multiplayer pileup.

And oh yes, Boston won, 2–1. Esposito scored both goals.

"Like it or not, that's the kind of thing that is going to make you a
team," Sinden told his charges afterwards. "Everybody has an identity
but us. Detroit are great forechecking; Montreal has all the speed and
players. Toronto is clutch and grab. Maybe that's our identity—'Don't
mess with us.'" The black-and-blueprint for Boston was in place: fight
me, fight my gang. "Bobby Orr made a rule that no one was ever to be
in a fight alone," Sanderson told a reporter back in the day. "You were
only alone until the second guy got there. If you hit one of us, the closest
teammate was going to clock you—just drill you in the back of the head,
cross-check you or sucker-punch you—*pow!* Whatever it took."

The division of labour was soon apparent—Esposito, Orr and a suddenly efficient power play that included Johnny Bucyk and Fred Stanfield
looked after the *pow.* The rest of the Bruins (with Orr's eager assistance)

handled "whatever it takes." The Bruins kept getting badder and better—764 minutes in penalties and 182 goals in 1966–67; 1,031 penalty minutes and 259 goals in 1967–68; 1,281 penalty minutes and 303 goals in 1968–69; 1,184 minutes in penalties (down, but still leading the league) and a whopping 460 goals in 1969–70 . . .

Esposito's goal-scoring output went from 35 to 49 to 43 to—it seemed incredible at the time, like running a three-minute mile—a whopping 76 goals in 1970–71.

The Bruins also led the league in tall tales. Arrested for drinking and driving, Wayne Cashman used his one phone call to order in Chinese from Kowloon's, in Boston. At training camp in London, Ontario, Turk Sanderson finished evenings at the Campbell Tavern (Esposito loved the pickled eggs) by running through a parking lot and diving through his open motel window. A handful of Bruins gathered one night to watch Turk do a perfect dive and tuck into an open window. "Watch this," he told teammates, assuming a sprinter's pose. And then he took off. The players disappeared like a break shot in pool, however, upon hearing a loud crash and astonished screams.

Turk dove into the wrong room, interrupting a civilian card game.

The Bruins story of all time had Esposito recuperating at Mass General after surgery. In burst a masked surgeon—Orr in blue scrubs. "OK, wop-po, you're coming with us." Acting on Dr. Orr's orders, teammates wheeled Espo out the door and into an elevator. The kidnappers peeled off exit railings to ram their fallen comrade's gurney out of the hospital. Finally, they were bobsledding Esposito through icy Boston streets. "Turning, stick out your hand," Orr instructed Phil at one point. Minutes later, they arrived at Bobby's bar, the Branding Iron, for yet another Bruins team party.

Years later, the *Boston Globe*'s Kevin Paul Dupont would comment: "Was this really a team, or some type of brotherhood that had come together years after signing a blood oath in the backwoods of Canada? From afar, one had to wonder. They could be seen partying at Polcari's down the street from the Garden or the Elbow Lounge on the Boston/

Brookline line. The next night, they would line up, five across, pummelling any Canadien, Red Wing, Blackhawk or Maple Leaf who rubbed
one of them the wrong way."

"Even in an airport, they were loud and always carrying on," remembered referee Hood. "You could see them all together, joking and fooling around."

Lots of clubs stiffed rookies with team meals. The Bruins tied
Sanderson to a restaurant chair before slipping him the bill. Bucyk routinely cut Esposito's suspenders as he climbed into his jersey; all the guys
enjoyed the ensuing vaudeville act—hockey's leading scorer racing onto
the ice with his pants sinking to his ankles. Johnny McKenzie competed
in wild-cow milking contests in the off-season and showed up for hockey
practice in shower clogs, smoking a cigar. Orr's two-drink minimum led
to rocky mornings. "Pass the salt," rookie Jimmy Harrison asked Hodge
one breakfast. "You got a broken arm? Get the salt yourself," Hodge
snarled. Harrison did so, firing the shaker at his grumpy teammate. Eddie
Johnston entered the fray, breaking his hand. For laughs in practice, Ted
Green manoeuvred some rookies into the corner and then took a home-
run swing over their head, just to see the look of horror in the kids' eyes
when his stick exploded against the glass.

The Wild Bunch was wilder still with other teams. Chicago's Pierre
Pilote believed the Bruins were hell-bent on revenge because they'd
spent so long in the league basement, taking beatings from everyone
else. Classic victim-turns-bully pathology. But it was more than that:
except for Orr, the Bruins were cast-offs. Bucyk arrived in a trade from
Detroit years earlier. Goalie Gerry Cheevers and defenceman Green
were cut loose by Toronto and Montreal. "You know, you think about
the Bruins of that era, they were guys nobody else wanted," McKenzie
told writer Jay Moran in the book *The Rangers, The Bruins and the End
of an Era*. "New York didn't want me. Esposito and that group, nobody
wanted them. And two or three other guys came that nobody else really
wanted, but we were all rebels, we wanted to play hockey . . . and we
became real close friends . . . Harry could see what was [going on], he

put the right guys together and he changed them around but once he got them set . . ."

With their black-as-night, black-as-coal jerseys, the Bruins were rowdy, taunting buccaneers. "Cashman would come up to me, rubbing his hand across the blade of his stick, and say, 'I'd like to cut someone's eyes with this,'" Hood recalls. The big, blond winger did the same to Bob Myers. Both refs called Cashman out: *Let's go after the game.* Cash would just laugh. Boston was the only NHL club with 1,000 penalty minutes in the 1967–68 season. Montreal collected 698; the Pittsburgh Penguins, 548.

"The Bruins put pressure on you," Hood told tell me, shivering at the memory of long-ago battles. "Normally, you do a game, you'd have maybe 50–60 decisions; what kind of penalty—major, minor? With Boston, you had twice as many decisions. Bench-clearing brawls most games. And Sinden complained about everything; it was always the other team's fault. I always got the feeling Harry disrespected me. It was the same with some of the Bruins players. Howe, Hull, Béliveau, they realized referees had a job to do. With the Bruins, it was tough. Frankly, Bobby Orr could be a real asshole . . . Esposito, oh boy, what an actor, always playing to the crowd. He'd get tangled up with somebody and fall down, then throw up his hands like you missed something."

(Espo's act did not go unnoticed by Hollywood. Years later, he claimed Francis Ford Coppola offered him the role of Connie Corleone's whiny, vindictive husband, Carlo, in *The Godfather*. But Espo turned it down. After he scored 76 goals one season and cashed in all his bonuses, he stopped working summers. Hollywood could take a hike.)

If the Bruins were rude to hockey's police, they could be downright sacrilegious with other players and teams. Going into the 1969 playoffs against the reigning Stanley Cup champion Montreal Canadiens, Sanderson predicted a Bruins upset, making his infamous "they don't have the guts to beat us" comment. No one in hockey had talked like that before. Bruins rookie Jim Harrison caught Gordie Howe with his head turned in late 1969, belting him to the ice. Harrison then stood over

Mr. Hockey, the sport's most legendary performer, pausing to think . . . and then kicked Howe's stick 30-feet down the ice.

Fuck you.

That never used to happen, either. NHL players just didn't taunt referees or bait Stanley Cup champions. Rookies never ridiculed Hall of Famers. No percentage in it. Bad karma. As folksinger Jim Croce warned in a bouncy hit from the period:

> *You don't tug on Superman's cape*
> *You don't spit into the wind*
> *You don't pull the mask off that old Lone Ranger*
> *And you don't mess around with Jim.*

The Big Bad Bruins didn't care about professional etiquette. The Bruins believed in their own narrative: referees were wrong; the opposition was asking for it. They were finally winning, a playoff team, the most exciting, most talked-about club in hockey. Boston Garden fans were in heaven. God was indeed on their side . . . playing all-star-calibre defence, in fact. Everybody was just going to have to deal with it. The Bruins weren't about to change. Not now that they were finally winning.

Maybe, as NHL president Clarence Campbell suggested, the brute, purposeful savagery was a sign of the times. That the ecstatic, swooning violence in films like *Bonnie and Clyde* (1967) and *The Wild Bunch* (1969), along with what was happening on the TV news (the October 1970 crisis in Quebec, riots in the United States), had something to do with a score of reckless skaters dressed in black, bashing around enemy players.

Didn't a man dressed in Bruins black win a 1969 Grammy Award for singing, "I shot a man in Reno, just to watch him die"?

Or maybe it was like Bruins goalie Eddie Johnston said at the time: "Let's face it, we're just a bunch of kooks and degenerates who get along." Either way, the Boston Bruins transformed hockey into something more thrilling, but also more violent than it had ever been. And make no mistake, the Bruins might have complained about referees, about other players on other teams always starting fights, but everyone watching, even little kids following the game at home on TV, knew it was on them.

In the from-the-mouths-of-babes department, the *Boston Globe* received the following letter on March, 14, 1970, with the headline JUST LIKE WAYNE:

> *Never again will I be a believer when someone points to the harmful effects of television violence on children. Yesterday, my two sons, ages 7 and 6, were playing street hockey in our driveway. An argument developed and one hit the other with his stick, thankfully with no serious injury. When I tried to explain to the guilty one that it was terribly dangerous to do this his answer was, "But it's OK, Ma, I saw Wayne Cashman do it on TV."*
>
> *I rest my case.*
>
> *Gail A. Barry, Whitman*

Although Espo missed out on a movie career, he did make an impression (as in long-lasting bruises) on kids as a pitchman with his "Mylec" indoor pucks and street hockey balls, available everywhere in and around 1970. The pucks were useless, but the bright orange balls were extremely popular, even if they became harder than algebra in cold weather. Catch one on the upper leg and you'd walk around with an angry welt—it felt like someone had a hand on your thigh—for 48 hours.

"GET QUINN! GET QUINN!"

Toronto Maple Leafs vs. Boston Bruins, April 2, 1969

Maybe NHL president Clarence Campbell was right: the NHL was no more than a cracked mirror to a disintegrating society. Anyone opening a newspaper on Wednesday April 2, 1969, must have figured the sky was falling. The Vietnam War had spread to Cambodia. British troops were on their way to break up a brewing civil war between Catholics and Protestants in Northern Ireland. Back in the States, massive coordinated Vietnam protests would take place that week in New York, Washington, San Francisco and Los Angeles. At the same time, the trials of Rosicrucian stable boy Sirhan Sirhan and petty thief/occasional stag movie director James Earl Ray played out on the front page. (The previous year, Sirhan assassinated presidential candidate Robert Kennedy; and, after undergoing plastic surgery in preparation for flight to Rhodesia, Ray killed civil rights leader Martin Luther King Jr.)

Toronto papers detailed domestic troubles as well: in Montreal, Pierre-Paul Geoffroy, the firebug and "workers' society" advocate for the Front de libération du Québec (FLQ), was sentenced to over 1,000 years in jail* for blowing up 31 banks, federal institutions and, when feeling lazy, the odd mailbox. Quebec and Canada were going through a painful divorce, it seemed. Some believed separation was already . . . how you say . . . fait accompli. The night before the first game of the Boston Bruins–Toronto Maple Leafs opening round playoff series, Quebec singer Pauline Julien appeared at Toronto's Massey Hall. When she attempted a song in English, someone yelled, *"En français."* Julien stopped. "In another country, I always try to do a little bit in their language," she explained.

But the big front-page story before the Leafs–Bruins opener, both in the *Toronto Star* and the *Tely* (*Toronto Telegram*) was a Tuesday morning bank robbery.

DENTIST SHOT CHASING GUNMEN IN $18,000 HOLD-UP

Two masked robbers entered the Bank of Commerce at Sherbourne and Wellesley, calling for customers to drop to the floor. A teller fainted. After stuffing their bags with loot, the crooks tore off out the bank, with branch manager Allan Dow in pursuit. "Hold up, stop those men!" the banker shouted. Jack Langdon, a health department official visiting a nearby dental clinic, took after the villains down an alley, knees pumping. One robber turned and shot the dentist in the groin with a luger.

"He was always honest," Langdon's mom advised the *Tely*. "Maybe too honest."

There could be no escaping gunfire and civil insurrections in the sports pages. Wednesday's dailies carried the tragic story of Hamilton Tiger-Cat receiver Ted Watkins. Months earlier, the African-American footballer had walked into a Stockton, California, liquor store, falling

---

★ Although Pierre-Paul Geoffroy was given 21 consecutive lifetime sentences, he would be paroled in on February 15, 1981, after serving 12 years.

quickly into an argument with Fred Earle Larsen, the store manager. Larsen ended the fight by pumping four bullets into Watkins, letting the athlete bleed out by the cash register. Ted's brother Clifton was shot in the parking lot, but he escaped. Neither was armed. And Clifton was eventually cleared of robbery charges. Still, there was no official probe into Ted Watkins's death. Elsewhere in sports, there were more stories on a recent game that turned into a civil insurrection. *I went to a revolution and a hockey game broke out,* to paraphrase comedian Rodney Dangerfield.

Over the weekend, the Czechs and Soviets met at the World Hockey Championships in Stockholm; this came six months after 200,000 Russian troops had invaded Czechoslovakia. Everyone in Prague watched on TV as their guys manhandled the Soviets, winning 4–3. Vaclav Nedomansky lifted the Russian net of its moorings after the winning goal. The victorious Czechs also refused to shake hands at the end of the game. In the Czech capital, hundreds of thousands assembled in Namesti Square, chanting, "Four-three, four-three." Growing drunk with victory, they attacked Soviet army barracks and ransacked the office of the Soviet state airline, Aeroflot. There would be arrests, beatings and reprisals. Few seemed to care.

"Four-three, four-three . . ."

Hours after the Prague furor, another hockey riot: close to 1,000 Bruins fans stayed up all night Monday, lounging about the North Station concourse in sleeping bags, playing cards or watching *Laugh-In* on portable TVs, waiting for the last Leafs–Bruins tickets to go on sale. Campers stretched awake Tuesday to a pleasant surprise—Bruins president Weston Adams Jr. arrived with coffee and crullers. But when the 24-year-old grocery store heir departed, fans discovered there was another ticket queue—the real one. *They'd been in the wrong line!* All they got for their 12-hour vigil were free donuts and the chance to try out "sock it to me" jokes† on police called in to quell what rookie

---

† A popular Monday night variety show, *Rowan & Martin's Laugh-In* (1968–73) was stocked with familiar running gags and catchphrases ("you bet your sweet bippy").

Boston Globe reporter Peter Gammons described as an ugly mob scene.

Even fans with tickets arrived in a wicked mood for Boston's playoff opener. Some chanted anti-Toronto slogans. Weeks earlier, during a game at Maple Leaf Gardens, Pat Quinn had knocked Bobby Orr down, kicking him in the arse. Like Orr, Quinn was working-class Irish (his maternal grandmother went by the name Snooze Ireland). Another brewing conflict: Bruins coach Harry Sinden didn't like his Leafs counterpart, Punch Imlach. Harry was just making a name for himself, and Punch could never remember what it was. "The young fella coaching the other team" was how Imlach referred to his 36-year-old rival. That was the real tension between the clubs: Toronto was old school—NHL royalty. There was a portrait of the Queen the size of a drive-in screen in Maple Leaf Gardens, not to mention 14 Stanley Cup banners (compared to Boston's three). And Bruins fans could see on TV how Toronto fans dressed for games, all la-di-da in suits and fedoras, wives draped in mink. *Wives? Mink?* The Boston Garden was a men's tavern. Dress code: windbreakers and scuffed desert boots.

Leafs owner Conn Smythe once roamed his palace after games, making sure it was spotless, nary a peanut shell on the floor. He would even send notes to fans who failed to dress in style—*No ski jackets!* By comparison, strolling into the Boston Garden, even for a Stanley Cup playoff game, felt like wandering into a drunk tank on New Year's Eve. For one thing, you could never tell what organist John Riley (another Irishman!) was playing. *Is that "The Stars and Stripes Forever" or "Jumpin' Jack Flash"?* Flasks were commonplace—drunks, too. Sometimes, after game's end, an over-refreshed Bruins patron would jerk awake, seeing monkeys. For decades, there had been rumours of an escaped simian tribe, refugees from Frank Buck's 1936 "Bring 'Em Back Alive" show,

---

One recurring feature had celebrities, from John Wayne to President Richard Nixon, asking "Sock it to *me?*" The gag was usually handled by cast member Judy Carne, who would be tricked into saying the phrase ("It may be rice wine to you, but it's still sake to me") and then would be dunked with water.

living in the shadowy netherworld above the Garden lights. After the building shut down for the night, the monkeys would swing down to the floor, feasting on trampled hot dogs and stale beer. Hearing a sudden noise, a snoozing fan or soused press box reporter would open his eyes, face to face with a beyond-hungry, shivering monkey reaching to grab a salty shelled peanut out of the crinkly cellophane bag beside him.

I once shared a drink with folksinger/rounder/sports fan Loudon Wainwright III, who spoke wistfully of the gamy pleasures of the old Boston Garden. "During the Bobby Orr years, I lived in Boston with my wife [folk singer Kate McGarrigle], a big Montreal Canadiens fan," Loudon recalled. "She first took me to a Bruins game; we sat up with the rowdies"—beside the kinds of guys who did your bidding all day: bus drivers, doormen and waiters. Bruins fans were smart and funny, with great, expressive faces; like children or drunks, their emotions were close to the surface, the folksinger said. They would get pissed off, wanting to kill somebody; then, a minute later, Orr or some other Bruin would score and there'd this eruption—*Hey-hey, we won!*

"What a rollercoaster those games were," Wainwright said. "I loved it."

Not as much as close to 15,000 swooning Bruins fans enjoyed the Toronto–Boston playoff opener. Loved it right up until the rollercoaster broke late in the second period, exciting a wave of anarchy that might have ended, if God hadn't intervened, in a gangland execution.

As always, the Bruins came out starved for goals. ("When they drop the puck . . . the Bruins think it's raw meat," Philadelphia Flyers GM Bud Poile said at the time.) The Bruins were particularly ravenous at home. The team had not won against the Leafs in Toronto, with Queen Elizabeth primly staring down, in 22 games—nearly four full seasons! And yet the last time the Leafs were here in Boston, the Bruins had walloped them, 11–3. Even at home, though, Bruins were accident-prone; so intent on glory that they often left their goalie to fend for himself. In pregame skate-arounds, Johnny McKenzie liked to whack netminder Gerry Cheevers on the pads, calling out, "See you after the game."

"You little bastard," Cheevers would shout. "You better do some backchecking tonight."

Tonight, it would be Ken Hodge who let his man get away after the puck was dropped. Brit Selby was in alone on Cheevers. Years earlier, while still a Leafs farmhand, Cheevers had practised without a stick, developing an aggressive flopping style and gunslinger-fast glove hand. This particular duel, Selby shot first. Still, Cheevers outdrew him, snaring a high drive in his trapper. The crowd let out a grateful cheer. Minutes later, off-season cowboy McKenzie calf-roped a Leaf, and then Dallas Smith took a foolish tripping penalty. Two-man advantage, Leafs. But Cheevers was a blur between the pipes, throwing a twitching body part at a half-dozen Leafs chances, diving on rebounds, then jumping to his feet, offering an open trapper containing the puck to referee John Ashley.

I think this belongs to you.

"Cheevers was a beauty," referee Bruce Hood told me. "Someone would shoot the puck over the glass, I'd point past the blue line and say, 'Faceoff outside.' Hearing this, Gerry would go, 'But Bruce, we can't play outside—there's no ice!' He was always joking. One time, minute to go, close game, he makes a great glove save and hands me the puck. 'Mind if I go to the bench and tape an Aspirin to my hand here, Brucie?' He tells me, 'Think I broke a finger.' Then he gives me a big wink. Oh, Gerry Cheevers—everyone called him 'Cheesy'—was a beauty."

Tonight though, Cheesy would only be intermittently involved in the action, as Boston took over early. And completely. After the Leafs' Bob Pulford was booked for interference, Esposito won a draw to Orr, who made a smart pass to Johnny Bucyk. Big Phil saw the rebound first, and then the hands that once snapped open brassieres without Catholic schoolgirls noticing went to work, quickly firing a loose puck past an amazed Bruce Gamble. Seven seconds; that was all the Boston power play needed to work. Next shift, Espo set up Bucyk. Two–nothing. Later in the first, Esposito undressed the Leafs defence, pulling Gamble with them. Three–zero. The onslaught continued in the second. Bucyk and Derek Sanderson made it 5–0. Turk didn't celebrate upon scoring; he just floated past teammates on one skate—the old flamingo pose. Growing cranky, Leafs coach Imlach threw out enforcer Forbes Kennedy. On the ensuing penalty, Esposito waltzed around a fallen Quinn, gave goalie Gamble a head shiver—"the old Latin swerve," an admiring press-box wag commented—and tucked the puck into an empty net.

Esposito's hat trick made it 6–0. The Garden ice quickly disappeared under hats—ball caps, woollen toques, fedoras. At least one spectator resisted the custom of flipping his lid when a home player collected his third goal. What with the Blackhawks out of the playoffs, Chicago coach Billy Reay—the Tulip, Esposito's former boss—was in the crowd, scouting, also wilting a little every time former Hawks Esposito, Ken Hodge or Fred Stanfield scored. They all did, too. Esposito ended up with four goals and two assists in an absurdly lopsided 10–0 Boston win. And after the game, big Phil administered the *coup de grâce,* severing the Tulip's stem. A Boston reporter asked how come Phil couldn't score like this for the Blackhawks in the playoffs.

"I never played in the playoffs for Chicago," Phil complained. "I played a total of one period in four years of playoffs and [then] they benched me."

A complete and utter fib—not that anyone was paying attention. Not to Esposito's four goals, to Boston's win, or to what would turn out to be George Imlach Custer's last stand for the Leafs. No, the story of tonight's game, what everyone would remember about the game, was not the score, but how the rollercoaster that was big-league, NHL hockey went off the rails, tumbling into wild air . . . not once, but twice inside a 20-minute period that, what with all the fights, took close to two hours of real time.

The first derailment occurred late in the second period. Saviour Orr took off with the puck behind the Boston net, speeding through a narrowing tunnel along the boards. Circling Bruins winger Hodge flew by on his right. Leafs checker Selby was there to his left. It was a tight gap, but Orr, who grew up playing neighbourhood hockey—15 on 15—along the frozen waters of Parry Sound, never worried about negotiating shifting traffic.

Teammates, fans, they were the ones who worried.

"He gives us the screaming meemies," Bruins trainer Frosty Forristall told *Sports Illustrated*. "He'll take a defenceman right across the goalmouth with him, full speed, a few inches from the post." Indeed, Orr's drag-strip courage, the way he courted danger, was part of his allure. That's what lifted fans from their seats—speed, more speed and the hummingbird-quick swoops and swerves that got Bobby out of seemingly impossible traffic jams. Not tonight, though. Bobby had his head down, skating as fast as only he could. And so he never saw the blazing headlights coming his way.

The Leafs' Pat Quinn, Snooze Ireland's towering grandson, hoofed in from the blue line—20, then ten, then five feet away . . .

Wincing linesman George Ashley watched it all happen, right in front of him.

"It was awful, like watching two trains on the same track coming straight for each other," Ashley told me over the phone years later. "Bobby Orr was really moving. And Quinn was a great big boy. He caught Bobby full on and both went flying . . . Quinn, though, he was the only one who got up. And I tell you, that building in Boston, which was usually so loud you had trouble thinking, got real quiet all of a sudden."

At first, everyone feared the worst. The NHL's director of officiating, Scotty Morrison, watched from the press box. "If [Orr] doesn't get up, we don't get out of here alive," Morrison told himself.

On the ice, Hodge hurried to Orr, carefully placing a glove under the head of his fallen, absolutely out-cold teammate. Within seconds, the rest of the on-ice Bruins, including Esposito, were sharks circling Quinn. Fans were up and jeering. A chant soon broke out: "Get Quinn! Get Quinn!" The big Leafs defenceman was also unhappy to hear that he had received a five-minute penalty for elbowing. "He thought it was a clean hit," Ashley recalled. "Pat kept saying that he had his arm to his body."

Film evidence suggests the Leafs defender was right. The elbow in question came away from his body *after* contact with Orr. He probably deserved two minutes for charging (and maybe three for breaching the peace, toppling a civic monument).

Didn't matter whether it should have been a major or a minor penalty—not to horrified, furious Boston fans; seeing big Quinn in the penalty box, sitting there complaining while their darling boyo lay splayed on the ice, arms outstretched like our saviour on the cross—it was all too much!

"Get Quinn! Get Quinn!"

Even the Boston cop in the penalty box, ostensibly there to protect visiting players, started in on Quinn.

Look at him out there, you coulda kilt him.

It was a clean check.

You shunt'a run the kid like that.

The Bruins waved their sticks over officials' heads at Quinn as the chant grew louder, more people joining in every chorus. "Get Quinn! Get Quinn!" A gathering crowd pressed against the glass behind the penalty box. Someone threw beer at the Leafs defenceman. "GET QUINN!!" Angrier fans aimed looping punches over the divide. A shiny metal object bounced off the Leafs defenceman. He picked it up—a tavern waiter's metal change-maker!—before encountering another blinding waterfall of beer. "Get Quinn! Get Quinn!" Now the Leaf couldn't see, but he could sense the fans almost on top of him. The irate policeman grabbed him in a choke hold—maybe to pull Pat to safety; then again, perhaps just to make the vigilante mob's work easier. To hell with this, Quinn thought as he threw off the officer and smashed the fan-covered glass with his stick. Then he jumped out of the penalty box before it became a coffin. He'd take his chances with the Boston Bruins. At least he was sure they weren't carrying knives or guns.

Pretty sure, anyway.

In the dressing room after the second period, Punch Imlach reminded players, "OK, boys, we got to play here [tomorrow night]. So let's go out there and show them something."

Ten minutes into the third period, with Orr long gone to the hospital, it was 9–0, Boston. And the Quinn riot continued. "Get Quinn!" the fans hollered every time the Leafs defencemen hit the ice. "Get Quinn!

Get Quinn!" Led by Sanderson and Ted Green, the Bruins took runs at the big defenceman at every opportunity, exciting more vengeful cheers. Tired of what he was seeing, Imlach patted tough guy Forbes Kennedy on the shoulder. "Start something, Forbesie," Punch said.

Cue the rollercoaster!

Kennedy came from Canada's toughest neighbourhood—New Brunswick's Memramcook Valley. His dad worked as a screw in Dorchester Penitentiary—maximum security. Around the NHL, it was said that Forbesie could outdrink a table of sailors and show up the next morning for practice, breathing Colgate and ready for work. Utterly fearless and purposefully mean, hockey's Lee Marvin had the perfect resumé to settle (and, if needed, start) riots.

As expected, Kennedy did what every hockey cop was supposed to do in this circumstance, travelling in a straight line to the Bruins' toughest player, Ted Green.

Let's go.

Except Terrible Ted couldn't go—he had a broken hand under his left glove. Now, here was where the Bruins were different, more selfless, better teammates—better friends, maybe—than most teams. Cheevers was minutes from his first playoff shutout. And, being a goalie, Cheesy got enough punishment from goalmouth scrambles—slicing and dicing skates and sticks. Besides, fighting was just not his style; indeed, the face Cheevers wore in public, hockey's first Halloween mask, was the result of wily self-preservation. Tired of taking practice shots one morning— this was years earlier—Cheesy feigned injury, retiring to the Boston dressing room for a cigarette with trainer and all-around Bruins abettor Frosty Forristall.

Coach Sinden eventually stomped in after him, ordering him back on the ice.

You're not fuckin' hurt.

Am fuckin' so.

Thinking quickly, Forristall decorated Cheevers's mask with a few Magic Marker stitches. Joking proof that he was actually hurt. The look

caught on. With every whack to Cheevers's noggin, Forristall administered more stitch marks. Soon, Cheevers was wearing a mask that looked
like a railway switching yard.

The point here is that the last thing that Gerry Cheevers wanted to
do in the dying minutes of a blowout was risk injury fighting a hard case
like Forbes Kennedy. But seeing Kennedy set sail for a vulnerable teammate, Cheesy decided, *Oh hell, I better go rescue Greenie.*

This was how the Boston Bruins rolled.

Dashing from his crease, Cheesy gave Kennedy a chop across the
prow with his stick. Forbesie wheeled to face his surprise attacker and,
you guessed it, took a stick to the face from Greenie. Now he was bleeding and beyond mad. It was one against two. Probably, the Leafs forward
should have just packed it in. Or at least waited for help. But this was
Forbes Kennedy, born in the shadow of a Maritime penitentiary. Besides,
it was 1969. There was something in the air. In fact, the hit single by
Thunderclap Newman, "Something in the Air," would hit the airwaves
in a couple of weeks. In a couple of days, 300 students would take over
the Harvard University Administration Building across the Charles
River from the Boston Garden.

> *Hand out the arms and ammo*
> *We're going to blast our way through here.*

Forbesie started swinging. Like Sonny Liston. He nailed Cheevers,
knocking off his Frankenstein mask. Then he again made a beeline for
Green, only to be grabbed by Johnny Bucyk. Struggling loose, the Leaf
resumed throwing punches. Linesman Ashley stepped in his way. After
the game, battling a headache, Ashley would write the following game
report on Manger Hotel stationery:

*Around the 16-minute mark of the third period a fight broke out between
Forbes Kennedy and Gerry Cheevers of Boston. In the process of breaking up
the fight I ended up with Kennedy, the other official, Matt Pavelich, ended up*

with Cheevers. After getting the combatants separated and well apart from one another, Kennedy started moving towards Cheevers once more. As I moved closer to Kennedy to stop him from getting after Cheevers again, I was met with a fist that moved up from his hip, catching me flush on the chin. The force of the blow knocked me onto the seat of my pants. By the time I got to my feet, Kennedy and Cheevers were going at it once more.

With that punch, Kennedy's NHL career was over, but that didn't mean he was through. In addition to fighting Cheevers, Forbesie grappled with Eddie Johnston and Johnny McKenzie and, when the scrum moved along the boards, an army of angry fans. One spectator reached over the glass and conked him with a beer. Two other ticket holders, one wearing a tan leather jacket, took turns hurting their hands on Kennedy's rock-hard skull.

No fighter wants to be pinned in the corner—that's been true since the Marquess of Queensbury. Like Quinn in the period before, Kennedy spun from the boards (and fans), finding McKenzie, ready and willing to go, near centre ice. Instantly, the two men began trading windmilling blows.

Kennedy's freakout lasted a full 45 minutes—no commercial breaks on TV at home. During that span, both teams emptied their benches. Fights broke out everywhere—although no Bruin took on Quinn, a fact that greatly frustrated fans, who continued to call for his capture and torture.

"Get Quinn! Get Quinn! GET QUINN!!!"

On local TV, Bruins colour man Don Earle brought everything back home, commenting, "No, you're not watching a rerun of last summer's [riotous] Democratic convention." This was hockey.

Or was it?

On Thursday morning, the Toronto papers were crowded with tut-tutting editorials. The line it is drawn. The curse it is cast. Hockey had been irrevocably wounded. Ruined, maybe. Here was Charles McGregor from the *Toronto Telegram:* "Well how about that sports fans? Did you enjoy your television visit to the Boston Zoo last night? Did you really enjoy seeing Canada's national sport prostituted once again before an audience of millions on TV in living colour?" Colleague George Gross added: "Boston Garden turned into a lunatic bin last night. The only thing missing was the straitjackets."

Canada's national sport prostituted?

We should note here that the hookers and fighters, every one of them Canadian, pretty well took the game in stride. Although Orr and Quinn remained grumbling enemies for some time*, there would be no hard feelings between the Bruins and Kennedy. Boston goalie Eddie Johnston shouted, "Open your mouth, Forbesie," when fans doused his old friend and former teammate with beer. Hearing that Kennedy would be suspended and fined a whopping $1,000, a sheepish Cheevers contacted the league. "I told them I'd started it all, I was the instigator, and it was unfair that Forbesie was suspended," he would tell Montreal *Gazette* reporter Dave Stubbs years later. In the dressing room, a chuckling Imlach searched for his one-man army. Finding the exhausted Kennedy slumped in his stall, too tired to lift his arms, Punch exclaimed, "Geez, I told you to get something started. I didn't mean World War III."

And if the Maple Leafs were sensitive to the plight of rookie defenceman Pat Quinn, they didn't show it. On the bus after the game, the team cruelly forced Pat to walk the plank, making him the guy who had to get out of the Greyhound to buy a case of beer for the ride to their Boston hotel.

Hey Pat, looks like the cashier has her head down. Just run her and grab the beer.

Yeah, and don't forget the Slim Jims.

No harm done. The papers were making an iceberg out of an ice cube, players figured. Of course, NHL president Clarence Campbell had a different perspective. Horrified by what he was watching on *Hockey Night in Canada* (channel 6 in Montreal), Campbell booked a flight to Boston for the following morning. "Mr. Campbell was quite upset,"

---

* Bobby Orr and Pat Quinn eventually patched things up and became grand friends, as the Irish say. But it would take a few decades.

linesman Ashley remembered. "This was a serious transgression—hitting an official." A room in the Boston Garden was set aside for Kennedy's hearing. Ashley and a fuming Campbell waited for Kennedy and a Leafs representative, who turned out to be the team's assistant general manager and chief officer of laundry and morale, King Clancy, a former star and, like Campbell, an ex-referee.

Clancy did all the talking—something he was very good at. The diminutive King could usually talk himself and his team out of any trouble. Once, decades ago, right here in the Boston Garden, the then Leafs defenceman got into a fight with Bruins star Eddie Shore. Well, maybe not a fight. The Boston legend was on his hands and knees after a spill. Skating past, Clancy couldn't help himself; he leaned over and bopped Shore on the chin. Shore jumped up and confronted Clancy.

"Why, I'd like to see you do that again!"

"Sure, Eddie," Clancy cheerfully offered. "First, get on your hands and knees."

Today, though, Clancy couldn't joke his way out of trouble, despite trying to butter Campbell up.

*What a game, eh Clarence? All's you hear about is their injuries. Esposito's this. Orr's got a bad knee. Sanderson's all sick. Well, if any of these guys are sick or hurting, I'm the first Chinaman named Clancy.**

No sale.

"Mr. Campbell was upset when he saw Kennedy because he didn't look at all sorry," Ashley recalled. Why? What *did* he look like?

"Forbesie came in . . . oh boy, he was wearing cowboy boots and smoking a big cigar."

Campbell fined Easy Rider Kennedy the aforementioned $1,000, suspending him for four games. That turned out to be the rest of the playoffs for Toronto, as the Bruins easily handled the Leafs, 7–0, on Thursday

---

* Clancy actually made this observation, including "Well, if any of these guys are sick or hurting, I'm the first Chinaman named Clancy," to reporters before game two in Boston.

night (they'd now beaten Toronto by a cumulative score of 29–3 in three consecutive home games). The two clubs returned to Maple Leaf Gardens on the weekend, with Boston finishing the Leafs' season with 4–3 and 3–2 wins. This was not a good time for Toronto bankers. The week began with Allan Dow's Bank of Commerce being held up at gunpoint on Tuesday morning and ended with the Saturday night firing of Punch Imlach—who, before turning to pro hockey, had worked as a young clerk at the Dominion Bank at Queen and Broadview.

Forbes Kennedy never played in the NHL again.

But for the grace of God, Pat Quinn might never have breathed again.

Orr was released from hospital Thursday morning, his head still ringing, having been diagnosed with whiplash and a concussion. He'd play that night, assisting on the first of seven Boston goals. But first, he had to rejoin his teammates, who were holed up in a hotel outside Boston.

Walking into the hotel lobby that morning, Orr caught sight of an approaching stranger—a big guy, menacing, maybe the son of the guy who took a lead pipe to boxing legend Ray Arcel near the Boston Garden back in '53.

BOSTON BRUINS NICKNAMES (A Checklist)

Gerry Cheevers: *Cheesy*
Eddie Johnston: *EJ*
Bobby Orr: *God*
Dallas Smith: *Dilly Dally*
Rick Smith: *Panda*
Garry Doak: *Sammy*
Don Awrey: *Bugsy*
Ted Green: *Greenie* or *Greenburg* (reporters called him Terrible Ted)
Phil Esposito: *Espo*
Wayne Cashman: *Cash*
Ken Hodge: *Bam Bam*
Fred Stanfield: *Fritz*
Johnny Bucyk: *Chief*
Johnny McKenzie: *Pie*
Derek Sanderson: *Turk*
Wayne Carleton: *Swoop*
Garnet Bailey: *Ace*
Don Marcotte: *Marcottie*
Mike Walton: *Shaky*
Jim Lorentz: *Lorenzo*
Eddie Westfall: *18*

PART ONE

"Do you want me to take care of Pat Quinn?" the man asked.

Orr stared at a real enforcer, swallowing hard. "No thanks," God stammered. "I'll take care of him myself."

GANGS OF NEW YORK

New York Rangers vs. Boston Bruins, May 11, 1972

No one remembered the shift *before* Bobby Orr's magic moment—Peter Puck flying through the air a split second after winning the 1970 Stanley Cup for Boston. Bobby's innocent jump for joy turned into time-capsule material when a St. Louis defender, Noel Picard, in an *aw-shit* moment after the goal, lifted Bobby's skates, sending him sideways, mouth agape, belting out a "hooray" for the ages.

Snap! Hockey's first manned flight was captured forever by Boston *Record-American* photographer Ray Lussier.*

---

* Lussier was given a spot at the east end of the Garden for the fourth game of the Blues–Bruins final series. Correctly presuming that Boston would score in overtime at the west end, he changed places, taking a seat from a photographer who'd gone to get a beer and hadn't made it back from intermission. "Get out of

The thing is, the shift before Bobby's big goal was even better, if obviously less productive. It was a tie game, remember, with the Bruins one win away—*one win away!*—after three decades of wandering the wilderness. Everyone watching at home on TV that hot Sunday Mother's Day afternoon hoped the game would soon end so Dad could scoot out in time to pick up a bucket from the Colonel and spare Mom having to make dinner. The players were eager, too: the Stanley Cup was in the Boston Garden, ready for the taking. With ten seconds left in the third period, the Blues' Terry Crisp[*] took a desperate slapshot on Gerry Cheevers, who rapped the puck into the corner with his blocker. Circling his own net in traffic, Orr grabbed the loose puck . . .

Eight seconds left. Protocol dictated that Bobby play it safe—bang the puck off the boards and then join in the silent countdown. No sense trying to do the impossible and risk turning the puck over and having the other guys score and win.

But impossible was Bobby Orr's middle name.

Though at the end of a long shift, Bobby curled behind his own net, racing up the left boards with the puck. Orr was full speed at his own blue line . . . warp speed at the centre red line. Brothers Barclay and Bill Plager, the Blues' best defenders, waited nervously, widely spaced inside their line, inviting Orr into a collapsing tunnel. Bobby dipped his right shoulder, indicating he might just do that, and then, when Bill and Barclay pulled together, he changed direction—*instantly*—pouring

---

my seat," the photographer complained a few seconds after the goal. Lussier had been in his seat a minute, maybe. "No problem," Lussier responded, "I already got what I want."

[*] Crisp was from Parry Sound, Bobby Orr's hometown. And in truth, all his slapshots were "desperate." A very good defensive player, he couldn't shoot very hard at all. Considering that Parry Sound was a town of 5,000 or so at the time, it's kind of incredible to think that three Parry Sounders were in uniform in the 1970 finals. The third player was Blues forward Gary Sabourin, who was on the ice when Orr scored his famous overtime goal.

around Bill. Glenn Hall hurried out to cut down the angle. Two hummingbird dips later, Orr was around the fallen goalie, around the empty net, getting ready to . . .

The buzzer sounded—overtime! In eight seconds, Peter Puck had skated through an entire team. Only problem was, he needed nine to score.

In the dressing room after regulation play, Phil Esposito talked about wrapping this up pronto. "Let's put them out of their misery . . . first shift," he said, inciting vigorous assent from teammates. Harry Sinden sensed his club's stampeding overconfidence and thought, *Whoah, let's not get ahead of ourselves and let the Red Baron* (the Blues' best player, Red Berenson) *ruin our afternoon.* "OK, boys, Sanderson line starts," the Bruins coach called out. Turk tossed away his Export "A," smiling *all right.* Boston was putting out its checking line to begin overtime. Theoretically, Harry was playing it safe.

Bobby Orr, though, never played it safe. Thirty-five seconds into overtime, the Bruins had the Blues penned in. The puck wobbled free off the half boards to the left of Hall. The Blues' Larry Keenan had the angle on the puck and a step on Orr, who in charging in from the blue line was breaking a cardinal rule of hockey. If Keenan slapped the puck off the boards, he had a breakaway. Besides, hockey *rear*-guards weren't supposed to be in this deep. In 1970, defenceman were like table-hockey players, trapped in the grooved furrows of their assigned territory. Everyone except for Bobby Orr. Hockey's first protean player, Bobby assumed whatever shape was needed to improve his team's chances. He could and would play goalie, block shots, jump up to lead the rush, set up plays, and score.

All on the same shift sometimes.

But that wasn't what made him the greatest player of his era, according to Ted Williams. Years later, the legendary baseball player appeared on a WBZ-TV talk show with Bobby and Boston Celtics basketball star Larry Bird. The moderator, Bob Lobel, struggled to explain Orr's dominance. Losing patience, Teddy Ballgame blurted, "Anticipation, that's what made Bobby great . . . He knew what was going to happen before everyone else."

What happened next would be a case in point. Orr saw the puck roll loose, saw Keenan charge and teammate Sanderson float free behind the net. He absorbed all this and knew instantly that, while Keenan would get to the puck first, he *should* be able to block the clearing shot, which is exactly what happened, with the puck dropping conveniently at Orr's feet.

Now Bobby glanced at Sanderson while taking notice of Berenson approaching. At the same time, a sweet pocket opened between goalie Hall, with his fanny underneath the crossbar, and big Picard standing guard a little farther out in the slot, in search of trespassing forwards. Bobby took in all of this at once and knew, without thinking, what to do. In the same motion, he shovelled the puck to Sanderson while slipping past Berenson, hurrying to the momentary gap in the Blues' defence.

No one saw him until it was too late. They followed the pass instead—the old misdirection play. Orr and Sanderson performed the give and go, a trick older than "Cyclone" Taylor. Without looking, Turk feathered a pass back to where Bobby would soon be, in the cleared opening outside the crease. Orr knew not to tee up the pass, which would give Hall a chance to set himself; he just shot, sensing that a space would open between the goalie's legs when he moved to cover the open side.

Before Hall turned fully to face his surprise guest, Orr's shot bulged the back of the net. Boston had its first Stanley Cup in 29 years.

It was crazy after that. Fans spilled onto the ice, swallowing the team. Sanderson punched a small man with Elvis hair. And then apologized: "Geez, sorry, Dad." Sharp as always, Harold Sanderson snapped, "First person you've hit all series." The Bruins shifted easily into party mode—their natural default position—hitting the Branding Iron, Orr's restaurant in Charles River Park ("western-style steaks, man-sized drinks, nightly entertainment and dancing in lounge") after the game. There, in the company of wives and "A" girlfriends, they worked hard to replenish lost bodily fluids before waking Monday morning to join 200,000 close personal friends at a street-party blowout, a parade ending at Boston's City Hall Plaza. Even police guarding the Bruins on their open-convertible, magic-swirling-ship parade route drank too much. "Wayne Cashman and I, we got ourselves a policeman's motorcycle," Johnny McKenzie would remember years later at a Bruins reunion. "I was up front riding and Cash was sitting behind me. The cop, he had about 50 beers in him and he was sitting in the sidecar."

Wash where . . . wash where you're going.

At City Hall, Louise Day Hicks, a big-haired, 54-year-old city councillor who ran for mayor of Boston in 1967 on an anti-busing slogan ("You know where I stand"), got so carried away she lassooed "Bam Bam" Hodge* with her arms, slipping off his tie. *C'mere, big boy!* Mayor Kevin White was in the middle of a toast to the Bruins when Pie McKenzie poured a pitcher of beer over his head. The Bruins partied the way they played—big and bad. Still, they had their first Stanley Cup. And the core of the team was still so young. Minutes after combining on the Cup-winning goal, Sanderson and Orr, both 22, lingered in the trainers room, drinking chocolate milk.

"Well, Four, whaddya think?"

Bobby was quiet a moment.

"Well, no practice tomorrow. No one left to beat."

No, not this year, but championship teams were counted on the fingers of both hands in the second half of the 20th century: the Toronto Maple Leafs and *Les Glorieux,* the Montreal Canadiens, had won nine of the ten Stanley Cups in the '60s (final score: 5–4, Montreal); Detroit finished in first place in seven consecutive seasons in the '50s, accumulating four championships. Their primary rivals that decade, Montreal, accumulated five titles during that same stretch.

How many Cups would the Orr–Esposito Bruins collect?

---

* Ken Hodge was nicknamed "Bam Bam" because of his hard shot and close resemblance to the super-strong kid, Bamm-Bamm Rubble, in the animated TV series *The Flintstones* (1960–66) and *The Pebbles and Bamm-Bamm Show* (1971–72).

After a quarter-final loss to the Canadiens in 1971, Boston got its chance for a second championship in '72. Unlike the four-game sweep of the expansion St. Louis Blues in 1970, the finals this time would be a fair fight—Bruins against the New York Rangers. Each team boasted two good goalies, with a flamboyant number one—Cheevers and New York's Eddie Giacomin. Both had a star defender—Orr and Brad Park. And New York's top line of Jean Ratelle, Rod Gilbert and Vic Hadfield was nearly as good as Esposito's unit.

Making the series more interesting still, the teams had a shared history. They despised each other—hated each other in a vicious, deeply personal manner that perhaps only the pre–politically correct 1970s could permit. Here's how Rangers coach Emile "the Cat" Francis described to me his entrance to the first game of the 1972 Stanley Cup:

> *I get out of our dressing room and there are three cops. "Mr. Francis," one of them goes, "we're going to escort you to the bench." What the hell? I tell him, "No way, I'm going to walk across the ice there like I always do." "I'm sorry, sir, our orders are to escort you, please come with us." OK, I respect the police and everything, I go with them: long way, all around the rink. People, fans, they're swearing at me left and right . . . men, women, boys, girls, everyone screaming. Finally get to the bench, I look up, there's this big sign and you know what it says? "Kill the Cat." Kill me! Welcome to Boston, eh? Anyways, end of the first period I turn to the cop behind me and go, "Know what, this time I'm going to walk across the ice by myself, you don't mind." Geez, I take two steps onto the ice and some son of a bitch throws a beer bottle from the balcony, just misses me, smashing there on the ice.*

Stan Fischler is a good person to explain how the Bruins–Rangers rivalry got so out of hand. Fischler was vice-president of the Rangers' fan club in the early '50s before turning to journalism with the *Brooklyn Eagle* and Hearst's *New York Journal-American*. Beginning in the late '60s, he experienced the Boston–New York rivalry firsthand as a literary double agent, writing bios on Boston and New York players—*Bobby Orr and the Big Bad Bruins; Derek Sanderson: I've Got to Me;* and *Brad Park: Play the Man*—books that turned up the heat, providing bulletin-board ammunition for what was then the NHL's most compelling rivalry.

Mr. Fischler has the floor:

"Speaking on behalf of Rangers fans, let me say New York hated the Bruins because it was felt that Boston always seemed to prevent New York from making the playoffs with, no way of getting around it, dirty work," he told me. "There was always a little Big and Bad with the Bruins. After the war, you had Boston's Milt Schmidt, a very tough player, sometimes more than tough, injuring Edgar Laprade, the Rangers' best forward, a beautiful, clean player—didn't record a single penalty several years, you can look that up.* And then in 1965, Ted Green, a very tough guy, went after little Phil Goyette, spearing Phil in the kidney. He almost died; again, another blow to the Rangers' playoff chances. After the Goyette incident, I went into the dressing room and Rangers president Bill Jennings was there. To say he was mad is an understatement. 'I think the Boston Bruins have animals on their team,' he said. 'When bruins run wild in Maine, the state declares a bounty for shooting the bears. I declare a bounty on Ted Green.'

"Strong stuff. I contacted Ted Green for a comment. His response was succinct and to the point: 'Go to hell,' he says."

Fans carried the rivalry forward. "This was around when New York began to change—there was a breakdown in society," Fischler declared, speaking in a slightly nasal, tell-it-like-it-is manner reminiscent of his fellow Brooklynite, the broadcaster Howard Cosell. "I've written a book about our subways† and can tell you 1969 was the year

---

* Laprade's rap sheet was spotless in 49 games in 1945–46, in 42 games in 1950–51 and through 60 games in 1954–55. In 500 NHL games, he spent only 42 minutes in the box.

† *The Subway and the City: Celebrating a Century* (New York: Frank Merriwell, 2004).

graffiti shows up on cars; shows up everywhere . . . you had mob rule."

Indeed, when the Amazin' Mets won the World Series in 1969, fans rushed the field, pulling up turf. Squatters occupied New York's Lower East Side, burning cupboards for heat in winter. The punk club CBGBs opened in the Bowery in 1973, giving refuge to the Ramones, New York Dolls, Television, the Dead Boys and Patti Smith. In movies of the day, New York was invariably a cesspool—as evidenced in Martin Scorsese's

NEW YORK COPS TO FIGHT FANS: DROP DEAD

New York in the mid–'70s was in desperate need of Batman. Crime was up. Cops were threatening to go on strike. In late 1975, city lawyers were in the state supreme court, filing a bankruptcy petition. New York begged for and did not receive a bailout from President Gerald Ford, leading to the famous *Daily News* headline FORD TO CITY: DROP DEAD. A year later, Yankee Stadium played host to a Muhammad Ali–Ken Norton championship fight. But all anyone remembers today were the punches thrown outside the stadium. New York police picketed the September 28, 1976, title match, looking the other way when hoods attacked and robbed fans exiting subways, taxis and limousines for the ball park. Actor and fight fan Telly Savalas was roughed up. Legendary sportswriter Red Smith had his typewriter stolen. Expecting a big demand for rush-ticket buyers, promoters had kiosks surrounding the Stadium ready with 18,000 admission passes. But fans hopped back into their vehicles when they saw what was going on. Only eight walk-up tickets were sold. Reporter Jerry Izenberg recalled: "I had guns pointed at me. I was absolutely convinced that night I was going to die." The announcer on the closed-circuit telecast of the fight likened the action outside the stadium to a scene from the movie *A Clockwork Orange*. The actual title fight was a mess, too, as Ali somehow won a controversial 15-round decision few witnesses believed he deserved.

Taxi Driver and *Mean Streets*, along with the crime dramas *The French Connection, The Seven-Ups, Up on 110th Street* and *The Taking of Pelham One Two Three*, all of which were released between 1971 and 1976.

The ugliest moment in New York sports history occurred in September 1976, when police looked the other way as looting gangs groped and pillaged wealthy patrons at the Muhammad Ali–Ken Norton heavyweight championship fight.

Misbehaviour also became an art form at hockey games. One night in the early '70s, Ted Green and the Bruins visited Madison Square Garden. Ever-gracious Rangers fans set loose a welcoming balloon-a-gram to Green. As it settled, becoming legible under the lights, spectators leapt up, cheering. The blimp read DROP DEAD TED. Then there was the time in Boston, during the national anthem, when a Bruins fan took advantage of a lull to extend a shout-out to the Rangers' Brad Park.

> *Whose broad stripes and bright stars, through the perilous fight*
> *O'er the ramparts we watched, were so gallantly streaming*

"We're gonna kill you, Pah-uk!"

> *And the rockets' red glare . . .*

Bruins fans hated Park for calling out God: "One myth about Orr is that he's a gentlemanly and clean player," Park complained in his book, *Play the Man* (co-authored by Fischler). "Actually, Orr can be a hatchet man just like his Boston teammates." Park suited up with the Bruins in the January 25, 1972, All-Star game in Minnesota, setting up Pie McKenzie with a breakaway pass that led to the tying goal. The exhibition game happened to arrive three weeks after Park's book. Number 19 and his Bruins buddies turned their backs on Park when he tried to join in their way-to-go celebration.

When I ask if the Bruins–Rangers war in any way resembled an out-of-control high school feud, Fischler laughed. "Well, they were young.

Park, Orr and Sanderson were around 20 when I worked with them. That was a big, big difference about post-expansion hockey. Suddenly, players were younger—kids! Know how today, young people say 'awesome'? Back then, it was 'super.' Everything was super with Bobby. I first met him, he picks me up at Maple Leaf Gardens and drives me up to Parry Sound. That night, he and his dad, we all get in a boat loaded down with beer and go to their little island—had a sauna, I remember, and we all went skinny-dipping at midnight. Like I said, talking with Bobby that day, everything was 'super.' Parry Sound was 'super.' The fish, swimming, everything was 'super.'"

The Bruins were super, too. No one could turn it on like the Black and Gold. Before taking on the Rangers in the 1972 finals, Boston swept St. Louis in the semifinals, outscoring them, 38–8. Earlier in the season, the Bruins were down 6–2 to the California Golden Seals. Former Bruin Wayne Carleton skated by McKenzie at one point, chuckling, "You guys just don't have it tonight." Pie advised his teammates of the remark in the second intermission.

Final score: Boston 8, California 6.

Prior to the Stanley Cup finals, reporters tried to solve hockey's most perplexing riddle: Why did the Bruins play so brilliantly for stretches and then book off work, taking it easy? "The Bruins, one of sport's most freewheeling teams, have faith in their ability to turn it on under game conditions," offered the *New York Times*'s Gerald Eskenazi. The *Boston Globe*'s Harold Kease cut to the chase: "Bruins lead the NHL in optional practices." By contrast, the Rangers were the NHL's fittest team. "Heck, you know how Emile Francis works his clubs, behind closed doors, secret plays, works them hard," Esposito admitted to the *Times*. "And you know how Tom Johnson has problems with us."

Could it be that the Bruins sometimes simply ran out of gas?

The Bruins were again inconsistent—at times brilliant, occasionally half-asleep—during the first game of the 1972 Cup finals. After New York's Dale Rolfe opened the scoring, Boston responded with a machine-gun clip—four fast goals. Two came on a penalty kill late in the first period, as Sanderson slipped between Hadfield and Ratelle to beat Giacomin, and then Bam Bam Hodge followed with a scoring blast. Sanderson and Orr almost teamed up for a third shorthanded goal seconds later. When the Bruins picked up another penalty in the second, the Rangers' Pete Stemkowski shouted from the bench, "Let's decline it."

Nolo contendere—New York was a beaten team. After Giacomin made an easy save, Bruins fans let out a mock cheer—"Eddie, Eddie." Hodge's hat-trick goal made it 5–1 Boston, with little over a period left. The Bruins were in high clover; their fans were ecstatic—the impossibly expensive drafts (three bits a beer—75 cents!) were going down smooth as honey. Boston had the game wrapped up. New York hadn't won in Boston all year, after all, and the Bruins had taken three straight in Madison Square Garden by a score of 25–4. The Big Bad Bruins looked to be well on their way to their second Stanley Cup.

Emile Francis wasn't dead, but the Cat was in the bag and the bag was in the Charles River.

"Yeah, that was a funny game," Francis remembered, chuckling. "The Bruins were all over us. But I told the boys, 'Forget about the score, keep skating. Win the next shift and see what happens.'"

What happened was that the Bruins stopped working. Rod Gilbert tipped in an open-net power-play goal to make it 5–2 late in the second. Hadfield scored to open the third. Walt Tkaczuk tallied. Next shift, the Rangers dumped the puck behind Boston's net. Dallas Smith and Orr both made a move and froze—*I got it, you take it.* Stemkowski darted between them and passed in front to Bruce MacGregor. Tie game. The Bruins had coughed up a four-goal lead in ten minutes and then had to hang on to the ropes, exhausted, as Bruins fans looked on, drowning in sweat. Luck was with them today, however. With two minutes left, on a harmless-looking counterattack, Ace Bailey squeezed past Park and beat Giacomin to restore Boston's lead. Next shift, Hadfield rung one off the post in the dying seconds.

With press from all over North America in Boston for the Cup finals, there wasn't enough air to breathe in a jam-packed Bruins dressing room after the game. Still, leave it to Turk Sanderson to find oxygen when reporters appear. "It was the kind of a game that people in Amarillo, Texas, would love," Sanderson said, stripped to the waist, leaning back in his dressing room stall. "We're ahead 5–1, Rangers score four to tie it up. The people out in Amarillo will think this is what playoff hockey is all about. Well, it was stupid. We should've never scored five goals, and they should've never tied it."

After that, Turk landed a few strategic insults. Sanderson sometimes had his most effective shifts *after* games. In the 1970 playoffs, Turk infuriated the Rangers by fabricating a story about New York putting a $5,000 bounty on his head. In response, the Rangers forgot about hockey and took turns running Sanderson. When Turk scored the final goal in a 4–1 win in New York to knock the Rangers out of the playoffs, Rangers fans set fire to their own building, dousing the mezzanine in flames.

"Sanderson was the best agitator in the history of hockey," Fischler said. "He was the smartest player—street-smartest—I ever met. Funniest, too. He would read you and then pick at and destroy you."

"He could get under a team's skin, all right," Emile Francis agreed, chuckling.

Now Sanderson pretended to defend an old enemy as a pretext to dissing the Rangers power play: "Hey, don't blame Giacomin on [my] goal," he told reporters after game one. "His forwards bailed out on him and he had to move out to get me."

Then he insulted Giacomin.

"Once he was moving, he was easy to beat."

Reporters pressed in for more as Esposito returned from the shower, naked as a tomato. "Hate to break up your press conference," Espo interjected, "but I gotta get dressed, if you don't mind, so could you please break it up so I can siddown?"

With Eddie Johnston and Gilles Villemure replacing Cheevers and Giacomin and teams contrite after a night of stupid Amarillo hockey, Boston and New York returned to traditional playoff values in game two—lots of hitting and checking. The Bruins emerged with a 2–1 win.

When the series travelled to New York, the Rangers responded with a convincing 5–2 victory as Park collected two goals and as many assists. "You saw tonight why Brad Park is the best defenceman in the NHL," Francis proclaimed. But even in a game in which Park bested Orr, he was still upstaged—this time, by his own fans. *New York Times* columnist Dave Anderson sat with his notebook open in the Boston end during the warm-ups, following the antics of angry fans who gathered behind the Bruins net, mouths open, hollering obscenities.

Anderson also took inventory of the items thrown at Bruins players—toilet paper rolls, batteries, apples, coins, staples. In the third period, a can of shaving cream bounced the moustachioed Sanderson's way. A bag of ice hit Cheevers. Anderson's subsequent report was widely syndicated. Soon, everyone was writing about abusive Rangers fans, going way back. The *Montreal Star*'s Red Fisher recalled the night, years ago, when a Rangers fan fired a hard-boiled egg from the balcony, KOing Rangers goalie Gump Worsley.

"Ah, it was awful that night," Francis says, recalling game three of the Rangers–Bruins Stanley Cup finals. "I remember leaving the bench to tell security to take down a sign that said SANDERSON EAT SHIT. Imagine that—family place and everything."

The series' fourth game, again in New York, saw Orr's response to Park's brilliant turn. Bobby scored the game's first two goals, fought Park to a draw and then risked his health jumping in front of a slapshot. A Stemkowski blast caught him bang on his oft-injured left knee, a joint already swollen with floating cartilage. Orr almost passed out from the pain, and there was a difficult moment on the bench when trainer Dan Canney applied a bag of ice to Orr's leg, wrapping it tight to his knee. The star defenceman panicked, insisting that the wrap be removed— *now, now.* "Bobby doesn't like anything on his knee," Canney explained to reporters after the game.

Orr missed half a period and then returned to kill a penalty. Travelling into the Rangers zone at reduced speed, drawing Park close, he flipped a perfect pass to Don Marcotte, who sliced the puck over Giacomin for a

3–0 lead. Again, New York roared back, making it 3–2, but they could get no closer. The Bruins were now up 3–1 in the series and had the Rangers at home, with the Stanley Cup in their own building. Boston was crazy in anticipation. The nearby racetrack, Suffolk Downs, had installed 12 new colour TVs before the playoffs so that race fans could bet the ponies while keeping an eye on the Bruins. A Norwood town meeting to settle the community's annual budget was cancelled for lack of quorum—everyone was at or watching the game. That afternoon, a big cardboard box arrived in the Bruins dressing room. FROM CITY HALL, it read. *What—a gift for Bam Bam Hodge from Cougar Councilwoman Louise Day Hicks?* The Bruins gathered around, poking and prodding. Finally, someone opened the package and a college-aged fan popped out, begging to watch the game. The laughing Bruins slapped the kid on the back and found him a ticket.

The fifth game was typical of the series: the Bruins started strong and then wilted. Boston was up 2–1 going into the third period. The champagne was on ice; the fans on their feet, cheering. But then the wrong Bobby scored two goals—the Rangers' Bobby Rousseau. The Rangers won 3–2, setting up a sixth game in New York (and sparing New York the agony of losing two title matches the same day; Wilt Chamberlain, with 29 rebounds and eight blocked shots, led the Los Angeles Lakers to a fifth-game championship series win over the New York Knicks later that Tuesday night).

Esposito was furious after Boston's loss. "Rangers think they're going to beat us in the next two games, they're full of Park spelled backwards—that's Krap," the league's best scorer insisted, showing off a flair for spelling that had eluded him in his Catholic schoolboy days in the Soo.

"Oh boy, I thought we had them," Coach Francis would say four decades later, letting out a whistle. "Esposito was mad because he hadn't scored all series, eh? And Orr was hurt. That shot he took in the knee." Then there was the matter of fitness. Although the Rangers were still down three games to two, New York had outscored Boston 10–2 in the second halves of games this series. Francis had worked his team all season for this moment. "We'd have two practices a day, some days, once in the morning, once in the afternoon," he said. "Then, late afternoons, mostly in the playoffs, we'd go to the film room until six o'clock. At six, we'd all eat together."

The Bruins, meanwhile, had some days off. Morning skates other days, just to sweat off beer and smokes. "Hey, it worked for them, it worked for them," Francis said. "They were champions, a great team, but, yeah, I thought we were ready to take them at that point. I really did."

Not in the first period of the sixth game, they weren't. Again the Bruins came out flying; they were even the better team while short-handed. After Hodge was called for hooking, Orr, playing at two-thirds speed, threw a high, arcing backhand from deep in his own end that seemed destined to hit the time clock but dropped down the other side of centre, a perfect long bomb, to a streaking Ed Westfall, whose break-away attempt was foiled by Villemure. As always, the Bruins were deadly when they enjoyed a man advantage. Ten minutes in, the Bruins power play set up shop inside the Rangers zone: Hodge and the Rangers' Rod Seiling wrestled for the puck in the corner. Esposito left the slot to help, sneaking the puck behind the net to Bucyk. He waited before snapping a return pass to Hodge, now free to the left of the crease. The winger had a shot. Esposito was available in front. But no, Hodge backhanded the puck to the point.

"He's got a shot in close, but passes back to Orr," Francis said. "That tells you something, eh? But I'm not worried at the time because it's not a very good pass, Orr has to stretch to get it and we have [Bruce MacGregor] right on him. Orr's trapped. Except, oh boy, he does this little backwards twirl or something. [I tell Francis that *Hockey Night in Canada* play-by-play man Danny Gallivan would've called it "a spin-erama."] OK, he does whatever you call it, that spin, and suddenly he's all alone. Where'd we all go? And then he fires this perfect shot—perfect shot—inside the post.

"I mean, what are you going to do, someone scores a goal like that—what? How do you defend against a play you never seen before?"

No film record of the sixth game of the 1972 Boston–New York final remains except for a private Rangers recording. Watching that footage helps answer the eternal question: How would Orr's career have progressed if creaky knees had allowed him to play at reduced speed? The answer: he'd have turned into the second coming of Doug Harvey, playing the point in a rocking chair, making quick passes instead of speedy rushes; on defence, he'd have drawn advancing forwards to him as if on a string. Even at two-thirds speed, Orr would be the most effective skater on the ice this evening, with the barging, long-armed Esposito and Park for the Rangers battling for runner-up. Bobby's only real enemy was himself—the blackout Irish temper that took over again near the end of the first period when Cashman threw a mean elbow at Billy Fairbairn; this after Gary Doak of the Rangers was called for a minor penalty. Orr figured the officials should have spared Cashman. His head snapped as he snarled something at referee Art Skov.

In response, the ref threw his hands to his hips.

That's ten minutes, Orr.

Hearing his sentence, Bobby turned into Yosemite Sam. Fortunately for Boston, Cashman, Dallas Smith and Mike Walton interceded, grabbing flailing superstar body parts. Still—boy, what a temper—Orr pushed the scrum towards Skov.

That's enough or you're gone for good, Four.

The Bruins somehow managed to get a still-screaming Orr to the penalty box. With that, the game changed, the ice tilting in New York's favour. The second period would be all Rangers, with the puck pinballing around Boston's net. Ratelle, Gilbert, Hadfield and Tkaczuk had chances. Park was fabulous, headmanning the puck, freezing Bruins with little head fakes and dishing no-look passes to suddenly open forwards.

Poor Brad. In the fifth game of the series, back in Boston, the perpetual runner-up for the Norris Trophy (four times to Orr, twice to Denis Potvin) made an astonishing play. Killing a two-man penalty, he raced Orr for the puck, tipping the puck past his nemesis, and then dashed the length of the ice with a posse of Bruins in pursuit. Pausing briefly in front of Eddie Johnston, he found an open top corner and fired an *almost-perfect* shot that clearly beat the Boston goalie, chiming off the crossbar. No goal. On the bench afterwards, cameras showed Park bent over, exhausted, tasting copper, unable to catch his breath. Now, in the second period of the sixth game, he made another great play. Jumping in from the point, Park collected a pass from Gilbert. Bruin Carol Vadnais jumped out to greet him, with Cheevers right behind. Brad shifted his weight to his left foot as if to shoot, pulling both Vadnais and Cheevers to the ice, then quickly went to his backhand, adroitly flipping the puck towards an achingly wide-open top corner.

Except Cheevers, climbing to a knee, threw up his glove, knocking a sure goal out of the air—like an outfielder jumping over the fence to snare a certain home run.

As he should, Park followed his shot in, looking for a rebound that wasn't there. And then he swore in disgust.

Fuck!

The Bruins somehow got through the second period unscathed. Early in the third, Rolfe was sent off; now it would be the Bruins' turn with a man advantage. Boston enjoyed a phenomenal 30 per cent success rate on the power play this season. Again, they made it look so easy: Esposito beat Tkaczuk on a draw, scything a pass back to the point. Remembering Orr's first goal, Rod Seiling raced to the blue line, blocking the route to the boards. But Bobby moved to the middle of the ice. Drifting between the circles, he allowed a scrum to materialize in front and then lowered his head, golfing a low screamer that entered the net in the exact same place as his last goal.

Although the public address announcer described the second goal of the game as "Bobby Orr from Phil Esposito," Orr informed referees—they were on speaking terms again—that it went in off Cashman. "Never touched it," Cashman would tell reporters after the game.

A little birthday present from Bobby, then: a Stanley Cup–clinching goal. Cashman managed to score a real goal of his own, on a nice setup from Esposito with under two minutes remaining, giving Boston a 3–0 win.

And their second Stanley Cup in three seasons.

"Yeah, when Orr got that second goal you knew," Francis sighed. "Bobby Orr, I tell you, he was the best I ever saw." I remind the old Rangers coach that he called Park the best defenceman in the NHL earlier in this series. "He was the best defenceman in the NHL!" Francis laughed. "The best defenceman not named Bobby Orr. Listen, Brad was a great player. One of those guys, you're watching sometimes from the bench, you stop being a coach—you're a fan again.

"But lemme tell you a story: one time, Brad's agent [Martin Blackman] probably read what I said about Brad in the papers. He goes, 'Brad's as good as Orr; he should be paid like him.' I just look at him and say, 'Here's the phone, pick it up and call Boston. If you can make the deal, Park for Orr, I'll give you another 15 per cent of whatever you make on Brad's contract.'

"No, Bobby, he was the best."

What President Richard Nixon might have called the great silent majority of New York fans gave the Rangers a standing ovation as they left the ice that evening. For good reason: the big New York sports stories the following day would be 41-year-old Willie Mays returning from San Francisco to play for the Mets, and Francis's team bowing out in the finals. To put the Rangers' achievement in perspective, the last time New York reached the NHL championship series, in the spring of 1950, "Buck" Mays was playing for the Birmingham Black Barons of the Negro leagues.

Other Rangers fans—Nixon's antagonistic, alliteration-prone vice-president, Spiro Agnew, might have called them nattering nabobs of negativity—were also in the house, however. And they were far from happy with seeing the hated Bruins crowned champions. The 1972 Stanley Cup final would end with Orr picking up the puck up to hand a Cheevers a keepsake of his shutout win. Smith, Hodge and Cashman joined the scrum. Seconds later, an irate party crasher in a Rangers blue jacket appeared, ready to raise a little hell, raise a little hell. The last image of Emile Francis's game film would be Pie McKenzie veering from the celebration to elbow the interloper, bowling him to the ice.

Private party, fella.

What would a '70s Bruins–Rangers game be without a gallon or two of spilled venom? Boston reporters required a police escort to get from the press box to the dressing room after the game. Meanwhile, down where the drunkards rolled, outside on Seventh Avenue, the Bruins bus was surrounded by angry, pounding fans.

"Bruins suck! Bruins suck!"

Irate fans crowded together *inside* the Garden, too, jeering, waiting for the Bruins to finish celebrating. Down the hall, Cat Francis was asked about the fans. "Hey, I wouldn't pay $15 to see many games, but if you took all the fans from Boston and New York and put 'em in Yankee Stadium and let 'em go at it, I'd pay $15 to see that," he chuckled to reporters. His only laugh that night. It was different in the Bruins room, where the beer and laughter were overflowing. (The always-cheap Bruins apparently "forgot" to bring champagne.) Asked how the Bruins had managed another championship, Cheevers removed a cigar from his mouth and volunteered, "Clean living, boys." As the Bruins emerged from their quarters, the angry crowd surged forward. Police took out their night sticks.

"Bruins suck! Bruins suck!"

One Rangers fan, a big kid, managed to break through the thin blue line, screaming his way towards public enemy number 16. "Sanderson, you're an asshole," he shouted. Turk saw the extended knife in time to lift a carry-on bag he was toting. The blade found leather instead of Sanderson. A split second later, a hustling cop took down the fan with his club.

"Hey, thanks," Turk said.

"Look, I think you're an asshole, too," the policeman said. "Just doing my job."

With the Bruins finally all aboard the bus, fans again broke police lines, rocking the big vehicle—"Bruins suck, Bruins suck"—until the players were safely on their way to the airport and home. Well, not safely. Some 3,500 fans (and 50 cops) squeezed into Boston's Logan Airport to greet the Bruins when they returned home at two in the morning.

Usually, when Bruins-mania got to be too much, the team sacrificed its superstar, who was famously patient with fans. It happened again tonight.

"Number Four, up in front," Turk shouted as they were getting off the plane. "Well, at least somebody take my garment bag," Orr laughed. The way it usually worked, Bobby descended into the melee, plucking a pen from his pocket. He'd sign 20 or so autographs, kibitzing with fans, while other Bruins shot by. Then "Sorry guys, gotta go," and Number Four chased after teammates.

Not tonight—or rather, this morning. When Orr waded into the crowd, admirers started grabbing at his clothes. Outside the building, fans were stomping cars and smashing windows. "They would have killed us if they could get us," Esposito told the *Boston Globe*. "We were terrified. All of us were mobbed. If anyone had been knocked down . . . he would have been trampled to death . . . I don't understand it. They came to cheer us and they want to kill us. I don't know."

Derek Sanderson did, though. Turk always knew what to do.

"Do you like this topcoat?" he asked an Eastern Airlines mechanic.

"Yeah."

"It's yours. Just give me your overalls."

"What?"

"Give me your overalls, your hat, your headphones and those two batons."

And so Sanderson skipped through the crowd, disguised as a flight mechanic.

Later that Friday afternoon, the Rolling Stones released *Exile on Main Street*, kicking off their 1972 U.S. tour.* In Boston, meanwhile, there was another Stanley Cup party. Maybe the road lives of the Bruins and Stones weren't that different. Girls flashed their breasts at Boston players on their way to City Hall. There was another beer fight with the mayor. Esposito would wake up three days later in Florida, with no idea how he got there.

---

* The Stones played Montreal and Boston on consecutive nights July 17 and 18, 1972.

And like with a superstar rock group, there was always another show for some Bruins to do. Orr's agent, Alan Eagleson, had arranged a summit meeting between NHL all-stars and the Soviet national team for the following August. Esposito told Team Canada he wasn't coming—too tired—but then he got a call from God. "Phil, I cannot play in this series with the Russians because of my knee," Bobby Orr said over the phone. "We really need you to play."

"Are you asking me?"

"Yeah, we really need you."

"Count me in."

THE TOP TEN IN *BILLBOARD* MAGAZINE
May 12, 1972

1. THE FIRST TIME EVER I SAW YOUR FACE—Roberta Flack (Atlantic)
2. I GOTCHA / A MOTHER'S PRAYER—Joe Tex (Dial)
3. OH GIRL—The Chi-Lites (Brunswick)
4. I'LL TAKE YOU THERE—The Staple Singers (Stax)
5. ROCKIN' ROBIN—Michael Jackson (Motown)
6. BETCHA BY GOLLY, WOW—The Stylistics Featuring Russell Thompkins Jr. (Avco)
7. LOOK WHAT YOU'VE DONE FOR ME—Al Green (Hi)
8. DAY DREAMING—Aretha Franklin (Atlantic)
9. BACK OFF BOOGALOO—Ringo Starr (Apple)
10. A HORSE WITH NO NAME—America (Warner Brothers)

THEM AGAIN

Montreal Canadiens vs. Boston Bruins, April 8, 1971

I n 1970, little Julie Hadfield wrote Bobby Orr, requesting an auto-
graphed photo. Younger brother Jeff already had an Orr jersey. Kids
naturally respond to the idea of a superhero—a supreme force that
imposed order in a hostile universe. What was remarkable about Orr and
the Big Bad Bruins was that they prompted childlike wonder in hockey
players, too. Prior to the 1972 playoffs, Julie and Jeff's dad, Vic Hadfield
of the New York Rangers, crowned the Boston Stanley Cup champions.
"Bruins are unbeatable," Vic told reporters.

Before defeating Hadfield's Rangers in the finals, Boston brushed
aside St. Louis. "Our team is awed by the Bruins," Blues coach Al Arbour
sighed. "We see Orr and Esposito and Bucyk out there and wonder what
we're doing playing on the same ice." The Bruins had won in 1970 and
would win again in '72. A Cup in 1971 would have given them three in
a row . . . tilt in a slot machine . . . hockey immortality. Boston players

figured the '70–71 team was their best ever. So did the new hockey math. Before these guys, a 50-goal year was Mount Everest. Ninety points, dreamland. NHL scoring champ Gordie Howe totalled 95 points in 1952–53; the Habs' Dickie Moore and Jean Béliveau led the league with 96 and 91 in '58–59; Boom Boom Geoffrion and Béliveau racked up 95 and 90 in 1960–61; Bobby Hull, 97 in '65–66—teammate Stan Mikita also reached 97 twice in the '60s.

Those were the best seasons for any NHL player—ever.

Then, in 1970–71, the Bruins forced the NHL record book into a shredder, establishing 37 new marks. Esposito collected 76 goals and 76 assists—152 points! Somehow that didn't look right. Neither did Orr's 102 assists. The league's top four scorers were Bruins. No centre had ever approached Espo's 152 points. Orr's 139 points were the best for his position. Bucyk, with 116 points, shattered Hull's record for left wing. Hodge's 105 was now tops for right wingers.

Boston also established a record for wins—57. Should have been more, too. The Bruins ripped off a 13-game winning streak, outscoring opponents 85–29, clinching first place with a March 21 victory over Philadelphia (Orr picked up a hat trick, the team's 14th of the season, another record). Afterwards, the Bruins were ready to blow past their two-drink minimum. "Too bad we didn't get Hodgie his 100 points," Esposito shouted. "Know what Espo forgets?" Cashman interjected, "The 100th point could be an assist." The dressing room howled. Esposito was the league's premier net-hanger. That season, he set a record for shots on net—550. No one has approached that figure since. "Hey, let's take a vote to see who has to stay sober so he can play Sunday," Pie McKenzie said. Talk soon drifted to other matters. Like Sanderson's hair, now the length of an Old Testament prophet. "Couldn't pay me enough money to cut [it]," Turk reported. "This company offered to pay $10,000 for a television commercial, eh? I told them no. So they offered me $15,000. I told my father I turned down $15,000 for the haircut and he said, 'You're crazy.' But I said, 'Listen, after taxes it's only $8,500.'"

Distracted, content, the Bruins lost their mojo—one drink led to another led to four straight defeats, including a home loss to the expansion Buffalo Sabres followed by an embarrassment in New York where the team was outshot 52–18. *Hic!* No matter, seemingly: Boston splashed cold water on their faces and closed the season with three convincing wins, drubbing Toronto and Montreal in their own buildings, 8–3 and 6–3, before returning home for the season finale, a 7–2 beatdown of the Canadiens.

Clobbering the Habs was important. Boston wanted to send a message to their first-round playoff opponents: we're the Stanley Cup champs . . . *us, not you.* Montreal was the greatest team in pro sports—12 championships since the war. Was it possible the Bruins could ever take their archenemy too lightly?

Yes, it was. Maybe because the Habs had already been written off—were dead and buried, according to some. When they failed to make the playoffs in the spring of 1970, the Montreal *Gazette* blew taps: R.I.P.—A STANLEY CUP PLAYOFF DYNASTY: 1949–1970, read a front-page headline. Midway through the season, Montreal had won but 19 of 40 games. Standard-bearers Béliveau and Henri Richard, along with fiercely competitive corner cop John Bowie Ferguson, were near the end. No one had been able to replace Toe Blake behind the bench: Claude Ruel, who believed Los Angeles was situated on the Specific Ocean, didn't work out, and current coach Al MacNeil couldn't speak French, antagonizing a province flirting with separation.

GM Sam Pollock—Trader Sam—had a plan: by slickering (the only word for it) the California expansion teams, the Canadiens had amassed nine first-round picks in the drafts between 1970 and 1972. Help was on the way. But Sam was a bad loser. Giving up on the '70–71 season wasn't an option. He had a secret weapon in the minors. Still, the playoffs were no cinch the way the team was playing, so in January he pulled off a greatly beneficial but expensive trade,* sending a promising young player,

---

* The trade for Mahovlich made Pollock very nervous, according to *Ottawa Citizen* sportswriter Jack Kinsella. After work that day, Sam arrived home with bad

Mickey Redmond, to Detroit for Frank Mahovlich—the Big M, a sensitive, easily discouraged superstar who, when motivated, could electrify a team. Sam made sure Frank was psyched, sending MacNeil and Ron Caron, Pollock's assistant, to meet Mahovlich's plane when it arrived for a game in Minnesota. Sam also boned up on his Group of Seven so he could talk to big Frank about Canadian art, the player's off-ice passion.

Boy, that Lawren Harris is something, eh Frank?

Arriving in Montreal, Frank was never happier. Or better. He rejuvenated Béliveau and Ferguson while persuading young brother Pete to mend his ways. At least, Pete put away his lighter for a while (to break up the monotony of road trips, the Little M crawled around hotel lobbies setting fire to teammates' newspapers). When Montreal's best defender, long tall Jacques Laperrière, with his funny, egg-beater skating style and extension-ladder reach, returned from injury, the Canadiens were themselves again. Scoring goals better than anyone—except Boston.

Beating everyone—except Boston.

Now, in the playoffs, they had to somehow get past the Bruins. Who were home licking their lips. "I'm not saying we're going to skate out there and run them down," Bruins defenceman Don Awrey told reporters after Boston outslugged and outscored Montreal 13–5 the final week of the season. "But you have to wonder if they've been destroyed psychologically. The two games had to do something to them. They were bad beatings."

Curiously, the Bruins' minister of counterespionage had nothing but nice things to say about his first-round playoff opponents. It figured. Back in the '68 and '69 playoffs, when Montreal was on top, Derek Sanderson professed contempt for the "gutless" Canadiens, hoping to infuriate and disable the solemnly proud *bleu-blanc-rouge*. Now, with the Bruins prohibitive favourites, Turk was a sweet-talking mom tucking baby into bed.

---

news. "We're broke!" he told his wife (Kinsella's sister). "What do you mean we're going broke?" Mrs. Pollock exclaimed. "I just signed Frank Mahovlich today for $60,000," Sam shuddered.

"Béliveau was my hero growing up," Sanderson advised reporters. "Love the guy."

Love, love, love.

Pollock and the Canadiens had their tricks, too. On Sunday, March 15, 1971, the Habs' secret weapon was coming down from a 9–2 thrashing by the Hershey Bears. Oh well, back to the books. A Cornell grad finishing off his studies at McGill's law school, Ken Dryden had a full Monday-to-Friday course load in Montreal before racing to Halifax to tend net for the Nova Scotia Voyageurs on weekends. Before returning to Quebec this Sunday, however, the goalie was told Pollock wanted to have a word.

Uh-oh—he had let in at least three softies against Hershey.

How's school going, Ken? Can you play around exams?

Yes.

We want you to play for the Canadiens.

The rookie wasn't sure he had that right. Dryden was such a secret weapon that not even he was aware of Montreal's plans.

Pollock's call came on the last day that minor leaguers could be called up and still be eligible for the playoffs. The Habs wanted to hide their big secret weapon until the last possible moment. No one could argue the "big" part: five years earlier, the Stanley Cup finals between Montreal and Detroit included three goalies, Roger Crozier, Gump Worsley and Charlie Hodge, listed as five feet, eight inches, five-seven and five-six. The biggest goalie in NHL history the moment he slipped on a Canadiens uniform, Dryden stood six feet, four inches—nine inches taller than Habs regular Rogatien Vachon—with arms that went from here to Halifax.

The youngster also had valuable experience in hostile Boston Garden. At Cornell, he played 25 games for the Big Red in Boston, winning every time. This summer, he had also lined up summer work with Nader's Raiders, a consumer group taking on the automotive industry. General Motors employed detectives and hookers to sidetrack Nader's investigations. If Dryden was willing to stand tall against Big Bad General

Motors, Pollock figured he was probably good to go against the Bruins.

To ensure that Dryden remained a playoff surprise, the Canadiens were careful about how they employed him in his six-game audition. While Number 29 did not play Boston, he started against good teams. Dryden's performance against the NHL's second-best club, a 2–1 road win over Bobby Hull, Stan Mikita and the Chicago Blackhawks, convinced the Canadiens to go with him in the postseason. "We thought we would try another goalie [that] hadn't been shell-shocked by the Orrs and Espositos," Pollock would later say. And so Dryden asked a friend to cover for him at McGill by taking notes for him during class, and he ventured off on on his first-ever extended NHL road trip—a pair of playoff road games in Boston.

Of course, it didn't matter how Dryden played if the pumping heart of *Les Glorieux*—veterans Béliveau, Ferguson and Richard—weren't circulating blood and energy to the rest of the team. A former altar boy, Béliveau was the team's spiritual leader, a link to the team that captured five straight championships to end the 1950s. Legend had it that a Canadiens rookie once tossed his jersey onto the floor after a game and *Le Gros Bill* jumped to his feet, trembling.

"This jersey never touches the ground!" big Jean thundered.

Before the first playoff game in Boston, Béliveau provided another leadership seminar. The players were in the dressing room fretting about Boston—Orr's skating, Esposito's shooting, Cashman's elbows. Jacques Lemaire kept going on about the Bruins. Finally, Béliveau had enough. "We have to play our game," the captain said. "Don't worry about their game."

Montreal's game was skating—the Flying Frenchmen. Al MacNeil had an idea how to further speed Montreal's game. The rookie coach wanted to mix lines and have his team play shorter shifts, the better to tire and confuse the Bruins. Richard, normally a centre, would be put on wing to intercept Orr as he swung around the net. A variety of centres playing short shifts would keep Esposito, who liked to stay out forever, at bay.

If MacNeil's strategy failed, there was Plan B: Pollock's secret weapon, the biggest goalie in the world—a rookie with yet-undetected weaknesses.

Lo and behold, the plan worked perfectly in the playoff opener. Montreal outskated—and outhit!—Boston. Speedy Yvan Cournoyer was the most dangerous man on the ice, with the possible exception of elegantly swooping condors Frank and Peter Mahovlich. Esposito, meanwhile, went 0 for 11 against Dryden, while Orr became so frustrated that at one point he blew up at an official, throwing linesman Ron Ego out of the way to get at John Ashley. The result: a ten-minute misconduct, although Pollock would lobby for capital punishment (a playoff-long suspension): "You can bet if John Ferguson threw down an official he wouldn't play again this year," the GM told reporters.

All this, and still somehow Montreal lost. Cheevers was fabulous, erasing all but one Habs chance. Orr scored an early power-play goal—another inch-high, inside-the-post blast from the point. Ferguson replied. And that was it for most of what was a terrific hockey game until Cashman tipped in a Dallas Smith pass midway through the second period en route to a 3–1 Boston win. Cheevers was named first star after stumping the Canadiens with an assortment of astonishing saves, including a marine roll across the crease to rob Reggie Houle on an open-net chance.

The effervescent Bruins netminder also provided the best postgame quotes. When told that his opposite number visited law school libraries between games, Cheesy cracked: "That's good. At least I'll never run into him off the ice." And where would Gerry spend his off day? "I start every day the same way, with the Lord's Prayer," the goalie said, giving reporters a wink. "'Our Father, who art in heaven, give us this day our daily double.'"

Gerry would be hitting the racetrack.

Elsewhere in the winners' dressing room, the Bruins were cackling. Someone came up with a new nickname for Don Awrey, the Bruins defender who got into a second-period scrap with Montreal's handsome, diffident winger, Marc Tardif (hockey's Alain Delon). Awrey grabbed Tardif's sweater at the neck, twisting and twisting until the winger's face was the same hue as his scarlet jersey. Then Tardif's legs folded and he collapsed, struggling for breath. Trainers hoofed it in from the bench to give him CPR.

Now Bruins called Awrey "The Boston Strangler."

Anecdotal evidence suggests that in the six-, 12- and 14-team NHL, professional hockey was a loosely affiliated fellowship, hardly the carefully segregated industry that is today's game. When he coached the Canadiens, Toe Blake golfed with announcer Danny Gallivan and played cards with scribe Red Fisher. Once, after a Saturday game with the Blackhawks, the Leafs arrived in the middle of a frigid night at Dearborn Station in Chicago. Taxis were scarce at the train station, so coach Punch Imlach and sidekick King Clancy squeezed into a cab with referees John Ashley and Neil Armstrong. Minutes later, Imlach nudged Clancy and both hopped out at the LaSalle Hotel. "You guys got in first, you pay the bill," Imlach said, sending the cab away. Later that night, Ashley whistled a parade of Leafs to the penalty box. When goalie Johnny Bower came to the bench for a break, Imlach handed him a fiver and said, "Tell that son of a bitch Ashley to lay off. I'll pay for the cab."

Once upon a time, reporters, players, coaches and referees were all, if not buddies, at least co-workers with a shared enthusiasm and phobia— love of hockey and fear of having to find a real job. All of which explained how the following argument could take place.

"Who you starting in nets tomorrow's game?" *Montreal Star* reporter Red Fisher asked old friend—and Bruins coach—Tom Johnson at the Garden the day after Boston's 3–1 first-game win.

"Eddie Johnston."

"Are you nuts? Cheevers was the only reason your team won last night. He was the best player on the ice."

"Before the series started, I promised Eddie I'd use him in the second game. If I don't, I'll lose him for the rest of the playoffs."

"It doesn't matter what you promised Eddie. If you lose him, you lose him. You go with the players who can win for you, and last night Cheevers won the game."

Johnson shrugged. He was the coach.

How crazy was New England for the Bruins in the spring of '71? So crazy that when Orr received a misconduct penalty in the Montreal-Boston playoff opener, fans went berserk. "Ashley's a bum! Ashley's a bum!" they shouted, jumping to their feet. Programs and bottles soon littered the ice. One protestor hung on to his beer and instead reached into his mouth, firing his dentures at the ref. "Aa—eed's a umm! Aa—eed's a umm!" It was a time to remember that *fan* was short for *fanatic*. The *Boston Globe* ran charcoal cameos of the Bruins ("maybe the best hockey team ever") that spring. For the series against Montreal, the *Globe* featured guest columns from the *Montreal Star*, the Montreal *Gazette* and, for *l'opinion française,* French pieces, in the language of love, with accompanying translation, courtesy of *La Presse*. Too much wasn't enough.

Young fans wearing army fatigues, in from the suburbs, from Revere, Lowell and Dorchester, hung around the train station overnight, waiting for same-day tickets to go on sale the next morning, broiling chickens over garbage cans and haggling with scalpers. Balcony tickets were going for $30 a pair; good seats, $100 and up.

"I remember when balcony seats were 40 cents," one fan told the *Globe* upon learning the scalpers' prices. Not that he wanted back up with the seething Gallery Gods. "Last time I was there somebody threw a beer bottle, hit me in the head."

Jubilant Bruins fans felt no need to throw things—no tantrums, no false teeth, no chrome- plated tavern change-makers—in the first two periods of the second Boston-Montreal playoff game. After another late-for-work Bruins opening (Yvan Cournoyer waltzed around a sliding Ted Green and outwaited Johnston to give Montreal an early 1–0 lead), Boston came dramatically to life, humiliating the Habs with a full demonstration of their talents.

As always, Number Four led the way. In a dizzying 20 minutes, the Bruins counted five goals, with Orr collecting four points. After Cournoyer's marker, Bobby materialized with the puck in front of the Canadiens' net. Aware that Orr liked to bang low shots in off the post,

Dryden dropped to the ice, only to have Bobby snap one under the cross-bar. A minute later, Green tipped in a neat pass from Hodge. Early in the second, Montreal's Terry Harper went off and Boston showed off their power play—big bodies in constant motion, sending no-look passes onto the sticks of swirling teammates. The Habs penalty killers staggered—kids stepping off a too-fast merry-go-round. Dryden made consecutive saves on Stanfield and Orr, but got his legs tangled on a spin-around shot from McKenzie. Five aside now, Orr, Esposito and Cashman combined on a smart three-way passing play. Seconds later, Orr rid himself of fore-checker Bobby Sheehan with a head shiver, then walked in alone. Dryden jumped out, pads splayed. Orr dropped his head for another short slap-shot. Following through, though, he noticed Sanderson hurrying towards the crease. The bullet pass hit Turk's stick blade, deflecting into the open net.

Five–one, Bruins. The scene at the Garden was like V-J Day—drifting confetti, horns, bear hugs and kisses. Cue the monkeys . . . it seemed certain there'd be an all-you-can-eat floor buffet in an hour or so.

But . . . but, despite being up by four and all over Montreal, the Bruins exhibited the lawless bravado that sometimes got them in trouble. Green chewed out referee Art Skov, picking up a ten-minute miscon-duct. Bruins would rack up 45 minutes in penalties this evening to Montreal's 17. Yes, the Bruins made life hard for the Habs, but they were also making the game difficult for themselves, playing at a man disadvan-tage to a proud, increasingly angry Montreal team.

They were tempting fate, displeasing the hockey gods—a group that historically favoured *le bleu-blanc-rouge*.

It could be argued the Bruins threw away their record-breaking '70–71 season late in the second period: Henri Richard, the Rocket's younger brother,* chipped the puck past Dallas Smith, then swung past

---

* Henri Richard once found himself being ground into the boards by Chicago Blackhawks winger Dennis Hull, Bobby's sibling. They came up screaming, grabbing and pulling, staring into each other's eyes. Little Henri connected with

Sanderson before fooling Johnston with a backhand deke. Five–two Boston. Scarlet sweaters raced to surround little Henri, but before they arrived, a fuming Sanderson cruised past and pulled Richard's feet out from under him with his stick.

Up went Skov's arm. Two minutes.

Sanderson complained—*Hey, it's an accident.* The Canadiens' Phil Roberto made a beeline for Turk, windmilling punches. He too was sent off—five aside. With Orr, advantage Boston—except the Bruins wouldn't lay off Skov, who eventually handed them a bench penalty. As the period ended, Ace Bailey also received a ten-minute misconduct.

The *Boston Globe*'s Jerry Nason worried that Sanderson's upending of Richard could potentially be a series turning point: "The old Canadiens reacted like the ol' Celtics when playoff opponents tried to get physical with an aging [Bob] Cousy," he wrote in his postgame report. Indeed, if *Le Gros Bill* reacted with wounded horror at seeing a Canadiens sweater thrown carelessly away, imagine his fury at seeing a red jersey (with a Richard inside!) tossed to the ice. Making matters worse, in the third period, Cashman took a tree-chopping swing at Frank Mahovlich, breaking hockey's 27th commandment: Thou shalt not wake up the Big M.

And so, as 14,908 fans looked on in horror, the Montreal Canadiens and Frank Mahovlich, who had combined for 13 Stanley Cup wins in the previous 15 NHL seasons,[*] surged to life. *Les Canadiens sont là.* Suddenly 25 again, Béliveau scored two goals and set up Ferguson for a third. Lemaire stole a lazy back pass and raced the length of the ice to beat Johnston. The Bruins mounted impressive counterattacks, but Dryden (all six feet, four inches of him) stood tall. With three minutes left, the Big M grabbed a pass intended for Orr and bolted down the left side.

---

the most personal insult. "My brother's better than your brother," the Rocket's younger brother told the Golden Jet's younger brother.

[*] Mahovlich won four Stanley Cups in Toronto in the '60s. The Canadiens collected nine championships from 1956–71.

Bobby put his head down but couldn't make up any ground on barging Mahovlich—an Olympic sprinter in the home stretch.

It was a nightmare. The fastest player in hockey, Orr skated all out, only to fall farther and farther behind. The Big M wound up upon hitting the circle to the right of Johnston, golfing a slapshot in off the far post. Now it was 7–5, Montreal. Boston had given up six goals in just over 20 minutes.

Poor Eddie Johnston. He just didn't have it tonight; kept falling to the ice on every Montreal rush, like a slapstick comedian in an old Mack Sennett silent movie who slipped over and over again on the same banana peel.

After Mahovlich scored, Orr materialized on our TV screens, lifting his stick over his head. Just before he broke it over the crossbar (Bobby had been on the ice for five Montreal goals), cameras tactfully moved away to find the Big M accepting congratulations from excited teammates.

We've beaten Boston—in Boston!

Or had the Bruins beaten themselves? After the game, Bruins coach Tom Johnson talked of "a complete defensive collapse" and called for a voluntary practice the next morning at 10:30.

Only fourth liners Don Marcotte and Ace Bailey showed up.

Let's fast-forward five years for a moment, shall we? Don Cherry would be the Bruins' coach by then. After a game, he too called an optional workout. By this time, the Bruins had traded for Brad Park and Jean Ratelle. The oft-injured Park strolled into the Garden to a memorable scene: "As I walk into the dressing room," Park would recall, "Cherry [had Rick Middleton] by the throat, with his feet off the ground, yelling, 'When I call an optional, it is for [veteran] guys like Park and Ratelle, not for a 23-year-old asshole.'"

Harry Sinden could also be tough on the Bruins. Yes, he gave them plenty of slack when he was coach. He had a routine the players loved. Sitting at the front of the team bus as it wheeled away from enemy rinks, he would hear a player, always the same one, snap open a beer—*pfft*.

"Hey, no beer on the team bus. Who's just opened a can?" Sinden would bark, feigning outrage. "C'mon . . . who?"

"I did," Bobby Orr would say.

"Drink up, everybody," Harry would sing.

Still, Sinden could lower the boom. During the 1968 preseason that saw Boston morph into the Big Bad Bruins, the team dropped two lop-sided home games in London, Ontario. As the Bruins got dressed after the Sunday afternoon game, discussing where and what to to eat, Sinden burst into the dressing room, fuming. Harry knew what the players would be doing for dinner—tasting their own bile. Sinden called for a Sunday evening practice: a vigorous two-hour skate around London's Treasure Island Gardens. Lap after lap. Everybody who wasn't named Bobby Orr (recovering from knee surgery) suffered through the drill.

Much has been made of Tom Johnson's decision not to start Cheevers in the second game of the '71 Boston–Montreal quarter-final. That game was the series, the theory goes. A hot Cheevers would've stopped the Cup-bound Montreal Express from ever getting out of the station. The stunning second-game upset encouraged the Canadiens to believe they could win. And so they did—four games to three. Flip that second game around . . .

But here's the thing: Boston did come back! After dropping a 3–1 decision in game three in Montreal—a contest Dryden stole—the Bruins righted the ship, clobbering the Canadiens 5–2 (Orr picked up a hat trick, including an astonishing goal where, anticipating Luke Skywalker, he snatched a Dryden goalmouth-clearing pass out of midair with his light sabre, depositing a backhand in the wee sliver of available net). Next game, the Bruins romped at home, 7–3. At this point, Boston had the momentum; Orr was flying and Cheevers was on his game. And then the team failed to show up in Montreal, losing 8–3.

These were the Big Bad Boston Bruins, a team that could do the hardest things easily—score exquisitely choreographed goals in bunches, outperform the other guy in areas of the rink where character was king. (Who could outwork Esposito in front? Outmuscle Cashman in the corner?) That said, boy oh boy, were the Orr-Esposito Bruins ever an up-and-down crew—a beautiful, sometimes ugly-scary Bipolar Express.

The Bruins overwhelmed Montreal for 35 minutes of game two, outscoring the Habs 5–1, only to give up six unanswered goals the rest of the way. The team dominated games four and five, outscoring Montreal 12–5. In games six and seven, it was the other way around: five goals for, 12 against.

Boston's problems were as glaring as their strengths. The Bruins were talented, but undisciplined; determined, but maybe not dedicated. More than anything, the team lacked leadership . . . wisdom. The missing Stanley Cups can invariably be attributed to mistakes, coaching or front-office blunders.

Yes, Cheevers should have been in nets for that second game against Montreal. He had played too well in the series opener. Boston should also have been more wary of their historic rivals—more respectful . . . *carefuller.* Turk should have never messed with Henri Richard.

You don't tug on Superman's cape . . .

Hard as it is to believe, Cheevers would later admit that Boston had underestimated Montreal—forgot who they were dealing with. "The Flying Frenchmen go glassy-eyed when they think of their tradition and pride and all that bullshit," the goalie advised biographer Trent Frayne. "They suddenly acquire adrenalin not available to other teams."

And yes, yes, the Bruins might have been more professional; after their second-game collapse, every Bruin should have been at practice next morning, getting mad at themselves, and then at the Montreal Canadiens. Instead, only benchwarmers appeared. "There were some others I thought should have been there," Coach Johnson tactfully complained to reporters at the time.

Why weren't they?

"Harry Sinden got fired and Tom Johnson didn't have the same kind of approach to coaching," Ed Westfall would tell broadcaster/author Dick Irvin, years later. "Things weren't as disciplined . . . It wasn't that we didn't take Montreal seriously . . . that year we didn't take ourselves seriously."

Sinden's momentary loss—he would later return as GM—was devastating. The coach had asked for an $8,000 raise after taking the Bruins to the Cup in 1970. He was offered $5,000, bringing his contract to $22,000 (most NHL coaches were making $30,000 at the time). The Bruins figured, *Close enough, this guy loves hockey too much to work in the real world.* They evidently didn't know Harry Sinden. Once, while playing senior hockey for the Whitby Dunlops in the late '50s, Sinden met GM/coach Wren Blair for a beer after a game to talk contract. Harry knew the team's star centre, Bob Attersley, received 7 per cent of the gate—$180 a contest, tops on the team.

"I'm giving you 6½ per cent," Blair advised Sinden.

"Fuck you. I'm a 7 per-centre."

"Fuck you, too. As far as I'm concerned, you're worth 6½ per cent."

Hearing this, Sinden left his beer and contract offer on the table, making for the door. "For Christ sake, Harry," Blair called after him. "Half a per cent is going to be worth eight bucks. What's the big deal?"

"It's not the half per cent, it's the principle," Sinden said, slamming the door.

That bloody-mindedness was what the Bruins needed. Tom Johnson was a terrific, tough player. All Howie Meeker ever remembered of the famous overtime goal that teammate Bill Barilko scored to give Toronto the Stanley Cup in 1951 was Montreal defender Johnson smashing his face into the glass behind the net. ("How do you like that, you big son of a bitch?" Meeker shouted when both men were suddenly bathed in red from the blinking goal light.)

But Johnson wasn't the son of a bitch the Bruins needed behind the bench. He wore a bow tie, had a droll sense of humour, made an effort to get along. Johnson was a superb fixer—the guy who could call in favours, phoning sportswriter Red Fisher to enquire about Esposito. Later, in 1975, after big Phil and Carol Vadnais were traded to New York for Brad Park and Jean Ratelle, the Bruins realized, uh-oh, they'd made a mistake. Vadnais had a no-trade clause. The deal was void. Johnson, the assistant GM by that time, was sent behind enemy lines to work out a deal with the Rangers' Emile Francis and Vadnais's agent.

Johnson was a valuable organization man, but Harry Sinden was the guy who could look into players' eyes and tell them what they had to hear. *Lookit, Derek, I need you to stay out of the penalty box tonight. Phil, quicker shifts out there—c'mon, we got some pretty good centres on this team.* Sinden was the only son of a bitch who could tell the Big Bad Bruins what to do. "You just cost us the Cup," Sanderson told management when Sinden was allowed to walk.

Turned out he was right.

THE WHA, PART ONE

Even though the NHL league guide kept tabs on former players who drifted into the American and Eastern Hockey Leagues, no record was kept on those who jumped to the WHA, including such former NHL greats as Gordie Howe, Bobby Hull and Frank Mahovlich. The new league, which lasted from 1972 unti 1979, began with lots of bright (as in colourful) ideas, including fluorescent blue pucks. Pink ones, too. Problems arose, however, when it was discovered that dyes cause rubber to cure, changing a puck's density and shape—shots hopped around crazily. Another wild idea: goals scored in the last minute counted for two. The Minnesota Fighting Saints drafted state governor Wendell Anderson. Winnipeg selected Soviet premier Alexei Kosygin. Referee-in-chief Bill Friday hired former Satan's Choice bouncer Ron Asselstine as a referee.

Only the Asselstine move worked out.

The Bruins had other management problems. Weston Adams Sr. did a wonderful job of reviving the franchise when he took over in 1964, bird-dogging Canada, stockpiling talent. But too often, Bruins recruits ended up playing for other teams. Montreal's Ken Dryden and Philadelphia's Bernie Parent combined for eight Stanley Cups in the 1970s. Both had been drafted and then traded away by the Bruins. Future 50- and 60-goal scorers Rick MacLeish and Reggie Leach were also sent packing.

Critically, Boston didn't see a rival league, the WHA, coming in the fall of 1972. The New York Rangers, Montreal and Philadelphia hung on to valuable assets. The Bruins lost Cheevers, McKenzie, Sanderson, Green and Mike Walton . . . although maybe Walton's departure was more an act of self-preservation. A friend of Orr's, "Shakey," fit in too well with Boston. The fast-moving centre surprised teammates by springing from a hotel pool diving board in full hockey gear—cannon-balling right into the water. Just another fun-loving night on the road for the Bruins. In St. Louis, the Bruins responded by playing a water gag of their own on Shakey, waiting on a balcony above the hotel entrance, holding heavy, overflowing buckets. When Walton appeared, he was greeted with a tumbling waterfall. Leaping out of the way, the hockey player smashed through a plate-glass door and sliced himself open from knee to chin. Doctors needed five pints of blood and 200 stitches to fill and sew him back up.

That story makes you wonder if the Bruins' real problem was that the team had somehow become compromised by its crazy, doomed environment—the falling-down Boston Garden and its lost tribe of midnight rambling monkeys. The team was by now inseparable from its brawling, working-class fan base. By the mid-'70s, many of the Manger Hotel's 400 rooms were occupied by homeless squatters; crime was rampant in the area. Fight manager Ray Arcel wasn't the Garden's only mob victim. Like the team they loved, Bruins fans included a few "enforcers." Like the muscle man who offered to take care of Pat Quinn for Bobby Orr.

Don Cherry would remember a game when a fan started getting on a made Bruin. "There's a guy sitting [across the rink from our bench] who's all over Phil Esposito one night," Cherry told writer Leigh Montville. "I'm just standing behind Phil and Wayne Cashman at the bench. I can hear Cash say, 'Don't worry about that guy, Phil. He'll be taken care of.' . . . Pretty soon, two big guys come along and talk with the guy and he leaves and never comes back."

Hey, buddy, what say we get some air—hot in here.

I'm not hot.

We're not asking.

In the 1973 crime movie *The Friends of Eddie Coyle*, Robert Mitchum (in the title role) is drawn to the Boston Garden by a conniving stoolie. The Bruins and Blackhawks are playing. At one point, Eddie returns to his seat with an armload of beer. We can tell from his heavy eyes he's had a few already. But when Eddie looks down and finds Bobby Orr on the ice, all his troubles lift away. "What is he, 24 or something," Eddie says, smiling, lifting a beer to heaven. "Greatest hockey player in the world: Number Four, Bobby Orr. What a future he's got, huh?"

Minutes later, Eddie is shot and killed, dumped in front of a bowling alley in Quincy.

As it turned out, Bobby's career would be over by age 27. Bad knees. Derek Sanderson succumbed to alcoholism, moving from the WHA Philadelphia Blazers back to Boston, then on to the New York Rangers, St. Louis, Vancouver and Pittsburgh before resorting to sleeping on a park bench. "Turk Sanderson was the most underrated player on Boston as far as I'm concerned, and a real loss for them," Stan Fischler would tell me. "Good two-way player, a little bit mean. Great agitator, he could read people better than any hockey player I ever met. Get them off their game."

Why couldn't Turk read himself?

Fischler thought about that for a second. "Lemme tell you a story— you know Leo the Lion?"

Metro-Goldwyn-Mayer's lion mascot, showed up roaring before all their films?

"Yeah, that's the one; he goes to a psychiatrist. Psychiatrist says, 'What's wrong?' Leo says, 'I don't know, but every time I go to work,

I have to sit through a three-hour movie.' You're asking me what's wrong with Derek Sanderson? I don't know, I'm not a psychiatrist . . . But I'll say this: Boston lost a lot of its swagger when he left."

And maybe the Bruins busting Esposito out of the hospital isn't as funny a story as we first thought. Esposito blew out a knee in the second game of the 1973 playoffs. He was petrified upon arriving at Massachusetts General—it was the first time Phil had been to a hospital since his appendix almost burst. After operating on Esposito the next morning, Dr. Carter R. Rowe received a panicky alert over the hospital's public address system: *Dr. Rowe, please call Phillips House 5. Urgent.* He quickly phoned back.

"Is this Dr. Rowe?"

"Yes, what's the problem?"

"Dr. Rowe, I don't know what to say—Phil Esposito is not in his room. And neither is his bed." When the doc arrived in Esposito's room, TV reports already had an unknown party rolling a bedridden patient into a bar across the street from Mass General. Acting on a hunch, Rowe phoned the bar. Bobby Orr, instigator of the great Bruins hospital kidnapping, answered.

"Doc, don't worry, we are handling Phil just like a baby," Orr assured Rowe. "He's having a beer, and we will have him back in 15 minutes."

In truth, the Bruins never got Phil back. He would never be the same. Not that the kidnapping hurt his career. But you have to wonder if the team's relentless pursuit of night life, shore liberty and happy hour eventually cost them. The Bruins would win only two Stanley Cups, a fraction of what most hockey dynasties yield. Then again, no team ever connected with a fan base like the Boston Bruins. With Bobby Orr—adopted son Number Four—leading the way, the Big Bad Bruins made happy hour last ten long years in Boston, from 1966 until 1976.

Some happy hours are happier than others, it must be said.

Asked to provide a colour piece about game seven of the 1971 Habs–Bruins series, played on a Sunday afternoon, 21-year-old *Boston Globe* reporter Peter Gammons took to the city's working-class taverns—to the

Blarney Stone on Dorchester and the Elbola Lounge on Beacon Street. There, customers arrived from Mass to watch the game, loosening their ties to wade into row after row of Seagram's V.O. shots and draft beer chasers. After Hodge scored early on for Boston, the Habs came back— two quick goals by the Big M and Reggie Houle.

Two goals inside three minutes, and six months of record work by the Bruins had disappeared.

John Ferguson banged Boston players around. "No way it would've happened if Sinden was here," a Blarney Stone drinker mused. "These Frenchmen smell money, money, money," a guy the end of the bar added. Someone else suggested that the Bruins needed to get Phil's brother, goalie Tony Esposito, from Chicago. As the game wound down, patrons stared off. It was bad enough just listening. Orr lost the puck in his end at one point. Sanderson tried to get the Garden crowd and his team going but lost a fight to Ferguson. Four–two, Montreal . . . with time running out.

At the Elbola Lounge, Bruins fans disappeared into drinks. "I've played here for four years," piano man Larry Matthews told Gammons, "and it's never been like this. Everyone here is dead."

Especially the on-screen Bruins, lost in a familiar bad dream, chasing the Canadiens but forever a step behind. Goddamn Canadiens. Here, the entire city, the whole league, figured the Bruins would be fighting it out with New York and Chicago in the 1971 finals—the Rangers and Blackhawks were, after Boston, the top-rated teams in the NHL. And then the Bruins go and get stabbed in the back, killed by an ancient adversary in the opening round. The game still had a few minutes to go, but Eddie the bartender knew hockey season was over in Boston, and so he braved the elements, walking outside to take down the tavern's WATCH THE GAME IN COLOR sign. Gammons tagged along, asking if the Bruins loss would be bad for business. "Tonight, they'll drink out their miseries," the bartender shrugged. "Tomorrow, they'll drink and watch the *Monday Night Movie*. Boston is a city that is thirdly for politics, secondly for sports, and but most of all it's a city for drinking."

WHA TEAMS

Alberta/Edmonton Oilers*
Chicago Cougars
Cincinnati Stingers
Calgary Broncos**
Cleveland Crusaders
Minnesota Fighting Saints
Dayton Arrows**
Houston Aeros
Denver Spurs
Ottawa Civics
Indianapolis Racers
Los Angeles Sharks
Michigan Stags
Baltimore Blades
Minnesota Fighting Saints***
New England Whalers*
New York Raiders/Golden Blades
Jersey Knights
San Diego Mariners
Miami Screaming Eagles**
Philadelphia Blazers

Vancouver Blazers
Calgary Cowboys
Ottawa Nationals
Toronto Toros
Birmingham Bulls
Phoenix Roadrunners
San Francisco Sharks**
Quebec Nordiques*
Winnipeg Jets*

* Played all seven seasons without relocating

** Never played

*** Folded before the end of the 1975–76 season. Cleveland moved to Minnesota the following season, reviving the Fighting Saints name.

THE BRUINS ARE COMING, THE BRUINS ARE COMING

Canada vs. Soviet Union, September 28, 1972

Why was Frosty Forristall boot-skating on the Luzhniki Stadium rink, giving Leonid Brezhnev, General Secretary of the Central Committee of the Communist Party of the Soviet Union, the finger? And why was the Boston Bruins trainer, a former U.S. marine, dressed in a red polyester jumpsuit set off by a white belt—a look known in Canada at the time as "the full Manitoba"? Shuffling alongside Frosty was Alan Eagleson, Bobby Orr's "older brother." Minutes earlier, Forristall and Eagleson had fought their way through the spectators to get at a goal judge who had failed to acknowledge a Canadian score in the final game of the 1972 Summit Series in Moscow. That was when the *militsiya* grabbed them. After that, Frosty and the Eagle crossed the ice on their way back to the Team Canada bench, giving all of Russia the finger (Eagleson used his thumb—*Up yours, Ivan*). Locals put two fingers in their mouths and shrieked their dissaproval. Imagine 12,000 people hailing a cab. All but one Team Canada supporter responded with "*Da, da, Canada, nyet, nyet, Soviet.*"

The missing Canuck was in prison, sentenced to Siberia for impersonating Bobby Gimby[*] by leading the Canadian contingent with sputtering bugle calls. OK, the guy might also have smashed up a hotel bar. But more on that later; let's get back to Forristall. The Bruins trainer had been drafted onto Team Canada by Harry Sinden. The ex-Bruins coach was calling the shots for Canada. In fact, this was very much a Boston show. Esposito, Ed Johnston, Don Awrey and Wayne Cashman were also here. There'd have been more Bruins, too, except Orr was hurt (knees again) and, though chosen, Gerry Cheevers and Turk Sanderson couldn't play because they'd jumped to the WHA.

Orr and Canada's best playing Russia on a world stage! That had always been the Eagle's dream. He and Orr were up at Eagleson's Georgian Bay cottage in the summer of 1966, listening on radio as 100,000 Wembley Stadium fans cheered England to a 4–2 win over West Germany in the World Cup of soccer. Hearing the applause, Eagleson asked, "Why can't we have a World Cup of hockey?"

Six years later, Eagleson was in a position to make something like that

---

[*]   The former musical director of *Hockey Night in Canada*'s postgame show, *Juliette,* trumpeter Bobby Gimby was commissioned by the Canadian government to whip up a bilingual pop song celebrating the country's 1967 centennial. And by God, he did just that, writing a punishingly cheerful, breakfast cereal–sweet ditty that became an AM hit. Try as we might, we couldn't forget the first verse: *Ca-na-da (one little, two little, three Canadians) / We love thee (now we are twenty million) / Ca-na-da (four little, five little, provinces) proud and free . . .* Gimby and schoolkids performed the song everywhere at the time, earning Gimby the title "The Pied Piper of Canada."

happen. The Eagle was executive director of the NHL Players' Association, hockey's top agent and a growing friend to NHL owners. If the league didn't want WHA players in the series, that was OK with Al, who called Canada's team "the NHL All-Stars." The name didn't resonate with the Canadian Amateur Hockey Association; Terry Hill, a recently hired Detroit-born employee of the Toronto ad agency Vickers & Benson, came up with "Team Canada." Whatever. As long as *most* of Canada's best pros could finally play the Russians, winners of three straight Olympic hockey golds. Eagleson, who advised friends he expected to be prime minister someday, wanted a global Summit Series for patriotic reasons. But there was also something in it for him.

Question: What do you do when you have a finger in every pie in hockey?

Answer: Build a bigger bakery.

Hill's first name for Canada's best was "The Dream Team."[†] But boss Terry O'Malley said that was "too cocky and think how stupid the name will look when Canada loses the first game." Few thought that could ever happen. The *Globe and Mail*'s Dick Beddoes crowed that if Russia won a single game, "I will eat this column shredded at high noon in a bowl of borscht on the front steps of the Russian Embassy." Sinden tried to convince players to take Russia seriously. Showed film of them destroying opponents. Hired former Canadien John Ferguson, with his John Wayne glare on, as assistant coach. Nothing worked. It didn't help that Team Canada's advance scouts gave the Russians bad grades. Players were small and couldn't shoot, they said. Goalie Vladislav Tretiak was a sieve.

If Team Canada was unprepared, Russia had been planning for this series since Josef Stalin put his propaganda department in charge of athletics in 1946. Stalin also made his son Vasily the manager of the first

---

† Though too showy for Canada, the "Dream Team" designation was deemed just right for the star-studded 1992 United States Olympic basketball team that featured Michael Jordan, Charles Barkley, Magic Johnson and Larry Bird.

national hockey team. They were hardly starting from scratch. Before
the NHL was born (1917), 34 Russian teams competed in a nationwide
bandy (ball hockey) league; in fact, the country had been playing a sport
like hockey since Peter the Great stickhandled the frozen Neva River in
the 1700s. After World War II, the Ministry of Sport took to creating the
perfect hockey team. Almost 4,000 sports schools trained 1.3 million
athletes, creating superheroes to inspire the proletariat. Muscle biopsies
determined a child's optimum sport. Top hockey players made it to
Moscow Dynamo, sponsored by the KGB (secret police) or, better yet, a
military all-star squad, CSKA Moscow—better known as the Red Army.

Beginning as kids, players trained and worked on the same line,
developing a telepathic rapport. Even a married athlete like Russia's best
hockey player, Valeri Kharlamov, worked out 11 months a year, six days
a week in a barracks outside Moscow. No TV, phones, women or booze.
Kharlamov and linemates Vladimir Petrov and Boris Mikhailov had
grown up together, season after season—soccer in the summer, hockey
in winter.

If Valeri's scalp itched, Boris or Vladimir scratched it.

Maybe if Harry showed Team Canada footage of Russians training.
Canadian stars golfed in the summers, staying longer than they should
at the 19th hole. Their Russian counterparts would run staircases with
teammates draped around around their necks. Stickhandle tennis balls
while skipping rope. Lift weights. Run for miles. They probably had
another advantage: in the summer of 1974, Philadelphia Flyers coach
Freddy Shero travelled to Russia for a hockey symposium. One aspect
of Soviet training intrigued him. "Forty days before a big event," he
would tell *Sports Illustrated*, "Russians require their athletes to give a
pint of blood, which they then regain naturally. It's a program designed
to build strength."

It was also cheating—blood doping. Because he didn't know better,
Freddy left out the part where the blood was reinfused into athletes a
week before a high-endurance event, greatly increasing a player's aerobic
capacity.

In other words, the Big Red Machine was likely running on super unleaded, while Team Canada puttered along on regular fuel. Didn't help that the Canadian players weren't in shape yet. Phil Esposito balked when a trainer asked if he stretched before workouts. "I just started laughing," Espo remembered, years later. "I'd never stretched in my life."

At first, it looked as though Dick Beddoes was right. In the Summit Series opener in Montreal, Esposito scored 30 seconds in; Paul Henderson tallied minutes later. But then the Big Red Machine whirred into gear. Anatoli Tarasov, the father of Russian hockey, had improved the sport by increasing its tempo—faster skating, more puck movement. Canada outshot Russia 32–30 in the first game. That would mean nothing to Tarasov, watching back in Moscow. He counted passes, not shots. He believed in motion and misdirection, players hopping lanes at full speed, making relays to open spaces filled with charging red jerseys until all that was left was an open player with an empty net.

Russia tied it quickly. "What do you think?" Gary Bergman asked defence partner Brad Park as they puffed off the ice at the end of the first period. "We're in trouble," Park replied, catching his breath.

"Yeah, they're coming at us in waves," Bergman groaned.

They could also shoot. And Tretiak had lightning-quick reflexes. Custer at Little Big Horn had better scouts than Team Canada. In the dressing room between periods, Cashman looked at Esposito, who shook his head. For the rest of the game, it was all Russia. Team Canada doctor John Zeldin took his eight-year-old into the Canadian dressing room after the 7–3 Russian win. "I saw the cold and naked posture of defeat—gloom, despair and self-pity," he told the *Globe and Mail* years later. "[My son] was so frightened by the mood that he held my hand the whole time." The morning after Russia's surprise victory, the Montreal *Gazette* ran an Aislin cartoon of NHL president Clarence Campbell sneaking off to a pawn shop with the Stanley Cup.

After the humiliation, Sinden and Ferguson stumbled back to the Queen Elizabeth Hotel and snapped open a couple of beer in Harry's room. *What are we going to do? Once they relaxed, Russia beat us 7–1.* The coaches would have to earn their pay now (Eagleson gave Sinden $15,000 and Fergy $10,000 for the series). They would do that and more, for even in absorbing a terrible loss, Sinden and Ferguson detected a flaw in Tarasov's master plan:

The Big Red Machine had no reverse.

"They didn't use their point men much in the offensive end and their wingers were beating our D-men in the corners," Sinden concluded. "We decided to have our centre cover the two ineffective point men and bring our two wingers down low to help the D-men." The strategy worked. Canada won 4–1 in Toronto and tied the Russians 4–4 in Winnipeg before succumbing to fatigue and dissilusionment, dropping the Canadian finale in Vancouver, 5–3. Sinden's club could still win the series, but—this was another surprise—they already seemed to have lost the country. No more Team Canada; they were the NHL All-Stars again. Vancouver spectators applauded Boris Mikhailov, Russia's star of the game. Canada's best, Phil Esposito, received a derisive cheer.

What did Russia think, watching Canada welcome and applaud the visiting Red Army? Certainly, their players enjoyed the spoils of victory, mainlining North American culture. Soviet athletes watched *The Godfather* in Montreal and John Wayne's *The Cowboys* in Winnipeg. "The Russians . . . loved their Coca-Cola,"* according to Team Canada trainer Rick Noonan. "I'd hand out a hundred and more bottles after practice . . . Also, when they left a hotel room, everything came with them— soaps, shampoos, there wasn't even any toilet paper left."

"I loved Canada," defenceman Yuri Shatalov would tell the *Globe and Mail*. "The fans were so enthusiastic—and sometimes in our favour."

The Summit Series was turning into a Soviet propaganda win. To that end, their delegation included a gatekeeper (Igor Sharikov), whose lone job it was to ensure that the Canadian TV feed to Russia cut away before ads—beer commercials that made Canada look like a college mixer populated by blindingly attractive models.

★ Coke didn't begin bottling operations in Russia until 1985.

When you're smiling, say Labatt's Blue, the beer that smiles with you. It's the true one, brewed for you one . . .

But wait . . . something happened at the end of the Vancouver game that changed everything for Canada—how the series was viewed, what it meant. After fans began turning on Team Canada, Esposito told his teammates in the second intermission, "I've got to get named a star here"—just so he'd be handed an open microphone afterwards. In the third, Esposito earned the postgame spotlight by setting up two goals, working himself into a telegenic lather—proof that what he was about to say was true.

"For the people across Canada, we tried," Esposito told viewers. "We gave it our best. For the people who booed us, Jesus, all of us guys are really disheartened and we're disillusioned and we're disappointed in some of the people. We cannot believe the bad press we've got, the booing we've gotten in our own buildings. If the Russian fans boo their players like some of the Canadian fans—I'm not saying all of them— some of them booed, then I'll come back and apologize to each and every Canadian. But I don't think they will. I'm really, really, I'm really disappointed . . . What the hell, we're doing the best we can. They've got a good team, let's face facts. But it doesn't mean that we're not giving it our 150 per cent . . . Every one of us guys, 35 guys who came out to play for Team Canada, we did it because we love our country . . . We came because we love Canada. And even though we play in the United States and we earn our money in the United States, Canada is still our home and that's the only reason we came."

Heartfelt, with a touch of maple syrup—to say I love you, Canada, right out loud—Esposito's address stirred passions; 3,000 fans, carrying 6,000 Canadian flags, spent $800 for a return trip to Moscow to watch "their boys" play the second half of the series. On the flight over, they prepared themselves by singing "O Canada."

True patriot love in all thy sons command . . .

But before landing on the dark side of the moon, the Union of Soviet Socialist Republics, Canada played tune-up games in Sweden, alienating that country with Big Bad Bruins hockey. Canada won the first game 4–1 and managed a tie late in the second game when big Phil scored a shorthanded goal. (Vic Hadfield took a major penalty for attempting a tonsillectomy on Swede captain Lars-Erik Sjoberg.) The team left the ice to the shrieking of a breaking train—10,000 whistling Swedes. Canada's ambassador apologized, calling Team Canada "hooligans."

OK, maybe, but the players stood closer together now. Vilified underdogs, mortally afraid, but still cheerful, giddy at times, leaning on and jostling each other. In a Stockholm bar, a gay man hit on Bobby Clarke (oh, those misleading Shirley Temple curls). Bobby told his admirer he was barking up the wrong hockey player, but said the guy over there with two women, Rod Gilbert, that was the fella he wanted. *But the women?* He's a whattayacallit . . . bisexual, Clarke explained and then sat back, enjoying his beer. When Guy Lapointe's wife back in Montreal gave birth, Team Canada bought a two-four and joined together in a leafy park, laughing, sharing stories, drinking the heart right out of a beautiful fall afternoon. In Moscow, travel plans would go awry. Eight hundred steaks, beer and soft drinks shipped from Toronto all but disappeared. Wives were shunted to bad hotels. Phones rang in the middle of the night. When Phil Esposito ripped his out, a repairman appeared minutes later.

Ham fixing, OK?

Being hockey players, Team Canada laughed, complained and got on with it. In Moscow, they stayed at the Hotel Ukraina, a cardboard-brown monstrosity from the Stalin era; the elevators were without a 13th (bad luck) or 21st floor (KGB offices, worse luck). Players—and Canadian fans—might receive a call in the middle of the night inquiring, in perfect BBC English, "Do you want a Russian woman?" The drunk and curious would find themselves trapped in a honey pot, some nightmare misadventure out of a John le Carré cold war spy thriller. Again, the players grumbled and laughed off the inconveniences. "We should camp outside in the hills beyond the city," Frank Mahovlich warned his teammates.

"The Russians will start construction in our hotel at 4:00 a.m. just to ruin our sleep."

"But Frank, most of our guys won't be in bed by then anyways," Lapointe rightly pointed out.

In addition to playing hockey, the members of Team Canada were forced into an unfamiliar role—cultural ambassadors. The Bolshoi Ballet was on the team's itinerary. "We have to go, Phil?" goalie Tony Esposito moaned to big brother. "You can always leave at halftime," Phil shrugged, as if it were a football game. The great Plisetskaya, whose admirers included Khrushchev, Robert Kennedy and Warren Beatty, was dancing *Don Quixote*. It was the theatrical event of the season. But Team Canada sat with arms folded, bored out of their trees. "That it?" Frank Mahovlich asked writer Canadian writer Jack Ludwig at the end of of the first act. "Why were the dancers always on their toes?" Stan Mikita joked. "Why don't they just get taller dancers?"

They were having a horrible time. They were having the time of their life. In the anxious moments before the fifth game of the Summit Series in the Luzhniki Stadium rink, tiny dancers from the Moscow Ice Ballet presented the players with rose bouquets. When he was introduced to the crowd, big Phil stepped on a fallen petal from a subversive "red" rose and—*oops*—slipped, landing on his ass. Recovering, he performed an elaborate stage bow. Brad Park skated forward, joining in the comedy, helping Phil to his skates.

That would be Esposito and Park, formerly sworn enemies with the Bruins and Rangers. No longer NHL all-stars, the Canadian players were a team now.

After all this, Sinden's team played brilliantly, torturing Russia with piranha-like forechecking, skating into the third period of the fifth game with a comfortable 3–0 lead. The outnumbered Canadian fans even outperformed their Soviet counterparts. When Russian fans chanted, "*Shaibu, shaibu*" ("pass the puck"), Canadians returned the volley with, "DA, DA, CANADA! NYET, NYET SOVIET!" Pierre Plouffe, a Canadian athlete who finished fifth in waterskiing at the 1972 Munich Games, was there, trumpet in tow. Apparently, bugling in public was *zapreshchennyy* (forbidden) in Russia. Authorities attempted to seize his instrument. Fellow Canadians protected Plouffe by passing the bugle around.

I am Spartacus.

Alas, Team Canada suffered a Bruinesque collapse in the third period. A deflection, sloppy clearing attempt (Park), tip-in and ghastly defensive blunder (Rod Seiling), all inside five minutes, gave the USSR a 5–4 win. Sinden shattered his coffee cup against the dressing room wall afterwards. Canadian players left the ice with their heads down. But not for long. Sound the trumpet. As the players passed by, Pierre Plouffe led fans in a stirring rendition of you know what. Three thousand Canadians, including future Ontario premier Mike Harris, were up and singing:

> *With glowing hearts, we see thee rise*
> *The true north strong and free . . .*

Esposito's speech had kicked in. Supportive telegrams, some 50,000 of them—one from Brampton, Ontario, with a list of 10,000 names—began arriving in Moscow from far and wide, Oh Canada. How much did all this help? Not much, Winnipeg writer Jack Ludwig would suggest in his provocative journal of the series, *Hockey Night in Moscow.* Ludwig reported that, by the time they got to Russia, Sinden's team was an emotionally self-sufficient army. After all, they called themselves not Team Canada, but Team 50, a reference to the number of players and staff who had travelled to Europe (and a tribute to their favourite drink—Labatt 50 being the most popular beer in Canada at the time).

Perhaps the most meaningful message after the crushing defeat came from Red Berenson, a bench player. "Guys, we can win this," the Red Baron told teammates, puncturing the gloom of the dressing room. "Tonight, we showed we're better than they are." That helped. But a strategy devised by coaches Sinden and Ferguson after the game was more beneficial still. Convinced that Russia's Achilles heel was defence— their inability to play without the puck—Coach Sinden skated with a whistle during scrimmage the next morning. Players had to hold the puck or pass to a teammate until Harry whistled. No dump and chase. No more what-the-hell slapshots from way out. "Puck possession," Sinden implored his team. "We've got to hold on to the puck. Long as we've got it, they can't score."

Ludwig made note of one practice instruction that was calculated to infuriate players while reinforcing Sinden's "pass, don't shoot" message. When a Canadian player went off script, an angry voice filled the Luzhniki rink.

"Shaibu, you cunts!"

Pass the fuckin' puck!

Something clicked. Team Canada beat Russia 3–2 in a bruising, bashing game six. Canada did all the bruising and bashing . . . all the whining and sitting in the penalty box, too, taking 31 minutes in various infractions. Compared to four minutes for Russia. One play was shown repeatedly after the game on Russian TV—Bobby Clarke taking out Kharlamov with a mighty two-handed slash; this after coach Ferguson pointed out that the Russian star had a bad ankle, and that maybe someone should "give him a little tickle."

Hooligan!

More than one, too. Reports surfaced of Canadian tourists defacing Lenin's Tomb with happy-face stickers and graffiti. WINKLER, MANITOBA, RULES! Worse news for Russian coach Vsevolod Bobrov—Canada had now outplayed Russia in consecutive games. And the young goalie for the USSR, Tretiak, was looking tentative, hiding in his net instead of challenging shooters. With the outcome of the series now in doubt, the hosts of what in Russia was being called "The Friendship Games" began playing mind games with their guests. The morning after their first Moscow win, the Canadian players showed up for 10:30 practice to find schoolchildren twirling about their rink.

So sorry . . . big mixing-up.

Dennis Hull was dispatched to scatter the kids by booming slapshots off the boards. (Bobby Hull, it is said, could fire a puck so hard it might travel through a car wash without getting wet; Dennis shot even faster, the joke went, but might not hit the car wash.) Suddenly, Team Canada's practice was on again. At least one member of the Canadian entourage was the worse for wear, however. The previous night, trumpeter Pierre Plouffe had been arrested for disturbing the peace, capping off a rollicking evening that suggested Team Canada and its fans were closer than Ludwig believed. Plouffe celebrated the game-six win with Ferguson, Awrey, Phil Esposito and Pete Mahovlich at the Hotel Intourist. At one point, Pierre went off to buy more hooch, was told the bar was closed, accidentally (his story, anyway) smashed a few things, eventually getting into a fight before being hauled off to prison. Upon release at 6 o'clock the next morning, he found Pete Mahovlich waiting at the jail, making sure he was OK.

Not for long. Back at his hotel, Plouffe was again arrested and brought to court, blindfolded. As he was led to a bench, he heard his mom sobbing. "What's wrong?" Pierre asked.

"You've been condemned to five years in Siberia."

Prison guards were more lenient than the Russian justice system; before game seven, they dragged a portable TV into Plouffe's cell. Canada's bugler enjoyed what he saw, for this would be the night that Phil Esposito began wearing out the USSR. A lifetime of training hadn't prepared the Russians for the greediest capitalist scorer in hockey. The Big Red Machine came out flying for the first period, scoring twice. But Phil wouldn't let them stay ahead. There is a *Peanuts* cartoon from the period that has Charlie Brown returning from a baseball game in a sour mood—a squiggle decorating his forehead. "What's wrong?" he's asked. "We were winning until some big kid showed up," Charlie complains. Phil Esposito was that big kid. He killed penalties, worked the power play, skated with a French (J.P. Parisé–Yvan Cournoyer) and English (Bill Goldsworthy–Pete Mahovlich) line. And when he got hold of the puck, the Russians couldn't budge him. It was like trying to push a parked car. Twice in the first period, Phil beat Tretiak with the same post-up move: Espo stood with his back to the defence in the slot, grabbed a pass from a teammate and then arsed his way towards the crease, forcing the helpless defender towards his screened goalie. Though he couldn't possibly see the goalie's position, when Espo whipped around to take his shot, the puck invariably headed for an unguarded area.

The game was thrillingly close until, with two minutes left, Paul Henderson, recovering from a concussion and playing against doctor's orders, scored the goal of his life on—speaking of Don Quixote—a one-on-four rush that maybe, had he been in his right mind, he would never have attempted. Canada won, 4–3. The series was even, three games apiece along with a tie.

But the gamesmanship had just begun. After the match, Russian coach Bobrov complained, "[Gennadiy] Tsygankov cost us the winning goal." Why would a coach take the unusual step of blaming a player for a loss? Because in Russian hockey, Tsygankov played for Tarasov's Red Army. Bobrov was covering his superiors' asses here. If the USSR lost, fans might well ask why the father of Russian hockey, winner of nine straight world titles, wasn't coaching. Hadn't Anatoli Tarasov led the national team to a gold medal that spring? And where was Tarasov's on-ice alter ego, Anatoli Firsov, the Soviet league MVP in 1968, 1969 and 1971? Shouldn't he have been playing, or at least available to replace the injured Kharlamov?

All good questions. A persistent rumour had it that Tarasov had been replaced as national coach for refusing to throw the final game of the 1972 Olympics. Unbeaten, the USSR went into the match against Czechoslovakia with the gold medal sewn up. A loss to their Eastern bloc ally would mean the Czechs took silver and Russia's cold war nemesis, the United States, bronze. *More glory to the communist states of Central and Eastern Europe.* A sportsman, Tarasov refused to go along with the charade. Russia won the final, 5–2, giving the U.S. silver. Tarasov was fired. The fanatically loyal Firsov would also be removed from the national team.

With an if-we-lose alibi awkwardly in place, the Soviet Union Ice Hockey Federation took steps to ensure that the home side didn't surrender the eighth game of the Summit Series. A Czech and a Swedish referee, Rudy Bata and Uve Dahlberg, were to officiate the final match. But that morning, both referees, including Dahlberg (Canada's choice), mysteriously developed food poisining.

"I just saw him at breakfast," Eagleson screamed.

Ah yes, bad egg . . . very sick.

The Russians hoped to replace Bata and Dahlberg with two Germans, Josef Kompalla and Franz Baader—"Badder and Worse," Canadian players called them. Hours of wrangling led to what, for Canada, was an unhappy compromise—Rudy Bata and Josef Kompalla (both essentially Soviet choices). Canada was skating on thin ice here and knew it. Weeks earlier, in Munich, the American basketball team had lost the gold medal to the USSR in a maze of Russian-red tape. With his team down a point, U.S. collegian Doug Collins stood at the foul line with three seconds left. His first shot was good. Then, just as he attempted his second free throw, the Russians blared their timeout horn. Surely a technical foul. Collins hit the shot anyway. *America won!* Except the referees permitted the unauthorized timeout, allowed an illegal substitution and reset the time clock. Russia took the game on a buzzer-beater, 51–50. The U.S. protested, of course. A five-member tribunal adjudicated. Two members upheld the American protest. Three Eastern bloc officials didn't.

More glory to the communist states of Central and Eastern Europe.

Politics frequently intruded in sports in the '60s and '70s. Around the world, athletes were pawns in greater, deadlier games. Muhammad Ali was stripped of his heavyweight title in 1967 by the U.S. government for refusing to serve in Vietman. Czech–Russian hockey matches of the period made Bruins–Rangers games seem like morning skates. In July 1972, America's Bobby Fischer and Russia's Boris Spassky faced off for the World Chess Championship in Iceland. In a game of brinkmanship the Russians knew well, Fischer forfeited a match because of intrusive cameras. Might have quit the tournament altogether except for a telephone call from U.S. Secretary of State Henry Kissinger, who told him, "America wants you to . . . beat the Russians." Months later, in Munich, several members of the Israeli Olympic team were kidnapped by a

Palestinian terrorist group, Black September. On September 6, three weeks and a day before Team Canada and Russia completed the Summit Series, ABC sportscaster Jim McKay famously broke the bad news to the world: "We just got the final word . . . you know, when I was a kid, my father used to say, 'Our greatest hopes and our worst fears are seldom realized.' Our worst fears have been realized tonight. They've now said that there were 11 hostages. Two were killed in their rooms yesterday morning, nine were killed at the airport tonight. They're all gone."

Blood was in the air in Moscow before game eight of the Summit Series. "I'm not too proud of it, but there's no doubt in my mind I would have killed those sons of bitches to win," Phil Esposito later confessed. It would take exactly 250 seconds for the game's first death threat. Kompalla called three penalties against Canada—*bang, bang, bang*. Russia scored on a two-man advantage. Then Parisé hauled down Alexander Maltsev. "Two for interference," the German ref shouted. "Guy was carrying the puck," Parisé hollered. Entering the penalty box, he found Peter Mahovlich already there and decided to go for a skate to cool off while barrister Phil Esposito plead his linemate's case to Kompalla.

C'mon, three fuckin' penalties in four minutes.

Maybe it was the steam-kettle whistles, thousands of them, that set Jean-Paul Parisé off. Canadian fans, meanwhile, chanted, "Let's go home." Whatever it was, when Kompalla signalled a misconduct, Jean-Paul lost what what was left of his mind. "You're going to die right here," he screamed, taking a swing at the ref's head with his stick. He checked that swing before it landed, but on the Canadian bench, Coach Sinden was now throwing everything overboard, as if he was captain of a too-heavy ship entering the horse latitudes. First, a stool skidded across the ice Kompalla's way. Next, a chair. Ken Dryden skated past the flying debris to the bench.

"Take it easy, coach."

"Kenny, you haven't stopped a puck in seven games. Get back in your net."

Sinden later admitted this was all an act. Well, mostly. His team couldn't win if it continued drawing penalties. He was going to stick it to the referees every time they pulled something. The refs would have to call the game.

Too late; they already had. Referee Rudy Bata advised a Russian off-ice official in the penalty box, "The game is over. We can play no more."

But the Russians didn't want that. They were trying to build relationships with the West. Besides, the series was proving to be a lucrative venture. More would surely follow. But not if, like the recent Olympic basketball misadventure, it looked like the fix was in. "Rudy, be so kind and finish the game," the Soviet official said smiling. "We have to play and we have to finish in regular time. Please try." Bata reluctantly continued.

The Ugly Canadian act worked. Afraid for his life maybe, Kompalla swallowed his whistle. For the rest of the contest, the penalties would be even. It would be a magnificent back-and-forth game, extremely close, with the Russians up by two, 5–3, going into the final period. And then the gamesmanship began anew. "C'mon, let's tie it up and get out of here," Brad Park remembered players shouting in the dressing room. Then a grim-faced Sinden advised the team that couldn't happen. The Russians had informed Eagleson that, in case of a tie, the series would go to Russia because they'd scored more goals—Olympic rules. Eagleson pitched a fit.

These aren't the fuckin' Olympics.

Sorry, international hockey. You can read the rules, please.

Team Canada could only only lose or win. Death or glory. Back home, a nation turned its frightened eyes to Phil Esposito. During the series' final broadcast from Moscow, TV analyst Brian Conacher called Phil "the heart and soul of Team Canada." Always before, he had played in someone's shadow. Bobby Hull's in Chicago, Orr's in Boston. For the first time in the series, Orr had practised with Team Canada earlier in the day. "Gentlemen, start your engines," John Ferguson shouted, beginning the workout. There were excited rumours. But Bobby's engine wouldn't turn over. No, it was all on Phil. Had been all series. Certainly, he kept his team in this game, scoring Canada's opening goal in the first period.

He'd either scored or assisted on the team's first goal in five games this series. Now, as teams prepared to meet their fate, he reminded everyone, "We've got to score early, guys."

Big Phil took care of that himself on the first shift, grabbing a lacrosse pass from Pete Mahovlich, throwing it down to his skates and whacking a drive past Tretiak. Ten minutes later, he accepted a long bomb from Park outside the blue line. Six Russians were back. Everybody. Esposito veered to the middle, avoiding three defenders, snapping a high shot that Tretiak blocked to the side. Phil then beat two more Russians to the rebound, banging through a series of legs and sticks to shove a blind pass to Cournoyer, who tied it up. Except the goal light didn't go on. Canadian fans at the game leapt in the air anyway—including a trumpet-less Pierre Plouffe, released from prison this morning but forced to sit ("and don't move") among Russian military police. Back on the ice, there was no time to celebrate or even wonder what the hell was going on. "They've got Al!" Phil heard Pete Mahovlich shout. Now Phil raced to the other side of the rink to rescue Eagleson and Frosty Forristall, who had embarked upon an ill-conceived charge through uniformed police to turn the damn goal light on themselves. Watching Mahovlich and Esposito battle military police, an American reporter passed Jack Ludwig in the press box, shaking his head.

"They can't let this go by."

But they did. And with a little over a minute left, in a moment millions of Canadians would remember more fondly than their first kiss, Big Phil did it one more time, beating two Russians to the puck to the side of the net, then turning himself inside out to chip a puck on goal. A startled Tretiak kicked out a fat rebound. Play-by-play man Foster Hewitt, who began his career in 1923, calling a game between the Toronto Argonaut Rowing Club and the Kitchener Greenshirts for *Toronto Star* radio, made his final-ever TV hockey call:

"Here's a shot. Henderson made a wild stab for it and fell. Here's another shot [Esposito's]. Right in front. They score! Henderson has scored for Canada."

Afterwards, Canadian invaders enjoyed the fall of Moscow. "Fuck Russia, fuck Russia," fans inside the Intourist Hotel chanted. Plouffe remembered Eagleson shouting that Team Canada's win was a victory for capitalism. Team 50 players drank way too much beer and vodka. Harry Sinden would choose his lineup for Saturday's exhibition match with Czechoslovakia* on the basis of who could make it down the airplane steps in under ten minutes.

Back home, Canada had a group hug. Paul Henderson and Phil Esposito were received as heroes upon their return. A cartoon in the *Toronto Star* by Duncan Macpherson proclaimed Esposito the first Italian prime minister of Canada.

The same newspapers that had ridiculed Team Canada welcomed players home as conquerors—heroes of the free world. Russian players have always scoffed at the suggestion the Summit Series was an ideological war. "I have heard what the Canadians think, this is laughable," Alexander Yakushev once said. "For us, this was not a battle it was a game."

Understood. Still, it must be said that Phil Esposito, the player most responsible for defeating Russia in 1972, never would've been able to play for the Soviet Union had he been born there. While in Moscow, Ken Dryden and author Jack Ludwig, who could speak Russian, took an afternoon off to search for Anatoli Tarasov, deposed father of Russian hockey. They never found him. Perhaps the Soviets wanted it that way. But the six-foot, four-inch Dryden did get to meet an official of the Institute of Physical Culture and Sport. Upon meeting Dryden, one of the sport scientists, a small, bald man, announced: "You are too tall. We would never allow a man of your length to become a goalie."

"There are advantages," Dryden laughed. "My reach . . ."

---

* Serge Savard scored with four seconds left in the game to give Team Canada a three-all tie with Czechoslovakia. Coach Harry Sinden wrote in his diary afterwards, "Lady Luck is all over me. I mean, lately she's really had a crush on old Harry J."

The Soviet scientist shook his head. "The advantages," he said, "could never make up for the disadvantages."

So there.

A question, then: If Ken Dryden was too tall to be a goalie, what would muscle biopsies have revealed about Phil Esposito's hockey potential? That he was overweight, slow. And a sports psychological profile? That he displayed oppositional behaviour; had a megaphone where his mouth should be? No, Phil Esposito would've never made it in Russian hockey. It's astonishing the ugly duckling ever became a star for the Boston Bruins. Remember, he didn't make Junior A on his first try. Still, he went on to score 76 goals for Boston one season. Got his own bumper sticker in New England: *Jesus Saves . . . and Esposito scores on the rebound.* The Summit Series would remain his greatest hour. One of the reasons we remember the Bruins as such a great team, something close to a dynasty, is the freelance work Esposito did for Team Canada in 1972. Wayne Gretzky, who was 11 when he watched the series, a 368-goal scorer in peewee hockey in Brantford, Ontario, would return to the '72 series for the same reasons film fans continue to watch *Casablanca*. When Esposito revisited the Soviet Union in 2012 to be honoured on the 40th anniversary of the series, Gretzky sent Espo a congratulatory text, saying: "You deserve it. I watch the eight games all the time. You were unreal. Best I've ever seen a man play."

So maybe we shouldn't make so much of the Bruins winning only two Stanley Cups. Yvan Cournoyer, who won ten Cups for Montreal, once said that winning the Summit Series was worth five Stanley Cups. That would make seven championships for the Boston Bruins' second-best player of the era.

There would be another, less formal tribute to the hero of the 1972 series: the name Esposito eventually found its way into Russian street slang. Apparently, whenever a luckless Russian hooligan accidently burns himself on the stove or cuts himself on an unexpectedly sharp knife, he winces and shouts out the worst curse imaginable:

"*Esposito!*"

GOD'S LAST GAME

Canada vs. Czechoslovakia, September 13, 1976

He was the kind of guy who could get in a revolving door behind you and still somehow come out ahead. The son of a millworker from Northern Ireland, Alan Eagleson grew up as fast as he could—a Celtic Duddy Kravitz. "I'm going to be a minister," he told his parents, "only I won't make sermons. I'll take the collection plate and leave." He skipped grades and made it into the University of Toronto before he could shave. There, he made friends and contacts (was there a difference?), slugging everyone in his way. Cheering on the home side at a college basketball game, he noticed a trombone player from Queen's University issuing a blubbery squeal whenever a U of T player attempted a foul shot. Al took care of that with one punch. At age 30, the Eagle was a quadruple threat—lawyer/agent/sportsman/Ontario Member of Provincial Parliament. On the side, he befriended and formed a partnership with Toronto Maple Leafs players. Come summers, he also played baseball, sliding hard into every base. His cleats were always up, even at Queen's Park. Once, a fellow MPP asked, "Al, did you steal my *Sports Illustrated*?" "Yeah," Eagleson replied. "That's why I'm rich and you're poor."

Al was playing ball in Mactier, Ontario, in the summer of 1964 when the quick-handed third baseman on the other team, MacLaim Construction, approached him after the game.

Hi, name's Doug Orr. Don't know if you heard a my son, Bobby.

Doug, is it? Put it there . . .

Al and Doug were from the same patch of Northern Ireland—Ballymena. That made them family, Eagleson said, collecting another hyphen. Pretty soon, he was Bobby Orr's older brother/agent. The Eagle did a lot for Bobby, negotiating the richest contract for a rookie in hockey history—$70,000 for two years, with a $25,000 signing bonus. He assisted other players, too. Eagleson helped form and became executive director of the NHL Players' Association in 1967. When Al took over, players were making around $18,000; upon his departure in 1991, the average salary was $276,000. He organized the 1972 Summit Series and five subsequent Canada Cups. At first, the Soviets insisted they'd only deal with NHL president Clarence Campbell (who hated the idea of international hockey). Then Eagleson sent a magic telegram overseas:

"Mr. Campbell is a representative of capitalist owners. I represent the player-workers."

Open sesame.

But as much as Al helped players, he did more for himself. Eagleson knew his adopted younger brother wasn't a good long-term investment. Twelve knee surgeries. To paraphrase Hemingway, Bobby Orr fell apart gradually, then all at once. He couldn't turn as quickly after a June 1972 operation. After that, his accelerator occasionally stalled. But Bobby was so good, so smart with the puck, that he still managed to accumulate over 100 points a season. By the spring of 1975, however, there was little cartilage left in his left knee—just bone on bone. The end of Achilles was near.

The fatal arrow came ten games into the season; not on the ice, dodging trouble, but innocently, in a diner, as he was finishing a coffee. Looking at his watch, he realized he had to dash to get to the airport for a game in Chicago. Jumping from his chair, Bobby felt his knee lock. It had done that before, but this time was different—worse. He'd never play another shift for the Bruins.

The injury came at a bad time. Orr's contract was almost up. Boston knew he couldn't play much longer, but they were willing to make him a partner, offering close to 19 per cent ownership of the team (worth $50 million today). Nevertheless, Eagleson recommended that Orr sign with Chicago for more money up front (five years, $3 million).

Finding Bobby rehabbing on an exercise bike, Bruins president Paul Mooney tried to convince Orr to stay in Boston. "Bobby, can I speak to you a minute?"

"Fuck off, Paul. You're trying to drive a wedge between Al and I."

"Just let me talk to you for 30 seconds."

"Fuck off. Don't talk to me."

Many people tried to tell Bobby that Eagleson wasn't looking out for him; that there was something dead-fishy about Eagle's empire. He was too cosy with owners . . . wore too many hats. But why would Bobby believe any of that? How could Eagleson be a crook? He was a lawyer—not only that, but a former MPP, president of the Progressive Conservative party of Ontario, backslapping pal of the 17th and 18th prime ministers of Canada, John Turner and Brian Mulroney.

He was also Bobby's older brother, right? . . . *Right?*

Bobby signed with Chicago, where he was miserable and almost always injured. A devastating portrait of the superstar in exile by Earl McRae appeared in *Quest* magazine. McRae was in Eagleson's office when Orr phoned. Al rolled his eyes. "Take a message," he told his secretary. Elsewhere in the article, Bobby was with Chicago teammates in a Vancouver bar, mixing it up with Canuck players who wandered past. He ended up in a punch-up with Hilliard Graves. Afterwards, Orr called Graves over. "I'm glad you hit me," he said. "I deserved it. I've been acting crazy lately. I don't know what the hell's wrong with me. I'm so frustrated. I've been looking for something. I don't know what."

Without hockey, Bobby Orr was a ship without a sail. Eagleson recommended that he sit out the 1976 Canada Cup that autumn. His allegiance was to the Chicago Blackhawks. But Bobby suspected he only had a few games left. Why waste them on the Cleveland Barons? Orr's roommate for the 1976 tournament would be ascendant superstar Guy Lafleur. They hit it off in the manner of like-minded kids thrown together at summer camp. Lounging in their room, mowing through beers at night, they compared magic tricks and discussed the nature of their improvisational genius. How much was from up above, how much from hard work? Lafleur moved about as they talked—fidgeting, smoking, searching the window. They were inside because Bobby couldn't go out, couldn't even practise—could hardly walk. So he passed the hours in a chair, legs swathed in ice, chatting with Guy, waiting for another country to conquer.

In his last meaningful hockey series, Bobby was half the performer he once was and still the best player on the ice—first star of the Canada–US, Canada–Sweden and Canada–USSR games. He accepted an Inuit carving from a suited Gordie Howe (decked out in glistening white shoes) after the contest with Russia, a 3–1 win that put Canada in the finals against a surprise opponent: Czechoslovakia. How could anyone know, watching the two men out there on the ice laughing that night, that Old Man Winter, who scored his first NHL goal two years before Bobby was born, would survive another five seasons of hockey, while Orr, who still might pass for a college student, was close to the end?

In the first of the best-of-three final against Czechoslovakia, Bobby astonished us for the last time. Fittingly, it was a Boston reunion. Phil Esposito was on the 1976 edition of Team Canada, too. Espo was now a New York Ranger. Traded because he had become too much (and too little) for the Bruins. It was one thing for a 70-goal scorer to stay out on the ice as long as he felt like it; quite another for a 30-goal guy. Coach Don Cherry complained that young André Savard might go "sturl" sitting on the boards waiting for Espo to come off. Predictably, the hero of '72 chafed at reduced ice time in 1976. "Don't you fucking say good morning to me," is how he greeted coach Scotty Bowman one day. "I don't like you. You don't like me. We have a job to do for our country, and I'll be here for that, but don't you dare be a hypocrite and try to be nice to me."

Both Bobby and Phil were out for a power play, with their team up 2–0 midway through the opening game of the Team Canada–Czech finals. Everyone else on the ice for Team Canada was a superstar—Bobby Hull and Lafleur up front, Denis Potvin alongside Bobby. But they would have little to do but watch the magical last shift of the duo that had made the Big Bad Boston Bruins the greatest show on ice for eight seasons.

Bobby slipped a pass to Espo behind his own net and then watched, just like old times, as big Phil hopped up the middle. At centre ice, without looking, Esposito flipped a backhand to Orr, who caught the pass in mid-stride with his right skate. That was DNA kicking in. Robert Orr, Bobby's grandfather, probably made that play a thousand times as a professional footballer in Ireland. At the Czech blue line, Phil stalled, knowing what would happen next as Orr, changing speed and direction, suddenly accelerated past two Czech defenders.

Where'd everybody go?

It was a two-on-one now. Esposito rushed to open space, stick on the ice, waiting. Orr looked his way, pulling goalie Vladimir Dzurilla to the middle, and then artfully tucked a backhand into the vacated short side. The Maple Leaf Gardens crowd jumped to its feet, screaming—everyone's wish, an Orr goal, having been granted. Bobby and Phil met behind the Czech net for the last time.

Atta bee, Bobby.

Phil.

Probably, there was some grateful laughter and a curse or two in there, too. A few shifts later, Bobby assisted on roommate Lafleur's goal to make it 4–0. Later, in the third period, he scored his second goal of the game. Canada wrapped up the tournament by virtue of a 5–4 win two nights later, with Prime Minister Trudeau, his wife, Margaret, and their boys in attendance at the Montreal Forum. No one had to ask who the tournament MVP would be.

Number four, Bobby Orr.

Following the 1976 Canada Cup, Orr managed 20 games for Chicago and suited up for four games in 1977–78. That was it. Upon retiring, Bobby discovered he was bankrupt. The corporation his older brother-agent had set up for him wasn't recognized by tax authorities. He'd also have to sue the Blackhawks to receive a third of the money owed him. Almost half of that total went to legal fees. He separated from Al Eagleson on April Fool's Day 1980. Later, Eagleson criticized Orr for "living beyond his means."

That didn't sound right, coming from a guy who lived in a Rosedale mansion with seven washrooms. Who had a helipad at his Georgian Bay cottage. Rubbing it in with Bobby and other players would turn out to be a big mistake for Alan Eagleson.

Everyone knows you never want to start a fight with a hockey player.

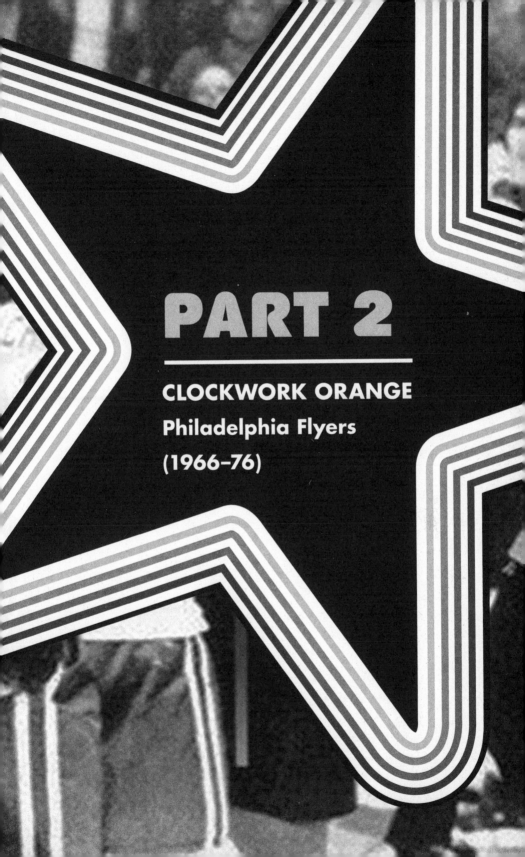

PART 2

CLOCKWORK ORANGE

Philadelphia Flyers

(1966–76)

A 99-POUND WEAKLING

No joke, Philadelphia's first NHL team were Quakers. William Penn (1644–1718) was a learned, religious man, a Quaker, and the city he created on the shores of the Delaware was to be a utopia—hence, Philadelphia, from the Greek *philos* (friendship) and *adelphos* (brother). Still, to honour Penn's memory by dressing a hockey team in lemon jerseys with *Quakers* in a swirly script drooping down the front would prove bad for business. Philadelphia was a multi-ethnic, working-class hive in 1930, at the start of the Quakers' lone season. Local Italians invented cheesesteak; native Germans, soft pretzels. Citizens were also notoriously quick to anger. A *New York Herald Tribune* reporter noted that Philadelphia fans began making "caustic remarks" in the third period of the Quakers' first home game, a 3–0 loss to the New York Rangers in November.

What's a matter, guys, forget to eat your oats?

The Quakers won four of 44 games that season. Few cared when the team left, or took notice when the orange-and-black Flyers arrived in

1967. Flyers executive Ed Snider arranged for an introductory down-town parade—20 people showed up. Defenceman Ed Van Impe stared at one onlooker, trying to figure out whether he was a hockey fan. The guy gave Eddie the finger.

Put him down as a maybe, Van Impe decided.

"Philadelphia fans would boo funerals," Philadelphia Phillies pitcher Bo Belinksy famously said. He wasn't kidding. For the team's 1972 home opener, Phillies owner Bill Giles dreamed up a properly gaudy, '70s-style, Evel Knievel-esque publicity stunt—a winged waterskier, Kiteman, was to schuss down an 80-foot ramp from the upper deck of Veterans Stadium, flying into wild air, floating to home plate with the ball in his hand.

Stee-rike one! Your 1972 Philadelphia Phillies baseball season is underway.

Alas, a blast of wind blew Kiteman off course and he crashed into fans on the railing of the upper deck. There Icarus lay, tangled in his beauti-ful, foolish arms. "I thought he was dead," Giles would say. And Philly spectators, how did they respond? "The fans were booing lustily," Giles remembered. When it turned out Kiteman wasn't kaput, when he gamely staggered to his feet and lobbed the ball like a grenade over the railing, hoping for the pitcher's mound but only making the lower deck, specta-tors complained even more loudly.

You call that an arm?

Mind you, Philadelphia teams gave followers reasons to jeer. The Phillies lost a record 23 straight games in 1961. ("Spread out, guys, so they can't get all of us with one shot," advised pitcher Frank Sullivan when the team returned home from one road trip.) Even when local teams won, the city often lost. The Eagles took the NFL championship in 1960. The league's head offices, then situated in Philadelphia, were moved to New York the following season. The basketball 76ers, led by a Philly kid, Wilt Chamberlain, won the NBA championship in 1967. Months later, the giant known as the Big Dipper insisted on a trade from his hometown to L.A.

Famously hostile to strangers, Philadelphia became a punchline for stand-up comedians of the period on Merv and Johnny.

The premier daredevil of the '70s, Robert "Evel" Knievel, attempted 75 elaborate motorcycle jumps between 1965 and 1980 without ever fulfilling a career-long dream of vaulting the ten-mile-wide Grand Canyon. (He received the name Evel from cops upon being thrown in jail as a boy for stealing hubcaps. Apparently, the prisoner in the next cell over was a man named Awful Knofel.) What a surprise—the frequently hospitalized (433 bone fractures) professional hot dog was a former hockey player. He played for the Charlotte Clippers of the EHL in 1958–59 but quit because he couldn't stand bus rides. No, Harleys and hustling were more E's style. His greatest hockey feat would be conning the Czech national hockey team into playing the Butte Bombers prior to the 1960 Winter Olympics. Evel was tossed from the game at the start of the third period. In a related incident, a masked bandit stole the gate receipts minutes later, disappearing on a chopper. One of Knievel's lesser-known stunts took place at Maple Leaf Gardens in 1974 when he was allowed five penalty shots on Toronto Toro goalie Les Binkley during an intermission. Knievel scored three goals on the WHA goalie, although reports suggest Binkley mightn't have been trying that hard.

"Hey, I spent a week in Philadelphia yesterday."

"I went to Philadelphia last Tuesday, but it was closed."

Though they didn't like strangers, Philadelphia took right away to the Flyers . . . enjoyed the fast, unpredictably violent thrill ride that was hockey. Crowds jumped to capacity by the end of the first year. And the Flyers finished on top of the expansion division before being eliminated early in the playoffs, terminated by the St. Louis Blues and brothers Bill, Barclay and Bob Plager—precursors of *Slap Shot*'s Hanson Brothers.[*] In the series' final game, Noel Picard, the big battleship (six foot one, 200 pounds) who cruised the Blues' blue line, caught Flyers' speedboat Claude Laforge (five foot eight, 160 pounds) with a sucker punch.

Watching Laforge there on the ice, motionless, a halo of blood spreading around his skull, Flyers owner Ed Snider shook with rage. Ed was a disciple of Ayn Rand, the author/philosopher who believed "[man's] highest moral purpose is the achievement of his own happiness." Mentor Jerry Wolman, who brought Ed into the sports business in the early '60s, hiring him on as vice-president and treasurer of the NFL Philadelphia Eagles, believed his protege skated across his throat in taking over the Flyers. Wolman was in a financial bind at the time, his assets exposed. Snider made his play. The son of a grocer, Snider knew what you had to do with eggs if you wanted to make an omelette. No one could argue Ed wasn't the better man for the job; he loved hockey and was prepared to invest in the team. Snider figured Canada's winter sport was right for Philly while he was in Boston on business—this would be 1966—and saw a long, boisterous lineup for a Bruins game. "Must be a good team," he observed.

"No, last place," Snider was told. "But they got this rookie . . ."

---

[*]   The Plager boys were something else. Dad Gus Plager, a Kirkland Lake, Ontario, gold miner, settled clan arguments with makeshift boxing mitts (tea towels or washcloths stuffed in socks). Gus refereed Bill, Bob and Barc's matches, hollering out commentary all the while. Neighbours called the old man "Squirrel" Plager because it appeared he was raising a bunch of nuts.

Last place and fans are lined up, happy? Maybe hockey was Philadelphia-proof.

Snider heard fans booing St. Louis when they beat up his Flyers in the spring of 1968. But he knew Philadelphia. Knew they'd soon be heckling his guys if the Flyers didn't toughen up. Bleeding winger Laforge was not yet in the hospital when Snider gave GM Bud Poile and coach Keith Allen their marching orders. "We may not be able to come up with the great skaters and great shooters and great talents because we're an expansion club and it's going to take us a while, but we can come up with guys who can beat up other guys," Snider snarled. "I never want to something like that happen to a Philadelphia Flyer team again."

They listened, but maybe didn't hear. Early the next season, on November 8, 1968, the Blues again visited Philadelphia, winning 8–0. The Plagers didn't record an assist, but they were nevertheless instrumental in the victory. "Every time we played Philadelphia we warned Ed Van Impe, 'Don't touch Red Berenson or we'll kill you,'" Bob Plager would later tell the *St. Louis Post-Dispatch*. The following are excerpts from fabulous St. Louis play-by-play man Dan Kelly's broadcast of the game:

Berenson around Van Impe . . . right in on goal . . . he shoots, he scores!

McCreary ahead at centre to Berenson . . . Berenson knocks it by Van Impe. He has a break. Berenson shoots, he scores! Another great goal by the redhead!

Henry, a great pass to Berenson . . . he shoots, he scores. The hat trick for Red Berenson!

Here's Camille Henry, ahead to Berenson, who has a break at centre. Berenson in . . . he shoots, he scores! Berenson has four in a row and the Blues lead 4–0!

Van Impe, who has broken his stick, is back to get it. He lost it to McCreary. He's in with Berenson. Berenson shoots, he scores! Berenson has scored his fifth goal and the Blues lead 5–0! What a night for the redhead!

Ahead for McCreary. Van Impe lost it to Berenson. Berenson has a break! One man back! Here he comes! A shot . . . he scores!

In fairness to Philadelphia's toughest player, Van Impe did break his stick across Berenson's legs on Red's fifth goal. But you get the picture. Owner Ed Snider certainly did, again and again. In the first round of the 1969 playoffs, the Blues trounced the Flyers on the scoreboard and in the corners, winning four straight, outscoring the Flyers 17–3.

Five weeks after the Red Baron recorded his six kills, Snider received another lesson in Philadelphia civics, looking on as Minnesota Viking quarterback Joe Kapp picked apart the molting Eagle defence on the final game of the 1968 regular season. Winners of two games that year, the Eagles tried to placate the crowd by hiring a halftime Santa. There was a blizzard that day, however, and Santa didn't show. (Philly reindeer didn't work in snow—it was a union thing.) Someone in the organization spotted a scrawny teenager, Frank Olivo, in the sixth row of Veterans Stadium, wearing a ratty Salvation Army Santa oufit. Pitiful cotton-batten beard.

Kid, you gotta help us here.

Olivo obliged, circling the field, spreading halftime holiday cheer. *Ho-ho-ho . . .* Fans were hardly in a festive mood, however. It was freezing, no one had scraped the outdoor seats free of snowdrifts, and the Eagles had missed the playoffs. Again. Catcalls and snowballs spilled down from the stands. Santa saw a fan in the lower seats pack an iceball and shook his fist, hissing, "You're not going to get anything for Christmas." That was it. Santa was then forced to flee an avalanche of snowballs.

That'll be us soon, Snider figured. The Flyers' problem was simple, the owner remained convinced. His team wasn't nearly as scary as its Halloween-orange-and-black jerseys. Much of their talent came from the Quebec Aces. Philadelphia had bought the club Jean Béliveau made famous for $700,000 prior to expansion, and in so doing cornered the market on French-Canadian players not quite good enough to play for the Montreal Canadiens. "I finally get [a French-Canadian player] and he can't skate," coach Keith Allen complained about the team's best forward, André Lacroix, who formed a line with shifty Simon Nolet and Jean-Guy Gendron. A pacifist, Lacroix racked up four minutes in penalties during the 1968–69 season. Nolet was not much worse: eight minutes' worth of holding and interference calls. *Girls' penalties. We're still the Philadelphia Quakers,* Snider grumbled—*the NHL's 99-pound weakling. Do I have to say it again? Get me some tough guys!* Now GM with the departure of Bud Poile, Keith Allen (ironically, a former Saskatoon Quaker) heard his boss loud and clear. In the NHL 1969 junior draft, held in Montreal, Allen went wild–wild west, using late picks on Prairie toughs—Waldheim, Saskatchewan's Dave Schultz and Moose Jaw's Don Saleski. The team's second pick (at Western Canada scout Gerry Melnyk's pleading insistence) would be Allen's real coup, though: a scrawny, whip-smart, win–at-any-cost centre.

The last hockey player to wear the number 16 for Philadelphia had been Noel Picard's leaky punching bag, Claude Laforge. The new one was a teenager who would very soon become the heart, soul and spleen of the Flyers franchise, another westerner, Flin Flon, Manitoba's Bobby Clarke.

Yes, the Dark Side was coalescing, pulling together like curdling storm clouds on the horizon. Next draft, the team took Bob "Mad Dog" Kelly with its second pick. In the fall of 1971, Allen hired Fred Shero, a very successful career minor-league coach who won two International Hockey League championships with the St. Paul Saints and as many Calder Cups, first with the Buffalo Bisons and then with the Omaha Knights.

But don't let the Knights and Saints stuff fool you. Freddy's teams were mean as a toothache. In fact, he prefered calling his Minnesota club "Shero's Magnificent Malconents."

The Flyers played on Broad Street, and their belligerent style would one day win them the nickname the "Broad Street Bullies." Still, in support of NHL president Clarence Campbell's contention that hockey violence was a sign of the times, the first instance of Broad Street bullying involved not a single Flyers player.

The date was Thursday, January 6, 1972. Three days earlier, Frank Rizzo, Philly's granite-tough police chief, had been sworn into office as mayor. (Rizzo's most memorable stump speech: "I'm going to make

Attila the Hun look like a faggot.") Richard Nixon would announce his bid for re-election as the American president on Friday. That same day, police located time bombs in safe deposit boxes in eight separate banks in New York, Chicago and San Francisco—the work of lunatic yippies (a radical, politically active hippie).

A violent struggle was going on for America's soul. Over the Vietnam War, civil rights, women's rights, you name it. "Bang a gong, get it on," T-Rex sang that week on the radio.

That Thursday, the St. Louis Blues were in town to play the Flyers. The hated Blues! Fans, even local security, were in a bad mood. As the second period ended, St. Louis was down 2–0. A jubilant Philly crowd stood cheering. Blues coach Al Arbour hurried from his bench to the exit ramp to argue with referee John Ashley. Before completing his submission, he was drenched with beer by a spectator. More cheers. Two Blues—Bob and Barclay Plager—leapt into the stands after the beer guy and were soon surrounded by 40 club-swinging riot police. More Blues—John Arbour, Floyd Thompson and Phil Roberto—joined the melee. John Arbour received a cut to the head that required 40 stitches. Coach Arbour had the shirt ripped off his back, his jacket torn and, later in the training room, ten stitches sewn into his skull. After having their wounds tended to, most of the Blues returned to the ice. As they exited the dressing room, Mayor Rizzo's police took names and numbers.

Always alert to possible trouble, Bob Plager remained behind with brother Barclay and told Blues trainer Tommy Woodcock, "Go out and lock the door."

"That everybody?" the cop asked Woodcock when the door was closed.

"Yeah," the trainer lied.

Minutes later, the Plagers sneaked back to the bench. Led by a furious coach wearing a tie over his T-shirt, the Blues roared back with goals by Roberto, Garry Unger and Gary Sabourin to win 3–2. Minutes after the game, Al and John Arbour (no relation), Thomson and Roberto were arrested (for assaulting police officers) and spent the night in jail. The

Plagers would have been in there with them except police figured they had taken a powder. Blues owner Sidney Salomon Jr. called the incident the "worst case of police brutality I've ever seen."

Solomon hadn't seen nothing yet. Dave Schultz, Don Saleski and Moose Dupont soon joined the Flyers. "Is there any NHL rule against having a whole bunch of policemen on the same team?" Snider asked GM Allen at one point.

No, there wasn't. The 99-pound weakling had vanished. All trace of Philadelphia Quaker blood would soon be gone. Bruce Banner was turning into a carrot-coloured Incredible Hulk. After their January 1972 victory, the St. Louis Blues would not win another game in the Philadelphia Spectrum for 17 years.

PUCK FINN

Taking a break from chores, Flin Flon, Manitoba, housewife Yvonne Clarke looked out her window one winter morning, watching children play hockey in the park across the street—little columns of frozen exhaust rising from bobbing heads. Smiling, she said to herself, *Why, one of those little Dickens looks a lot like my Bob. Couldn't be, I guess, he's in class.* A minute later, the phone rang. It was the school.

Mrs. Clarke, it's about Robert. I'm sorry to say he's been suspended again . . .

Another misconduct—gone for three days this time. Mrs. Clarke—Bob's principal, too—had it all wrong, though. School for Robert Earle Clarke was the hockey rink. Life cooped up in a classroom, trying to figure out whether St. John's was the one in New Brunswick or Newfoundland, all that memory work and math, counting something other than goals and assists—*that* was the penalty box! At age eight, Bob fibbed about his age to play indoor Tom Thumb hockey with older boys. Years later, a teenager now, he stayed home when his parents took kid sister Roxanne on a one-week, end-of-summer holiday. This would be in 1965. Bob had a job pumping gas, saving to buy a pair of custom skates—a whopping 60 bucks. That was what they cost in Brandon, Manitoba, anyway—a nine-hour drive away. Bob needed new skates because he'd be trying out for the Flin Flon Bombers, the local junior team, in a couple weeks.

Make sure you look after the house, Bob. No going anywhere.

Sure, Mom.

Throw some water on the lawn, if it doesn't rain.

Right, Dad.

Hours later, Bob was on the road, hitchhiking, dragging girlfriend Sandy's nine-year-old little brother, Bill McIntyre, with him. They were on their way to Brandon, of course. Bob wanted those skates—*now!* It turned into an epic, four-day journey. There'd be lots of walking between rides, catching lifts with passing truckers and teenagers looking for adventure. Fast highway driving and conversations with strangers made difficult by wind and Top 40 music streaming in and out of open windows.

So, where you boys off to?

Brandon, to buy skates.

What's new pussycat, whoah-ow-oo-oo . . .

There would be consequences for being Puck Finn, missing school and lighting out for Weyburn and Selkirk to play hockey on nights so cold players had to thaw out block-hard frozen equipment (stored under the bus) before getting dressed. Upon being taken in the 1969 NHL draft by the Philadelphia Flyers, Bob would be visited by a momentary panic.

"I honestly had no idea where Philadelphia was. I didn't know whether it was on the West Coast, the East Coast or in the middle somewhere," he admitted to *Sports Illustrated*. "I actually got a little scared when I thought about going to a city I didn't know anything about."

He may not have known where he was going, but Bob Clarke sure as hell knew where he was from: Flin Flon, Manitoba. He was a western kid, wild as grass.

"Best in the West and least in the East," sports columnists in Ontario and Quebec would write in weighing the chances of the western representative in Memorial Cup and Canadian Football League Grey Cup games in the '60s. Fans, teams and players west of Ontario knew and hated that. They also knew how to count. Ontario and Quebec teams won 34 of 40 Memorial Cups from 1944 through 1974. Eastern CFL teams garnered 29 of 40 championships in the same period. In the NHL, the Detroit Red Wings, the West's team, with stars Gordie Howe (Saskatoon), Norm Ullman (Provost, Alberta) and Terry Sawchuk (Winnipeg), hadn't won a championship since 1955.

No, it was always Montreal and Toronto, with rosters of Ontario and Quebec stars winning the Stanley Cup (23 times in the 30 years from 1944 through 1973). Montreal did have some westerners, it was true. "French fire power and Prairie brawn" was the Habs' well-advertised recipe for success. In the '60s, that would be "big, burly" Ted Harris, "scrappy" Terry Harper and hockey's reigning heavyweight champ, "belligerent," "bellicose" John Ferguson (all adjectives courtesy of *Hockey Night in Canada's* Danny Gallivan).

Brawn meant corner muscle. Montreal French skaters got all the glory. Western players, the cuts and bruises.

Eventually, *western* became a hockey adjective. It meant combative, resentful and a little bit mean—born with a pebble in your skate, maybe. Players knew they had to scrap to play junior. Future *Hockey Night in Canada* host Ron MacLean was culled from the herd in his early teens. "I was playing midget Triple A in Red Deer, [Alberta]," he would tell a reporter, years later. "This was in 1975. And western hockey was the roughest in Canada. One game, I'd hurt my thumb playing football, but that probably didn't matter. I got into an altercation with another player. He dropped his gloves. I just skated away. I later got cut from the team."

Making it out of western junior hockey to the NHL required true grit. When asked by Toronto sportswriter Dick Beddoes about the slash that put Russian star Valeri Kharlamov out of the 1972 Summit Series, Bob Clarke shrugged and said, "Dick, if I hadn't learned how to lay on a two-hander every once and a while I never would've left Flin Flon."

Who could say if it was nature or nurture? Bob's dad arrived in Flin Flon as a teenager during the war, landing a job at Hudson Bay Mining and Smelting. Cliff Clarke sweated and toiled 5,000 feet underground, hooking up the big blasts that loosed shards of zinc and copper. Come winter, he wouldn't see the sun from Monday to Friday.

In four decades working in the mines, Cliff Clarke only missed a half shift of work.

Son Bob had the same work ethic. Patty Ginnell, the legendary coach of the junior Flin Flon Bombers, first saw the kid in juvenile. First thing he noticed were the big round glasses and buck teeth. Patty knew Clarke was diabetic. Skinny, too. All of that said—*sorry kid . . . next.* (What would Russian sport scientists have concluded?) But the Bomber coach never listened to league officials. He once slugged a referee and tried to get around the ensuing suspension by wearing a false moustache and beard (the old Inspector Clouseau disguise!). So why would Patty bother paying attention to a bunch of fool doctors? The proof was right there out on the ice. Bob could skate forever on his shiny, new $60 Brandon skates. Ginnell also noticed how the youngster used his stick. That he could check, pass, shoot and catch toboggan rides on faster players with that Sher-Wood. Do whatever the hell he wanted.

"Bob had a real good stick," is how Patty put it.

Like most good talent evaluators, Ginnell wore X-ray specs; he could see inside a player's heart. Forget about his kidneys, all that diabetes stuff; Bob worked his tail off every shift. Anyone could see that. And like every great player, the puck followed him around. Bobby Clarke, or Clarkie—soon everyone was calling him that—was a hockey player.

A playmaker, not a scorer, though. Bobby needed a sniper on his wing. Ginnell found that scorer, ironically, in a stay-at-home defenceman with a deadly slapshot. Born into a large Ojibway family, Reggie Leach grew up in Riverton, Manitoba, 300 miles north of Winnipeg. He was a goalie at first (no money for skates) before graduating to the blue line, where he earned distinction as a puck-carrying defenceman who could score.

Like Bobby Clarke, Leach had a disease. Bobby was diabetic, Reggie, an alcoholic at age 12.

"There were a lot of white people and a lot of Indians and Metis [in Riverton]," Reggie explained in Don Marks's documentary *They Call Me Chief.* "On Friday night, people would go downtown to socialize (or in more simple language, to get drunk). There was a white bar on one side of the street, and an Indian bar on the other. At midnight, people would spill out of the bars and it was like *Twelve O'Clock High.*"

Some of Reggie's siblings didn't make it through to the next morning.

"I lost one brother that froze to death in Riverton," he would recall in *They Call Me Chief.* "I had another brother that wrapped himself around a telephone pole, and I had a sister that, I don't even know what it was, froze to death in a car . . . fell asleep. And I had another brother who strangled himself to death."

Siggy Johnson bought Leach the skates that allowed him to excel in "The Smelter," what everyone called the Riverton hockey rink. The appliance store owner also talked Reggie into getting out of the little freshwater fishing town. The moment came at a local diner, one of those places where everyone works a toothpick at the end of a club sandwich, waiting for a coffee refill and the cheque. Siggy sized up his luncheon companion and asked, "What do you want to be?"

"A hockey player," Reggie said, still lost in his food. *Everybody knows that.*

Siggy must've thought about what he would say next for a while.

"Reggie, you can either get out of town right now or you can stick around and be a bum the rest of your life."

That got Leach's attention. Before long, the teenager set off, stick and skates over his shoulder, in search of a junior hockey club. He struck out with the Weyburn Red Wings, but caught on with Ginnell's Flin Flon Bombers. At first, Patty saw the dark, curly-haired 16-year-old as a stay-at-home defenceman who could work the point. But that didn't work out. "You're too fast for a [stay-at-home] defenceman," Ginnell told Reggie. "Besides, you're never at home." Next game, Leach was on

Bobby Clarke's port side, snapping expertly placed passes past startled goalies. The press soon dub him the Riverton Rifle. With Clarke furnishing the bullets, the teenagers dominated western junior hockey, commencing an on-and-off 16-year partnership that would make both famous ... notorious, too. In the 60-game 1967–68 junior season, Clarke-Leach combined for 299 points and 456 penalty minutes. They sometimes misbehaved off the ice as well. One night, trying not to laugh or make any noise, Bobby and Reggie climbed into a Brandon, Manitoba, hotel window from a fire escape after a night of carrying on. There, sitting on a bed waiting for them, was Patty G.

"I don't care if you're from Flin Flon, you're gone," Ginnell told Clarke. Traded. The boys pleaded and begged. Maybe tried to force a tear. Patty wouldn't budge. He wouldn't trade or suspend them, either, mind you. Ginnell just wanted to scare the boys. The Flin Flon Bombers liked to do that to other teams. One game, Patty's Bombers wrapped police tape around the visitor's bench, suggesting it would soon be the scene of a murder investigation. No one liked playing in Flin Flon. With Ginnell barking approval, Bombers finished their checks into the second row of the Whitney Forum. Squeamish visitors developed an allergy to playing in the Manitoba–Saskatchewan border town, contracting a 24-hour virus that became known as "the Flin Flon flu."

The high and low times continued in the NHL. "I played 960 games in the NHL and I was probably hung over for about 400 of them," Leach would later admit. There were plenty of blackout nights. Come morning, Reggie staggered out of bed and grabbed the paper outside his hotel room door, anxious to see how he and the team did the night before.

Two goals and an assist! And we won—all right!

The morning of May 6, 1976, Flyers teammates discovered Leach in his room, still passed out cold—stiff, unmovable ... a car on blocks. Reggie missed practice, suffering through a two-pots-of-coffee hangover. Coach Fred Shero didn't want to play him that evening. The rest of the Flyers players talked him into it.

The Riverton Rifle scored five goals that night, a playoff game against the Bruins.

And then went out afterword to celebrate.

Reggie couldn't miss any games because of drinking. Not skating alongside Bobby Clarke. Bobby played through every kind of injury, once using DMSO—dimethyl sulphoxide, a controversial wood industry by-product that gave users "bomb breath"—in order to stay out on the ice. One night in Philly, skating against the Bruins, Clarke took a Rifle shot to the head. Like most great goal scorers, Reggie had a quick release; the puck was off his stick and over the goalie's shoulder in an instant. This night, however, Reggie was off balance when he fired the puck and instead of hitting the net, the Riverton Rifle's shot creased Clarke's temple before banging hard off the glass. Bobby staggered and shook his head, sprinkling blood over his jersey. Righting himself, he then skated to Leach, tapping him on the pads.

Let's go.

After completing his turn, Clarke raced to the dressing room for repairs. (He'd take more than 100 stitches to the face that season.) Later in the game, he scored his 1,000th NHL point. Pictures in the papers next day showed him wearing what looked like a butcher's bib. He never even bothered to change into a clean uniform.

Clarke and Leach weren't the only westerners on the Philadelphia Flyers. GM Keith Allen and defenceman Ed Van Impe both hailed from Saskatoon. Ross Lonsberry was born in Humboldt, Saskatchewan. The son of Russian immigrants, coach Fred Shero—Frederick Alexander Schirach—was from Winnipeg, same as former Montreal Canadiens defender Ted Harris, now also a Flyer. Brothers Joe and Jimmy Watson were from Smithers, British Columbia. Backup goalie Bobby Taylor was a Calgarian. Tom Bladon and Jack McIlhargey were from farther up the line in Edmonton.

Then there were the Flyers' committed troublemakers, a pack of wild dogs straining on the leash, all of them on a single forward unit: Saskatchewan-born Dave "The Hammer" Schultz and Don "Big Bird"

Saleski, along with centre Orest Kindrachuk, a kid out of Nanton, Alberta.

The Boston Bruins had one westerner on the team that won the 1972 Stanley Cup: Winnipeg's Ted Green. The Habs had no one from the West on their 1976 championship team. Counting their GM and coach, the Flyers employed 13 western Canadians.

The mid-'70s Philadelphia Flyers embodied Western Canada. All the clichés about the West—the restless yearning, resentment and reckless high spirits—were true of the Flyers. Young men from rural Canada, the Flyers insulated themselves from big-league pressures with horseplay and jokes. In airports, Kindrachuk and Saleski crawled up baggage carousels; minutes later, teammates found their clothes coming at them in scattered clouds. At bars, captain Bobby Clarke dropped his fang dentures into teammates' rum and Cokes. Only two Flyers played for Patty Ginnell, but the entire Flyers lineup, which included players out of every tribe in Canada—from First Nations (Leach) to oversized French mammals (Moose Dupont)—might identify with the following, an ode to rough-and-tumble Flin Flon that found its way, drunken spelling and all, into a local newspaper in the 1930s.

Our Town (Anonymous)

It's boulevards are barren rock
With patches here and there
Of Polular stumps and rounded lumps
Of muskeg, brown and bare.

It's little shacks and houses
Are every shape and size,
Some way down in the muskeg brown
And some up in the skies.
A mill, some shops, a hoistroom,
A head frame out of line,
An assay lab and a bunkhouse drab
And a dump, make up the mine.

The motley population,
Has come from East and West
Alsase-Lorraine and rich Ukraine
Hong Kong and Budapest.

Spaghetti-eating 'Talians,
And garlic-eating Jews,
Yonsons tight and Finn's who fight
And Scotsman chasing booze.

The streets are never empty
The cafes never close
There's myth and song the whole day long
From blanant radios

The parlqur seems like bedlam
With raucous shouts and roars
While hjsty calls #nd sounds of brawls
Float through pool room doors

But yet, with all it's ups and downs
I do not sulk or frown
If the price of Gold will only hold
It's God's own very town.

In spirit, the Philadelphia Flyers were all Flin Flon Bombers. And Bobby Clarke was the native-born captain who kept them in (and out of) line. But if Bobby learned his hockey on the Prairies, in battles against Red Deer and Moose Jaw, he took his officer's training in service overseas—in Stockholm, Moscow and Prague. Clarke was, by his own estimation, the 35th—or last—man chosen for Team Canada in the Summit Series with the Russians. He was an afterthought, a scrimmage partner for more established centres. But he worked hard, harder than anyone else, and found his way to Canada's second line, with Paul Henderson and Ron Ellis.

Even in practice, coaches Harry Sinden and John Ferguson marvelled at Clarke's competitive fury—the sharpness of his stick and tongue. The 22-year-old called out anyone who didn't put in sufficient effort. One scrimmage, Vic Hadfield—an established 50-goal man, but also a player who came into camp out of shape—skated out to take a faceoff on Clarke's line.

"Where do you want me?" he asked Clarke.

"On the bench, Vic," Bobby snapped.

Clarke drew the Russians' top line, facing off against Vladimir Petrov while keeping an eye peeled for the great Valeri Kharlamov at left wing. When the latter proved too fast for Canada's defence, Clarke took it upon himself to fix things. Everybody saw the public execution: galloping at top speed to catch Russia's Number 17, Bobby took a full swing and hit the Russian speedster where it would do the most harm, snapping his right ankle.

Like Patty Ginnell said, the boy could do anything with a stick.

Not everyone approved. "Hockey changed when Clarke broke the Russian's ankle," referee Bruce Hood would tell me. "It stopped being hockey and started being something else, something more like . . . I don't know what you'd call it . . . war, maybe. How do you call what Clarke did 'sports'? He took that back to Philadelphia, too, with all their enforcers, or whatever you want to call them. That was the beginning of the Broad Street Bullies."

The Flyers recognized the change in Bobby upon his return from Moscow. "That series pushed his development," teammate Joe Watson would remember. "Clarkie came back more confident because he had proved he could play with the world's best players. He had even been one of the leaders. He became a real presence in the dressing room after that." A presence on the ice, too! Just as Cliff Clarke had been responsible for hooking up the blasts that shook loose valuable minerals a quarter mile below the surface of the earth back in Flin Flon, Bobby Clarke was now coordinating the big body-explosions that blew up in rinks across North America.

It happened like in a western movie: the Flyers would ride into town spoiling for a fight. Bobby was the guy on the lead horse, squinting into the sun, figuring out how to bust into the local Wells Fargo. The plan, always improvised, usually began with a calculated provocation—a face wash, a spear, a wild elbow. The other team retaliated, as expected. And then the Flyers bench emptied, alive with manufactured rage, justified in beating the hell out of smaller, more law-abiding teams.

Afterwards, the Flyers galloped off, waving their hats in the air, two points safe in their saddlebags, heading off for the next town, another job down the line.

There had been players who were beyond rough and tough before. The notorious Cleghorn brothers—Sprague and Odie—left a trail of wounded hockey players and civilians in the Roaring Twenties. Sprague claimed to have sent "50 stretcher-jobs" to the hospital. Recovering from a broken ankle, Sprague was arrested for beating his wife with a crutch. A horrified Lady Byng, wife of Canada's governor general at the time, created the "gentlemanly play" trophy that bears her name in response to his villainy. Still, there were only ever two Cleghorns on a team. In the 1974–75 season, the Flyers could put out a five-man unit—Van Impe, Dupont, Saleski, Schultz and Kindrachuk—that accumulated 1,133 penalty minutes over the course of the regular season and playoffs. The Hammer alone was responsible for 656 minutes—almost half a day in the penalty box.

What made the Flyers unique was how much of their mayhem was premeditated. Maybe it wasn't choreographed, mapped out with salt and pepper shakers on a saloon bar, but still, when the Flyers fought, they did so as a team, with players assuming defined roles. These were coordinated attacks with an ever-changing cast of lookouts, guards and button men. Former referee Bryan Lewis would always remember the night of October 25, 1974, when the Wild Bunch descended on the California Golden Seals in Oakland.

"Some guy on the Golden Seals, Mike Christie, hit Don Saleski," he told me. "Knocked him over. And boy, the whole Philadelphia bench were suddenly on the ice, all of them going for Christie. We tried to get him to the penalty box to protect him. But they went for him there, started fighting again. There were so many Flyers protecting the box, no one could get in at first to break the second fight up."

According to *The Sporting News*, "The fight, which took nearly 40 minutes to break up, centered around the California penalty box, where defenceman Mike Christie was the victim of a beating . . . administered by Philadelphia's Orest Kindrachuk, Bob Kelly and Don Saleski." Kelly and Saleski bulled past the official scorer. Soon it was three on one, Saleski, Kelly and Kindrachuk whaling away at Christie, while Schultz and other Flyers blocked the penalty box door. Minutes later, the Seals' Jim Neilson and Len Frig, along with officials Lewis, Ryan Bozak and Leon Stickle, broke through to find Christie beaten and bloodied on the penalty box floor.

But it wasn't the referees who ended Christie's misery; it was Flyers captain Bobby Clarke. "That's it, that's enough," referee Lewis remembered Clarke shouting at Kelly, Kindrachuk and Saleski. The Flyers fighters immediately stopped pummelling Christie. Then Bobby nodded to the beaten Golden Seal. "Get him off the ice," he instructed Lewis.

"No doubt about it," Lewis said, "Bobby Clarke was the field general, the guy who called the shots on that Flyers team."

Clarke seldom fought himself. His job was to create mayhem and scoring chances and, after that, to protect every lead. "Clarke, you're sick," Chicago Blackhawks defenceman Keith Magnuson once screamed at the Flyers captain, perhaps referring to Clarke's diabetes. "I can't help that, you dummy," Clarke replied. "But you're stupid, Maggy, and you can do something about that. Now fuck off, or else I'll send Schultzie after you."

The rest of the NHL didn't like the way Clarke outsourced fighting. But with Hound Dog Kelly, Big Bird Saleski, Moose Dupont and Dave "The Hammer" Schultz around, what could they do? Referee Ron

Wicks, who got along with some Flyers but never Clarke, remembered a night when Boston's Wayne Cashman had to contend with Bobby's bodyguards.

"Clarkie, you better hope you're never traded from this team because you'll be fuckin' dead in a minute," Cashman told Clarke, skating away. When Wicks laughed, Cash gave him a little wink.

What made Bobby Clarke so tough? Part of it was Flin Flon, yes—Patty Ginnell and Cliff Clarke, his explosives-wielding miner dad. But some of it, too, probably had to do with Bobby being diagnosed with diabetes at age 14. When kids learned about Bobby in the '70s, they read about his hockey exploits—all the trophies and parades—and how, because of his health, he would swig pop between periods, sometimes downing a bowl of ice cream after games to keep his energy up.

Boy, that's the life, young fans figured.

But being diagnosed a diabetic in 1963 must've felt like a death sentence to a kid whose life was hockey. At the time, Bobby was told he couldn't play anymore—not as a forward, anyway. "Goaltender, maybe," a Flin Flon doctor told his mom, "long as he's not too active." In other words, he could be a bad goalie. As for the NHL, forget about it.

Patty Ginnell saw Bobby playing 40 minutes a game and figured that diagnosis couldn't be right. The Bombers paid for Clarke to go to the Mayo Clinic, where Bobby was tested and finally assured that, with proper care, he could play professional hockey. Whenever a scout came to watch Clarke play, Ginnell waved the Mayo Clinic report at him. Scouts would smile and nod, but remain unconvinced. Being declared a diabetic was a "Boy Named Sue"* kind of thing. Bobby had

---

* Johnny Cash heard "A Boy Named Sue" during a songwriter party at his Tennessee home in April 1969. Bob Dylan sang "Lay Lady Lay" and Kris Kristofferson played "Me and Bobby McGee," while couple Graham Nash and Joni Mitchell performed "Marrakesh Express" and "Both Sides Now." But it was "A Boy Named Sue" by Shel Silverstein that caught Cash's ear. He brought the lyrics to a concert he was giving in San Quentin prison the next day—a concert

to fight his whole life to convince everyone he was good enough to play.

And so Bobby played every shift like he was auditioning for a job. Still, the best hockey player from Western Canada since Johnny Bucyk, the only kid ever to receive a 9 for character from legendary western scout Lorne Davis,† passed unclaimed through the first round of the 1969 draft. The Flyers' rookie western scout, Gerry Melnyk, formerly a Detroit Red Wing and Chicago Blackhawk, went to bat for Clarke. "He's a hell of a hockey player," Melnyk told Alex Davidson and Eric Coville, his eastern counterparts on the Flyers. "I just came out of the game [he'd played the year before in St. Louis] and this kid is a better player than I ever was."

"What about the diabetes?" Davidson and Coville wondered. They wanted a kid named Bob Currier, a big scorer in Ontario, healthy as a horse. Flyers GM Keith Allen went with his senior scouts. Lo and behold, Bobby was still there in the second round, 16 choices into the draft. Sam Pollock of the Montreal Canadiens, the league's savviest talent judge, had passed on him twice.

"We gotta take Clarke now," Melnyk said.

"His health."

---

that was being recorded for release as an album. Months later, the song was number two on the charts, where it would remain stalled behind the Rolling Stones' "Honky Tonk Women" for weeks. "A Boy Named Sue" was the story of a boy given a girl's name by his absentee father, who knew he'd have to "get tough or die." Silverstein said the song was inspired by his friend, humourist Jean Shepherd, who was forced to fight his way through grade school because of his feminine first name.

† Saskatoon-born Davis, a loyal scout who died on the job at age 77 in 2007, still working for an Edmonton Oiler team he'd helped make into Stanley Cup champions, gave two juniors a grade of 9 during his 40-year career. Clarke earned it for work ethic. Mark Woolf, a Medicine Hat Tiger who never made the NHL, got a 9 for shooting. Davis left his sport with a record that will never be broken. He went his entire hockey career, including stops as an NHL player in Montreal, Detroit, Chicago and Boston, without raiding a hotel mini-bar.

"I don't give a damn if this kid's got one leg; he's the best player I've ever seen at this level. He'll right away be our best player," Melnyk reassured the Flyers. The team's eastern scouts winced. *The kid's sick.* But GM Keith Allen, a westerner himself, saw the fire in Melnyk's eyes. "Let's listen to this guy," Allen said. Melnyk explained again about how Clarke had passed some test at the Mayo Clinic. He had seen the bloody affidavit from the hospital. At this point, Allen had team owner Ed Snider phone a Philadelphia doctor, who concurred with the Minnesota medical research centre's analysis of Clarke.

As long as he looks after himself . . .

A minute after the Flyers chose Clarke, the Detroit Red Wings approached the Flyers table, sniffing around for a trade. Then, what do you know, Pollock appeared. The draft was in Montreal, at the Queen Elizabeth Hotel; maybe Sam had a few restaurant recommendations for the Flyers contingent. Before leaving, though, he had another message for Keith Allen: *If you're interested, we could put together a nice little package for the kid from Flin Flon.*

Montreal, and Detroit too, had hoped Clarke would fall to a later round. When Pollock appeared, Allen knew he'd made the right choice. Others still weren't so sure. "Some skeptics are certain to accuse the Flyers of cruelty, forcing Bob Clarke to play such a rugged sport at his own risk," *The Hockey News* reported after the draft. Bobby, meanwhile, loathed talking about his diabetes. *Boring.* As far as he was concerned, it just wasn't an issue.

Bobby Clarke didn't have Bobby Orr's philanthropic streak. Who did? But there would be two instances when the Flin Flon Bomber softened in public, lending a helping hand. One season, he and the Flyers spent Christmas in Chicago. After beating up the Blackhawks, they returned to the dressing room. While teammates shouted and hollered, Clarke whistled over *Chicago Tribune* reporter Bob Verdi. That day, the *Trib* had run a story about a South Side mother with no heat in her apartment, no Christmas presents for her kids.

"You know that lady in your paper this morning?" Clarke asked, reaching into his pants for a wad of cash and handing $250 to Verdi. "This is from the guys. Make sure it gets to her, eh?"

"She's a perfect stranger," Verdi laughed.

"It's Christmas."

Clarke's other Good Samaritan moment was more telling. An NHL linesman at the time suffered from diabetes. He had a seizure on the road. Clarke approached referee Bryan Lewis offering to help. "He arranged to have an airplane bring in some kind of machine," the referee said. "Looked after everything." The human moment didn't change Clarke's relationship with Lewis. "Hey, Lewie, that's a horseshit call," Bobby shouted whenever the referee whistled down a Flyers player. And Lewis and Clarke inevitably fell into arguments during faceoffs.

Bobby always cheated, moving first.

"He was super-competitive, had as much drive as any hockey player I've ever seen," Lewis told me. "He had one goal: to get his team to the Stanley Cup. I can remember him to this day, at the faceoff circle, trying to get an edge. I'd tell him to back up and he'd snarl, 'C'mon, no one paid 20 bucks to watch you drop the puck.'"

That was Flin Flon talking. *Let's just do this.* After he won his first Stanley Cup with the Flyers, Flin Flon invited Bobby home. The town wanted to have a big day for him, load him down with gifts. At first, the hockey player didn't want to do it. "We told Bobby when he was here on vacation in June that we wanted to have a big testimonial dinner for him at the end of summer," Pat Ginnell told *Sports Illustrated*. "But he told us he wouldn't hear of such a thing. He got mad in fact, and said we didn't owe him anything, that he owed us everything. We argued about it for a few days. Finally, Bobby suggested that we hold a benefit game instead, with all the money directed to youth hockey in Flin Flon."

What a surprise: Bobby would rather play hockey than have to make a speech with good clothes on in front of a couple hundred people.

And what a heartwarming gesture, giving back to the community, lending a helping hand to the next Bobby Clarke out there—some deserving youngster who dreamed of making it out of Flin Flon and into professional hockey. Twenty-six hundred locals turned up at the Whitney Forum to cheer their native son. Of course, in the first minute of play, the next little Bobby Clarke, a kid named Robbie Watt, knocked the old Bobby Clarke flat.

Hey, the kid was from Flin Flon, right? Same name, too: Robert.

"Do that again, kid, and I'll take your fuckin' head off," Bobby said, rising from the ice. Uh-oh. Pat Ginnell jumped from the bench and wondered if (maybe even hoped that) the two would go at it. Beside him, the Flin Flon Bomber trainer, Jim Bryson, let out an appreciative chuckle. He'd seen Bobby like this before. But the kid stood down and Bobby Clarke relaxed. The rest of the game was good, fast-paced hockey.

Until the final minute, when Bobby found Watt skating with his head down at centre and decided to say goodbye, hammering the teenager to the ice.

"Owwwwww," the crowd groaned.

"Ah yes," Bryson said, smiling. "That's our Bobby."

ANATOMY OF A MURDER

The following is referee Bryan Lewis's penalty breakdown for a single interlude on the night three Philadelphia Flyers harvested California Golden Seal Mike Christie in the penalty box.

PHI—Kindrachuk, minor (roughing), 8:20
PHI—Kindrachuk, major (fighting), 8:20
CAL—Christie, major (fighting), 8:20
PHI—Kindrachuk, 10-minute misconduct, 8:20
PHI—Kindrachuk, game misconduct, 8:20
PHI—Saleski, major, fighting, 8:20
PHI—Saleski, 10-minute misconduct, 8:20
PHI—Saleski, game misconduct, 8:20
PHI—Schultz, 10-minute misconduct, 8:20
PHI—Schultz, game misconduct, 8:20
PHI—Taylor, minor (goalie leaving crease), 8:20
PHI—Kelly, double minor (roughing), 8:20
CAL—Christie, 10-minute misconduct, 8:20
CAL—Christie, game misconduct, 8:20
CAL—Frig, major (fighting), 8:20
CAL—Frig, 10-minute misconduct, 8:20
CAL—Frig, game misconduct, 8:20
CAL—Neilson, 10-minute misconduct, 8:20
CAL—Neilson, game misconduct, 8:20
CAL—Simmons, minor (goalie leaving crease), 8:20

SMOKE ON
THE WATER

Flyers rookie Kevin McCarthy wondered why Freddy Shero didn't seem to like him. Two months into the season and Coach still hadn't said boo. Ah, he's just weird, don't worry, you'll love him, teammates advised. And then at practice one day, McCarthy looked up and found Shero skating beside him. "What section of Winnipeg you from?" the coach wanted to know.

"Uh, St. James."

"Any problems with the sewers?"

"As a matter of fact, yeah."

"Not surprised; I helped on the sewers when I worked for the city, eh? Really sloppy work . . . cut corners. We knew they'd never last." With that, Shero skated away, chuckling.

Gone like a puff of breath disappearing on a window.

The coach everyone called "The Fog" came from Winnipeg's North End, the same Eastern European neighbourhood as NHLers Bill Mosienko and Wally Stanowski. Born to Russian immigrants, Frederick Alexander Shero (né Schirach) started life in a large Depression-era family. Four of 12 siblings died in childbirth. The young Russian experienced prejudice growing up. Like many quiet, intelligent kids, he found friends in books. In Dickens, Shakespeare and, later, the Russian masters Tolstoy and Dostoyevsky. Sports were a way to fit in. Freddy quarterbacked the football team at Isaac Newton High—the high school that served Winnipeg's immigrant population—to a city championship. Winters, he played junior hockey. During the war, he would become lightweight and middleweight boxing champ in the Royal Canadian Navy. He eventually played for the New York Rangers (1947–50), but for some reason the boxing champ refused to fight. "Isn't my nature," he told GM/coach Frank Boucher. Teammate Emile Francis remembered that "he was always in libraries." Freddy also played violin and attended the University of Manitoba in the off-season (history and Russian lit.)—this while working for the city, imitating sewer worker Ed Norton of TV's *The Honeymooners*. Come hockey season, Shero also took correspondence courses in law.

"I was minus-five as far as personality [growing up]," Freddy would say of his formative years. "I had so much fear in me."

Shero was different at a time—the *Father Knows Best* '50s—when fitting in really mattered. He didn't. A bad back forced him to retire. What could he possibly do? The lifelong loner stuck with what he knew, hockey and schooling, drifting into the life of a minor-league coach in the Rangers organization. There was a string of championships, but no callup from the parent club. Probably because the cup of coffee Freddy walked around with at the rink wasn't always filled with coffee. That and . . . well, he talked and acted funny.

Sometimes Freddy played dumb. "I remember Shero coaching in the minors, in St. Paul," former referee Ron Wicks told me, laughing. "One of his players scores three goals and fans throw hats on the ice. I go over to their bench and Freddy asks, 'What's with all the hats?' My linesman explains the custom of throwing hats after three goals. Freddy keeps shaking his head. 'Is that so? . . . Really?' And I remember thinking,

'Freddy's one of the smartest guys I know; no way he doesn't know about hockey hat tricks—he just wants to figure out the linesman, keep him talking.'"

The Fog also loved putting people on. Asked to list his hobbies for the Rangers press guide, he wrote down "violins and boxing." *Violence and boxing?* St. Paul Ranger Buzz Deschamps remembered the time Bob Plager, a star on the team, was badly injured, lying on the ice. "Who's Number Five?" Freddy wondered behind the bench. "Plager," Deschamps replied. Shero looked down at his pad, like he was searching his lineup card, and remarked, "Oh, I hope he's not out too long. He's one of our better defencemen."

Shy but far from insecure, Shero adopted a public persona that allowed him to come and go as he pleased. Purposeful eccentricity, startling people, was the Fog's all-purpose social strategy. Sometimes the loopy non-sequiturs were a way to meet people. Coaching in Shawinigan Falls, Quebec, he stopped in at a drugstore one day. "Can I help you?" an attractive salesgirl asked. "I love you," Freddy answered.*

Freddy and Mariette Gelinas were married three months later.

Other times, Coach Shero simply slipped away from an unwelcome task in a sour fog. Once, during a press conference, a reporter asked Freddy the optimum age for hockey players. Shero took a deep pull on an ever-present Lucky Strike (unfiltered), chewed on the question awhile, and then offered, "I wish I had got married sooner. I'm old now and they're still kids."

The press conference was over.

Maybe it was just as well that GM Keith Allen never interviewed Freddy for the Flyers coaching job. That instead, he simply looked at

---

* Freddy's Shawinigan goalie, future Boston netminder Eddie Johnston, insists he introduced Fred Shero to his wife. Eddie was going out with Mariette's sister at the time. Who knows? The love-at-first-sight story is the one Shero told Philadelphia sports reporter Jack Chevalier. Johnston does, however, confirm that Freddy proposed to his future bride on their first date.

his record—a Quebec Hockey League championship with Shawinigan Cataracts, International Hockey League and Central Pro Hockey League trophies in St. Paul and an American Hockey League title with the Buffalo Bisons—and figured this Shero guy must be a pretty good coach. He was from the West, too—had to be a hard worker. Who knows what would've happened if Freddy had shown up for a formal job interview in his standard outfit of the time—tinted glasses, Fu Manchu moustache, plaid jacket—and then mumbled his way through proceedings, failing to make eye contact and missing the ash tray with his cigarette?

"I thought he was an odd guy when I first met him," owner Ed Snider would always say.

As it would turn out, the characteristics that made Freddy a great minor-league coach worked even better on the Flyers, perhaps because Philly was still an NHL expansion team with a roster filled with cast-offs. For Freddy, there was no such thing as an unwanted forward or defenceman. Frederick Alexander Schirach cherished hockey players the same way his literary hero, aristocrat Leo Tolstoy, appreciated serfs. "I truly love everyone who ever played for me, from Shawinigan to Philadelphia," Freddy always said. Life toiling in the minors, trying to stretch three-dollar-a-day meal money for a ten-game road trip with card games in the backs of buses, losing, then having to bum food on the final days of the journey ("You going to eat all those chips?"), that was life itself for Shero who, by the time he reached Philly at age 46, had spent most of his working life riding the buses.

Stories of small towns and big-dreaming hockey players were among Freddy's favourite topics. Like the time a Long Island Duck took a penalty just so he could sit next to—and take in the perfume of—actress/jazz canary Doris Day at a Los Angeles rink.

"You'd meet him in the hotel bar on the road, where coaches always drank," referee Wicks recalled, "and Freddy would call you over. 'Hey Wicksy, sit down, buy you a beer . . . Where you from? Sudbury? I knew so-and-so from there . . .' He was always curious, not just about hockey;

he just liked to talk—about what he was reading, books . . . about life. He was cerebral, is what I always say about him.

"But he was weird," Wicks continued, laughing. "Next time you saw him at the rink—before a game, maybe—you'd say hi and he would walk right past you, like he didn't see you. That was why they called him 'The Fog,' I guess."

Once, after a penalty-filled Flyers–Rangers playoff game in 1975, Shero was chatting with reporters in a Madison Square Garden hallway when the NHL's supervisor of officials, Danny McLeod, happened by. "Hey Mac," Shero shouted, "if they thought this game was tough, they should try playing in Kingston." McLeod, formerly coach of the Kingston Aces, laughed. Freddy was probably doing a little damage control here, reminding McLeod that hockey was a rough game before McLeod reported on a contest that saw Shero's Flyers wade into the stands after fans. Still, the Flyers coach always enjoyed talking about his minor-league days. And former players loved the guy, even if they never quite got around to figuring him out. For years, the Shero family pet was a duck—a gift from a St. Paul player. And years later, when Ray Shero, Freddy's son, settled into his own hockey career, he couldn't believe the number of people who would approach him, volunteering a tale about bumping into his father somewhere.

That was because, after games, Freddy wandered downtown streets throughout North America by himself, dropping into saloons, shopping for poetry in the language and laughter of everyday citizens. The strangers who approached him were inevitably hockey fans.

Hey, what are you doing here, Freddy?

Same as you.

Freddy Shero's lifelong goal was to make hockey players happy, using everything he'd learned about the sport to ensure they made it to the top—became champions, were in heaven at last. For he had seen the promised land: Shero's last minute as an NHL player was spent on the bench in the Olympia, the Old Red Barn on Grand River Avenue in Detroit—double overtime, game seven, Rangers vs. Red Wings, spring of 1950.

Detroit's George Gee won a faceoff from Buddy O'Connor and got the puck to Pete Babando, playing out of position. "He just rifled it and it went through about 35 legs and nobody saw it—it just went into the net," is how Freddy always recalled the goal, punctuating the tale with a sour grunt.

Minutes earlier, the Rangers' Jack Gordon had chimed the puck off a post past Harry Lumley.

Freddy would go to his grave believing the Rangers should've won that Cup. If only they could have done a few things differently. He also realized "a few things"—a faceoff lost, an offside call, bad positioning or a blind pass up the middle—were inevitably what separated winners and losers. His teams, he vowed, wouldn't make those mistakes, at least not often as their opponents.

Freddy also knew what hockey players liked—respect, a good part in the play and the narcotic rush of winning (followed by a half dozen beer chasers). And he'd certainly long since figured out what they hated—losing, curfews, being embarrassed in public by schoolmarm coaches. All that and dull, endless practices.

Shero's genius, if you will, would rest in his giving the players everything they wanted in exchange for allowing him to play teacher (in his own peculiar way). Freddy had his rules—ten at first, just like the commandments. Number one: "Never go offside on a three-on-one or a two-on-one." The tenth commandment: "No forward must ever turn their back to the puck at any time."

Freddy quizzed his players incessantly. "Schultz, what's number three?"

"'Never throw the puck out blindly behind your opponent's net.'"

If a Flyer screwed up, he might find the latest mimeograph of the "Flyers bible" rolled in his glove next morning at practice. If the mistake cost the team a win, the message might be a pep talk: "Success is falling down nine times and getting up ten." Shero would never embarrass players. Knew that sticks and stones might break a player's bones, but bad names, like *loser*, that was what really hurt them.

He tried not to bore players. Remembered how, when he played, his mind would go on vacation during repetitive drills. The Flyers worked endlessly on breakouts. That was a hang-up of Freddy's. Flyers practised tic-tac-toe passing drills out of their end until the process became automatic. But not mechanical! Once he saw players going through the motions, simulating what he wanted, Shero would cancel practice. Instead, he'd stage a badminton tournament. Or dream up some stunt. Sometimes he had players race, pushing their goalies—Bernie Parent and the seldom-used Bobby Taylor—around the ice on chairs, like rickshaw drivers.

Occasionally, he'd just fast-forward to the final drill, a five-dollar contest in which players tried to perfect the wraparound play, wheeling from behind the net in an effort to stuff the puck past a shifting goalie.

Freddy would do anything to get a team alive and thinking. If they ended up laughing and having a good time, even better.

Shero was never more inventive than when it came to chalk talk. Other coaches used blackboards to draw plays or as an appointment calendar: *Team photo Friday. Get your hair cut.* For Freddy, the blackboard was an opportunity for a basically shy man to say something meaningful to players he cared about, but had difficulty reaching one on one. Whatever he was reading, or maybe a song he heard on the radio, or something that popped into his head at a bar, it was all grist for the mill.

Some messages were battle cries for hockey's toughest team.

If you keep your opposition on their ass, they don't score goals.

Some were sly reminders to the team's made guys, the goal-and-girl-getting scorers, of the contribution made by their unsung supporting cast.

When you have bacon and eggs for breakfast, the chicken makes a contribution; the pig makes a commitment.

Some were existential heart-to-hearts.

We know that hockey is where we live, where we can best meet and overcome pain and wrong and death. Life is just where we spend time between games.

Every now and then, Freddy's oblique communication strategies took the form of one-act plays, complete with props. One day, the Fog crept into the Flyers dressing room with a sloshing pail of water, placing it square on a training table. Saying nothing, he wandered off, leaving his team with a single thought: *Huh?*

The players were still gathered around the pail when Freddy returned. "Ricky, over here," the coach said. Ricky would be Rick MacLeish, the rare Flyer who could really fly. His nickname was "the Hawk," because of how he swooped. Freddy didn't like swooping. "Take the shortest route to the puck carrier and arrive in ill humour" was one of his mottos.

"Roll up your sleeve, Rick," Shero said. "I want you to put your hand in that bucket of water. Now pull it out. See the hole that's left."

Ricky did as he was told and then said, "There ain't no hole there, Freddy."

"Well, Ricky, that's how much we're going to miss you when you're gone."

MacLeish got the message: less swooping, more ill humour. Public criticism was rare for Freddy, and almost always directed at a star, a 50-goal scorer like MacLeish. As for the grunts, the pigs that provided breakfast bacon, Shero championed them endlessly. Once, during the Flyers' Stanley Cup reign, NBC picked a Flyers–Bruins match for its Sunday game of the week. *Bobby Orr and Phil Esposito against the other Bobby, Bobby Clarke, and hockey's best goalie, Bernie Parent!* is how the network sold the game. Minutes before the puck was dropped, NBC discovered that Bobby Taylor, who hadn't seen the ice in 35 games, would be starting in net for Philly.

"Freddy, how can you do this to us?" a network executive complained to the Flyers coach. "Everyone is going to be tuned in to watch Parent. How can you start Taylor?"

"It was his turn," Freddy shrugged. Taylor would also start in Montreal on a Saturday night that season—another marquee game. Freddy's way of making sure the world knew that, even if he only started three games a season, Taylor was a card-carrying, dues-paid member of the Philadelphia Flyers.

Even though he often took refuge in a fog ("I don't live in the fast lane—I live on the off-ramp," he once told a reporter), Shero knew what worked best for his club. The Flyers had no curfew; they were free-range hockey players. Once, after a win in Chicago, the team bus pulled out of the "Mad House on Madison" and headed downtown. After a while, the players realized they weren't returning to their hotel.

"Hey, where we going, Freddy?"

Shero remained quiet until the bus stopped in front of the Flyers' favourite watering hole, Hennessey's.

"Way to go, Freddie," the players screamed, hurrying en masse into the club. "See you back at the hotel," Shero said, wandering by himself to a bar across the street. Freddy never drank with players.

And if Coach Shero tied one on that night, he made sure the fog had burned off in time for work next morning. That too was part of being a hockey lifer, a pro.

Bobby Clarke prided himself on being the team's hardest worker. He was captain, after all. Players took their cues from him. One morning, Bobby had trouble sleeping and headed to the rink way early—nine in the morning.

But he wasn't the first Flyer at the Spectrum. There was a noise coming from Shero's office, a little shoebox off the team dressing room. Bobby peeked in to see what was going on. "[Freddy's] got last night's game on the fil-um," Clarke would recall, years later. "And he's watching. In those days, nobody watched fil-um. I go into his office and he's got an unfiltered cigarette in one hand and a Budweiser in the other."

How's the movie end, Coach? Good guys win?

We'll have to see, won't we?

"BERNIE, BERNIE"

Scientists at the Russian Ministry of Sport employed calipers and tape measures to determine a young hockey player's optimum position. In a 1957 Montreal suburb, evaluators were more casual. *"Patiner!"* a Rosemont coach shouted early on in his team's first practice. *Skate.* With that, kids raced around the rink, single file, while someone's dad studied a stopwatch. A swift, sure skater made the journey in a dozen seconds. *"Avant,"* the coach decreed. Plenty fast, maybe the next Rocket Richard— *forward.* Another kid flew the course in 17 seconds. *"Défenseur!"* Next up, wearing too-big skates (they belonged to an older brother), Bernie Parent ankled around the boards in just under half a minute.

"*Gardien,*" the Rosemont coach shrugged. It would be a lifetime sentence:

Goalie.

That was OK with Bernie. He happily stood between galosh-goalposts in Rosemont street-hockey games; enjoyed hearing shooters moan when he picked tennis balls out of the air. Not only that, but his favourite

Canadien was goalie Jacques Plante—Jake the Snake. Incredibly, Plante's sister, Therese, lived next door to the Parents on Bruxulles Street. Young Bernie hid in the shrubs when Plante visited, breathing in the magnificence of the Canadiens goalie's smouldering, jauntily upturned cigars.

Ah, the sweet smell of success.

Just how good a goalie Parent might be would become a matter of prolonged debate. Not good enough for the Montreal Junior Canadiens, apparently (Rocky Farr, André Gagnon and Rogatien Vachon beat him out there). Bernie was instead signed by Boston and sent to the Niagara Falls Flyers, where he played with Turk Sanderson in the fight-filled 1965 Memorial Cup—intimation of impending thunderstorms. After winning the Memorial Cup, Bernie was summoned to Boston. His first memory of the Garden was of a beer bottle sailing over his head. While the young goalie failed to shine in Beantown (Harry Sinden figured him for a party boy), he did impress Marcel Pelletier, future Philadelphia Flyers personnel director, while playing with Boston's farm team in Omaha. When the Bruins failed to protect the 22-year-old goalie in the 1967 expansion draft, Philadelphia shocked the hockey world by selecting Parent with its first pick. If the Flyers needed a goalie, why not grab a bona fide Stanley Cup winner like Glenn Hall? observers grumbled. Actually, Philly did want Hall, left unprotected by Chicago, but he was asking for too much money—$50,000.

"I don't make that much money," GM Bud Poile laughed.

"You're not a goalie," Hall laughed back.

Philly went with plan B—Bernie. Parent played well alongside Doug Favell in the very first Flyers season; the duo even led the NHL in goals against at the all-star break (sharing $125 league prize money!). They also topped the NHL in laughs. During practice, Favell once dropped his catching glove to snare a wobbling Terry Crisp slapshot. After a Flyers win, Philly radio play-by-play man Gene Hart asked Parent why defenceman Ed Van Impe was so effective at clearing the crease of enemy forwards.

"Well, Gene, he fart a lot," Parent said.

Though technically skilled, with lightning reflexes, Bernie sometimes lacked focus. (Could be all those *Three Stooges* episodes he watched
before games.) And his early NHL resumé was blemished by one awful
moment: the last game of the 1969–70 season. The Flyers, playing the
Minnesota North Stars, needed a tie to make the playoffs. The game was
still scoreless with just a few minutes left, and the puck was in Minnesota's
end. Bernie, playing great, was doing some housekeeping, clearing snow
from his crease. *Concentrate,* he told himself. *C'mon, keep it together.* North
Stars defenceman Barry Gibbs lofted a clearing pass from deep in his end.
Bernie had his head down, was still talking to himself, when the winning goal bounced past him into the net.

Parent was very good his first four years in Philadelphia, but might
not be the goalie to lead them to the Stanley Cup, the Flyers concluded.
So in 1971, Philly included him in a three-way deal involving Boston
and Toronto, getting back Rick MacLeish, a top junior scorer from the
Bruins. Bernie was devastated. He loved Philadelphia, had just bought a
house there. In Toronto, though, he would meet the inventor-technician
who turned him into the best goalie in the world (and turned him on
to ten-dollar cigars!). Jacques Plante, Bernie's childhood hero, was the
Leafs' number one backstop. Though sullen and vain as a peacock, Plante
was also a goaltending genius, a true pioneer. Before Plante, goalies played
like suspicious security guards blocking a store entranceway. And they
never, ever left their post. While with Montreal, Plante slipped behind
the cage to stop passes curling around the boards, or raced to the blue
line to bang pucks out of an attacker's reach. Hockey's first roaming goaltender was also the first in his profession to wear a mask, infuriating
Montreal coach Toe Blake.

Only bank robbers wear masks, Toe complained. Shooters will think
you're afraid.

"I am," Jacques said.

Then there was his pre-game fussing: with the Leafs, before the
opening faceoff, Jacques trimmed his finger and toenails and did up his
stick with exactly 17 strands of tape on the blade and knob. These weren't

superstitions. Three decades into his hockey career, Jacques was still searching for perfect balance in the net. He would take the same care making a save an engineer did in making a bridge. In Chicago, years earlier, he once bolted from the net before a game, spooked, shaking his head. "This net is ¹⁄₁₆ of an inch too big," he told the referee.

While Blake reached into his pockets for another Rolaid, referees brought out a tape measure. What do you know? The net was ¹⁄₁₆ of an inch too big.

Another idiosyncrasy: Jacques liked to bang on the pipes behind him before leaving the net; the pings worked like a ship's sonar, allowing the goalie to get "a feel" for where he was.

At age 42, Plante figured he knew everything about goaltending. He also realized his playing career was almost over. The seven-time Vézina winner saw in Parent, a fellow Quebecer, a worthy successor. His hockey son! Sure, they were almost related; Bernie grew up next door to his sister, after all. And so Jacques took Bernie aside, teaching him everything he knew.

Why are you pushing off your left foot in the net?

Am I?

Yes, push off your right foot. That way, your glove hand is steadier. Now, where will Bobby Hull shoot first time down the ice?

Dunno.

First shot will be high around your head. That's to scare you, eh? Get you standing up straight; after that, he'll go low to the corners. Orr . . . where does he go?

Ah . . .

Before he arrived in Toronto, coaches would talk to Bernie about concentration. Plante stressed anticipation—understanding the flow of the game, working with teammates (Jacques was the first goalie to raise his arm to signal icing to his defence). Though Bernie improved steadily under Plante's tutelage, the results weren't always there; the Leafs were a mediocre team. Then the goalie bolted to the undermanned Philadelphia Blazers of the WHA. That he signed with the Pennsylvania team revealed just where his heart was (he once even showed up at a Flyers practice).

The WHA didn't work out, though. The Blazers failed to honour his contract. Bernie wanted out of the new league, but not back with the Leafs. So Toronto shipped his rights back to the Flyers for a draft pick (who would turn out to be Ian Turnbull).

His first game back, Parent shut out Toronto, 2–0. Two days later, he blanked the New York Islanders. "He's the best goalie I've ever had," Freddy Shero beamed. Upon Parent's return, Freddy took him aside and admitted, "I don't know anything about goaltending, so you're on your own." But he wasn't—not really. For the first time in his pro career, Parent was part of a defence-first, winning team. In the 1973–74 season, Bernie finally became heir to his childhood hero, Plante. He set a league record for wins, with 47, recording a league-high 12 shutouts.

The new and improved Bernie Parent was more studious. He had adopted some of Plante's ritual preparations, watching films the night before contests, compiling a list of shooters' tendencies. And prior to games, he always had the same meal: a 16-ounce porterhouse steak, medium done, with ten mushrooms . . . not nine, not 11—ten mushrooms. Still, Bernie never lost his joie de vivre. Signed on to do a TV ad promoting a local bank, Bernie advised viewers to put some "moa-*knee*" down and get a free, pumpkin-coloured, Bernie Parent Flyers "jack-*kett*." Before signing off, he stared into the camera, ad libbing what became his signature cry: "Some fun, eh?"

That Bernie still watched *The Three Stooges* before games only made him more of a Flyer—a team that now boasted five eye-poking, hair-pulling brawlers: Schultz, Saleski, Van Impe, Kelly and Dupont.

Hello, hello, hello, hello, hello . . . HELLO!

Philadelphia was a Stooge stronghold, in fact. Larry (Louis Feinberg), the blinking, Brillo-haired stooge, grew up not far from the Spectrum. A museum, the Stoogeum, is now located in Ambler, just north of the city.

For teammates, getting Bernie back was like having an old girlfriend return from a wildly successful makeover. "We couldn't believe how much he'd improved," centre Bill Clement commented at the time. "We were like—wow!" With every save, the legend of Bernie Parent II grew.

"Bernie, Bernie," 17,077 Spectrum fans chanted, sometimes 30 times a night. Parent knew he'd really made it back with the Flyers when Dave Leonardi, the sign guy who held up large messages on cardboard for all to see, began hoisting a custom-made Parent sign: "Only the Lord saves more than Bernie Parent."

What Philadelphia appreciated most about Parent was his cocky assurance. The city had been without a dependable, year-after-year winner since the long gone Philadelphia Athletics, with baseball stars Jimmy Foxx, Al Simmons and Lefty Grove, way back in the Roaring Twenties. Parent acted as if he expected to win. Up a goal with seconds left in a game, he would skate out to consult a teammate. "I feel like pizza after the game— two slice, maybe," he'd say. And then he'd return to his net, banging both posts with his stick to establish who and where he was. Everyone on the bench saw the defencemen laugh and relaxed—Bernie's got this.

Parent fascinated Shero. For his pre-game nap, Bernie slept with a 200-pound English mastiff named Gus. Other players went to a bar or movie to clear their heads. Bernie grabbed a pocket full of Cuban cigars, along with his bow and arrow, slipping into the Jersey woods behind the Atco Raceway in search of deer. Away from the rink, he battled nor'easters in a 45-foot ship, the *French Connection,* decked out in a white hat, rain jacket and khakis. What he called his "Hemingway look."

Fred Shero never drank with players . . . except Bernie Parent. One night, the two men were throwing them back at Bernie's home bar in Cherry Hill, New Jersey. Afterwards, Shero had to get home to Bala Cynwyd, north of Philly. Guys with nicknames like "the Fog" aren't great with directions. And Freddie had had a few. Delighted with the situation, Parent gave his coach overelaborate instructions.

Go wes' on Graham Avenue to Highway 644.

West, Highway 644 . . . got it.

Continue onto NJ 70.

Hold it, NJ 70—shit, maybe I should get a pen here.

Pas de problème—just listen, my friend: now you get onto US 30, crossing into Philly . . .

What, another highway?

It would take Shero hours to negotiate what should have been a 20-minute drive. Next morning at practice, Freddy was grumpy, no sleep, bags under his eyes. "If Bernie Parent told Christopher Columbus which way to go, he never would've discovered America," the coach complained to his team, who would hold their laughter until they got to Rexy's, a blue-collar Jersey bar frequented by welders, pipefitters and, fitting right in, the Philadelphia Flyers.

THE WHA, PART TWO

The WHA was even rougher than the NHL in the '70s. The Birmingham Bulls sometimes started games with a lineup that included Gilles "Bad News" Bilodeau, Frank "Never" Beaton, Steve Durbano and Dave Hanson, a quartet that ended the season with 21 goals and 1,062 penalty minutes. The Bulls smuggled Beaton out of the dressing room in an equipment bag to avoid the police one night.

Success somehow didn't taste as sweet in the new league. When Gordie Howe's Houston Aeros won the Avco Cup one season, Houston decided to throw a Texas-sized wingding. City fathers arranged for the team to rajah down the parade route on huge, swaying elephants. Everything was waves and cheers until the elephant in front of coach Bill Dineen seized up and shivered, depositing five pounds of you-know-what on the pavement. Good thing these things don't fly, Dineen chuckled. At which point, his elephant scooped up the spreading pile, tossing it over his head onto the coach's lap.

STAIRWAY TO HEAVEN

Philadelphia Flyers vs. Boston Bruins, May 19, 1974

reddy Shero's first season with Philadelphia (1971–72) ended with a punishing shock: in the last minute of the final game, the Flyers and Sabres were locked in a two-all tie. If it stayed that way, Philly was in the playoffs. Shero had Bobby Clarke on the ice to take care of the newly formed "French Connection"—Gilbert Perreault, René Robert and *Ree-char Mar-taen*. When Bobby chased Perreault off the ice, the Flyers bench stood, watching the clock—*seven . . . six . . . five . . .* At the count of four, Sabres defensive specialist Gerry Meehan lobbed a desperate shot in from the blue line. Doug Favell reached for a puck that somehow disappeared, rematerializing in a tent-like bulge behind him in the net.

As Favell crumpled, Mariette Shero, watching on TV back in Philly, screamed, throwing a wide splash of coffee in the air. Now the Sheros' TV room smelt like Sanka. Fourth grader Ray Shero began to cry.

Tomorrow would be worse. "One of the most devastating days of my life," he'd remember. "Kids were saying the Flyers and your old man suck."

Even ten-year-old Philadelphians knew the routine: as soon as your guys lost, and they always did, start with the insults.

Predictably, owner Ed Snider wasn't happy. "This can't happen again," he told GM Keith Allen and Coach Shero, letting the implied threat hang in the air. Snider must have wondered about Allen after the deal that sent Bernie Parent to Toronto in return for big offensive threat Rick MacLeish. Some threat—Ricky managed three goals in his first two seasons in Philadelphia. As for Shero, players liked him, but did you really want a guy nicknamed "the Fog" piloting your team?

Allen shrugged off his owner's fury. *Hey, we didn't win* . . . The Philly GM was a pragmatic, take-charge guy who occasionally dropped into saloons and made like Sinatra. The Flyers' director of team services, Joe Kadlec, walked into the Washington Mayflower Hotel lounge one night to discover Allen sharing a microphone with actress/singer Gloria Loring. Three months after Philadelphia's loss to Buffalo, Allen found himself in another hotel, working yet another microphone. The NHL's 1972 junior draft was held at the Queen Elizabeth Hotel in Montreal. And on this fine summer afternoon, Allen belted every song out of the park.

First-round pick: Hall of Famer Bill Barber. Second round: All-Star defenceman Tom Bladon. Third round: All-Star defenceman Jim Watson. Fourth round: All-Star forward Al MacAdam, to be swapped for scoring champ Reggie Leach.

It got better: MacLeish suddenly blossomed into a 50-goal scorer the next season. Helmeted (bewigged, too) Ross Lonsberry and bearded Bill "Cowboy" Flett, wingers Allen had picked up from Los Angeles, turned into valuable contributors. Moose Dupont was acquired from St. Louis and fitted with contact lenses, greatly reducing an understandable propensity for making blind passes. Allen would soon be named sports executive of the year by *The Sporting News*. He also received a new nickname, "Keith the Thief," courtesy of *Philadelphia Daily News* sportswriter Bill

Fleischman. Boss Ed Snider would pretty well leave the saloon singer alone from here on in.

Fly me to the moon, and let me play among the stars . . .

Freddy Shero undoubtedly hated hearing from his owner. Loathed sitting still for a boss wearing cufflinks telling him how "his team" had to get tougher. Freddy wasn't a manage-up guy. His sympathies rested with the third-liners who did all the heavy lifting. Still, as he soaked in the bathtub, hour after hour, smoking—a favourite afternoon activity according to wife Mariette—or wandered bars alone nights, Freddy must have concluded Snider was probably right. According to Ron Wicks, Freddy's minor-league teams were always the toughest in the league. "You always knew you had your work cut out for you," the referee said.

The 1971–72 Philadelphia Flyers were only a *little* tougher than the Cup-winning Boston Bruins. With power forward Gary Dornhoefer and unpredictable, sometimes downright squirrelly defender Rick Foley leading the way, Shero's Flyers topped the NHL in penalty minutes (1,233)—a hundred or so up on Boston. The Bruins' success confirmed Freddy's belief that rough and rowdy was the way to go. But the Bruins, with Orr, Esposito and all their 100-point guys, were more talented than Philly.

That meant the Flyers had to be way bigger and badder than Boston.

Come training camp in the fall of '72, Freddy could see that rookies Bladon and Watson were sure, mobile defenders. Barber and MacLeish added speed and scoring. Allen's draft haul, an invigorating jolt of fresh, racing talent, meant Freddy was free to muscle up elsewhere. Two 21-year-olds who had wreaked havoc with the Flyers' minor-league team (the Richmond Robins), Dave Schultz and Don Saleski, graduated to the parent club. Shero also advised Bob Kelly that he expected a little more fight out of him. The Hound must have been relieved to know Dupont was now a teammate. When Kelly was a junior in Oshawa, he once got into a memorable brawl with Moose, then with the Montreal Junior Habs. Dupont tipped the Toledos at 255. And even in junior, Kelly played as if shot from a cannon. The two went at it like King Kong vs. Godzilla, heaving each other around the ice. The Hound was exhausted afterwards. Not Moose. "Good fight," he shouted as referees pried them apart. "We go again in Montreal."

If Big Bird Saleski, Kelly and Dupont liked fighting the way most kids enjoyed bumping cars, Hammer Schultz was something else again. He had been a goal scorer in junior, a solid citizen who married the mayor's daughter in Rosetown, Saskatchewan. Descended from Dutch-German Mennonites who left the Ukraine to escape Russian militarism, Schultz didn't fight—not at first. His favourite player growing up was butter-smooth Maple Leafs pacifist Davey Keon. But something happened to Schultz playing in blue-collar industrial towns in the Eastern and American Hockey Leagues. A big guy (six foot one, 190 pounds), he won some fights and enjoyed the rush of combat. He liked the cheers, too . . . strangers slapping him on the back and picking up the tab at bars.

Way to go there, Dave . . .

Because of his background, Schultz sometimes fought with himself after taking on NHL bruisers. Every brawl required a series of transformations. First there was the Incredible Hulk metamorphosis. His eyes would bulge seeing some tough escort Bobby Clarke into the boards. Growing LARGER, he bowled through traffic to get to the culprit. Mid-fight, Schultz was a crazy man—he spit, snarled, hammering away with his fists, and then, after it was all over, barked at referees and played to enemy crowds with wild, windmilling gestures. Hours later, the demon having fled, "Schultzie" would be a little bit vulnerable. He was once spotted by a Philly sportswriter alone in a hotel lobby, reading a popular self-help manual: *I'm OK—You're OK*, a book that began with a quote from poet Walt Whitman:

I contradict myself. I am large. I contain multitudes.

Schultz's swelling slugger act electrified his team, inspiring wolf-pack attacks. Fans at the Spectrum loved the way the newly energized Flyers went about their business. After so many Philadelphia teams had turned coward with the wind, the violence felt redemptive, like having big brother show up to settle a series of schoolyard humiliations.

Fans outside Philadelphia, though, especially in Canadian cities, hated Schultz for what he was doing to *their* sport. It was those Mennonite-to-man-killer transformations—all the chest swelling and crowd baiting. In filling the role of the pro wrestling bad guy, or heel, the Hammer diminished hockey, critics charged. NHL president Clarence Campbell despised the Flyers, as did Eastern Canadian newspapers and crusading politicians. Of course, all the bad publicity only served to make the Flyers closer. Every coach wants his team feeling like it was them against the world. Just as Harry Sinden welcomed the birth of the Big Bad Bruins, Shero rejoiced in his team finding a protective identity. He had a ready speech for snooping reporters: "We have no Rocket Richards on this team. Hitting is our game. Besides, 18 choirboys never won the Stanley Cup." Next came the inevitable throw to his minor-league days: "I used to coach a team in St. Paul, Minnesota, they called Shero's Magnificent Malcontents and we won the championship—easy."

Soon, Freddy's NHL team had its very own nickname. Just after Christmas 1972, the Flyers landed in boiling water in Vancouver. Saleski had a Canuck, Gregg Boddy, in a chokehold along the boards when a fan reached over, grabbing Big Bird's plumage. Outraged, substitute goalie Bobby Taylor jumped from the end of the bench, barging past startled spectators to whack Saleski's assailant before turning to slug a cop. Six more Flyers, led by Barry Ashbee, were by now over the glass, throwing punches, waving sticks and swearing. Not a good idea, what with the aforementioned cop, mad and getting madder, writing everything up. After the game, "The Vancouver Seven"—Taylor, Saleski, Ashbee, Flett, Joe Watson, Lonsberry and Ed Van Impe—were brought down to the station and charged with causing a disturbance by "using obscene language and by fighting with spectators with fists and wielding hockey sticks against and in close proximity to spectators."

Two months later, the Flyers returned to the scene of the crime for a rematch. The second game produced more rough stuff, with the Moose and the Hammer getting into a series of fights. Vancouver fans booed nonstop as the visitors crushed the home side, 10–5. When Dupont was given five minutes for savaging one Canuck, Clarke and MacLeish scored shorthanded goals. The Flyers were overwhelmed by reporters in the dressing room after the game. Not that anyone was saying much. The Flyers, particularly Clarke, were getting tired of defending themselves from charges that they were ruining hockey. Reporters got the quote they were looking for, however, when the Moose returned, naked, still wet from the shower, cigarette in one paw, beer in the other.

"It was a good day for us," Dupont mused, flicking away an ash. "We dint go to jail, we beat up their chicken forwards, we score goals and we won. Now the Moose drinks beer."

On the same road trip that produced the Christmas riot, the Flyers finally received the nickname that made them famous. On January 3, 1973, Philadelphia beat up the Atlanta Flames, 3–1. Philadelphia *Bulletin* reporter Jack Chevalier typed up his game report afterward. Back in Philadelphia, Pete Cafone scanned what was probably the last story to go into the paper before it went to bed. One passage caught the editor's eye: "The image of the Fightin' Flyers is spreading gradually around the NHL, and people are dreaming up wild nicknames. They're the Mean Machine, the Bullies of Broad Street and Freddy's Philistines . . ."

That's it, Cafone told himself, setting the headline.

BROAD STREET BULLIES MUSCLE ATLANTA

Soon, all of hockey was talking about the frightful, Halloween-orange Broad Street Bullies. The Flyers thrived on the attention. Before the Vancouver riot, Philly was 16–16–6, fighting to make the playoffs. Subsequent to Vancouver, the team went 21–14–5, finishing second in the NHL's West Division. They then won their first-ever playoff series, beating Minnesota, before shocking *Les Glorieux* first game of the semi-finals in a freewheeling, fight-free overtime thriller. Frank Mahovlich was checked by a puddle in the Habs' end and MacLeish hopped on the soggy puck, firing one past Ken Dryden. Montreal won the next four, however, going on to take their second Stanley Cup of the '70s. Though they'd lost, the Broad Street Bullies remained undaunted. "I can hardly wait until next year," rookie Bill Barber exclaimed.

Some teammates started a pickup game in a tavern that summer. In June of 1973, the "Vancouver Seven" appeared in a British Columbia court. Flyers attorney Gil Stein* took the septet to a bar to strategize. The boys nodded and sipped beer while Stein explained court proceedings. Midway through their lawyers' spiel, Ashbee lit a match, leaning over to set fire to Cowboy Flett's beard. Still nodding, Cowboy dunked his chin into a hissing beer glass.

"You guys are absolutely crazy," their lawyer groaned.

The Flyers showed up a week early for their fall 1973 training camp, skating at a rented rink in Voorhees, New Jersey. One reason for the team's almost palpable, kids-on-Christmas-morning excitement was the return of Bernie Parent, acquired by Keith Allen that summer in a trade with Toronto. An original Flyer, Parent was more than welcome at Rexy's, a Jersey hangout ten minutes over the Walt Whitman Bridge from the Spectrum. Back in 1967, Parent and his teammates cashed their paycheques at owner Pasquale "Pat" Fietto's ringing cash register, wolfing down sausage pies and, if they missed breakfast, a couple of orange juice and vodkas. Many Flyers still lived nearby at the $60-a-month Barrington Gardens. Now that some Flyers were making six-figure salaries, however, Fietto didn't have to cash many cheques. Still, players returned for beer (white wine for Parent) and pizza. They also liked giving Fietto "agita"— agitation. The owner couldn't count how many times he reached for his

---

*   Gil Stein eventually became the fifth and last president of the NHL in 1992, lasting a year before the arrival of Commissioner Gary Bettman.

drink and found someone's dentures staring at him from the bottom of the glass.

Porco dio, Bob Clarke!

Imagine a planet with a dozen Keith Moons and you have an idea of what the Flyers were like in the 1973–74 season. Coach Shero didn't have curfews. A former player, he remembered putting up with intrusive coaches. Sitting back in his tiny corner office at the Spectrum, pulling on a Lucky, he delighted in telling visitors about lunatic minor-league micromanagers: "[Eddie] Shore used to tell his players they'd lose 15 per cent of their strength if they cut their hair," Freddy said. "They couldn't shit the day of a game. They couldn't have sex after Wednesday night."

Did Freddy restrict his players' love lives?

"I tell my players when they can have sex, too. Any time they can get it."

Though a reluctant disciplinarian, Freddie was forced to lay down the law after a one-game road trip to Minnesota. The Flyers were savage practical jokers. Players returned from the shower to find a pant leg missing or maybe the sleeve of a sharp, paisley dress shirt gone. For a while, the Flyers took to pulling the heels off each other's cowboy boots. Because the team had only packed for a single night in Minnesota, players didn't have extra clothes or footwear. When Freddy looked around at the airport on the way home, he felt like Washington leading a bedraggled Continental Army into Valley Forge. Players were limping, clothes torn.

That's it! Any more ripping up clothes, you'll be doing it in Richmond.

Still, the Flyers continued tearing at each other. The *Bulletin*'s Jack Chevalier took notes on this exchange between the Flyers' chubby play-by-play man, Gene Hart, and forward Bob "Hound" Kelly on a ride to the game. Gary Dornhoefer and Rick MacLeish acted as scorekeepers. Action began as Hart entered the bus.

"No airplane today, Gene, so you won't need an extension for your seatbelt."

"Oh, Kelly, are you still with the team?"

"Will they have a TV lens wide enough for you tonight?"

"I've got a better chance of getting on camera than you, Hound."

"That's two-two—your turn, Mutt," Dornhoefer called out.

"Gene, it looks like your slacks are flared at the wrong end."

"I'd rather be fat than ugly like you. At least I can always lose weight."

"You're nothing but an educated derelict."

"That's four-three for the Hound," MacLeish decided.

"Those are pretty big words, Kelly, for a guy whose IQ matches his number."

"What's an IQ?"

If the Broad Street Bullies were rough on each other, they were murder on other clubs. Collectively, the team accumulated a record 1,750 penalty minutes in the 1973–74 season—up 500 minutes from Shero's first Flyers club. The Hammer got into 36 fights, spending ten hours in the penalty box that season. But it was more than fights and hit-and-run collisions; Saleski, Schultz, Van Impe, Orest Kindrachuk, Kelly and the Moose punctuated most whistles with a palmed glove to the face of opponents. Clarke and Schultz harassed other players verbally, too. All in hopes that the other guy would fight back, at which point he'd be swallowed up in an orange rockslide, two or three Flyers arriving at once, flailing away.

Ron Wicks spent the days prior to Flyers games lying in his hotel bed, watching the TV soap *As the World Turns*, rereading and underlining the rule book. Refereeing a Flyers game felt like being a traffic cop at the Indianapolis 500. "Sometimes you'd just feel like you should put a stick in the arm of your jersey and leave it up all night," Bryan Lewis told me. "We knew what was going on. They figured if they kept high-sticking and boarding, you wouldn't dare call them all. They figure, 'If we do it 35 times, [the referee's] only going to call 25—we get ten free shots.' Another thing they were masters of, particularly Clarke, was drawing the other guy into a fight—saying something, or sticking the hand in the other guy's face. Away they'd go, fighting. You'd have to send the other guy off, too."

Wicks won't talk about Clarke today, except to tell one story.

"I once called a penalty against Bobby and skated away with him still shouting at me. Seconds later the linesman skates by. 'Mr. Wicks,' he says, 'Bobby Clarke's chewing gum passed through his teeth, hitting you.' 'Where?' I said. 'In the back.' So I rang him up: 'Ten-minute gross misconduct.' Bobby was furious. Later, I get a call from [referee-in-chief] Scotty Morrison, who goes, 'gross misconduct?' I say, 'Clarke's chewing gum *passed through his teeth*, hitting me in the back.' Scotty says, 'That's pretty gross, all right.' I think Clarke got fined $100."

The Flyers were infamous now. Maybe even a symptom of troubled times. *Newsweek*'s April 30, 1973, issue had President Nixon and Watergate on the cover and a piece on the Broad Street Bullies inside. Both stories wondered if their subjects went too far. By the following spring, the Flyers were drawing more fans on the road than Orr's Bruins, not just in expansion cities, but in Montreal and Toronto. Everyone wanted to see a villain toppled, but these Flyers routinely disappointed enemies. The team dropped only two decisions in the last months of the '73–74 season, finishing first in the West Division. THINK STANLEY CUP bumper stickers began showing up all over Philadelphia in February.

Still, no matter how many wins Philadelphia racked up, critics only wanted to talk about how *bad* the team was. "Violence in hockey, violence in hockey," Keith Allen complained to a reporter. "I'm going to kill the next person who asks me about violence in hockey."

When commenting on his team's brutish ways, Shero baffled inquisitors with Runyonesque tales of minor-league hockey. Told everyone about one player he knew—why, the guy was born without an outer layer of skin. Oh boy, what a horrible thing—even slapping him on the back after a goal was more than the poor guy could endure. Another Shero tall tale: "In the old Western league, a guy named Bruce Lea used to be like a punching bag. Six-foot-three, weighed 210, but everybody clobbered him. Finally, he decided he had enough and hit back. Turned out he was a helluva fighter and didn't even know it."

Did he make the NHL?

"Nah, he had trouble with his wife and shot himself."

Freddy's perpetual fog bank and his team's occasional crime spree made it hard to get a fix on just how playoff-ready the Flyers were. Hockey people dropped in on a Philly practice and saw the team rushing around with three pucks or waltzing around the ice in pairs, pulling each other's arms. Sometimes Shero wasn't at scrimmages. Hell, sometimes it seemed like he didn't even show up for games. "Freddy was different," Wicks laughed. "He wore those tinted glasses so you couldn't see his eyes. And he never argued. Really, you didn't notice him behind the bench. Other coaches—[Scotty] Bowman, Don Cherry, Sinden . . . Bob Pulford was the worst—they would yell and scream, dare you to give them a penalty. Not Freddy. He never got upset . . . He let his team do that for him."

By now, everyone had heard about Shero's curious ways. How, like a fussing kindergarten teacher, he placed notes on rolled-up pieces of paper in players' gloves; that he tried telepathy to reach talented, undisciplined Rick MacLeish. Still, numbers didn't lie. The Flyers finished second in hockey in the '73–74 season with 112 points, one behind Boston. Montreal coach Bowman spoke for all of hockey when he said of Shero that spring: "Sometimes I think he doesn't know Wednesday from Thursday. Other times, I think he's a genius who got us all fooled."

Energized by an ecstatic, ravenous fan base, the Flyers overwhelmed visiting teams at home early in the 1974 playoffs, dispatching the Atlanta Flames by a combined score of 9–2 in two games at the Spectrum; Emile Francis's Rangers were next, and they too looked aimless and discouraged on Philly ice, losing all four matches, 16 goals to 6. On the road, away from roaring fans and Pat Fietto's sausage pies, the Flyers were far less confident, however. The Rangers beat them three times—all close games—at Madison Square Garden. And Coach Shero disappeared into a fog of war in Atlanta.

Freddy's evaporating act occurred Easter weekend. On Good Friday, the Flyers beat Atlanta 4–1, taking a three-nothing lead in the series. Maybe the team drank at their hotel, the downtown Regency, on Saturday night. Probably, they headed off to the Beer Mug, a nearby sports bar, to catch the Atlanta–San Diego ballgame. Days earlier, the Braves' Hank Aaron had tied Babe Ruth's career record for home runs—714. Everyone wanted to see Hammerin' Hank's 715th shot live. Freddy, being Freddy, ventured off by himself to drink things over at the Marriott, five blocks from the team hotel. Last thing he remembered was getting into an argument—something about the word *animal.* Then it was suddenly Sunday morning and he was back in his hotel room, unable to move his left arm, his face battered. Assistant coach Mike Nykoluk took over behind the bench that afternoon for a 4–3 overtime victory. (Schultz netted the winning goal.)

The Flyers, who heard their coach had walked into a telephone pole Saturday night, couldn't wait to hear Freddy's story. There was a fair bit of kidding at practice Monday morning back in Philadelphia.

Hey, Freddy, you forgot rule number one: No coach should ever turn his back to the puck in an enemy bar.

Hey, Freddy, what does the telephone pole look like?

Shero didn't disappoint. "I don't know if I got mugged or walked into a telephone pole," he told his team at centre ice. Next came the punchline: "From now on, when I go for a walk, I'm taking Schultz with me."

Although the Bruins finished a mere point ahead of the Flyers in the regular season, they were heavy favourites going into the Boston–Philadelphia Stanley Cup finals. It was an expansion-club thing. Last time someone other than an "original six" team had won the Stanley Cup was when the Montreal Maroons did it in 1935—"Rubber Ball" Bennett was prime minister of Canada at the time; Shirley Temple was Hollywood's biggest box office star. No one could imagine a new team winning the Cup. Why, it seemed like only yesterday that the Philly public-address announcer was explaining icing and offside to fans. Besides, Boston had hockey's two best players—Esposito and Orr. Again, the league's four top scorers were Bruins—Espo, Orr, Ken Hodge and Wayne Cashman. Plus, Boston had always killed Philadelphia. The Flyers' record against the Bruins, going back to 1969, was one win, 23 losses and four ties. And the Bruins were hot going into the finals—four straight wins against Toronto; 30 goals in six games against Tony O (Esposito) and the Chicago Blackhawks. Phil Esposito would be league MVP this season. Orr was tops in playoff scoring going into the finals.

"Orr just killed us," Blackhawks coach Billy Reay complained after the semifinals. "You can't give him the puck."

So what was Freddy's plan against Boston in the finals?

"We've got to give Orr the puck," Shero told his players before game one in Boston. "Give him the puck all he wants in his end and then hit him . . . tire him out. Same thing with Esposito." The Flyers greeted Shero's master plan with sidelong glances. *Is he serious?* Most teams tried to sideline hockey's two best players. Shero wanted to give them the puck. Finally, Terry Crisp broke up an awkward silence with "Whatever you say, Freddy." The team must have wondered if their coach was joking. It happened from time to time. Once, Shero had his players skating around on one leg during practice until Clarke complained. "Why the hell are we doing this? It's stupid."

"You're right," Shero shrugged. "I was just waiting for one of you guys to figure it out."

Still, Freddy was serious about feeding Orr and Esposito. "The more Bobby [Orr] has the puck, the harder he has to work and the more tired he gets," he told the *Boston Globe*. He also suggested that the Rangers, a team the Flyers had just knocked off, were better than the Bruins.

"How's that?" a reporter asked.

"Because they've got better players."

Freddy knew his incendiary comments would take the heat off his young team. But he really did believe that allowing Orr and Esposito to lug the puck all night was the way to go. Trying to cover Orr *and* the puck was too much work. Give Number Four the puck, the game gets simpler by a half, Shero figured. And the Philadelphia coach was confident he knew how to contain Esposito.

Shero hardly looked like a soothsayer in game one, as the Bruins dominated the first period, jumping to a 2–0 lead. The Flyers came back to tie the game, but Orr, the game's best player, golfed in the winner with 22 seconds left, inciting an ovation that undoubtedly awakened the circus monkeys high in the Boston Garden rafters. The Bruins got off to another 2–0 lead in game two, but it was a different Bobby who took over after that. The Flyers' Bob Clarke won 31 of 47 faceoffs, killed five penalties, scored the Flyers first goal, set up Moose Dupont's last-minute tying effort and then turned hero in overtime. He would get some unexpected help in extra play. Eleven minutes into overtime, a Bruins fan behind the Flyers' bench shouted, "Hey, Shero, put Schultz on so we can win this game."

Seconds later, the Flyers coach called for a line change, and Schultz was the first word out of his mouth. In his first overtime shift, the Hammer slipped a backhand pass to Bill Flett, high in the slot; his turn-around shot was gobbled up by Clarke, cruising in front. The Flyers centre hurried a backhand. Sprawling, Bruins goalie Gilles Gilbert made the save, but Clarke collected his own rebound and banked a shot into the net off a diving Terry O'Reilly, giving the now-dancing Clarke and the Flyers the win they needed in Boston.

Game three, back in Philly, drew big ratings in the United States, as 8.3 million Americans* looked on to see Philadelphia exhaust the Bruins 4–1. Following Shero's orders, the Flyers hammered away at Esposito and Orr. Bobby was evidently hurt, and an ineffective Esposito would be benched for most of the final period. Next game, it was more of the same: 4–2 for Philadelphia.

Flyers needed one more win. And the Bruins were reeling.

---

* More proof that slam-bang '70s hockey was popular in the United States: five of the six most-watched (on American TV) NHL hockey games occurred in this decade. The May 12, 1974, Flyers–Bruins game remains the sixth most popular NHL game on American TV, with 8.30 million viewers, trailing only game one of the Boston–New York finals in 1972 (8.51 million viewers), the seventh game of the 2011 Boston–Vancouver finals (8.54 million), the sixth game of the 1973 Montreal–Chicago finals (9.41 million), game six of the 1972 finals between Boston and New York (10.93 million) and the seventh game of the 1971 Montreal–Chicago finals (12.41 million).

As long as Orr was alive and skating, though, Boston remained dangerous. Up against a collapsing wall, down three games to one, the Bruins' Number Four was at his very best at home in game five, lugging the puck, absorbing elbows, shoulders and sticks, fighting past every form of intimidation, scoring twice and adding an assist in the second period, leading Boston to a convincing, dramatic 5–1 win.

Orr played over nine minutes in the first period. In the second, he was on for 14½ minutes–6 minutes and 31 seconds straight at one point. Bobby was headed for another 40-minute game until Bruins coach Bep Guidolin rested him late with a safe lead.

The decisive loss in Boston shook the Flyers, who realized that game six in their home rink was their one shot at the Stanley Cup. They hadn't beaten the Rangers in New York in the semifinals, and it had taken a last-minute score and overtime tally to steal one of the three matches in Boston. Bobby Orr in his own rink, game seven, with 15,000 ardent, cheering fans giving wind to his sails, was a prospect no Flyer wanted to consider.

"We know we have to win at home Sunday," Clarke said.

Like prizefighters before a title match, the Montreal Canadiens went to mountain hideaways prior to championship series—no distractions. Coach Shero, who believed life was a smorgasbord of welcome diversions, preferred that his team stay in the city. "Let the players look at pretty girls," he said. Still, before game six against Boston—the Flyers' title shot—he took his club to stay overnight in Valley Forge. The little town 18 miles north of Philadelphia was where General Washington rested his Continental Army in the winter of 1777–78. Maybe the Flyers' stay would provide them with a sense of destiny. At the very least, it would keep the players from having to talk about championship pressure, not to mention taxiing two sets of families around. Ed Snider had thoughtfully flown all the players' dads in for game six. Dave Schultz's pop, a mechanic, and Bob Clarke's underground-demolition-expert father were here. The Flyers owner had also arranged for Kate Smith, America's pre-eminent patriot, to belt out "God Bless America" before the big game. (She'd be on the Philly-based *Mike Douglas Show* singing "The Good Life" the following afternoon.)

The Flyers had begun playing "God Bless America" in the early '70s because fans, suffering from Vietnam fatigue, were tuning out "The Star-Spangled Banner." The team was now 39–3–1 when Smith's anthem was played, including a four-game win streak in the 1974 play-offs. Freddy preferred the Beatles to Irving Berlin and shrugged off questions about the importance of a celebrity visit with a familiar dodge. Sure, he'd seen stars before hockey games, lots of times—all in the minor leagues, of course. "Who's that big, busty blonde, about six-three, who used to be on TV?" Freddy asked reporters. "Yeah, Dagmar [a 1950s model], she dropped the puck for us one night in Buffalo and kissed our captain."

Being away at a hotel robbed Freddy of one pre-game ritual. At home in Cherry Hill, he sometimes woke in the night with an inspirational thought for players, at which point he padded downstairs to his basement office, fired up a Lucky and gathered his thoughts on paper. Freddy had been leaving notes for his team since the middle of the '72–73 season. The Flyers didn't take them all seriously. Sometimes, there would be a snide comment on the bottom of Shero's message chalkboard.

Not this morning. On Sunday, May 19, 1974, Freddy ambled into his home rink and dashed out one last note of encouragement for the team he had made his own.

"Win today," he wrote in chalk on the team's slate message board, "and we walk together forever . . ."

Afterward, he disappeared into his office to prepare for the game. Freddy had a note to himself tacked to the wall of his cubbyhole: "O, the despair of Pygmalion, who might have created a statue and only made a woman." In Greek mythology, Pygmalion carved a statue out of ivory that eventually came to life. The message was an ironic reminder that a coach's greatest creation—his team—remained, after all he had done, human and entirely fallible. Shero had always treated his team with respect. The daily notes were a shy, learned man's apology for not being able to say more. Verbal messages were often implied. He once invited Dave Schultz into his cubbyhole for a difficult talk.

"Hockey players can have three things," Shero told Dave. "Agility, skating and strength; you haven't got a lot of agility and you're not a good skater."

Schultz evidently got the message: be strong, real strong.

Freddy found it painful to spell things out for players, so he wrote them down instead.

"Win today and we walk together forever . . ." was a way of reminding the Flyers that they had an opportunity to achieve immortality. Beat the Bruins this Sunday afternoon, and Pygmalion's dream would come true. Flesh-and-blood players would remain preserved forever in their youthful glory, as lifelike statues outside wherever the Flyers play hockey in Philadelphia.

Watching an old NBC tape of the final game of the 1974 NHL season serves as a reminder of how good Freddy Shero's Flyers could be. There were no fights that day, and only a handful of minor penalties. The game began with a whoosh, both teams skating hard. No whistles. The first eight minutes take 12 minutes, including two TV breaks. The Bruins get a few early chances. The Moose gave away the puck. Johnny Bucyk was in alone. Parent made a deft save.

"Bernie! Bernie! Bernie!"

But the Flyers came right back. Midway through the period, they were the better, smarter team. At 14 minutes, MacLeish performed a nifty toe drag to slip past Al Sims. As he was being taken down, Ricky slipped a pass to Clarke, who hit the post. On the ensuing power play, the Flyers came close. There was a goalmouth scramble. The Flyers had been taught to take someone off with them upon getting a penalty—someone better than them, preferably. There was only one player better than Bobby Clarke on the Boston Bruins—Bobby Orr—and that was whom Clarke chose to tangle with.

"Two minutes, both of you, let's go," referee Art Skov shouted.

Advantage Philadelphia: it was four on three now, and while MacLeish could fill in for Clarke, no one would ever be able to replace Orr. MacLeish won the ensuing faceoff from Gregg Sheppard. From the point, Dupont directed a shot at the net, hoping for a rebound or deflection. Boston's Carol Vadnais, riding Bill Barber out of the play, threw out a skate, deflecting the shot away from the net.

Good play.

But MacLeish, floating behind him, managed to get a stick on the zigging puck, sending it zagging past an off-balance Gilbert.

Better play. One-nothing, Flyers.

After that, Flyers forechecking took over. Four lines and a quintet of rapidly shuffled centres (Clarke, MacLeish, Kindrachuk, Clement and Crisp) slowly and surely choked the life out of Boston's offence. Shero's answer for Esposito and his famously long shifts was to have three racing centres, a pony express, take turns pestering him. Orr was performing in a spiralling nightmare, with a Flyer everywhere he turned. The idea that Parent alone defeated Boston in 1974 is a myth. Yeah, he was great, but the Flyers dominated the second period that afternoon, outshooting Boston 14–9. The Bruins could muster only five shots in the third. But even these totals would be misleading. Most Bruins attempts were from well out. In 60 minutes, the Bruins had seven good opportunities on Parent. The Flyers enjoyed 14 excellent scoring chances on Gilbert.

Why were the Flyers so good at home? "If I was a player, I'd want to play in Philadelphia," referee Wicks told me. "The fans were always behind you, loudest rink in the NHL." With Philly fans shouting endless encouragement, the Flyers felt like they were skating downhill. Schultz, Saleski . . . Clarke and MacLeish, too, were a little faster in the Spectrum. "When you're playing down there, someone seems to be on top of you right away," Rangers winger Ted Irvine commented after a semifinal loss to the Flyers in Philadelphia. "The rink is just that much smaller."

"But I checked, the dimensions are exactly the same in both rinks— exactly," a New York reporter told him.

"Hmm, well, it doesn't feel that way."

And the Flyers were always hitting. "If you had to play one full 78-game season against the Flyers you'd have to retire," Ranger Pete Stemkowski commented after losing to the Flyers. "You'd be that tired."

The Bruins took three penalties, the Flyers only one in the third period of this, their title match. MacLeish, the best skater on the ice, overtook Carol Vadnais to nullify an icing, nearly scoring seconds later. Ross Lonsberry caught up to and stripped Johnny Bucyk of the puck to cancel a power-play try.

"Shero changes men every few seconds here," NBC play-by-play man Tim Ryan told viewers late in the third period. It was a shrewd observation. Freddy Shero would often be credited for innovations he made popular but that weren't really his own. The Toronto Maple Leafs, with Wild Bill Ezinicki, Bashing Bill Barilko and Gus "Old Hardrock" Mortson, won four Stanley Cups in the postwar years. Shero saw first-hand how they did it—by outmuscling the other guy. That was how his teams played. As for studying tapes, Maple Leafs owner Conn Smythe watched game film in the 1940s. And the Canadiens had a de facto assistant coach, Claude Ruel, tutoring Guy Lafleur and other young Habs before Shero hired Mike Nykoluk. Where Freddy did change hockey was in going to shorter shifts, speeding up the game. The former Canadian bantamweight champion realized that, just as boxers paced themselves for three-minute rounds, hockey players alternately charged and coasted through two-minute shifts.

But what if, instead of three-minute rounds, boxers could throw themselves into 60-second attacks? Similarly, what if forwards skated furiously for 40 seconds and then were replaced by another racing trio? One of Shero's "crazy" practice routines was to skate around with a bull-horn. Players had to go full out until the horn sounded.

Freddy blew his born every 40 seconds. Players became accustomed to getting on, skating full speed and then jumping off. That was why Freddy dared Boston to overuse Orr and Esposito. He'd overwhelm them with numbers and speed.

In the last five minutes of the 1974 hockey season, the exhausted Bruins would be penalized twice for grabbing passing Flyers. The Bruins knew they were a beaten team. Flyers winger Don Saleski overheard Phil Esposito skating to the faceoff circle, looking at Parent, muttering, "No way we're going to beat that guy tonight."

This being Philadelphia, the team did experience a last-minute malfunction. If you were a true Philadelphia sports fan, you remained ever prepared for disaster—superstars leaving, inexplicable losses, mascots crashing into the stands . . . and after that, a tidal wave of booing. The Flyers had twice ended seasons on horrific goals—Parent and Favell whiffing on last-second softies. Incredibly, with the whole world watching, it almost happened again that Sunday afternoon.

With time running out in the third period, Bobby Orr jumped from the penalty box* and found the puck in his own end, aiming a last-second, rink-long desperation shot at the Flyers net as the Spectrum crowd counted the game down.

Seven, six, five, four . . .

"I was looking at the clock, watching the seconds tick off," Parent admitted later. "*Pow!* The puck missed the net and hit the boards behind me."

Wouldn't that have been something, if Orr's 200-footer had gone in? But it hadn't. Just missed. It seemed incredible at the time. An expansion team with a weird, "minor-league" coach had won the Stanley Cup.

The next hour was a blur. Clarke and Parent tried to steer the Cup around the Spectrum but were crushed by swarming fans. The team retreated to the dressing room for champagne, beer and an early Father's Day celebration. Everyone's dad was there—lots of hugging

---

* Predictably, Orr went ballistic when given a questionable penalty for catching up to and checking Bobby Clarke on a breakaway with less than three minutes to go in a game in which the Bruins were down a goal. Art Skov made the call. After the game, the referee would ask Orr for his stick. No, it wasn't always easy being a superstar.

Before the 1970s, hockey hair came in one length (short) and two styles (plastered down or close-cropped, like iron filings called to attention by a magnet). Then Derek Sanderson happened. By the mid-'70s the Flyers were the hairiest team in hockey, with beards (Bill Flett), a wig (Ross Lonsberry) and one classic rock-star look (Bobby Clarke). Mostly, though, the team was an affront to good grooming. Together, Rick MacLeish, Hound Kelly, Moose Dupont, Hammer Schultz and Don Saleski resembled the mangy quintet who tormented Dustin Hoffman in the 1971 movie *Straw Dogs*.

and backslapping. The Flyers were dying to take their dads and the Cup to Rexy's, but they couldn't get close to their hangout, which was swarmed by Flyers fans. So they gathered at a bar in Haddon Heights, where everyone laughed at defenceman Joe Watson's story.

With 40 seconds left in the game, goalie Parent called him over. Watson expected to be told where to stand for the ensuing draw. Parent, though, gave him a wink and said, "We win tonight, the women are going to be lined up outside our door all summer long."

What Bernie didn't say was that they'd have spray paint. He would return to his own Cherry Hill residence that evening to find his house painted orange and black. Bobby Clarke's home was the scene of a mammoth block party. *People all over the world (everybody) join hands, start a love train, love train.* His family wouldn't be able to return home for days.

Still, even while they partied, at least one member of the relentless Flyers team continued to scheme and toil. In the Flyers dressing room after the game, GM Keith Allen was still working on bettering his club. Moving through a champagne mist, he approached Bobby Clarke, standing beside his father. After shaking their hands, he had a question for Cliff Clarke: *Tell me about Reggie Leach.*

What you want to know?

Well, I'm talking to California about trading for him. What kind of kid is he? I want to know if he'll fit in here.

Bobby Clarke had the answer to that question: *He'll score 50 for us.*

Days later, Allen made the deal. By then, the Flyers' coach was back in his ancestral homeland, travelling Russia. Hockey season was never over for Freddy Shero. Presumably, he was now telling Anatoli Tarasov about Doris Day and all the great guys who played for him with the St. Paul Saints, the Buffalo Bisons and his now favourite team, the Stanley Cup–winning Philadelphia Flyers.

TOP TEN '70S HAIRCUTS

1. Ron Duguay (Farrah, Cheryl, Bianca and Cher put their hands through hockey's first mullet!)
2. Guy Lafleur (go with the flow)
3. Bobby Clarke (*Frampton Comes Alive*)
4. Derek Sanderson
5. Garry Unger
6. Dave Hodge (former host of *Hockey Night in Canada*)
7. Bobby Orr
8. Darryl Sittler (the Ryan O'Neal)
9. Marc Tardif (the Alain Delon)
10. Tom Lysiak

THE SACK OF TORONTO

Philadelphia Flyers vs. Toronto Maple Leafs, April 15, 1976

I must not call Clarence Campbell an old fart.
I must not call Clarence Campbell an old fart.
I must not call . . .
　　　　—BOBBY CLARKE as Bart Simpson, Christmas, 1975

The Flyers were better than ever in the 1974–75 campaign. Worse, too. The team racked up 51 wins in the regular season, the most in hockey. Bernie Parent again took the Vézina. League MVP Bobby Clarke established a record for assists, with 87. On the other fist, Schultz spent more time in the penalty box than any player in league history—472 minutes in the regular season, 83 more in the playoffs. Moose Dupont picked up 325 minutes in overall penalties.

Two players: 880 minutes.

Some perspective: in Bobby Orr's rookie season (1966–67), the entire

Bruins team accumulated 764 minutes in penalties, while the New York Rangers and Detroit Red Wings spent 722 and 719 minutes, respectively, in the "sin bin."

The Flyers fought and won on beer, Rexy's pizza and . . . *Helsinki highballs?* While travelling Europe the summer of '74, Shero befriended a Finnish track coach who told him his runners had improved their times with pollen pills. Clarke tossed back a handful one day. "I never remember having so much zip," he would tell *Sports Illustrated.* Too much, maybe; next game, he almost killed Rangers defenceman Rod Seiling, a Team Canada roommate in 1972. "I speared him, pole-axed him and cut him close to the eye," Bobby admitted. He flushed the pills before calling Seiling to say he was sorry. It would be the Flyers centre's second *mea culpa* this season. Before Christmas, Bobby had apologized to Clarence Campbell for suggesting the 69-year-old NHL commissioner was too old to be running a hockey league.

That was the *baaad* Bobby. The good one would give the Sheros a fluffy white puppy for Christmas that season, a bounding Russian Samoyed to be named Cherry Hill, after the family's Jersey residence. The previous spring, Parent had given Freddy the keys to the Mustang he won for being playoff MVP. Shero pretended to be put out by gifts. "Hey, you owe me money," he told Parent upon discovering he had to pay tax on the Mustang. (Bernie looked after that too.) Of course, Freddy showed affection in his own way. His players won championships. He also gave his players what every employee craved—respect. The Pygmalion quote in his Spectrum office was a real tell. An avid reader of Shaw, Freddy must have known the line in *Pygmalion* where Eliza, the cockney flower girl turned duchess, credited her teacher, Professor Henry Higgins, with her transformation. "The difference between a lady and a flower girl is not how she behaves," Eliza says, "but how she's treated."

Shero treated players like sons he wanted to succeed. He installed Apollo weightlifting machines in the Flyers dressing room one year. This season, he took the guys to Temple University, putting them through tests. The idea was to get in better shape. "I'm afraid Freddy's in for a shock,"

Clarke said afterwards. "He's going to discover that nine of us ought to be teaching school and the other nine ought to be working as bouncers."

Freddy the Fog's most curious manoeuvre was teaching players how to think by pretending he himself didn't have a clue.

"How much time left?" Shero once asked his bench late in games.

"Two minutes."

"Where's Clarke?"

"Penalty box."

"OK, Clement takes the faceoff."

But that was all hockey shtick. Freddy knew where Clarke was and how much time was left. But by making his team stop to reflect upon Clarke's absence before ordering Clement onto the ice for a last faceoff, he was:

a) asking the entire Flyers team to work harder to compensate for the loss of their captain;

b) giving Clement a pat on the fanny by requesting he replace the league MVP;

c) reminding the replacement centre what he and the rest of the team expected;

d) which was a faceoff win and the puck whistled out of trouble.

All that in two words: "Where's Clarke?"

The absent-minded professor act came easily to Freddy, who regularly missed ashtrays with cigarettes and once locked himself out of the Spectrum after a game. But if anyone kidded him about being in a fog, Shero never pointed out the origin of the nickname: in 1948, in a muggy Minnesota arena, he was the only player who could follow the puck in a soupy haze. If people thought he was in a fog, let 'em. The truth was, for all his idiosyncrasies, with a hockey game on the line, the Flyers coach was as composed as Jack Nicklaus lining up a championship putt.

The Flyers would repeat as Stanley Cup champions in 1975, knocking off the Maple Leafs, Islanders and Sabres. As always, defence would be the key. In nine of 12 wins, the Flyers gave up one goal or none. Parent again won the Conn Smythe Trophy. Though there wasn't a heavyweight contender like Boston to conquer, for blue-collar Flyers fans, these playoffs were emotionally gruelling. Middle America was experiencing existential ennui, according to the big New York papers. *Bad news on the doorstep, I couldn't take one more step.* Saigon fell the day after the Flyers and Islanders began the Cup semifinals. The Vietnam War was in its death throes. Months earlier, shortly before 1974 training camps opened, Richard Nixon had resigned over Watergate, and now all the President's men—John Mitchell, John Ehrlichman, H.R. Haldeman, et al.—were trooping off to jail in handcuffs. Discotheque music blared on the radio. The number one song in April was a saucy Creole jumbo—(Philadelphia's own!) Labelle singing, *"Voulez-vous coucher avec moi, ce soir?"* More French—quiche was suddenly everywhere in restaurants. What the heck was going on? Real Flyers fans didn't eat quiche or do the hustle. It would get worse. A roaring fire destroyed Rexy's on Mother's Day, Sunday, May 11 as the Flyers lost 2–1 to the Islanders—their third straight defeat to the Long Island upstarts. The fire department couldn't pry one Jersey mother out of the burning building. She wanted to be there for the Philly comeback.

And come back they did. Kate Smith showed up to sing "God Bless America" before game seven of the Islanders-Flyers series. After Philly won 4–1, Islanders goalie Battlin' Billy Smith grumbled, "I should've skated over her wires." Flyers took it from there, delighting their constituency by clobbering the Buffalo Sabres and their fancy-skating French Connection line without incident, unless you counted the game in Buffalo that turned into a scene out of *The Hound of the Baskervilles* as an eerie fogbank, complete with a swooping-swirling bat, descended on Memorial Auditorium. Rick MacLeish tossed the bat over the boards with a bare hand.

"Ricky, you can get rabies from that thing," teammate Joe Watson hollered.

"What're rabies?" Rick shrugged.

The next dangerous moment in the Flyers' second Cup run came during their victory parade. Parent sat next to Mayor Frank Rizzo as the Flyers' orange flotilla wound through downtown Philly past two million gleeful, cheering spectators. While Bernie waved and shook hands, the unsmiling former police chief searched the crowd with narrowed eyes.

"Frank, what are you looking for?" Parent asked.

"Snipers," the mayor said.

Shero surprised his family at the parade windup—a packed, adoring JFK Stadium. Grousing about the travails of married life, Freddy had once let Philly sportswriters in on the story about how he told wife Mariette "I love you" the first time he met her, then admitted he hadn't been able to utter the three magic words ever since. "Mariette knows I love her," Freddy continued, mad at himself for his inhibitions. "I know women like to hear it, but I feel like I'm bullshitting when I say it." Except for right now, standing in front of close to 100,000 hockey fans at JFK.

"I love you, Mariette!" Shero shouted. "This is better than heaven. I think I'm the luckiest guy in the world."

Why shouldn't he feel that way? Nine summers earlier, the Flyers couldn't draw 20 fans to a welcoming parade. Now here they were, celebrating their second Stanley Cup in front of millions. Flyers charity softball games that summer attracted close to 20,000 fans, more than the Phillies drew some nights. Without question, the team had changed hockey. And not just by making it rougher. *Sports Illustrated* noted that it was Shero's tactics, not Schultz's elbows, that beat Buffalo: "Shero's plan became operative the moment Perreault, Martin and Robert skated out . . . The Connection was on the ice for 97 seconds, and during that time Shero threw three different lines at them. On their next shift of 106 seconds, the Connection faced another three lines."

Lester Patrick's Vancouver Millionaires startled the hockey world by becoming the first team to change lines on the fly, blowing past the Ottawa Senators to win the Stanley Cup in 1915. Soon, all teams were changing on the fly. Shero's innovation was every bit as consequential. *Sports Illustrated* quoted Scotty Bowman in Montreal and Boston's Harry Sinden as saying they would adopt the Flyers' quick-change system next season.

Still, it would be decades before Shero would get the credit he was due. Flyers owner Ed Snider, GM Keith Allen, even broadcaster Gene Hart would make it into the Hockey Hall of Fame long before Freddy. As would Flyers stars Clarke, Parent and Barber.

Arguably, the sticking point was the Hall of Fame's home base—Toronto. Specifically, the issue was what the Broad Street Bullies did to the Leafs in the 1975 and '76 playoffs at the Gardens, with Maple Leafs Nation, millions of indignant fans, watching. The '75 Leafs–Flyers quarter-final was a mismatch: four straight for Philly with a couple of Parent shutouts. As for rough stuff, the biggest injury was to Schultz's pride. Some Leafs fan hung a toy orange gorilla dressed in a Schultz sweater from the Gardens rafters. Signs referred to the Saskatchewan hockey player as "an animal."

"I admit it, I do change on the ice, even though I don't like fighting," a broken Hammer told reporters. "If the guys want me to shake things up, I do. If Clarke tells me to do it, or the coach, I'll muscle up. But off the ice, please make it clear, I'm no animal."

Though the Flyers took it (relatively) easy on the sub–.500 Leafs, saving their energy and elbows for better teams in coming series, Toronto fans were indignant, heckling their own players. In particular, they booed Jim McKenny, a player once thought to be the future of the franchise, all because he wasn't Bobby Orr. Mind you, Leafs fans also booed Number Four of the Bruins because he *was* Bobby Orr. They booed Bobby Clarke, too. At one point in the '75 playoffs, Bobby upended Lanny McDonald, skating off to let Moose Dupont deal with the angry Leafs rookie.

"Suck-suck-suck," Leafs fans chanted.

Clearly, this wasn't simply about Philadelphia. It was about the Leafs, in their beautiful Great Lakes–blue jerseys, outfits once worn by champions Syl Apps and Teeder Kennedy—being pushed around by an expansion team wearing orange softball jerseys. Maple Leafs fans hated the Philadelphia Flyers for what they were. And what the Leafs weren't.

Winners.

The '76 playoffs were different, though: Toronto youngsters McDonald and Darryl Sittler were now stars. Leafs Nation had also fallen for a Laplander, Borje Salming—an agile, effortless skater. Everyone knew BJ's story. The NHL's first European star was the grandson of a reindeer herder; dad Erland died when Borje was five. Toronto immediately took to the orphaned Swede. The puck-rushing defender was named a star in his first game at the Gardens. He wasn't yet fluent in English and had no idea what was going on when he was pushed back onto the ice for a final bow. He saw Sittler do a little circle and wave, so he did the same; hearing the cheers, his mournful face broke into a wide, little-kid grin.

Ping! Leafs fans all over Canada were in love.

Salming had sand in his game. After mixing it up with a Barrie Flyer, he was tossed from the exhibition game that Leafs scout Gerry McNamara saw him play in a Christmas tournament in Sweden in 1972. But the Barrie Flyers, a senior hockey team from southern Ontario, weren't related to Philadelphia's Flyers, who in middle of game three of the quarter-finals on April 15, 1976, with a Leafs win apparently a foregone conclusion, decided to stop playing hockey and, what the hell, take out the other team's best player.

These were the Broad Street Bullies at their outlaw worst. Before getting Salming, Flyers started a riot, collecting 16 penalties in the second period. They were running everyone and then throwing tantrums upon being sent off. With a few minutes left in the second period of a game the Leafs led 5–3, Saleski and Schultz sat in the penalty box, fuming over deserved infractions. Seeing the infamous, ornery westerners, both of them Stanley Cup champions, acting up in hockey's most famous building was too much for some Toronto fans. "The [fans] . . . were really giving to the players—the language was unbelievable," policeman Art Malloy would tell reporter Howard Berger decades later. "At one point, Schultz reached into the bucket of frozen pucks on the floor of the penalty box, picked up a chunk of ice and threw it into the crowd behind him. . . . Just then, some little five-foot-nothing twit from the next section down ran over and challenged Saleski."

Bobby Orr's voyage of discovery, as chronicled in a Topps hockey card booklet. Note that he's wearing a Bruins-yellow suit to visit a kid in hospital. That's our golden boy!

Bruins pile on Bobby Orr after his Superman-in-flight, Stanley Cup–winning goal in 1970. Bobby's abandoned glove and stick are in the foreground.

Flyers announcer Gene Hart speaks at a disastrous lunch thrown by Philadelphia for CSKA Moscow in 1976. Visitors were late, causing Flyers owner Ed Snider (holding chin) to fume. Fred Shero concentrates on getting ash into tray while plotting his team's revenge: *We'll show them a real Iron Curtain.*

High anxiety: Workers on a Hamilton sky-scraper watch the Canada-Russia 1972 finale. There would be no lunch bag letdown this day.

As seen on TV: Team Canada's Phil Esposito with Russian bodyguard in 1972.

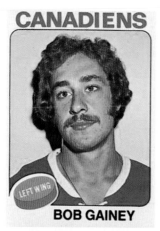

CANADIENS

BOB GAINEY

LEFT WING

RANGERS

BRAD
PARK

DEFENSE

NEW YORK
RANGERS

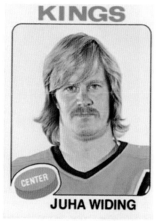

KINGS

JUHA WIDING

CENTER

BLUES

GARRY UNGER

RED WINGS

HENRY BOUCHA

MAPLE LEAFS

DARRYL SITTLER   center

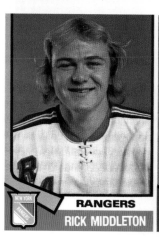

RANGERS

RICK MIDDLETON

NEW YORK
RANGERS

CANUCKS

GARY SMITH

SCOUTS

WILF PAIEMENT • R.WING

The helmetless 1970s were hockey's hairiest decade.

Who points with their middle finger? The ever mysterious Fred Shero tells Bobby Clarke what he wants done. Jimmy Watson looks on.

The Flyers and Vancouver Canucks duke it out in 1973. At the far left, looking on at a fight he probably instigated, is Flyers captain Bobby Clarke.

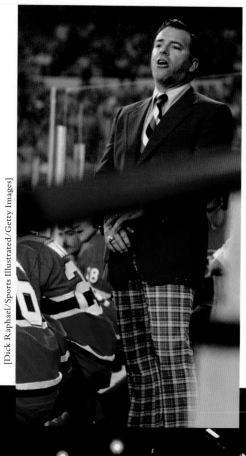

Scotty Bowman behind the bench, but not the times—blue plaid pants were "faire fureur" in 1977.

A winning smile: Bob Gainey accepts the Stanley Cup from captain Serge Savard in 1979.

Bobby Orr after winning the 1976 Canada Cup. The Czechs surprised Team Canada by offering to exchange jerseys after the game—a European soccer custom.

Wild and crazy Habs: Guy Lapointe and Yvon Lambert in the Stanley Cup parade. Their inspiration (inset): Dan Aykroyd and Steve Martin as *Saturday Night Live*'s swinging Czech bachelors, Georg and Yortuk Festrunk.

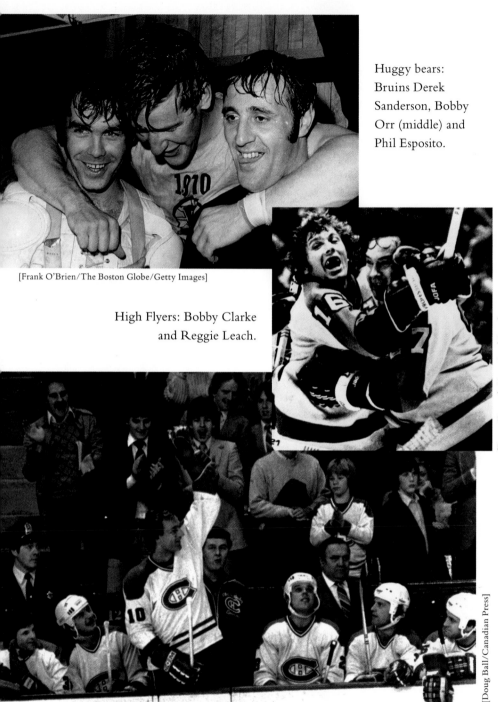

Huggy bears: Bruins Derek Sanderson, Bobby Orr (middle) and Phil Esposito.

[Frank O'Brien/The Boston Globe/Getty Images]

High Flyers: Bobby Clarke and Reggie Leach.

[Rusty Kennedy/Associated Press]

[Doug Ball/Canadian Press]

Meet the new boss: Guy Lafleur acknowledges his 1000th point in 1981. Just to the left of Guy's raised hand is 15-year-old Mario Lemieux, then a Midget AAA sensation with Montreal-Concordia.

"Get the stupid asshole outta here," Malloy hollered to his police partner, Mike Whitworth. Saleski was up now, waving his stick at the fans. Afraid the enraged Flyer might hurt someone, Malloy grabbed Saleski's whirling Koho.

"What are you doing? I've got to protect myself."

"Before they get you, they've got to get through me, so sit down."

Flyers reinforcements soon arrived: Joe Watson jumped the glass, whacking Officer Malloy with his stick. Oh my God, Joe said to himself, realizing what he'd done. Gardens fans let out an outraged howl. So did Ontario Attorney General Roy McMurtry, also in attendance. Watson, Hound Kelly and Saleski would be cooling their heels in a Toronto courtroom the following day, charged with possession of offensive weapons.

A fourth Flyer soon picked up his summons. Earlier in the period, Salming took out Saleski with a clean hip check, sending him folded in half, sprawling to the ice. The Flyers couldn't stand for that, and so they began attacking the young Swede at every opportunity. With time running out in the period, Borje retreated behind his net with the puck. Flyers forward Mel Bridgman bolted after him, elbow out, removing Salming's white Jofa helmet. It was a clear, unprovoked assault. Up went referee Dave Newell's arm. Justifiably angry, Salming found his attacker in front of the Leafs net and pushed Bridgman down. Flyer Jack McIlhargey appeared, cross-checking Salming. Bob Kelly also gave Salming a shot. Leafs fans were up and screaming. Then it was square-dance time: benches emptied and everyone grabbed a partner.

> *Ambulances and big black hearses*
> *Swing those doctors, swing those nurses!*

Minutes later, referee Newell, with the aid of linesmen John D'Amico and Ray Scapinello, appeared to have quelled the disturbance, but just then *Hockey Night in Canada* cameras found Bridgman throwing Salming to the ice. Though scrappy, Borje had little fistic experience, having previously wrestled more than fought Dave Schultz and New York Islander Garry Howatt. Kneeling over his victim, Bridgman landed 11 uncontested, piston-like blows to Salming's head. Borje's wife, Margitta, left Maple Leaf Gardens in tears; Gordon Sinclair, star of CBC's *Front Page Challenge,* followed close behind, telling his old employer, the *Toronto Star,* "I'm totally disgusted." After Newell hauled Bridgman off of a bleeding Salming, viewers saw the referee hollering at Bridgman, a rookie. We can only imagine what he was saying.

What are you doing? The Swedish kid doesn't fight. You want to fight, fight Tiger Williams. He fights. Fighters fight fighters. That's how the game is played up here, rookie.

Joe Watson clobbering a cop and Bridgman's seal-pup slaughter of Salming were replayed in Toronto on CBLT-TV (with Brian Williams), CITY-TV, CFTO and Global for days. Fans saw Bridgman land those 11 punches over and over, making a dreadful attack look even worse. Before all the replays ended, Leafs Nation, a constituency that included several national media outlets and maybe eight million fans, had learned to hate the Philadelphia Flyers.

After the game, Terry Crisp approached Officer Malloy, apologizing for his team. "Don't listen to them, you did your job and everyone's fine." Next day, Watson told the officer he was sorry. After this, he would drop by to visit Malloy whenever he was in the Gardens. All in all, the Flyers were pretty good guys, but it didn't matter: half of Canada (excluding much of the West) now hated Shero's team. Hated Shero, too. And the epicentre of anti-Flyers rage would always be the home of the Hockey Hall of Fame, Toronto. Part of the city's contempt was barely disguised jealousy, no doubt. The Gardens was where hockey became a glorious Canadian obsession; Toronto was where broadcaster Foster Hewitt first uttered the phrase "He shoots, he scores" in 1923. During Philadelphia Flyers broadcasts on WTFX-TV, channel 29, play-by-play man Don Earle shouted, "He shoots, he scores for a case of TastyKakes."*

---

* Pittsburgh baker Philip Baur founded a snack-food business in 1914, quickly

Hoo-boy, how could these vulgar, disorderly parvenus walk off with our Stanley Cup two years in a row? Leafs fans wondered.

Still, there was no getting around it: the Flyers too often made hockey an ugly spectacle, diminishing their chosen sport. Almost as disturbing were the delusional, self-protective lies the organization told itself in defence of unconscionable behaviour. Here was play-by-play man Don Earle on the Flyers home broadcast, summing up Bridgman's attack on Salming: "It was a thumping check that knocked the helmet off of Borje Salming. And Salming, I believe, was the one who threw the check, or at least banged him hard enough to rattle it loose."

Huh?

Some hockey fans back in the States could see how villainous the Flyers could be. In Boston, 11-year-old Conan O'Brien watched the Flyers whack and flay opponents. Years later, when he was writing for the TV show *The Simpsons*, he'd come up with a story featuring one of the very best (and, in some ways, worst) hockey teams of the '70s. A 1993 "Halloween Treehouse of Horrors" special featured a segment entitled "The Devil and Homer Simpson." In it, a slick, slippery lawyer/devil (Ned Flanders) put Homer on trial, hoping to steal his soul. Being the devil, Flanders cheated, stacking the jury with the most awful people in the history of the world. The devil cackled as he unveiled his evil allies.

"Benedict Arnold, Lizzie Borden, Richard Nixon . . . John Wilkes Booth, Bluebeard the Pirate . . .

A long beat, and then the punchline: " . . . and the starting lineup of the 1976 Philadelphia Flyers."

---

taking his business to Germantown in Philadelphia. His partner Herbert Morris's wife reportedly exclaimed, "What a tasty cake!" upon biting into one product. Soon, horse-drawn trucks were schlepping TastyKakes all over Philly. Flyers players once received a case of Kakes (containing between 18 and 24 Family Packs) for scoring a goal. Today, Flyers players donate the snack cakes to charities.

"TELL IT TO THE CZAR"

Red Army vs. Philadelphia Flyers, January 11, 1976

Gary Dornhoefer kept telling his Flyers teammates that the upcoming Sunday afternoon encounter between the Flyers and the Red Army was "just an exhibition." But on the morning of the game, he couldn't keep his breakfast down. At the Spectrum, Joe Watson passed anti-Soviet protesters carrying placards reading FREE SOVIET JEWS to find an accordion-sized message in the locker room. Look at this, he told teammates, unfurling a telegram with 4,000 signatures from his hometown. (How was that even possible? There weren't quite that many people in all of Smithers, British Columbia.)

Earlier in the week, at Maple Leaf Gardens, the Flyers had beaten the Leafs 7–3 and received a standing ovation. That's right, a standing O . . . *in Toronto.* Leafs fans followed the Flyers to their bus, chanting, "Beat Russia! Beat Russia!" Looking around, Joe Watson said to himself, *Holy shit, this really means a lot to everybody.* Yes, it did. Hockey's first Sunday afternoon Super Bowl would be viewed by untold millions in Russia, along with every hockey fan in Canada and the United States. And what a matchup! You had your Eastern champs, the Central Red Army, winner of 19 national championships, fortified by the inclusion of stars Alexander Maltsev and Valeri Vasiliev, both from Moscow Dynamo, against your Western champs, the Stanley Cup–winning Flyers, minus Bernie Parent, out with a neck injury.

The Broad Street Bullies vs. the Big Red Machine.

The Red Army had enjoyed its tour of North America to date, pushing aside the New York Rangers and Boston Bruins by lopsided scores—7–3 and 5–2—while playing Montreal to a thrilling, three-all New Year's Eve tie. Away from the rink, they'd managed to enrich themselves culturally, taking up three rows at a Montreal adult movie theatre (Cinema L'Amour); in Boston, they basked in hellfire, eyeing waitresses in tight black leotards at a hot disco called Lucifer's.

Do the hustle, ooh, do it, ooh, do it!

For the Flyers, the Russians were house guests from hell—complaining and late for everything. On the Saturday, the Flyers invited their opponents to lunch. Play-by-play man Gene Hart spoke Russian and had prepared gracious welcoming comments for owner Ed Snider. But the Red Army, bivouacked in a hotel five minutes away, rolled in more than a half-hour late for the ceremony. The Flyers sat there, fuming, filling up on rolls, sure that the Russkies were trying to mess with their afternoon practice. Earlier, the Red Army had asked that the Flyers provide them with extra sticks. They were running out, they said. OK, the Flyers wrestled up an assortment of Jofas. The Russians said they weren't good enough. Nor did they want the heavy glass pyramid sculptures the Flyers organization had created for them as goodwill mementos.

We play Team Canada, they give us gold watch—expensive, very nice. This glaz brick or something, ptttt . . .

When Snider saw Red Army players snickering during Hart's comments, he decided the hell with it, he wasn't going to say anything. The Flyers, meanwhile, tried to stare down the Soviets, employing fellow Philly heavyweight Joe Frazier's pre-fight penitentiary glare. "I hate the sons of bitches," Bobby Clarke told reporters.

After the strained luncheon, Shero, Clarke and assistant coach Mike Nykoluk (who had followed the Red Army on their tour) met to discuss strategy for the forthcoming title match. Freddy had also been watching the Red Army in his office late at night, chain-smoking, going over reel after reel of game film. And he had a plan: "We'll show them a *real* Iron Curtain," he told Clarke and Nykoluk.

Shero had seen how the Russians liked to set up big plays—lots of weaving drop passes, then—*boom!*—a long bomb to a breaking winger two lines away. They killed Montreal with sudden two-on-ones and breakaways. Shero's solution was to play the hockey equivalent of a football prevent defence—keeping his defence and two forwards back at the Flyers blue line, with a centre up forechecking. In the offensive zone, he wanted the Flyers to hang on to the puck in the corners, passing back and forth. The Russians didn't use the body, so they'd never get the puck off Dornhoefer, Saleski or Barber, he figured. Keep the puck around the boards, Shero told Clarke. If you have to kill the puck to force a whistle, go ahead; the Russians are lousy at faceoffs anyway.

And so, in one short session in the winter of 1976, Fred Shero anticipated two big coaching breakthroughs of the 1990s and 2000s—the neutral-zone trap and cycling in corners to weary and bewilder opponents.

A half hour before game time, the Flyers were beyond tense, ready to come out of their skin. It didn't help that Clarence Campbell, who had had nothing good to say about Philly in the past, came into their dressing room for a pep talk.

Boys, the whole league is depending on you. Hockey is a wonderful sport. And I know you will agree with me in thinking that it's our sport. As you know, no NHL team has been able to beat Red Army so far. That's why I'm . . .

When Campbell and other league executives exited the dressing room, Joe Watson stood up and shouted, "Screw these NHL guys! Let's win this for ourselves." Elsewhere in the Spectrum, Fred Shero recorded a message for *Hockey Night in Canada*—just him staring into a camera, stiff as a hockey stick: "As far as this game is concerned, it's going to be the highlight of my life. If we win, I'm going to be sky-high, and if we lose, I think it'll be worse than dying. I'm ready. My team is ready. And I believe we're going to win, thank you."

Eleven days into America's bicentennial year, the opening ceremony to the Red Army–Flyers game was a patriotic doozy—klieg lights found Soviet starters as they were introduced in what was an otherwise darkened, silent building. (Although if you listened carefully, you could hear some fan shout, "Y'guys are bums!" before Alexander Maltsev was announced.) Then the gum-chewing Flyers skated into the spotlight and a series of thunderous ovations. Bobby Clarke received the biggest welcome. The next-loudest roar was for Kate Smith, on tape, belting out what had been FDR's campaign song on the eve of America's entrance into World War II. Everyone in the Spectrum joined in singing:

> *God bless America*
> *Land that I love*
> *Stand beside her, and guide her*
> *Through the night with a light from above . . .*

When the puck was finally dropped, Maltsev won the draw and the Red Army carousel whirled into gear—12 short passes in 20 seconds before the Soviets lost the puck at the Flyers blue line. The Flyers carried play after that, following Shero's orders with characteristic brio. Saleski, Kindrachuk, Barber and Dornhoefer dawdled with the puck, elbows out, in corners, and the defence and back-checking wingers secured the Flyers blue line. The Red Army skated in circles, looking in vain for an opening. Flyers counterattacks were relentless; Shero's plan was working. Midway through the first period, the Flyers had directed 18 shots at the

Russian net, the Red Army just three long shots at the Flyers' Wayne Stephenson. Then came the game's defining interlude.

Killing a penalty, Clarke skated into the Russian end and was knocked flat by a suddenly *there* Vasiliev. Good, clean hip check, but the Spectrum let out an angry, expectant groan—*Hey!* No one messed with Bobby, not in Philly. Seconds later, Maltsev performed a dive when Van Impe escorted him away from the play. Up went a referee's arm. Now the Flyers were really mad; the crowd, too. On the ensuing power play, the Red Army failed to record a shot on net. Near the end of the man advantage, Moose Dupont demolished Alexander Gusev with a jolting check—*big roar.* Down at the other end, Barber took out Vasiliev with an elbow (not called) and then flattened Kharlamov with a powerful shoulder check, sending him flying—*bigger roar.* This was Flyers hockey, belting everything in sight, feeding on the enthusiasm of a delirious Spectrum crowd.

The Red Army still had the puck, attacking the Flyers end just as Van Impe raced from the penalty box. Boris Mikhailov held up along the right boards and fed a still-woozy Kharlamov. A speeding Van Impe got there at the same time, bowling over the Red Army's star forward. Van Impe was just under six feet; Kharlamov, five feet, eight inches. Maybe Van Impe hit Kharlamov with part of his elbow. Might've been a penalty, but it wasn't called.

Kharlamov squirmed, tried to get up, and then collapsed. Russian hockey players were plenty tough. Vasiliev, born in a Gorky slum, would play through the 1978 world championships with a tightening in his chest. Returning to Moscow, he finally relented to a cardiogram and discovered he'd suffered a heart attack. Still, Soviet players were also known to resort to theatrics, hoping to draw penalties. In fact, they were almost as bad as the Flyers' Bill Barber. (After a Barber bellyflop, referee Don Koharski once skated past the sliding Flyers forward and commented, "I hate to tell you, son, but the pool's frozen over.") Who knows how hurt Kharlamov really was. But referee Lloyd Gilmour lost any sympathy for the fallen winger when Russian linesman Yuri Karanedin glided by

Kharlamov and muttered, "*Ostat'sya vniz.*" Seconds later, linesman Matt Pavelich, a Croat from Sudbury, Ontario, who could speak Russian, approached Gilmour and said, "He told Kharlamov to stay down to draw a major penalty." Growing upset, Gilmour skated over to the Red Army bench and warned them that if they didn't return to the ice soon, he was giving them a delay-of-game penalty.

Coach Konstantin Loktev screamed at Gilmour through an interpreter, "We never play against such animal hockey." When the Soviets refused to budge, Gilmour gave them two minutes, as promised. With that, the Red Army filed out of the rink. Play-by-play man Bob Cole—like Keith Allen, a big Sinatra fan—made like Ol' Blue Eyes in the *Hockey Night in Canada* booth, as if he were ad libbing an ending for a Vegas showstopper: "They're gonna go . . . They're goin' home. They're goin' home—*yeah!* They're goin' home . . . Can you believe it?"

Two years earlier, the Soviet Wings had done the same thing in a game against the New Haven Nighthawks of the American Hockey League. Coach Boris Kulagin pulled his team to force the reversal of a penalty. Gilmour, though, wouldn't budge. Alan Eagleson, Clarence Campbell, Ed Snider and the Soviet delegation argued in the bowels of the Spectrum. The Flyers, meanwhile, stayed on the ice, skating and peppering untested Wayne Stephenson in the Flyers net. "Lookit, they're gonna play, they want the money," old Russia hand Fred Shero told his players. *Hockey Night in Canada* filled the 16-minute delay with commentary and commercials, including one for a Tom Jones *20 Greatest Hits* package on Tee Vee Records ($7.99 for a double vinyl record album, $10.99 for twin eight-track cartridges). On the ice, Philadelphia's famous sign man, the curly-haired, moustachioed Dave Leonardi,* sorted through his fat leather

---

* Dave Leonardi felt mute sitting behind the glass in the Spectrum—in that space, no one could hear you scream, to paraphrase the tagline to the classic '70s sci-fi movie *Alien*. So early in the 1972–73 season, he brought printed signs to games. The Flyers' radio crew soon incorporated his cartoon-balloon commentary into their broadcasts: TKO SCHULTZ after the Hammer won a fight or NEXT GOALIE

satchel of over 100 alphabetized placards, finding and holding up the perfect response to a sulking Red Army deserting its post:

TELL IT TO THE CZAR!

Shero was right. The Soviets returned when told that, if they quit now, they wouldn't get their share of the gate. Although the game was still scoreless, the Red Army was a beaten team. Seconds after the game resumed, Reggie Leach threw the puck into the Soviet end, arriving in the corner about the same time as Vladimir Lokotko. Bracing for a hit, the Red Army defender hurried a blind pass off the boards. Forward Vladimir Vikulov shied away from Barber at the point, and the Flyers' Number Seven lobbed a shot at the net that Leach, racing from the corner, deflected past Tretiak. Minutes later, Kharlamov got rid of the puck to avoid Ross Lonsberry, who intercepted his pass, catching MacLeish on a breakaway. The Hawk whistled a high shot over Tretiak's shoulder, prompting an involuntary shout from guest TV commentator Denis Potvin of the New York Islanders in the *Hockey Night in Canada* booth.

"Oh, perfect."

Early in the second period, the Flyers made it 3–0 with a man short (Dupont was in the box) as a falling Joe Watson flipped a rebound past Tretiak. A stay-at-home defender, Watson had scored only one other goal this season. As he skated past the bench, coach Shero shouted, "Hey Joe, you just set Russian hockey back 20 years."

Years later, Tretiak explained Red Army's desultory 4–1 loss against the Flyers, a game they were outshot 49–13, by writing, "Everything was turned inside-out. We did not play, we merely skated." Some argued that the Red Army caught the Philly Flu, a deadly strain of the original Flin Flon Flu. Maybe a few players did. But no one could argue

---

when the score got out of hand for Philly. Dave would become a minor star when American and Canadian TV crews began cutting to him during the action—yet another example of how fans intruded on sports action in the '70s.

that the great Soviet players—Kharlamov, Mikhailov or Vasiliev—were afraid of the Flyers. They had endured so much to get here. The Russian Hockey Federation played worse mind games on its own players than it did on its opponents.

A Russian biopic of Kharlamov released in 2012 would document how coach Anatoli Tarasov broke the mercurial star, the son of a factory worker and a Basque refugee from the Spanish Civil War. "The Spaniard" was too showy, too flamboyant, Tarasov believed. The coach was also offended by Kharlamov's declaration "I like to score beautiful goals." Other players were ordered to humiliate the young forward. Boiling water was poured on his hands. During Red Army games, Number 17 sat in the stands, fully dressed, doing penance for his athletic conceits. After a game, he was called onto the ice and forced to stand in front of the net while teammates took shots at him. After the firing squad, he couldn't move, let alone play hockey. Next game, he was allowed to join teammates on the bench, where he sat quietly until, midway through the game, the coach decided he'd been scrubbed free of ego and was ready to play selfless Soviet hockey.

"Petrov, Mikhailov," Tarasov called out . . . and then, finally, "Kharlamov!"

The Red Army weren't so much afraid of Dupont, Schultz and Saleski as they were fatally discouraged by the Flyers' blueline Iron Curtain— Shero called it his 1–4 defence (one roaming forechecker, four back at the blue line). For sure, Flyers hitting also took its toll. In the fall of 1974, Yvan Cournoyer told *Hockey* magazine the Flyers would never be able to keep it up. "The more they hit the more tired they get," he predicted. "By playoff time, the Flyers will be exhausted." Two and a half years later, the Flyers were still hitting. Still winning, too. They'd already beaten Boston and Buffalo for the Stanley Cup and had now knocked off the Red Army to win hockey's Super Bowl. After the final horn, the three stars, all Flyers—MacLeish, Dornhoefer and Saleski—took their ceremonial bows, while the game's only injured player, Clarke, recipient of an accidental Russian high stick, had the ugly gash on his forehead inspected. Before heading off to a refurbished Rexy's, the Flyers undertook one last diplomatic mission. With no interpreters, league officials or Soviet gatekeepers in attendance, they knocked on the Russians' dressing-room door.

"They were drinking straight vodka and beer," Joe Watson would remember decades later. "So we drank vodka and beer with them." Some players traded hats and clothing. For Clarke, it would be his second drinking session with Russian players. After game eight in Moscow in 1972, Valeri Vasiliev, wearing a lopsided grin, sought out Clarke, inviting him into the Russian dressing room. "They were all sitting around eating and drinking," Clarke later told the *Philadelphia Inquirer.* "Vasiliev got the bottle of vodka out, and we were chugging it."

Once you replaced pucks and sticks with vodka and beer, Russian and Canadian hockey players got along pretty well. That shouldn't have been much of a surprise. On a 1976 Canadian tour to promote a book and film series on Russia, writer/actor Peter Ustinov told the *Globe and Mail,* "Russians resemble no other people on earth more closely than they do Canadians. They share the Canadian sense of awe and loneliness living in a broad, unknowable country, and, like Canadians, take pride in their stubborn ability to survive winters that make the outdoors a killing ground."

OGIE OGILTHORPE

Near the end of the Philadelphia Flyers' championship reign, owner Ed Snider wrote a fan letter to libertarian firebrand Ayn Rand. "Dear Miss Rand, I have two sons in college and they've been taught all kinds of Marxist and socialist ideas, and I would love to have your philosophy taught in every Philosophy class in America . . ." The object of his affection summoned Snider to New York. They became friends. Months later, Rand's protege Leonard Peikoff delivered a lecture at the University of Pennsylvania entitled "The Virtue of Selfishness."

Snider learned about Rand at, of all places, an NHL meeting. The owners were deliberating over some deal—maybe the bailout of an expansion franchise (the Kansas City Scouts wilted and folded after two seasons, becoming the Colorado Rockies in 1976). "Why are we voting against our own self-interest?" Snider asked seatmate Peter O'Malley. The president of the Washington Capitals scribbled something on a scrap of paper. Snider unfolded the note: *Atlas Shrugged*. "Read it," O'Malley said. The 1957 novel hit Snider like a Dave Schultz check. In

Rand's future dystopia, supermen business leaders are brought down by socialist do-gooders. Vital industries collapse. Before long, the home of the brave is boarded up by regulators. Same thing could happen here, Snider believed.

Every year, the NHL introduced some rule to handicap the Flyers: in 1974, referees began calling bench minors if players didn't proceed directly to the penalty box. The gross misconduct penalty was a response to Bobby Clarke spitting at referee Ron Wicks (making it grosser still, Bobby chewed tobacco). The real bother was a 1976 league edict allowing for a game misconduct to anyone instigating a fight.

Still, the NHL was losing the battle against lawlessness. In the 1973–74 season, four teams exceeded 1,000 penalty minutes. That spring, the Flyers won their first Cup. The following campaign, 15 out of 18 NHL clubs smashed past the 1,000 penalty-minute mark, and police were now routinely being called upon to settle riots. Oh, how hockey had changed! From 1917 through 1967, only one NHLer had been arrested for on-ice violence: in 1922, Sprague Cleghorn was fined $50 for attacking Lionel Hitchman. Between 1969 and 1976, 16 players ended up in court—nine of them Flyers. When Toronto police threw the book at the Flyers during the 1976 playoffs, *Toronto Star* sports columnist Jim Proudfoot applauded the bust, writing an open letter to the Flyers in the voice of NHL president Clarence Campbell.

"Lawless and violence are now accepted in American cities," Proudfoot-as-Campbell wrote. "In fact, our American fans demand it: they get bored with anything less. But the one place they clamped down on us is Toronto. So kindly behave yourself in [Maple Leaf Gardens]."

The snooty anti-Americanism was a bit much. After all, the Flyers would be the last entirely Canadian team to win a Stanley Cup. And the week Philadelphia clobbered poor Borje Salming, police also broke up hockey riots in Quebec City and Vancouver. At Le Colisée, Rick Jodzio of the WHA's Calgary Cowboys was arrested for clubbing Marc Tardif of the Nordiques, leaving him with permanent brain damage. Days later, another Wild West saloon fight broke out during the BC/Alberta Junior

A finals between the Spruce Grove Mets and Nor-Wes Caps. There were 18 battles in all, including a bench-clearing brawl involving players and coaches. (Mark Messier's older brother, Paul, played for the Mets.)

Campbell hated the Flyers. He also believed the world was falling apart. Referee Ron Wicks was with him in the stands in April 1968 at the precise moment hockey turned into an indictable pastime: "I was [spare referee] in the crowd when Noel Picard of the St. Louis Blues ambushed [the Flyers'] Claude Laforge, then got into a fight with Ed Van Impe," Wicks said. "After that, he skated over to the Flyers bench and waved at everyone as if to say, 'Who's next?' Fans were hollering and the Philadelphia police were ready to move in. And I remember Mr. Campbell saying, 'I fear for a civil insurrection.'" Of course, to believe that hockey violence fed off the world let the NHL president off the hook—*Hey, it's not my fault.* Not that referees believed Campbell was responsible for what was happening on the ice. "Clarence no more ran the National Hockey League than that plant over there," an ex-referee told a meeting of members of the Society for International Hockey Research in Toronto in the fall of 2013. "The owners—[Chicago's] Bill Wirtz and Ed Snider—called the shots."

Campbell understood only too well that he served at the pleasure of owners. A former referee, he was fired by Leafs owner Conn Smythe in 1939, reputedly for missing a major penalty on Toronto star Red Horner. Stafford Smythe, president of the Leafs in the '60s, famously said of the distinguished NHL executive, "Where else could we find a Rhodes scholar, a graduate lawyer, decorated war hero and former prosecutor at the Nuremberg trials, who'd do what he was told?" Montreal GM Sam Pollock was more sympathetic. "[Campbell] guided the league through some extremely rough periods, especially between 1972 and 1975," Pollock once said. "There were rules in place, but . . . for whatever reason, maybe not the appetite [to pursue them]."

For whatever reason?

I asked Wicks to comment on a popular view of "what happened" to hockey in the '70s: that owners encouraged fighting to sell the sport in the United States. "That's one of those 'What do you think of my wife?' questions you should never ask or answer," he told me, laughing. "I made my living for a long time working for the NHL."

Colleague Bruce Hood would be more forthright. "You know, I think the league was caught up in a lot of different things," he told me. "There was expansion, trying to make the league work in new cities; there was the threat of the WHA . . . international hockey . . ."

So whose fault was it that '70s hockey so often required police intervention? Not Ayn Rand's, certainly. Hood would have the most reasonable explanation. "I think it just happened while people who should have been dealing with the problem were too busy doing other things."

The Flyers were worthy champions. A close inspection of their defining wins—the 1974 and 1975 sixth-game Stanley Cup final victories over Boston and Buffalo, along with the January 1976 Super Bowl defeat of the Red Army, reveals their mastery of disciplined, defence-first hockey. Collapse the final periods of all three games into a single match and the Flyers won 3–0, allowing 14 shots, while taking just four minutes in penalties. At the time, Philadelphia's greatness was acknowledged: Clarke would win three MVP trophies (as many as Orr or Mario); he was also named captain of the legendary 1976 Team Canada that included Orr, Phil Esposito and Bobby Hull; head coach Scotty Bowman's number one line for that tourney was Philly's L-C-B unit (Reggie Leach, Bobby Clarke, Bill Barber). After he masterminded the defeat of Red Army in January of 1976, *Hockey Night in Canada* was ready to give Freddy Shero the Order of Canada.

"Every Canadian has every right to be proud of [Shero], his system and all his players," said commentator Howie Meeker.

"Well, it is not done, it has never been done, but maybe it should have been done today, but I think Freddy Shero was star of this afternoon," concluded host Dave Hodge. Even Clarence Campbell acknowledged Philly's supreme achievement. "Our best beat their best," he said.

In time, though, the Flyers' accomplishments faded. Shero didn't make the Hall of Fame for almost 40 years. Outside of Pennsylvania, the term *Broad Street Bullies* would often be pronounced with a sneer. Partly this was because the Flyers were, well . . . ruffians. Here is Montreal goalie Ken Dryden's level-headed assessment of the team from his 1983 memoir, *The Game*.

> *The Broad Street Bullies were a hugely intimidating team. I saw the admirable and the contemptible side by side, the simple, courageous game they played, their discipline and dedication. Bobby Clarke, Bernie Parent, their no-name defence, Fred Shero. It was the way they turned a hockey wasteland into something vibrant and exciting. It wasn't the brawling and intimidation that turned me. It was their sense of impunity. They were bullies. They showed contempt for everyone and everything. They took on the league, its referees and teams; they took on fans, cops, the courts and politicians. They searched out weakness, found it, trampled it, then preened with their cock-of-the-walk swagger—"C'mon, ya chicken, I dare ya!"*

Further damaging their legacy, the upstart Flyers ran roughshod over hockey's eastern establishment—media centres crowded with pundits and historians. Moose Dupont stampeded Orr at the Boston Garden in 1973. New York would always remember Hammer Schultz punching out Dale Rolfe in the 1974 semifinals. In Toronto, home of the Hockey Hall of Fame, it was the keelhauling of Borje Salming during the '76 quarter-finals. Montreal would never forget a 1974 Sunday afternoon home game (an hour after high mass!) when Schultz KO'd John Van Boxmeer with a sucker punch; in the resulting brouhaha, police spilled onto the ice to shoo away *Allo Police* photographers.

Another group of storytellers ultimately damaged the Flyers' legacy. On Friday, February 25, 1977, Hollywood released an entertaining film that captured hockey's unruly, wayward drift. But first, the NHL provided a trailer. That Thursday, the mustard-coloured Los Angeles Kings, with recently traded Dave Schultz in the lineup, welcomed the Vancouver Canucks to the Fabulous Forum with open fists. There would be nine fights in all, including a bench-clearing brawl at game's end—40 players on the ice, 120 sticks and gloves tossed aside, 35 or so slow dances and eight actual fights, including three separate brawls involving Schultz and Canuck tough guy Harold Snepsts, who remained together like a couple in a bad marriage, unable to either stop fighting or let go.

Hours later, Paul Newman's *Slap Shot* opened across North America. The movie followed a hockey team that was literally fighting for survival, a very topical storyline at the time. In addition to the Scouts of Kansas City, the Cleveland Barons, San Diego Mariners, Jersey Knights, Indianapolis Racers and hornet-coloured Cincinnati Stingers were just a few NHL and WHA teams that came and went in the '70s. In the minors, there was more turnover still. In Virginia alone, you had and then you didn't have the Richmond Robins, Tidewater Wings, Tidewater Sharks, Virginia Wings, and Hampton Wings.

Slap Shot was the story of another Virginia team—the Charlestown Chiefs. Screenwriter Nancy Dowd planted a tape recorder on the bus and in the dressing room of brother Ned's Pennsylvania-based Johnstown Jets. (The club played in the North American Hockey League, a WHA farm system.) Though fictional, Dowd's story was as real as rent due—an aging minor leaguer, Reggie Dunlop, tries to save the Chiefs from foreclosure by turning hockey into a burlesque act, beating up every team in sight. His secret weapons: the Hanson Brothers, a dim-witted forward line who played slot cars in their hotel room by day . . . and demolition derby hockey at night. Almost all of the characters were based on real hockey players. In the mid-'70s, Johnstown was the very buckle of the northeastern rust belt, a region suffering from mill and mine closures. But it was also a hockey city; the Jets, a former Montreal franchise, had been around since 1950—Rocket Richard played there in a 1951 exhibition game. Now they'd resorted to goon hockey to stay alive. The Hanson brothers were inspired by Jeff, Steve and Jack Carlson, Minnesota siblings who played with toy cars, sported Buddy Holly glasses and amassed 754 minutes in penalties—not including suspensions, the odd week off for bad behaviour—during the Jets' championship 1974–75 season. Newman's character, Reggie Dunlop, was based on minor-league legend John Brophy, later a coach for the Toronto Maple Leafs—a silver-haired, beer-guzzling rogue who once, after being spat on by a fan leaning over the boards, responded by catching the perp with the butt end of his stick, freeing several teeth.

"Now spit, motherfucker," Broph hollered.

Slap Shot included one more notable real-life character. The king of the castle of minor-league hockey horrors, the player everyone feared more than having to find a real job, was Ogie Ogilthorpe. In real life, that would be Bill "Goldie" Goldthorpe, 18 times arrested, stabbed and shot in the stomach, but never rehabilitated, never tamed. Bob Costas began his award-winning career as a sports announcer for the North American Hockey League Syracuse Blazers and, decades later, remembered an encounter with Goldthorpe during an NBC broadcast of an NHL game.

We're riding the bus from Syracuse to some outpost . . . I made the mistake of sitting in my seat, I thought minding my own business, reading the New York Times, and this mere fact alone offended Goldthorpe and he reached over my shoulder, grabbed the paper from my hands and tore it up into shreds and let it fall like New Year's confetti on the floor of the moving bus. I probably should have let it go at that, but I was 21 years old, so I looked at him and I said, "Don't be jealous, Goldie, I'll teach you to read."

Blazers coach Ron Ingram and a makeshift SWAT team jumped in to protect the Syracuse announcer.

In *Slap Shot*, Goldthorpe's alter ego would be mentioned, always with a gulp, 20-some times before he was finally introduced: "Oh, this young man has had a very trying rookie season, with the litigation, the notoriety, his subsequent deportation to Canada and that country's refusal to accept him, well, I guess that's more than most 21-year-olds can handle . . . Ogie Ogilthorpe!" Another true story: one of Goldie's many arrests came after he got into a fight with a teammate on the tarmac of an airport in

Green Bay, Wisconsin. Two Canadian immigration officials were required to escort him back to his native Thunder Bay.

Slap Shot's best insider hockey joke occurs when Ogie finally jumps onto the screen and we see that he is wearing—what else?—a pumpkin-orange Philadelphia Flyers uniform.

[Bruce Bennett/Getty Images]

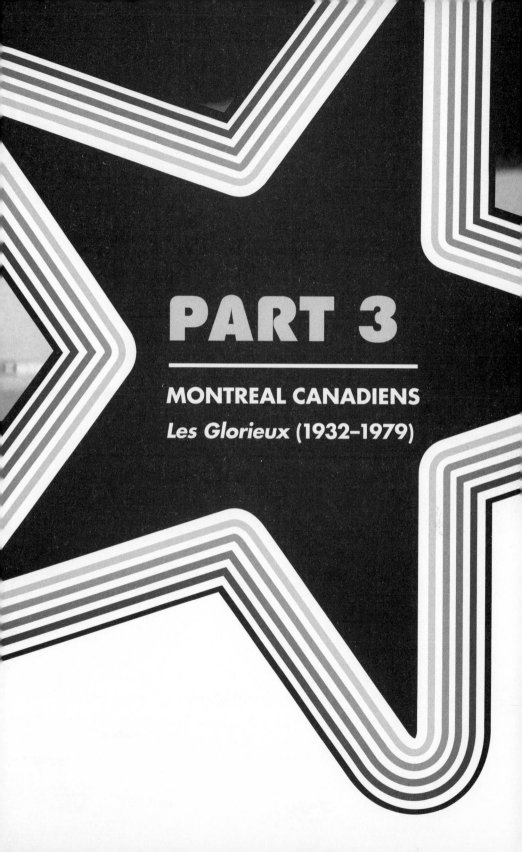

PART 3

MONTREAL CANADIENS
Les Glorieux (1932–1979)

A CIVIL WAR

In the fall of 1956, Montreal GM Frank Selke made a rare sortie into the Forum dressing room. "Boys, with Butch Bouchard gone, there's only one of you who should replace him as captain," Selke said. "I'm going to give each of you a ballot, and I want you to write one name on it. I'll be disappointed if you all don't vote for Maurice Richard." At the time, Butch was one of two great Habs leaders. The strapping defenceman also ran a popular restaurant, Chez Butch Bouchard, not far from the Forum. When the mob "requested" that Butch hire one of its guys to ensure that business ran smoothly, he invited a city crime boss to dinner. "Il lui a dit over my dead body," is how Butch remembered the meeting ending.

The obvious candidate to replace Bouchard was former defence partner Doug Harvey, a Montreal boy from Notre-Dame-de-Grâce (NDG) who ruled the dressing room with wisecracks and the occasional glare. On the ice, the perennial all-star was team quarterback. Hearing Selke endorse the Rocket as captain, players studied their skates. "Hell, there were times when Rocket couldn't captain himself," Bert Olmstead would later tell *The Globe and Mail*'s Dick Beddoes. The Canadiens accepted Richard as their symbolic leader, but, as Olmstead put it, "We went right on cementing around Doug Harvey."

Despite a diminutive frame and reserved nature, 60-year-old Selke went out of his way to befriend the volatile Richard. The two men hunted deer together in late fall, sometimes driving back to Montreal with a white-tailed stag atop their car, to be dropped off at Butch's restaurant. Days later, Canadiens players and wives would show up for a feast—venison, no doubt served with pearled onions, mushrooms and carrots stewed in red wine and cognac. There would be music—Butch's cocktail lounge was graced both by international (Charles Aznavour) and Quebec singers (Dominique Michel and Denise Filiatrault). These bois-terous team parties lasted into the wee hours. The Canadiens were big on celebrations; every Stanley Cup win—there were ten from 1953 to 1969—ended with a binge at coach Toe Blake's tavern at Ste-Catherine and Guy, an easy walk from the Forum. Hot sandwiches washed down with quarts of Molson Brador (6 per cent malt liquor!). Those driving home wisely signalled OK, for O'Keefe Old Vienna.

Upon retiring in 1960, Richard began an office job with the Canadiens, but that didn't work out—Rockets were only good when set afire, after all. Given little to do, he quit in 1964. Selke became nervous. Habs public relations director Camille DesRoches tried to placate him. "Richard is not God," he said.

"No, but in Quebec, he is very close to the pope," the GM sighed. The smartest, most successful GM of his time, Selke understood that the symbolic leader of the Canadiens had to inspire fans. *Les Glorieux* were at their best with a shouting crowd at their back, pleading for victory. That was why the GM had wanted Richard—a hero of the people—as captain in the first place.

In the spring of 1971, Selke's successor, Sam Pollock, was faced with his own tricky personnel challenge. After upsetting Boston and Chicago to take another championship, Habs captain Jean Béliveau retired, as did alternate captain John Ferguson. Montreal was in search of the next

Rocket Richard (though a new Béliveau would do). Fortunately, they had six (!) first- or second-round picks in the June draft; this at a time when Quebec was a virtual Cadillac assembly line of hockey talent. Someday, an enterprising scholar will explain why the 15-year battle for Quebec's soul, the simultaneous 1968–84 reigns of Canadian prime minister Pierre Elliot Trudeau and separatist Parti Québécois leader René Lévesque, would coincide with the most fertile period in French-Canadian hockey history.

Quebec's Michel Plasse, Réjean Houle and Gilbert Perreault were the NHL's number one draft picks in 1968, 1969 and 1970. Junior hockey's 1973 Cadillac Eldorado was Denis Potvin. Michel Bossy turned out to be the best player in the '77 draft. Raymond Bourque, as close as Boston would ever get to another Bobby Orr, arrived in 1979. The premier goalie of the modern era, Patrick Roy, landed with the 1984 graduating class. Every year, a new francophone 50-goal scorer would emerge, it seemed—Bossy, Marc Tardif, Jacques Richard, Pierre Larouche, Michel Goulet, Réal Cloutier, Luc Robitaille, Stéphane Richer and, best of all, Mario Lemieux arrived in the NHL and WHA between 1968 and 1984. Each registered at least one 50-goal season. In Verdun, three kids named Denis (Savard, Côté and Tremblay) were born on the same street—indeed, *on the same day* (February 4, 1961), growing up to become a famous junior line, *Les Trois Denis. Deux Denis* made the NHL—Côté and Savard. The latter enjoyed a 500-goal career.

Nor did the francophone hockey baby boom end in Quebec. Two-time MVP Bryan Trottier was a Métis from Saskatchewan. Hockey immortal Mark Messier sprang from a Franco-Albertan community—St. Albert. Michigan's Pat LaFontaine, son of French-Canadian parents, grew up idolizing francophone hockey players.

And how could you not count Wilf Paiement (class of '79), a Franco-Ontarian star whose professional wrestler father, Wilf Sr., broke the arm of a 470-pound bear in a 1938 Quebec City arm-wrestling exhibition?

To Montreal's great fortune, the 1971 junior draft represented the best ever French-Canadian graduating class. The highest-rated goalie

(Michel DeGuise), defenceman (Jocelyn Guevremont), and the three top forwards—Guy Lafleur, Marcel Dionne and Richard Martin—were all Quebecers. Lafleur and Dionne were reputed to be once-in-a-generation players . . . potential superstars, as good as Béliveau or Hull maybe. (In junior, Lafleur and Dionne even wore Béliveau's and Hull's numbers—four and nine.)

Despite the French hockey boom, few young stars actually played Quebec junior hockey. The province's best team, the Montreal Jr. Canadiens, operated in the Ontario Hockey Association (OHA), where they were very successful, breezing to Memorial Cups in 1969 and '70. Led by the dazzling Perreault, the baby Habs capped their second national title by humiliating Vladislav Tretiak in an exhibition game, outscoring the Soviet national team 9–2.

Montreal had moved its junior team to the OHA in 1961, it should be explained. The Ontario league had won eight of the previous 11 Memorial Cups at the time, and was rougher and more physical than the Quebec leagues—all in all, an ideal place to acclimatize francophone players to the NHL, the Habs figured. Given the sudden profusion of French junior talent, OHA teams had begun raiding Quebec in the late '60s. Michel "Bunny" Larocque and Denis Potvin, two boys from western Quebec, hopped the Ottawa River to star for the 67's. But the biggest defection would be St. Catharines Black Hawk Marcel Dionne, a squat, speedy waterbug who could pinball through traffic undisturbed, setting up and scoring goals in record numbers.

On his way to a second consecutive OHA scoring title in 1970–71, Marcel was totalled by Toronto Marlboro heavyweight Glenn Goldup—out of the lineup six weeks with a separated shoulder. Dionne returned home to Drummondville, crying for two days, then came back with a few weeks left in the season to score in grapelike clusters, winning the scoring race (over Toronto's Dave Gardner and Steve Shutt) going away, compiling 62 goals and 81 assists—an astonishing 143 points in 46 games.

One great French-Canadian junior stayed home, refining his game against the Trois-Rivières Ducs and Sherbrooke Castors. Oh, Guy

Lafleur was often tempted to leave. Almost did several times. The Ottawa 67's, Kitchener Rangers and Montreal Junior Canadiens had all come a-courting. In the summer of 1970, Dionne and his parents made a recruiting trip to Guy's hometown, Thurso, a pulp-and-paper town on the Quebec side of the Ottawa River. At one point, Marcel and Guy drifted away from parents and team officials. The hockey was better in St. Catharines, Marcel told Guy. So was the weather. (Protected by the Niagara Escarpment and warmed by Great Lakes Erie and Ontario, St. Catharines' average December temperature was 32 Fahrenheit, compared to 9°F in Quebec City.) Dionne's closing sales pitch seemed to seal the deal: "If you come to St. Catharines, with the two of us, our team will be unbeatable," he said. "We'll wipe out everyone. The Ontario players will have to stop saying that we Québécois are useless players."

Guy agreed to go, committing to St. Catharines loudly enough for all to hear. After the Dionnes left, though, he changed his mind, deciding to remain in Quebec City, where the 18-year-old had been a star nearly half his life. Both the boldness and hesitation were part and parcel of the player who saved junior hockey in Quebec. From the moment he strapped on skates, Lafleur would be an intriguing, compelling contradiction—a reluctant showoff, a loner who stood out in crowds. Here is a conversation between the youngster and his father after one of Guy's first games from what is the definitive study of Lafleur—*Overtime: The Legend of Guy Lafleur*, by Georges-Hébert Germain.

> *"Guy, did you play well?"*
> *"Yes."*
> *"Did you win?"*
> *"Yes."*
> *"Did you score?"*
> *"Yes."*

With that, Guy was gone: outside, dreaming about hockey—flying on skates, the wind cool in his face—even if he was up in his room, working on math homework. At age ten, Guy found a few loose timbers in the wall of the Thurso Singer Arena. On weekends, the altar boy would steal from home early in the morning, when it was still dark, skating on tiptoes across crunching snow, his mosquito-league hockey jersey on under his cassock. A minute after squeezing through his secret passageway, he was free, tracing parabolas in the wide, welcoming ice, banging the boards with cannon fire—slapshot after slapshot.

The artillery sounds woke up Ti-Paul Meloche, manager of the Singer Arena (and tenant in an attached apartment). Nursing a hangover, Ti-Paul shuffled with exaggerated care into his refrigerated office, throwing on the lights. Little Guy ended his imaginary game, coasting to a stop.

"What are you doing here?" Ti-Paul asked. "Does your father know you come here in the middle of the night?" Réjean Lafleur had been drinking with Ti-Paul at the nearby Hotel Lafontaine the evening previous.

"It's not the middle of the night, it's almost seven o'clock."

"Seven o'clock on a Saturday morning—that's still the middle of the night."

Yawning occasionally, Ti-Paul gave Guy a tour of the arena—showed him how to flick on the lights and work the skate sharpener, paint the blue and red lines. They made a deal: Guy could practise here before mass, as early and as often as he wanted, in exchange for help around the rink. One other thing: Guy couldn't tell anyone else about the loose timbers. The ten-year-old was ecstatic—*his very own rink*. And the confidentiality agreement wouldn't be a problem. Guy Lafleur was always very good at not telling people things.

Lights as bright as Guy's couldn't be kept under a bushel long, however. Lafleur was the best player at École Ste-Famille—both protege and hero to Brother Leo, the school's hockey coach. In 1962, Guy led the Thurso Mosquitos to a regional championship. He scored 41 goals in five games; would've been a lot more except a Lake Placid team refused to play if Lafleur were allowed to continue slapping the puck. In March, a peewee team from across the river in Rockland, Ontario, smuggled Guy into their lineup for the big Quebec City Pee Wee Hockey Tournament. Like the Orrs, the Lafleurs didn't own a car, so Guy walked through a snowstorm across the frozen Ottawa River at dawn, stick over his shoulder, to find car lights waiting for him at the other side. Though underage, he was a sensation in the Quebec City tournament, scoring 30 of his team's 48 goals. The highlight for Guy, though, was meeting and shaking hands with his hero, Canadiens great Jean Béliveau.

Guy would also lead the tournament in disappearing acts. Before and between contests, Rockland coaches and guardians were always searching for him, it seemed.

Where's Guy?

Dunno. He was beside me a second ago.

Well, go find him. He has to eat; we've got a game in two hours.

Teammates were sent to look. Before long, they always knew where to go. An article in the *Ottawa Citizen* in 1953 suggested that Thurso, with a population just under 2,000, was the smallest town in Canada with an artificial rink. Crowds six times the size of his hometown watched Guy in Quebec City. When he wasn't playing, Guy climbed to the top row of Le Colisée, dizzy but happy, staring down at the gleaming, boldly lit ice surface, and felt the shouting crowd's energy travel through him.

The ten-year-old must've felt like he was in heaven.

He would get better every game, and he played daily. Then there were the crack-of-dawn weekend solo concerts in the Singer Arena, where the youngster perfected a fluid, deadly slapshot. Future teammate Larry Robinson, another Ottawa Valley peewee, remembered a 1963 tournament in Montreal where Guy scored from centre ice, drawing amazed gasps from onlookers. The next year, on February 5, 1964, two days before the Beatles landed in America, Guy counted seven goals to lead his club to a Quebec City peewee championship. The city loved him. Tournament organizer Paul Dumont advised the Lafleur family that Guy was welcome to play with the Aces, Béliveau's old team, upon turning 15. Until then, in addition to all his ice time, Guy attended

Saturday night drama lessons. He and sister Suzanne lay on the floor at home, a few feet away from the blue-flickering TV screen, watching the Canadiens play on channel 9, CBOFT. His parents sat on the sagging corduroy couch behind them. Ti-Paul and Brother Leo, Guy's school coach, were also around, arguing hockey aesthetics, provoking an occasional grumble from maternal Grandfather Chartrand.

A dispassionate empiricist, Ti-Paul urged Guy to study the swooping Béliveau: see how he flew above the action, seeing everything, controlling play—himself too. He was a true master, unlike the reckless, frequently injured Rocket Richard. "Anyone at all could make him fall apart, just by calling him a 'frog' or a 'pea-souper,'" Ti-Paul said of the Rocket. That elicited a howl from Brother Leo, a man of God and so partial to stirring, injury-prone heroes. Leaping to his feet, the priest would launch into a defence of the Rocket.

Stop it! Richard inspired us—brought crowds to their feet.

Grandfather Chartrand agreed. "Hockey is half dead," he told everyone. "No one will ever take the Rocket's place, unless Guy does something about it."

Lafleur left Thurso for Quebec City at age 15. He wore Béliveau's number (four) while playing Rocket's position, right wing. For Quebec fans, he was both. This was his gift: Guy Lafleur was a blank, silent screen onto which everyone could project their dreams. Like Béliveau, another altar boy, he seemed obedient, glad to be of use. *Un bon fils.* Brother Leo wrote a religious pamphlet extolling the adolescent's virtues: "One of the best things about him is that he is French Canadian, and when he gets an idea in his head, he succeeds. Guy is a young man laden with talent and goodwill. He listens to the advice of his teachers and tries to follow it to the letter."

Guy was also the first kid to say no to Ontario, a virile hero who played home games close to the Plains of Abraham, where New France fell to British troops in 1759. Lafleur wore his hair long (but not too long) and sported bell-bottoms from Marquis de Brummell in Vieux-Limoilou. In the incense-scented head shops that sprang up in old

Quebec, his picture was there alongside rock heroes Jim Morrison and Mick Jagger.

So he was a rebel, maybe, a sovereigntist.

Quebec licence plates read JE ME SOUVIENS—*I remember.* But citizens at the time didn't have to go back to 1759 to recall a stinging defeat. Canadian troops roamed Quebec streets in late 1970. That October, British trade commissioner James Cross and Quebec labour minister Pierre Laporte were kidnapped by the Front de libération du Québec (FLQ). Abductors demanded $500,000 in gold and the release of FLQ bombers. Prime Minister Trudeau refused, and days later, his old friend and classmate Laporte was found stuffed into the trunk of a Chevrolet, strangled with his own gold neck chain. At the request of Premier Robert Bourassa, Trudeau sent troops into Quebec. Civil liberties were suspended. Almost 500 were arrested, many of them intellectuals and sovereigntists, including popular folk singer Pauline Julien, jailed for eight days. Most Quebecers were outraged by the kidnap-murder, some by the Canadian government's response.

The fevers of the day spread to hockey. In 1969, Paul Dumont, creator of the Quebec City peewee hockey tourney, took advantage of growing nationalism to convince 20 local businessmen to buy the Quebec Aces from the Philadelphia Flyers, while at the same time merging the province's junior leagues—the Metropolitan Montreal and Quebec Junior Hockey leagues. He also changed the name of the Aces to Remparts, referencing the walls of old Quebec City, thrown up in 1620 to protect the then village from Iroquois and British troops. Still busy, Dumont hired a new coach, Maurice Filion, a flashy, combustible leader nicknamed "Monsieur 100,000 Volts" by the press.

The success of the new Quebec Major Junior Hockey League rested on the shoulders and swerving hips of one pleasant, oddly withdrawn teenager. Though there were inexplicable lapses, Guy Lafleur let no one down. At 17, he reached the number the Rocket made famous—50 goals. Quebec City fans once nicknamed Béliveau *"Le Gros Bill"* after a French folk song. Now there were songs for Guy. At Le Colisée, French singer

Gilbert Bécaud's hit "L'important, c'est la rose" was turned into "L'important, c'est Lafleur."

But Guy was not above it all, an easy-soaring eagle like Béliveau. Not that he lost his temper like the Rocket. It was stranger than that: sometimes the young winger simply became lost, period. Nobody knew how or why. In his first season as a Rempart (1969–70), Lafleur counted 94 goals in under 50 games, drawing cross-Canada coverage. Guy seemed sure to become the first junior to break the unimaginable 100-goal barrier. And then, who knew why, he simply stopped scoring, going weeks without a goal. Fans created a song to help the 18-year-old find his way.

> Oh, if Guy would only score here
> I'd give him a fine hat
> Score, Guy, score
> Don't you hear the people?
> Don't you hear your fans?

With two games left, he remained stuck at 94. One hundred goals would have to wait until next year, it seemed. The Sherbrooke Castors were in Quebec City on February 17, 1970. Number Four finally scored . . . and scored again and again and again and again and again. It was ridiculous—six goals in one game! Number 100 came with three minutes left. Suddenly, it was New Year's Eve and St-Jean-Baptiste Day all at once in the Colisée. The ice was buried in hats and streamers. Crying fans sang, "Il a gagné ses epaulettes," the French "For He's a Jolly Good Fellow." The following year was better still—Guy fired 130 goals. The Remparts outdrew the Montreal Junior Canadiens three to one, attracting close to a half million fans. Indeed, the baby Habs now wanted to move back to their home province.

All because of Quebec's love affair with Guy Lafleur.

It was a relationship similar to the province's romance with the Rocket, except for a crucial difference: the fiery Rocket lit up "La Grande Noirceur"—the Great Darkness—a sleepy time when deeply conservative

Union Nationale premier Maurice Duplessis ruled Quebec. Lafleur became famous in the early 1970s, when Quebec's Quiet Revolution turned loud with thunderstorms. Like the Rocket, then, Guy was an antidote to his times—quiet, vulnerable even, while the Quebec around him exploded. Buffalo Sabres rookie Gilbert Perreault told GM Punch Imlach to check out Lafleur. Punch journeyed to Quebec City. Knowing an NHL GM was in the crowd, Guy had an off night. The American CBS television network's documentary division sent a crew, and the same thing happened. Montreal Canadiens assistant GM Claude Ruel, who knew Guy, advised GM Sam Pollock to approach Lafleur gingerly.

"The secret is to see him without being seen," Ruel said. "Like when you're hunting. If the deer spots you, it disappears."

This was a time of incredible highs and lows in French Canada. Bad weather, biblical storms, too. It rained almost every day in April 1971 (baseball's Montreal Expos had game after game cancelled), and on May 4, the relentless deluge ended in catastrophe. The earth opened under the village of Saint-Jean-Vianney, forming a splitting crater that was soon filled with a rushing river of liquefied clay, killing 31 citizens. That same week, *La Presse*'s Jean Pellerin worried that the province itself was about to disappear. "We can no longer say that 'Quebec is growing in hope, on the shore of a great river.' It is shrivelling up before our eyes. The pill has taken away the last precious weapon—a new generation."* More bad news: the trial of Pierre Laporte's murderers—the FLQ's Chénier cell—played out on front pages. And Ottawa had promised reprisals in response to further violence: "WMA ready if need arises Quebec told," read a Montreal *Gazette* headline.

"WMA" meant the War Measures Act. Quebecers were angry, nervous. *What next?*

Thank God for hockey. The Canadiens, with Béliveau and this college kid with sideburns, Ken Dryden, were en route to an unexpected

---

*   According to the blog *Demography Matters,* the Quebec birth rate dropped from 3.9 children per woman in 1960 to 1.4 in 1974.

Stanley Cup win. The Remparts, meanwhile, faced off against the St. Catharines Black Hawks for a Quebec–Ontario Memorial Cup semifinal. Unlike the Canadiens' playoff run, the junior series wouldn't be an easy, feel-good story within the province. St. Catharines had its own French players, including one star some scouts believed to be the world's top junior.

For many Quebecers, however, Marcel Dionne was a traitor—the guy who abandoned his homeland. The Dionne clan pretended to split up to facilitate Marcel's transfer to Ontario. Half the family, including mother Laurette and two sisters, moved to St. Catharines, playing house for a while to give Marcel resident status. Father Gilbert and the rest remained in Quebec. Divorce (*sin!*) was now added to the crime of treason; the Dionnes became pariahs in their home province. There was also the matter of esthetics. Lafleur was elegantly tall, beautiful. His English nickname was "the Flower." His French sobriquet, "*Le Démon Blond.*" (Again, Guy was whomever you wanted him to be.) Dionne was generously listed at five feet, eight inches. His nickname was "Little Beaver," the stage name of Quebec midget wrestling sensation Lionel Giroux. And where Lafleur glided, there was evident strain to Dionne's hectic skating style.

Quebecers looked at Lafleur and saw who they wanted to be. In Dionne, they found something closer to themselves, maybe.

The Dionne–Lafleur confrontation was so big in Quebec that a hockey game was shown on closed-circuit TV for the first time anywhere in the world. In Le Colisée, almost 6,000 nervous fans watched the opening contest, held in St. Catharines. Another 2,300 bought tickets in Verdun, outside Montreal. At first, French viewers wouldn't like anything they saw. Before the game, a cleanup crew was on the ice with shovels. Fans had thrown something on the ice.

Dead frogs! Again with the frog jokes; francophones were growing tired of the French gags that were so popular elsewhere in Canada in the '60s and '70s.

Hey, how do we know Jesus will never return in Quebec?
Because they'll never be able to find three wise men or a virgin!

When the ice scrapers finished up, French viewers really had something to worry about: St. Catharines stormed the Quebec net from the start. Goalie Michel DeGuise, a loaner from Sorel, kept it scoreless, foiling a series of shooters. The Black Hawks were all over the Quebec visitors. But it would be the Remparts who scored first. Their other star, Jacques Richard, found the net. Dionne finally broke through with a goal late in the first period, exciting rapturous applause. Quebec City escaped the first 20 minutes with a tie, but it didn't look good for the Remparts. Lafleur seemed to be having an off night. Maybe that was why the Black Hawks forgot about him early in the second. Open for an instant, he combined with Michel Brière on a dazzling give and go. First, Guy slipped a perfect pass to his centre inside the blue line, and then he raced to the net, performing a delicate goalmouth tap-in. After that, he was swinging around the cage, shyly collecting congratulations from teammates. Dionne responded, setting up another Hawks goal. It was Little Beaver's 500th point in 194 games for St. Catharines.

The play of the game came out of nowhere midway through the third. Quebec's Brière had the puck at centre, hesitated, and then found Lafleur. The puck was on Guy's stick and into the far-far-away net in a split second. A gasp from the crowd: *How on earth?* The St. Catharines *Standard*'s veteran hockey reporter, Jack Gatecliff, explained what happened in his game report the next day: "Lafleur, who plays in an almost lethargic manner until he has possession of the puck, took Michel Brière's pass just over the blue line, then labelled a rocket-like shot . . . that cracked Hulme's stick, then caromed into the net just under the crossbar."

Rocket-like . . .

A real Richard, Jacques scored again to give the Remparts a 4–2 lead. Growing frustrated, the Hawks turned nasty. Pierre Guité took on Quebec's Pierre Roy. Bob MacMillan pushed Lafleur around, itching for a fight. Guy backed away, and MacMillan hollered something. Quebec fans watching on big TV could see all this. Later, in the Remparts' victorious dressing room, Lafleur defended himself. I'm not a "chicken," he said. "I can't help my team getting penalties." Monsieur 100,000 Volts,

Remparts coach Filion, threw a charge into Remparts fans by accusing the Black Hawks of trying to *get* Lafleur.

Next game in St. Catharines, the Hawks did make Guy disappear, crushing Quebec 8–3. Dionne was spectacular: four goals. The Remparts star made a few nice passes, nothing more.

"Is that Lafleur out there?" shouted a fan watching the closed-circuit feed in Verdun.

"No, it's his sister," responded a wiseass nearby.

Before the series resumed in Le Colisée, Dionne told the Canadian Press, "It will be interesting to play in Quebec City to see what reaction fans have to me." *Interesting?* He and the Black Hawks booster club, 200 parents and well-wishers, apparently had no idea they were stepping into a twitching bear trap. Later that year, the movie *Mon Oncle Antoine* would open in Canadian theatres. The film contained a scene that captured the French-Quebec working-class resentment of English bosses. Winding up a boozy wake for a departed friend, a miner empties his beer, saying, "That's another one the English won't get."

The underclass rancour hinted at in Claude Jutra's movie would explode at Le Colisée. The St. Catharines fans' frog jokes and going after Lafleur, calling him "chicken," had angered the Remparts fan base. Maybe Dionne should have been more wary. As a French player, hadn't he been a marked man in Ontario hockey? When Toronto's Glenn Goldup broke Marcel in two, GM Stafford Smythe took the Marlie defenceman out to dinner. There was a French–English thing in Canadian hockey—a sometimes vicious snowball fight that went back forever.

Now, six months after Canadian troops occupied Quebec, an English team—a club trying to maim Lafleur, according to coach Filion!—were about to break into Guy's home. Get him where he lived, maybe. Dionne finally figured his team was in trouble when the Black Hawks climbed into a shuttle bus at the Quebec City airport. The driver was angry about something. Before long, he and Dionne were arguing. It got worse, way worse, when the Black Hawks took the ice for a pre-game skate hours later.

"Hey, Dionne, fuck off."

"Hey, Guité, you cocksucker."

Fans hurled English insults for maximum damage, ensuring that the entire team and booster club understood what they thought of French defectors. In the dressing room before the game, Marcel explained away the insults by advising teammates, "Well, that's not swearing to them. In the French language, you swear against the church. Their swear words aren't your swear words."

First shift of the game, Pierre Guité took a Quebec Rempart out along the boards. Up went the referee's arm. A penalty, maybe, but the visiting Black Hawks were unprepared for what happened next. Fans responded as if Guité had taken Fortier out with a bayonet. One jumped the boards and spit in Guité's face. Police were soon on the ice. The game finally continued, fans jeering every time Dionne had the puck. A steady barrage of missiles escaped the stands, aimed at St. Catharines players. *What's going on?* Black Hawks players and fans must have wondered. *This is our first game here, and they're treating us like lifelong enemies.*

Exactly.

Colisée organist Marcel Gagnon whipped the crowd into a further fury with abstract-expressionist versions of French folk songs. Material the Black Hawks faithful had never heard, all of it played at rock concert volume. Though bewildered, St. Catharines outplayed their hosts, out-shooting the Remparts 36–17, but goalie DeGuise was again heroic and Lafleur deadly—two chances and a pair of implausible, lightning-fast goals in the first period. The crowd was in full voice:

> *Score, Guy, score*
> *Don't you hear the people?*
> *Don't you hear your fans?*

The singing stopped late in the first period. Hawk Brian McBratney threw Brière onto the ice. Benches emptied. Goalies fought. Brian McKenzie grabbed Lafleur. Officials dove into wild scrums. On his way to the penalty box, McBratney aimed an elbow at Guy. That was it; the crowd turned on the Hawks and their supporters, a stranded outpost in the upper balcony. Players were soon drenched in beer and spittle. So were the St. Catharines fans. They couldn't believe it: everyone in Quebec City, one of the oldest and most beautiful cities in North America, had been so cordial, so nice . . . up until now, they later told the St. Catharines *Standard*. And then, out of nowhere—or so they thought—war.

Dionne's family was here. A pregnant aunt miscarried. Marcel was embarrassed, deeply hurt. The Hawks player was *un vrai québécois*—a Drummondville boy, child of a lumberjack. His family had a store there, sold beer. Marcel developed his legs peddling Molson on the front basket of his bike to homes and businesses. At home, there was always extended family helping unload inventory, one beer at a time. Marcel loved them all, but wanted a little space, yearned to see the world. Was that a crime? Popular with Hawks teammates, he learned to speak English playing hockey and reading roadside menus. "Pass the salt." "Pass the puck." His first full English sentence came on the team bus late at night in a snowstorm, everyone asleep except Marcel and the driver, Charlie, who pulled out to pass a car. Jerking forward, Marcel saw headlights growing larger.

"Jesus Crise, Charlie, no time, *no time!*"

What had Marcel Dionne ever done to be spit at? To have callers threaten, night after night, to kill his family?

That was Friday night at Le Colisée—a 3–1 win for the Remparts. The next game was uglier still—a vile sequel to the famous 1955 Richard Riot.* Back in 1955, NHL president Clarence Campbell's suspension of

---

* Although a Montreal bus driver had a heart attack and drove off the road upon hearing that Clarence Campbell had suspended the Rocket for the remainder of the 1954–55 season, there were no casualties in the 1955 Richard Riot. The disturbance would become bigger in the retelling, however. By the time the story reached Holland, headlines read STADIUM WRECKED, 27 DEAD, 100 WOUNDED. Not that the riot wasn't significant. Writing in *Le Devoir* days later, editorial writer André Laurendeau, in a story entitled "*On a tué mon frère Richard*" ("My brother Richard has been killed"), suggested the riot "betrayed what lay behind the

the Rocket had resulted in anonymous attacks, hate mail: "You British animal! Why did your vile ancestors set foot on our lovely land?" Next Montreal home game, fans attacked the NHL leader, hitting him with tomatoes, eggs, pigs' feet. Someone threw a canister of tear gas. Later, stores were ransacked, fires set, windows smashed. By morning, rivers of broken glass extended in every direction from the Forum.

Saturday, May 8, 1971, in Quebec City was worse, arguably. There was some evidence that the sequel riot was the result of fans blowing off steam. "Saturday night's all right for fighting," as Elton John would soon sing. There were dozens of French-on-French fights in washrooms and corridors—drunkards "[got] about as oiled as a diesel train," as Elton's song went. Mostly, though, the violence was premeditated, racially motivated bullying—500-to-one attacks on teenagers and innocent bystanders.

The game started out like any other—skating, hitting, close calls, overexcited fans. St. Catharines scored first and enjoyed an advantage in play until the second period, when Quebec jumped ahead. Lafleur swatted in a rebound. Richard scored. The crowd belted out the Remparts theme song, "Ils sont en or," encouraged, as always, by organist Gagnon's wild keyboard splashing. Fans harassed the Hawks bench—their fans, too—throughout the game, but the third period was when the trouble really started. Who could say why? Was it Lafleur's effect on his audience? Guy scored from just inside the blue line again, a mighty, crowd-pleasing blast, and then completed his hat trick next shift. Chapeaus were off and on the ice. The Hawks eventually pulled goalie George Hulme, replacing him with Keith Pallett. Flying down his wing again, Lafleur let loose with another blinding slapshot. The new goalie took it on the mask and spun sideways, collapsing. Teammates pulled him up, groggy. Down he went again. More noise. Maybe this was blood lust—fans anticipating and enjoying the death of a swooning opponent, everyone on their feet. Balcony fans were giving it to the Hawks' boosters; closer to the ice,

---

apparent indifference and long-held passiveness of French Canadians." Many believed the Richard Riot was the first act in Quebec's Quiet Revolution.

Dionne heard taunts and was dripping with beer, spit and ice cream. You could feel something was about to happen—the electrical charge that preceded a thunderstorm. The Black Hawks had had it. Remparts fans wanted more.

With three minutes to go, the Hawks' Bob MacMillan and Remparts' Bill Landers (two Englishers) exchanged glares and then punches. Finally, Le Colisée exploded. Benches emptied. Fights broke out. Fans jumped on the ice. Gladys Crowe, president of the Hawks' booster club, told the *Standard*, "Everyone around us was spitting, throwing golf balls, bolts [lifted from seats] and eggs and one lady had her hair pulled so hard that she wrenched her neck and will have to see a doctor."

On the ice, it was worse. Fans reached over the glass and took swings at Hawks players. Anything and everything was coming out of the stands now: more ice cream bars, beer, potatoes, tomatoes, an open penknife, nail clippers, ball bearings, D-cell batteries, dentures, women's undergarments, makeshift bombs—erasers studded with nails—and a woman's wig sewn shut, stuffed with a mickey and two apples.

Getting out of Le Colisée would prove even more dangerous. Brian McKenzie would tell Marcel Dionne biographer Ted Mahovlich about how Marcel turned from team captain to general of an evacuating army after the game.

We were leaving the ice and it was crazy. So Marcel says, "Don't go up in the stands. Bring your father, bring your brother, and we'll all go across the ice together." So we get across the ice and, as we're going under the exit, somebody throws some garbage at Mike Bloom's head. In retaliation, Bloomer comes up with his stick, chopping up from underneath the exit. Well, guess what? He cranks a cop—right over the eye! Then all hell broke loose. So we got everyone into the dressing room and Marcel says, "Lock the doors. Don't let them take Bloomer because they'll beat the shit out of him."

Minutes later, the team bus pulled up to a Colisée exit—door to door. The Hawks could theoretically step into the getaway van from their dressing room. But an angry throng blocked the corridor and another 2,500 fans pressed against the team bus, throwing beer bottles and rocks, smashing windows. Police pushed back the crowd in the hallway, allowing passage. Twenty teenage players and coach Frank Milne collectively took a deep breath, readying for a sprint, until police delayed the escape.

"You have to wait because they blew a tire on the bus."

"How do you blow a tire on a bus?" players asked. "You can't get through it with a knife. Do they have guns?"

With the situation worsening—was the crowd getting bigger?—it was decided to send the limping bus on its way, bracketed by howling police cruisers. "I told the kids to take it easy, lie on the floor of the bus and they'd be safe from the bottles," Coach Milne told the *Standard*. "But I can tell you they were a frightened bunch of boys." When the team finally arrived at a nearby Holiday Inn, police remained outside, scarecrows warding off honking cars that circled the hotel for hours. Once inside and all talked out, players slept on the floor, between beds, afraid of FLQ bombs they were sure would come smashing through the window any minute.

The series returned to Ontario the following week, where the revitalized Hawks handled the Remparts, 8–3, in a regionally televised game at a packed Maple Leaf Gardens. St. Catharines refused to return to Quebec City for game six, however; worried parents wouldn't let their sons go. Instead, the team offered to play games six and seven at a neutral Quebec site: the Montreal Forum. The compromise would mean the Hawks were forgoing the right to play a decisive game seven at home. Remparts refused anyway. Canadian Amateur Hockey Assosciation president Earl Dawson ruled in Quebec's favour, even though, when asked in an informal gathering after a press conference if he'd want his son to play in Quebec City as a visiting player, he answered, "No fuckin' way."

St. Catharines forfeited the series. Marcel Dionne's adopted team was further disappointed to learn that the CAHA permitted a national showdown between Quebec and the Edmonton Oil Kings, even though the body had earlier ruled there would be no Memorial Cup final because western teams allowed overage juniors. Now they had changed their minds, presumably to provide a feel-good finale to what otherwise would be a dishonourable end to the junior season. Quebec City welcomed Edmonton with parades and banners, and then the Remparts made quick work of the Kings, winning the Memorial Cup finale series, 5–1 and 5–2. No fights, no broken glass or death threats . . .

But what about the Montreal Canadiens and their first pick in the 1971 draft? In the last game between the Black Hawks and the Remparts, Dionne was far and away a better player than Lafleur. Little Beaver scored four goals; Guy was again missing in action.

The draft, to be held in Montreal, was three weeks away. Who would it be? Which native son would the Canadiens choose—Dionne or Lafleur?

HARVEST, PART ONE

The highways linking Quebec and Ontario travelled in both directions, and decades before Marcel Dionne created a stir by "defecting," hockey talent poured from Upper to Lower Canada. The idea of *Les Glorieux* was in fact an English moneymaking scheme. In 1909, James Strachan, manager of the all-Anglo Montreal Wanderers, remarked to Ambrose O'Brien, owner of the Renfrew Millionaires, "A club composed entirely of French-Canadian players in Montreal . . . is bound to be a success." The following season, O'Brien, a prosperous Ottawa Valley dairyman, sponsored Les Canadiens in the new National Hockey Association.*

---

*   A precursor to the NHL, the National Hockey Association was a five- to seven-team central Canadian league that ran from 1909–17. Teams included the Quebec Bulldogs, the Ottawa Senators and a handful of teams from Montreal and Toronto, including the Canadiens and the Toronto Arenas. Only the Senators, the Canadiens and the Toronto Hockey Club (later the Maple Leafs) were still around when the NHA became the NHL in the fall of 1917.

The Habs' first star, Newsy Lalonde, was an ex-newsboy from Cornwall, Ontario. His successor would be celebrated in a popular folk ditty:

Maroons, they have good hockey team
Those Maple Leafs is nice
But Les Canadiens they are the best
That ever skate de ice
Morenz, he go like one big storm
Sil Mantha's big and fat
They all are good but none is quite
So good as Joliat.

Joliat, he is my friend
I don't know him myself
But I knows a man who knows a man
Who knows him very well

So when I tire of travail trop
I put on coat of coon
And go to see Les Canadiens
Make mincemeat of Maroon

That was a very exciting game
The score she was a tie
And then my little Joliat
He get hanger in his eye

He take him puck at other end
And skate him down so fast
The rest of players seem dormir
As he is going past

That was the winning goal hurrah
The game she come to end

I yell bravo for Joliat
*You see he is my friend**

That would be Aurèle Joliat, a Swiss Protestant from Ottawa. Another Ontarian, "Big Storm" Howie Morenz turned hockey into a Montreal civic preoccupation. Playing alongside Joliat and Arthur Gagné, the Stratford Streak made the Roaring Twenties noisier still, playing the ukulele at parties and drinking in more than Montreal's bright lights. Stateside, the "Flying Frenchmen" became fashionable exotica, forerunners to Cirque du Soleil. In their hometown, they were soon an obsession. Morenz penned a (ghosted) column for the French daily *La Patrie,* cementing a relationship with fans. His death in 1937 after an on-ice spill was a catastrophe. Next day, the top two-thirds of *La Patrie* included only these words:

HOWIE MORENZ
EST MORT À
L'HÔPITAL HIER

Another hero was soon on the way. Native son Maurice Richard more than filled Morenz's skates, pushing the Allies' comeback win over Germany off the front page in the 1944–45 season with an unprecedented feat—50 goals in as many games! Author Roch Carrier recorded what it was like on Quebec rinks during the Richard era in his famous work, *The Hockey Sweater*: "When the referee dropped the puck, we were five Maurice Richards taking it away from five other Maurice Richards. We were ten players; all of us wearing with the same blazing enthusiasm the uniform of the Montreal Canadiens. On our backs, we all wore the famous Number Nine."

Though famous, the Flying Frenchmen really had yet to ascend to greatness. Nor were they really all that French. Aside from Richard, there

---

* I first encountered the Joliat poem in Mrs. Knight's English class at St-Médard School in Deschênes, Quebec, circa 1963:

were only four French-Canadians on the 1943 and 1946 championship teams.* No, the team truly became *Les Glorieux* upon the arrival of yet another Ontario-born game-changer. Not that many snapped to attention when Frank Selke, Maple Leafs owner Conn Smythe's long-suffering second-in-command, took control of the Canadiens in the sweltering summer of 1946.

War hero/millionaire/visionary Constantine Falkland Smythe invented the Toronto Maple Leafs, no question. Buying the troubled Toronto St. Pats in 1927, he undertook hockey's most successful makeover, changing team colours from pea-green to Great Lakes blue. For a new name and logo, the Military Cross winner lifted the maple leaf insignia from his service uniform. Roosevelt built the Hoover Dam to lift America's spirit during the Great Depression. Smythe erected Maple Leaf Gardens (1931), a winter cathedral where English Canada gathered Saturday evenings, listening to CBC Radio's *Hockey Night in Canada*. A new psalm entered the nation's prayer book: "Hello Canada and hockey fans in United States and Newfoundland, this is Foster Hewitt from Maple Leaf Gardens . . ."

But while the nervy Smythe was the face of the franchise, the diminutive (five feet, two inches), eternally reserved Selke was the backroom genius who made the Leafs work—assistant manager, chief scout, head publicist; he even edited the club program. When Smythe was off leading his own regiment in World War II, dashing off letters to newspapers in which he criticized Canada's war effort, Selke was home, quietly building a team that won four Stanley Cups from 1947–51. Upon returning from the war, Smythe reasserted his might, quelling a board coup he figured Selke had some part in. From then on, Smythe made his backup's life miserable—requesting, for instance, that he ask permission before leaving work.

---

* Francophones on the 1943 champions included goalie Paul Bibeault, Butch Bouchard, Leo Lamoureux and Maurice Richard. Bouchard, Lamoureux, Richard and Gerry Plamondon played on the '46 champs. Although I should mention that captain Toe Blake's mother was French.

"Lincoln freed the slaves," Selke scrawled on a note he slapped on Smythe's desk before heading off to take over the Montreal Canadiens in the summer of 1946. Five minutes into his new job, the Habs' new GM revealed both a decisive nature and awareness that he was in a new land. "Clean the toilets, this place stinks like a *pissoir*," would be his first (bilingual!) command. Selke had the Forum refurbished in hopes of turning a smoky men's club into a varied, profitable entertainment showcase. He'd need the money, for as he told Canadiens president Donat Raymond, "I'd like to inaugurate a farm system here. I'd like to put a team in every province to build up young reserves."

What Selke really wanted to do was kick Toronto's ass, beating his old team at its own game—one he had invented. With the Leafs, Selke grew the NHL's first junior system, getting the jump on competitors. Why wait for players to turn 21 to recruit by-then-expensive amateurs? Get them when they were 13, 14, for peanuts! All it took was hard work and a keen eye for talent to build a hockey empire.

In 1948, Selke expanded the Quebec Junior Hockey league from four to 11 teams. "[Before Selke, the Canadiens] owned four or five junior teams and controlled senior hockey too, but it was run like a bad orchard, they waited until the wind would blow apples out of the tree," Rocket Richard told authors Chrys Goyens and Allan Turowetz in the definitive study of the Canadiens dynasty, *Lions in Winter*. Before long, Montreal orchards dotted the Dominion. There were ten Canadiens farm teams in Winnipeg alone. The Habs' Regina Pats were the best western juniors in the 1950s. Twice, in 1950 and 1958, the Pats faced off against the Montreal Junior Canadiens in the junior finals.

The Habs also ran the NHL's premier executive development program. Montreal's 1950 Memorial Cup team was coached by Sam Pollock; in 1958, Scotty Bowman ran the juniors. Habs managers got results the old-fashioned way—by outworking opponents. At a wedding, Selke bumped into the coach of the Victoriaville Tigres, who told him, "Mr. Selke, I have a player who plays for me . . . you should sign. He's a big, strong fellow and will be an excellent professional one day."

Selke was soon on his way to personally sign up 15-year-old Joseph Jean Arthur Béliveau. In the spring of 1960, Bowman, coach of the Peterborough Petes at the time, spent an off day driving five hours to watch a bantam game in Gananoque, Ontario. *A bantam game!* Weeks later, he found additional time to drop by Parry Sound (another seven-hour return trip) to advise 12-year-old Bobby Orr he might look pretty good in a Montreal jersey.

At its peak, the Canadiens empire stretched from Halifax to Houston—750 teams. But it was in Quebec that the club collected its best players, youngsters called to action by Selke's captain/poster boy hero, Maurice Richard. *The Rocket Wants You.* The brilliance of Selke's master plan became evident when local teens enlisted with Montreal's junior clubs. Béliveau wore Richard's Number Nine for the Victoriaville Tigres in 1947. That same year, Boom Boom Geoffrion played for Laval Nationale, often against Dickie Moore's Montreal Royals. Afterwards, the 16-year-olds jumped onto the streetcar outside the Forum, dreaming of the big time. Moore hopped off at Park Ex; Geoffrion was ten minutes away in Mont-Royal.

In the spring of 1956, Béliveau, Boom Boom and Moore joined Richard and his kid brother, Henri "The Pocket Rocket" Richard, helping the Habitants to the first of five straight championships. To Selke and Quebec's delight, 13 Canadiens were Montreal-born; more than half the team, 12 players, French-Canadian.

Les Canadiens sont là!

The '60s brought more Stanley Cups (six) and arresting nicknames—the "Roadrunner," Yvan Cournoyer; the Gumper, goalie Lorne Worsley; and long, tall Jacques Laperrière. When Number Two, Laperrière, helped on a goal, the Habs' stirring public address announcer, Claude Mouton, demonstrated his chops, transforming the defenceman's last name into something wonderful: "Assisté par le numéro deux, Jacques . . . *le Paris hier!*"

The decade also brought looming disaster—expansion and the death of all NHL junior farm systems, which were to be replaced by a universal draft. It would be a problem Selke's successor, Sam Pollock, would have to solve. Like his former boss, Pollock was a remote, hand-wringing fret-ter. As a teenager, he dropped out of high school to help in his father's men's shop, finding time to run the Canadiens' off-season softball team—baseball was his real passion. Summer days, he would invariably be found at Delorimier Downs, watching the Montreal Royals. The Royals were the Brooklyn Dodgers' farm team, although Sam was a New York Giants fan. And what a fan! On Sundays, after church, he drove alone 100 miles to Plattsburgh in upstate New York to tune in Giant games, hanging on every word of broadcasters Russ Hodges and Ernie Harwell.

When Selke hired the baseball nut on as a Canadiens scout, Sam brought that same relentless fervour to hockey. Writer Trent Frayne would describe Pollock as an "ulcerous monk." The Montreal GM made two significant trades in his rookie season. In the first, Billy Hicke was sent to New York for Dick Duff, a useful veteran who helped Montreal to five straight Cup finals (and four championships). The other swap turned out better still. His first day on the job, at the 1964 draft in Montreal, Pollock sent defenceman Guy Allen and winger Paul Reid, two players who never made the NHL, to Boston for a goalie named Ken Dryden.

That was how Montreal's new GM worked. Like an expert pool player, Trader Sam always set himself up for his next shot, even as he drained an easy corner ball.

Pollock's gift was superior vision. Heading the NHL's expansion committee, Sam recommended a new, instant six-team league. Others wanted a few teams added intermittently. Pollock argued there was pub-licity value in going big. Besides, a separate division meant four expan-sion teams made the playoffs—fans would be happy. It was just good business. With the equivalent of a new league's worth of players on the way, Sam really went to work: *Listen, new teams will need players they don't have because they don't have farm systems,* he told other GMs.

Not like the Canadiens, colleagues joked.

OK, yeah, right, so I think—geez, I can't believe I'm saying this—I agree with Stafford Smythe [of the Maple Leafs]; I think we should eliminate junior sponsorship and go to a draft, like they do football in the States.

Oh boy, I sure wouldn't want to be in your shoes when you explain all this to your old boss, the little guy, Mr. Selke.

Now, wait a minute, I think fair's fair—we should be getting something back for our, ah . . . largesse. In return for dissolving our junior and minor-league teams, Canadiens should get . . . hmm, how about we get the first two picks in the draft for the first five years?

Two picks?!

OK, OK, two French-Canadian picks!

In reality, shutting down Selke's fabled farm system was a necessity. In 1959, Canadian sports fans enjoyed TV hockey once a week—on Saturday night. A decade later, with cable, sports programming was on the air most every night and weekend afternoon: NHL hockey on CBC, CTV and NBC on Saturdays, Wednesdays and Sundays; *les Expos* arrived in 1969, broadcasting games almost every day April through September; Canadian and American football clogged the airwaves fall and winter; golfers Jack (Nicklaus) and Arnie (Palmer) had their weekend armies; there was tennis, with the handsome John Newcombe; Saturday wrestling with Haystacks Calhoun and Bobo Brazil, as well as the Sheik, with his ever-present manager, Abdullah "The Weasel" Farouk. Once, the Montreal-owned Peterborough Petes were the only game in town on a Wednesday night. Now, fans in southern Ontario could watch the Habs play the Leafs on CTV or see *Le Grand Orange*, Rusty Staub, and the Expos challenge Willie Mays's San Francisco Giants on their CBC affiliate.

The universal draft was intended to destroy hockey empires. After all, the higher you were in the standings, the lower your draft choice would be. "The first one now will later be last, for the times they are-a-changin'." That was the way it was supposed to work, anyway. But not everyone in hockey recognized what was happening to their sport. Before anyone else, apparently, Sam Pollock realized that Bobby Orr, Brad Park and Bobby Clarke were the first gleaming nuggets in what would be a hockey gold rush. Bigger, better-fed (and -equipped) baby Boomers were the first generation to benefit from artificial ice and six-month hockey seasons everywhere—even British Columbia, southern Ontario and New England.

To ensure that expansion teams thrived, Sam recommended a five-year moratorium on trading draft picks. New teams should hang on to their lottery tickets. Tragically—for them, anyway—the new teams refused to listen. Suspecting that Sam might be pulling a fast one, keeping all the good, veteran NHL and minor-pro hockey players to himself, NHL teams rejected Pollock's proposal to ban the trading of picks.

Fine, then. Never interrupt the enemy when he's was making a mistake. In the late '60s, Pollock reinvented how the Canadiens did business, raffling off minor-league stars and aging veterans for draft lottery tickets. It was almost as if the Canadiens moved in the blink of an eye from being a feudal society to a high-frequency trading desk (swapping centres and defencemen instead of copper and oil futures). Between June 1, 1969, and May 29, 1973, Sam made over 60 trades. Sometimes, he was dealing known quantities—Frank and Pete Mahovlich were acquired in separate 1969 and 1971 trades for a pile of prospects. Mostly, though, it was the other way around, as Pollock swapped shopworn veterans for first- and second-round draft picks. From 1970 through 1976, he'd have 34 selections in the top 30. In 1971, Trader Sam found that he hit the jackpot: the number one draft pick overall.

Again, who was it going to be: Dionne or Lafleur?

HARVEST, PART TWO

Where was Guy?

It was Thursday, June 11, 1971, and Montreal's jam-packed Queen Elizabeth Hotel hadn't been this busy since John and Yoko's bed-in two summers earlier, when the newlyweds gave peace a chance in their suite, chanting about "ragism, tagism, this-ism, that-ism" with Timothy Leary and Petula Clark, among others. Today's big event was the NHL draft, held as always at the Queen Elizabeth. Montreal had the first pick overall, and everybody wanted to know whom the Stanley Cup champs were going to take. Only problem was, the time had come for Sam Pollock to make the big announcement and the guy he wanted wasn't there yet! Seated at the dais next to NHL president Clarence Campbell, Pollock acknowledged that Montreal was on the clock but asked for a three-minute time-out.

A buzz filled the room. *Is Trader Sam pulling another fast one?*

Who knew what was going through Pollock's mind? Two months

earlier, Sam had spent an off day during the Montreal–Boston playoff series driving to Quebec City. Just to see Guy Lafleur. At the time, the Canadiens brass were still torn between Guy and Marcel Dionne. Head scout Ron Caron liked Dionne. Habs assistant GM Claude Ruel preferred Lafleur, as did former coach Toe Blake. But none of them had final call. That was why Sam was driving up Autoroute 40—he hated to fly—plopped beside chauffeur Brian Travers. It was raining. The Expos were postponed again, so Sam couldn't find refuge in baseball, his favourite sport growing up. Instead, he chatted with Travers, listening to the bacon-frying sound of car tires on wet highway and wondering again: Lafleur or Dionne?

Remparts owner Paul Dumont was waiting for the Canadiens delegation, ready with two freebies—ringside seats. But Pollock waved him off, pulling lesser tickets from his coat pocket. He remembered Ruel's advice: *You have to creep up on Guy.* The Montreal GM wanted to sit up with the fans. Maybe they would tell him who to pick. Dumont shrugged. Small talk, a painful matter for Pollock, was exchanged. Spectators pointed. *C'est Sam!* And then Pollock and his chauffer lost themselves in the crowd.

Figuring this was just another playoff game (against Trois-Rivières), and not a formal audition before an NHL general manager, Lafleur was magnificent that evening—three goals and as many assists; unexpected blind passes to suddenly-*there* teammates. Everything was done at top speed, too. Pollock felt a poltergeist-like energy grip Le Colisée every time Number Four was on the ice. On the car ride home, the crowd's electricity was still coursing through him.

"We need someone like him," Sam said. "A player who plays for the people." Frank Selke had felt the same way about the Rocket. "These things have no price," the devout Scots-Irish Catholic continued. "It's a gift."

C'est un cadeau, as the French say. Maybe that's what Sam himself said. Unlike his former boss, Selke, Pollock was fully bilingual, born and raised in Snowdon, a Montreal suburb.

It normally took two hours to get from Thurso to Montreal. Less for Guy Lafleur, who loved cars and drove the way he skated—fast. But today, for some reason, on the biggest morning in his life, Réjean and Pierette couldn't even get their hockey-star son into his car. Guy tried on three suits—mod ensembles from Marquis de Brummel in Quebec City—then headed outside for a smoke and to shammy the morning dew off his Buick Electra, a gift from the Remparts. After that, he had a coffee and headed to his room, climbing into another suit and then trying on a series of ties.

"Bring them all, you can decide on the way," his father moaned, popping his head in the door. "Guy, are you trying to be late?"

He was. The 19-year-old hockey star was suddenly Benjamin Braddock, the Dustin Hoffman character in *The Graduate*, standing paralyzed on the end of a diving board, afraid to take the plunge and get on with the rest of his life. Ten minutes into the Lafleurs' pilgrimage to Montreal, the still-rising sun hurt the young hockey graduate's eyes. "I forgot my sunglasses!" Guy announced, turning the car around. *Mon dieu!* For sure they'd be late now, Réjean Lafleur told himself. Leaving the car, Guy told his parents he was going to try another suit while he was here.

"Guy, that will do," Pierette Lafleur announced. "We're late already. You're perfect as you are."

Still, Guy drove slowly. Usually, he was Gilles Villeneuve* on the road, squealing around corners. Now, Volkswagens and little old ladies from Chibougamau were flying past. "Guy, you'll have to speed up—we're going to be late," his father said, losing patience.

"So what?"

"So what!"

"It's a farce."

---

* Quebec racing driver Gilles Villeneuve was, after his friend Guy Lafleur, the most famous athlete in Quebec in the 1970s. A former snowmobile racer, Villeneuve won six races in his Grand Prix career before losing his life at the May 1982 Belgian Grand Prix. Prime Minister Trudeau walked his widow, Joann, out of the church at his funeral in Berthierville, Quebec.

The Lafleurs arrived in Montreal at midday, inching through bad traffic. Yes, they were going to be late. On Dorchester Boulevard at last, with the Queen Elizabeth Hotel in view, Guy realized he was in the wrong lane. Fortunately, a cop recognized him and parted the Red Sea, allowing Guy to swing around, stopping right in front of the hotel.

Guy Lafleur?

Oui.

Allons-y.

Inside the hotel, Guy seemed to relax. He was with applauding, beaming hockey fans and smiling hotel staff. A crowd's rapt attention always gave him confidence, reminding the youngster who he was. As the three Lafleurs entered the ballroom, Guy's parents stood back. Their boy was on his own now.

At the dais, Pollock was ready to speak. "The Montreal Canadiens pick . . ." And then he paused, milking the now-laughing crowd. ". . . from Quebec Remparts, Guy Lafleur!"

As if on cue, Guy appeared as Pollock intoned the word *Lafleur,* moving through the crowd, many of whom he now saw to be hockey players. He recognized a big red-headed kid he had played against in bantam—Larry Robinson. Guy nodded. Glad to be remembered, Robinson smiled. Everyone was smiling. Even the ulcerous monk, Sam Pollock.

Ready or not, Guy Lafleur was a Montreal Canadien.

THE GREATEST
TEAM EVER

We weren't a team that [said]—'Well it doesn't matter what the regular sea-
son is like, we'll turn it on in the playoffs.' The Montreal way was you play
in the playoffs the way you play in the regular season and you play in the reg-
ular season the way you play in training camp and the way you play in exhi-
bition games and the way you practise . . . We didn't lose. We were a team
that dominated not just the Stanley Cup playoffs, we dominated the regular
season; we dominated preseason. We dominated anything there was that could
be competed for.
—KEN DRYDEN★

They did so in front of a Forum crowd that had their backs. Should an
opponent think of tampering with Guy Lafleur, rising Habs fans let
out a prolonged holler: "*Heyyyyyy!*" Few referees could withstand such
peer pressure; a penalty was inevitable. One night, after Boston took yet
another early infraction, Bruins GM Harry Sinden jumped to his feet

---

★ Dryden quote from the TV series *Legends of Hockey*.

high in the Forum and made like the great Barrymore. "Death, taxes . . . and the first penalty at the Forum," he thundered.

Thanks to fans, to a province fighting for and against political independence and so in need of uniformed heroes, thanks most of all to hockey's Great Swami, Sam Pollock, the Canadiens were somehow better than ever in the mid-'70s. The team boasted not only the league's best scorer in Lafleur, but also its biggest, most airtight goalie, its best checking line, three of the NHL's top five defencemen . . .

Horses . . . horses . . . horses!

They raced and pushed each other, convinced of their historic mission; knowing too that Trader Sam would Air Canada their behinds to California if they didn't produce. They had a young, healthy 50-goal-scorer languishing in the press box many nights (Pierre Larouche) and a future Norris Trophy winner in the minors (Rod Langway). They were the finest professional sports team of their era—arguably hockey's best-ever collection of talent. *Et maintentant* . . . and now, here is the starting lineup of your 1976–79 Montreal Canadiens.

29. KEN DRYDEN

Today, he is hockey's beautiful mind—ex-MP and federal cabinet minister, lawyer, academic, author of *The Game*, a deeply felt valentine to hockey and *les Canadiens*. But when he arrived in the NHL, fresh out of McGill, all everyone talked about was Dryden's alien physique. "They let up every once in a while," Don Cherry would say of Montreal. "You'd get by Lafleur, the defence, and there'd be that octopus waiting for you." After losing to Montreal in the '71 playoffs, Gerry Cheevers refused to shake hands ("I've never congratulated a guy for beating me"), but asked a reporter to "tell that giraffe he had a hell of a series."

Seemingly with eight arms and legs as long as the St. Lawrence, Dryden's size and reach intimidated shooters. When play drifted to the other end, the big goalie stood loafing on his Sher-Wood, like all this hockey stuff was easy. The implacable calm belied an intensely competitive nature. In the 1973 finals against Chicago, the Habs missed a chance to salt away the Cup, losing at home in a wild shootout, 8–7. Toe Blake dropped by afterwards to give Dryden a pep talk, but he couldn't get close for all the reporters. Nevertheless, he heard the frustrated netminder complain about his defence.

Uh-oh. Toe tiptoed away. *It's not my team anymore,* he told himself. In the middle of the night, however, the old coach broke down and phoned Scotty Bowman. "You're going to have a problem with Dryden when that stuff hits the papers," he said. What should I do? Montreal's new coach wondered.

The kid is supposed to be frugal?

Yeah, I guess.

Tell him to take his defencemen out to lunch.

That he did, and the Habs won their next game—and the Cup—in Chicago. Paradoxically, as the Canadiens improved, Dryden's job grew more difficult. Tending net for a great hockey team was like being a lighthouse keeper: long stretches without action, followed by interludes of terror—a breakaway . . . a bad bounce leading to a two-on-one. Working inside a good, frothy sweat, goalies handled such chances automatically. But when you were cold, out of sync . . .

Dryden's gift was focus. Something he worked at, like a prospective law student cramming for LSATs. He checked into a hotel a day before the 1975 New Year's Eve game against the Red Army. Just to prepare mentally.

It helped that the great goalie eventually became a good sport. In his book *The Game,* Dryden recounted how once, sitting around after practice, teammates acted out his worst-ever goals. Players savoured every embarrassment. The time René Robert beat him on a softy. How about Bobby Schmautz? Did anyone remember that Lanny McDonald score from way out? Finally, Steve Shutt, as always, delivered the *coup de grâce*: "Hey, what about Bob Plager's goal?" Now everyone took turns describing a wobbly, bad-angle shot that dribbled off Dryden's trapper into the net with eight seconds left in a period. "*Câlisse,* Bob Plager," muttered Guy Lapointe. "It was so slow there were three minutes left when he shot it."

Dryden pretended to enjoy the attention. The Vézina winner also made an effort at fitting into Montreal. Dryden learned French (sort of) and deserved the Order of Canada he would receive one day just for going on *Apellez-Moi Lise,* a popular French late-night talk show of the era. He even appeared on Lise Payette's annual mid-'70s popularity contest, *Le Plus Bel Homme du Canada.* When singer Diane Dufresne stopped to sing him a song, staring for a second into his hazel eyes, the goalie reached into a burgundy leisure suit for a pocket-sized French-English dictionary, a prepared gag that brought down the province. *I guess not every Englisher from Toronto is a wet blanket,* Quebecers concluded.

MICHEL "BUNNY" LAROCQUE

Dryden's backup . . . and persistent competition, with a .701 winning percentage between 1974 and 1979. (Dryden's was .659, albeit against better teams.)

5. GUY LAPOINTE

19. LARRY ROBINSON

18. SERGE SAVARD

"The Big Three" were the steel foundation of the Habs' '70s dynasty—a trio of oversized, powerful defenders who played both ends of the rink with supreme effectiveness. Son of a firefighter and brother to a cop, Guy Lapointe was a master of male locker-room horseplay. Like all good jokers, Lapointe saved his best gags for rulers and kings. He filled referees' skates with shaving cream and climbed to the top of the Forum rafters, struggling with a garbage can full of water, which he then poured 100 or so feet, with the accumulating force of an exploding fire hose, onto the head of John Ferguson, hockey's heavyweight champion. Prime Minister Trudeau once breezed through the receiving line at a Forum Stanley Cup celebration until coming face to face with a grinning fool sporting a Prince Valiant haircut. *Felicitations,* the prime minister offered, shaking Lapointe's hand. A flicker of uncertainty then clouded the PM's eyes. *I suppose some labourers perspire quite freely,* the millionaire's son told himself. Wrong. Guy's hand was dripping with Vaseline.

On the ice, Lapointe was fearless, fighting when necessary, usually against the other team's designated hitters—Cashman, Schultz, Tiger Williams, King Kong Korab. The defenceman scored when he had to, too. "Go," coach Scotty Bowman would say, tapping his shoulder with the game on the line. With that, Number Five would jump onto the ice, grab the puck and take off, arousing teammates and fans.

Though hobbled, Serge Savard skated alongside Lapointe in the 1972 Summit Series against Russia. Because of injuries, he could play only five games. That Canada won four, tying the fifth, losing whenever he wasn't around, pretty well sums up his value to the team. A fine rusher early in his career, before suffering two broken legs, the big rearguard matured into an almost-errorless defensive specialist. Every now and then, though, Serge would just take off, his mouth open, sheepdog forelock parting in the wind, bounding up the right side. In 1969, Savard became the first defenceman to win the playoff MVP trophy. Ten years later, he showed up out of nowhere in overtime to knock in a game-winning goal in the finals against the New York Rangers. In between, he was, year in and year out, hockey's most capable stay-at-home defender.

Four stories high (six feet, four inches) and noodle thin, Larry Robinson was cut by his local junior team, the Ottawa 67's. All coach Bill Long could see was a too-skinny, not-yet-coordinated youngster. The farm kid who learned to skate pushing a milk stool around a pond finally made the OHA two winters later, filling out and growing up in a hurry. That he'd married a girl from the next farm over and become a teenage father undoubtedly hastened his maturation.

Pollock took him in the second round of the '71 draft, after Robinson had played a single campaign with the Kitchener Rangers. He was a project, the Montreal GM figured. Habs assistant GM Claude Ruel worked with Larry's footwork and positioning, while Halifax coach Al MacNeil encouraged the defenceman to take greater advantage of his strength, advising him to clobber the first forward he encountered upon joining the Canadiens in 1973. That he did, obliterating dumbfounded Minnesota North Star Bob Nevin.

Robinson didn't dress for the first round of the playoffs in his rookie season. Next series, facing the roughneck Philadelphia Flyers, Bowman kept him on the bench just in case. The second game went into overtime. His first shift that extra session, Robinson grabbed the puck as it rounded the boards and started moving. He was about to pass to a circling Frank Mahovlich. Big Frank saw that the charging rookie had a head of steam. "Take it," he hollered. And so the kid charged into the Flyers end, winding up for a blueline slapshot that goalie Doug Favell could only wave at. The Forum exploded. Suddenly a hero, Robinson didn't know what to do. He hopped, tossed his stick, throwing his gloves off. Watching the ungainly striptease, fans decided Larry was a dead ringer for the roller-skating yellow ostrich on the popular kids show *Sesame Street*. A new Montreal hockey hero, Big Bird, was born.

Ten months later, the Flyers again visited Montreal. Dave Schultz sucker-punched John Van Boxmeer, knocking him out. Minutes later, Robinson grabbed Schultz, holding him steady, as if measuring the Flyer for a casket. And then he went to work, hammering Broad Street's most famous bully to the ice. Robinson was now hockey's heavyweight champ—a hawk roosting on the blue line, waiting for opportunities to mete out justice.

Together, Robinson and Savard represented an evolved hockey species—size XXL all stars. When Serge, Larry and Dryden crowded the crease in goalmouth scrums, every one of them six-foot-seven on their skates, collectively 700 or so pounds, shooters found themselves paraphrasing the most famous line from the 1975 movie *Jaws*.

"We're going to need a bigger net."

23. BOB GAINEY

21. DOUG JARVIS

27. RICK CHARTRAW

6. JIMMY ROBERTS

GMs shopping for a left winger in the 1973 junior draft knew all about Morris Titanic and Darcy Rota, who had piled up 61 and 73 goals, respectively, for the Sudbury Wolves and Edmonton Oil Kings. Montreal bypassed both for Bob Gainey, a checker from the Peterborough Petes. No one knew why. Three months later, the mystery was solved.

Montreal played Boston in an exhibition game in Halifax. Bobby Orr raced down the boards, ready to unload . . . until Gainey caught up and hauled him down. *Caught Bobby Orr!*

Montreal GM Pollock prized speed and size. "I used to get phone calls from [Canadiens owner] David Molson. He'd say, 'Do you know about this junior, how many goals he has?'" Sam told me in a 1993 conversation. "And I'd go, 'But David, is he a good skater? How big is he?'" Pollock knew only so many forwards could fit onto a power play, and that defence won championships. Number 23 quickly turned into hockey's top defensive forward; Red Army coach Viktor Tikhonov called him "the best all-around player in the world."

Gainey changed hockey, creating a momentary category—superstar checker. In 1978, the league began handing out an award—the Frank Selke Trophy, no less—to its top defensive forward. Gainey won the Selke the first four years. With Gainey playing next to speedy faceoff artist Doug Jarvis and either of destructive whirlwind Rick Chartraw or forechecking piranha Jimmy Roberts, Montreal's top defensive line was the hockey equivalent of baseball's top closer at the time, the Yanks' burly fireballer, Goose Gossage. If the Canadiens had a one-goal lead in the game's last minute and Gainey and Jarvis jumped onto the ice, the other team knew the game was already over.

14. MARIO TREMBLAY

8. DOUG RISEBROUGH

11. YVON LAMBERT

If Montreal's number two line, centred variously by Jacques Lemaire, Peter Mahovlich and Pierre Mondou, tried harder, the club's third unit, featuring Mario Tremblay, Doug Risebrough and Yvon Lambert, was indefatigable and a little bit mean. "*La Kid Line*" skated every shift as if the three of them were looking for the guy who stole their car. Mario was 18 when he made the team and quickly earned the nickname "*Le Bleuet Bionique.*" That was because he never stopped moving and he came from Quebec's Saguenay region—*blueberry fields forever.* Nineteen-year-old Risebrough was more intense still, addicted to collisions. Lambert became known as "the French John Ferguson." A source of instant energy, the trio of young overachievers received regular ice time. And Lambert was rewarded with what, at the time, was a greatly appreciated local TV commercial for Dorion Suits, a haberdasher located next to a Poulet Frit à la Kentucky and a strip club in the Montreal suburb of Dorion. "Where you never 'ave any ass-el," according to pitchman Lambert. Presumably, he meant "hassle," which is exactly what the Kid Line was for opponents from 1974–79.

28. PIERRE LAROUCHE

A 50-goal scorer for Pittsburgh at age 20, traded to Montreal in 1977 as part of hockey's only multi-Peter trade—Pierre Larouche and Peter Marsh for Peters Mahovlich and Lee. In Montreal, Larouche often sat on the bench, an insurance policy in case centres Lemaire, Pierre Mondou and Risebrough stopped producing. Cutthroat internal competition was a defining characteristic of the '70s Canadiens. "Our practices are often tougher than our games," Steve Shutt complained/bragged at one point.

10. GUY LAFLEUR

20. PETE MAHOVLICH

25. JACQUES LEMAIRE

22. STEVE SHUTT

At first, Big Pete centred Montreal's top line. A six-foot, five-inch explorer who liked to carry the puck, Big Pete tired out defences with winding, rink-long expeditions before passing off to Lafleur or Shutt. The Little M wore out coaches, too. Hours before game six of the 1972 Summit Series in Moscow, he approached Harry Sinden with bad news. His left arm was in a sling. *Harry, I dislocated it, sorry as hell.* Sinden dissolved. Minutes later, Pete strolled by, a grin tugging the corner of his lips, wearing the sling on his right arm.

Joking wasn't something you did with Habs coach Scotty Bowman. And Pete eventually lost a step . . . too much partying—maybe he left it in a bar somewhere. He was then demoted to the second line, replaced by Lemaire, an older, wiser, two-way player content to allow *Le Démon Blond* and Shutt do more offensive spadework. That was not a problem; in his prime, Lafleur was a playmaking right winger who combined great speed with an Orr-like improvisational genius—a knack for spotting the open side street in every traffic jam.

Shutt would be a perfect fit on hockey's best line. He grew up in a Toronto suburb, playing hockey in a floodlit backyard rink crowded with every dreaming NHL wannabe in Willowdale. That was where he first learned to capitalize on a scoring chance in an instant, before some big kid knocked the puck away. With the Canadiens, he would slip behind enemy lines, redirecting passes and tipping in rebounds before

Steve Shutt should have an honoured place in Canada's Hoser Hall of Fame for being wingman to both Guy Lafleur and Geddy Lee, the lead singer with a tire squeal for a voice who fronts the All-Canadian rock band Rush. In fact, Lee always points out it is Shutt who introduced him to Rush's speedy guitar player, Alex Lifeson. (The boys all went to Fisherville Junior High in North York, outside Toronto.)

Before joining the Canadiens, Shutt was a star on the Toronto Marlboros, playing alongside Billy Harris and Dave Gardner, one of the most famous lines in Canadian junior hockey. From there, he went on to become *Les Glorieux*'s first 60-goal scorer, finding time in his spare time to create, along with teammate Larry Robinson, the Montreal Polo Club. Horses . . . horses . . . horses!

play-by-play men René Lecavalier or Danny Gallivan could even announce his presence.

15. RÉJEAN HOULE

6. PIERRE MONDOU

12. YVAN COURNOYER

Only five-foot-seven, with legs so muscular that he required specially tailored pants, Yvan Cournoyer was hockey's fastest skater for years. Many a defenceman caught a cold in his shivery tailwind. Yvan also played with unquenchable passion. You could sometimes hit the racing winger, but you'd never keep him down. Stop his bullet-hard shots, but watch how he fought for rebounds. "The Roadrunner" embodied what made *Les Habitants* great—burning speed and desire.

Acquired in a haul of draft picks for Terry Harper, Pierre Mondou helped Montreal's Halifax AHL farm team to consecutive championships before joining the parent club for an even bigger party in the spring of 1977. A skilled checker with speed and goalmouth finesse, Mondou centred the team's second line at age 22—his reward for being able to play Coach Bowman's deliriously up-tempo, mistake-free hockey.

"Pinotte" (peanut) to his teammates, Réjean Houle was a continuously happy, humble *travailleur*. Left wing, centre, right wing . . . didn't matter where or how much he played. If only Pinotte could be as good around the net as he was in the dressing room. Still, he scored 27 evenstrength goals in the 1977–78 season—same as superstar Marcel Dionne.

30. PAT HUGHES

31. MARK NAPIER

17. MURRAY WILSON

Fast, faster and fastest. Toronto-raised bit players whose dizzying speed, when called upon, kept the opposition off-balance and fatally discouraged. Napier emerged in the '80s as a top goal scorer.

2. BILL NYROP

3. BRIAN ENGBLOM

26. PIERRE BOUCHARD

24. GILLES LUPIEN

Big, bigger, bigger still, and hockey's first giraffe. Bill Nyrop (six-foot-two, 205 pounds) was an All-American boy whose dad ran the Federal Aviation Administration (FAA) for Eisenhower. Bill led his Minnesota high school hockey team to a state title and made backup quarterback at Notre Dame. By 1976, he was playing alongside Guy Lapointe. Strong and beyond dedicated, Bill hurried home after practice to lift weights. He looked to be a Habs blueline mainstay, but Montreal, big-city life, maybe it was the '70s, got to him. In the fall of 1978 he quit, leaving the Forum in a camper, heading off for a piece of Montana sky. Brian Engblom would be his replacement, equally big and faster.

Canadiens royalty, Pierre Bouchard was the son of former captain Butch Bouchard. Movie-star handsome, popular with teammates and good with the dukes, he was on the ice when Philly or Boston came to town. The biggest defender ever at the time, six-foot, six-inch Gilles Lupien was also good at the rough stuff, but lacked poise. To quote Mordecai Richler, "Lupien treats the puck as somebody else might being caught with another man's wife."

———

This was the last great and best-ever Canadiens team. Unlike the late-'50s dynasty, there were only four Montrealers—Lapointe, Lemaire, Savard and Bouchard. Still, you had 12 Quebecers. And Robinson came from a bilingual community in the Ottawa Valley. Besides, all the guys pulling the strings on the '70s-era Canadiens were Montrealers from the Selke years.

Although he'd hung up his fedora, former coach Toe Blake was vice-president ("They still haven't told me of what," he joked). GM Pollock never showed up in the dressing room, but he was at every game, high in the Forum, speaking sometimes into a walky-talky to former Canadien Floyd "Busher" Curry down at ice level. If Sam saw anything, he got word to Busher, who hurried to inform the coach. Messages sometimes got lost in translation. Once, with Montreal up 3–2 over Boston and time running out, Curry raced, panting, to the bench with the helpful suggestion: "Sam says don't let them score on you."

Pollock's business protege, Irving Grundman, was a butcher's boy who grew up plucking chickens on the Main. Right-hand hockey man Claude Ruel was another Habs lifer. "Piton," as he was known, convinced Pollock to draft Robinson and Gainey. Ruel also liked Lafleur over Dionne and believed Dryden was ready in the spring of 1971. Every morning, after the coach put the Habs through a racing, 45-minute practice, Ruel worked with the young kids, getting them ready to compete for championships. And when they did win, the '70s edition of *Les Glorieux* always remembered their roots, capping off Stanley Cup parades with a private team celebration at Henri Richard's Tavern at Park Avenue and Milton. "Every year I think they won't remember, but they always do," Henri would tell a reporter.

One other native Montrealer was responsible for getting the Canadiens to Henri Richard's tavern on time: their coach, William Scott Bowman.

RAIN MAN

Montreal was a city of male-only taverns in the 1970s. There were 700 in town, serving draft beer to working stiffs and on-the-lam husbands.* Joe Beef's was the place to go in St-Henri. (Back in the 19th century, original owner "Joe-Beef" McKiernan kept a basement zoo—a buffalo, some alligators, couple of parrots and monkeys.) Rymark Tavern on Rue Peel sold 150 pig-knuckle platters daily—sweet bits of pork wrapped in blubber and covered in spicy mustard. *Mmm-mmm-mmm!* Many former Canadiens had their own bars. Butch Bouchard's saloon was still around. Toe Blake, the Rocket and Henri Richard had their own taverns. Canadiens once gathered at Toe's after championships. But in the '70s, maybe because a waiter at Blake's once chased Ken Dryden's wife, Lynda, from the premises—*the nerve!*—they dropped into Henri's, on Milton.

The Pocket Rocket bought his place in 1960 from a milliner who went

---

* Women were finally allowed into Montreal taverns in 1979.

broke after the Catholic Church began allowing hatless women into mass. The Montreal centre redid the bar in a classic Habs motif—Canadiens hockey sticks on the ceiling, arborite tables in goal-light red. Upon retirement, Henri pulled beer, while younger brother Claude served as head waiter, settling bills with a metal change maker around his waist. When the victorious Canadiens came around, confetti still in their hair from downtown parades, the "Vest-Pocket Rocket" was everywhere, serving each and every backslapping Canadien, listening in as, like all workingmen in taverns, they complained about their boss.

One time in Oakland, Claude—écoutez-moi . . .

Keep in mind, we haven't lost a game on the West Coast in years—not in Los Angeles, Vancouver . . .

Larry and Serge, they show up late for morning practice . . . who cares . . .

Scotty Bowman, that's who! Before the game that night, he starts giving Larry and Serge the business: Well, I guess some players on this team think they're better than everyone else, he says. Figure they don't have to work as hard . . .

Then we go down deux–zero . . .

I get a pickled egg; get a chance there, Claude . . .

End of period, Scotty—oh boy! To hell with you, you guys, he says, you're not going to play, fine . . . me, I don't coach. That's it! C'est tout!

Just stands there, arms folded, rest a the night . . .

Ha! We score six goal—bing-bang-boom—to win the game. Bowman-là, he just stand there behind the bench, eating ice like peanuts, you know.

One time—I'm serious—we lose a game in the States, we're coming through customs, Scotty, he's fuming, tells them to check our bags, there's something fishy . . . like we're, I don't know, smugglers or something. He takes off, leaves us there for hours.

Tell him about the stick, the one in Chicago.

Oh yeah. What Scotty does is he gives a broken game stick to the elevator guy, tells him, he goes, "Any my players who comes in after midnight, have them sign it." We all sign, right? Nice guys and everything. Next morning, the guy shows Scotty the stick—we're all busted! Ah, there's no pleasing the prick. 'Member St. Louis?

Hoo-boy—19 and 72, do I ever!

We're in the Hilton—there's a fire, eh? Fire department comes. We get a ladder, all the guys, throw it up to Scotty. He's standing there on the ledge, trapped on the fourth or fifth floor. Can't get out, flames licking his arse. We're holding on to the ladder. Smoke everywhere. Trainer, Bob Williams, shimmies up to get him. Comes down, we're all clapping, laughing. You OK, boss? Think he'd laugh or thank us? Cripes, first thing he does he's breathing clean air again, he starts counting all the players, makes sure nobody broke curfew.

Me, I wish he jump.

He's unbelievable. Ever get a coach like that, Claude?

Oiy-oi, believe me, I know. Scotty is my coach, Hull-Ottawa Canadien. Make us wear a 'at everywhere.

He was a Montreal boy, working-class Verdun—grew up on a street lined with 26 tenements. Two kids from his block on Fifth Avenue became safecrackers . . . probably ended up inside the medieval walls of Bordeaux Jail in north Montreal. Scotty wasn't meant for crime, though. His dad, a fine soccer player in Scotland, was shop foreman for a lead furnace company; never missed a day's work in his life. The old man laid down the law at home, too. Young Scotty couldn't stay up to listen to the end of Canadiens or Maroons games on the radio. Dad left the final score, who did what, on a sheet for him to read in the morning. Scotty had his father's round face, the same high forehead, but his temperament—that was his mother's. Jean Bowman once threw her cards in the fire after losing at euchre.

At 17, Scotty was a real go-getter; had his own horse and milk-delivery route in summer. Attended Verdun High come fall. Played centre for the Junior Canadiens, too. But he was just another skater. Coach Sam Pollock didn't use him against Andy Bathgate and the Guelph Biltmores in the last games of the 1952 Eastern Memorial Cup finals. An uncharacteristic vanity allowed Scotty to perpetuate the rumour he was forced to quit hockey because of a fractured skull. That was a bit of a stretch. Biographer Doug Hunter makes a convincing case that, while Scotty was injured, clipped by a high stick, he missed but a single game. No, being realistic,

understanding there was no future for him as a player was the real reason
Scotty hung up his skates. He wouldn't give up hockey, though. He hung
around the Canadiens, encouraged by Sam Pollock, who saw something in
him (maybe himself). Scotty started off as Sam's assistant, watching as
Pollock stormed through games, throwing chairs onto the ice, hitting the
boards with his hand so hard one night that he broke his watch. Scotty
had an outside job as well: selling paint for Sherwin-Williams. Before
long, he had all the chips memorized: *Marshmallow White. Dorian Gray.*
Still, the best time of his day was always lunch, when he dropped in on
Habs coaches at the Forum—first Dick Irvin and later Toe Blake.

"Good if you can get a team laughing before a big game," Irvin told
him one time. That wouldn't be much help to Scotty. Younger brother
Jack, later an accountant and referee (he'd officiate the civil war between
St. Catharines and Quebec City at Le Colisée in 1971) was the funny
Bowman. And youngest brother Martin, a future English professor, was
the storyteller.

Blake was more helpful. Before games, he let Scotty in on his plans
for next game.

You're probably not going to see your friend Terry Harper much tonight.

Toe, he was your best defenceman against Chicago Saturday night.

*Bobby Hull, he's great against. Mahovlich gives him problems. Probably be
using another right-handed defenceman, Jimmy Roberts, more. Who knows—I'll
start Harper, see how he looks.*

Getting the right matchup was how you won, Blake told Scotty.
What left-handed centre should you put out against Stan Mikita for a
faceoff with the game on the line? Béliveau was your best guy, but
Backstrom gave Mikita fits. Keep both out there for the faceoff, maybe,
one on a wing. Tell Backstrom to be aggressive, and if he got thrown out,
then you had Béliveau. Wait—no, referees respected Big Jean. Have *him*
take the faceoff, maybe he can cheat; he gets thrown out, then you go to
Backstrom. That was the smart play.

The smart play, remembering who had done what against whom,
while remaining alive to the dynamics of a particular game, that was the

way Toe coached. That sounded good to Scotty, who had the memory of an elephant: paint chips, the names of the kids in the neighbourhood, how certain goalies, defencemen and forwards did against certain teams, Scotty remembered everything.

His first official coaching job was helping out Pollock in Hull-Ottawa, where he drank in as much sports as he could. In addition to being an assistant and then head coach of the Memorial Cup–winning Hull-Ottawa Canadiens, he lived in a boarding house on Holmwood, in Ottawa, with Kaye Vaughan and a bunch of football players from the Ottawa Rough Riders. (Yes, a boarding house. Scotty made $250 a season coaching at the time.) Saturday afternoon, he'd be at Lansdowne Park, watching the Riders take on Sam Etcheverry and the Montreal Alouettes, or Dick Shatto's Toronto Argonauts. After Ottawa, Scotty coached in Peterborough, where he first exhibited Pollock-like theatrics, getting himself suspended for pantomiming paying off a referee one night. He would take the Petes to a Memorial Cup final his first season. In the early '60s, he was back in the national capital, watching Russ Jackson quarterback the Riders and coaching the Hull-Ottawa Canadiens of the Eastern Professional Hockey League. After that, Sam sent him to Omaha to coach Montreal's top farm team. He was again successful—perfect, in fact, taking the Omaha Knights to eight straight wins before quitting. He couldn't take Nebraska. Nobody talked hockey in football Cornhusker country.

When expansion arrived, Scotty finally graduated to the NHL, assisting GM/head coach Lynn Patrick in St. Louis. The Blues got off to a bad start. Scotty was working behind the bench, handling the defence. One night in Philly, the team had a one-goal lead late in the game. Scotty didn't like the lineup Patrick had sent out and suggested replacing one forward. Seconds later, the winger in question allowed his man to score. The Blues lost again. In the middle of the night, Scotty got a call from Patrick.

"Scotty, you gotta take over the team."

He checked with mentor Pollock in Montreal first, who told him, "If you don't take it, someone else will, and what if he's successful?" Probably, Scotty was always going to take the job. He just wanted to share the good news with Sam; showing deference and maybe showing off, hoping to impress the coach who'd once benched him. Bowman would be an instant success in St. Louis, taking the Blues to two straight Stanley Cup finals losses against—who else?—Montreal. Showing his true colours maybe, Bowman tried to beat the new Canadiens team with the old one, talking Dickie Moore and Doug Harvey into comebacks, trading for Red Berenson and signing Jacques Plante—every one an ex-Hab. Moore told reporters Scotty was a better coach than Toe. Sam filed that away, no doubt. And what did Pollock make of all the stories about what a hard-ass, what a strutting martinet, Scotty could be? According to Montreal hockey reporter Al Strachan, here was how assistant coach Bowman greeted St. Louis Blues recruits at his first training camp, in the autumn of 1967: "There's not one of you belongs in the NHL. There's 40 of you here, 20 of you are going to be in the NHL, though you don't deserve to, so it's going to be the 20 that work the hardest. That's it, let's get on with it."

Scotty was always hard on players. Hard as the ice he chewed during games, reaching down for a handful from a pail behind the bench. One time, while coaching the Montreal Junior Canadiens in the mid-'60s, he didn't like the way the team played against the Niagara Falls Flyers. Next morning, the boys were on the bus again, seven hours up the 401. Only on the return trip home, they stopped in Kingston.

What we doing, Coach?

Grab your equipment. You'll see.

After the loss to the Flyers, a furious Bowman had booked practice time for his team in Kingston. He would race the teenagers hard for an hour. Then everyone jumped back on the bus for Montreal.

Pollock probably smiled hearing all these stories. He was the same way. Once, when Sam ran the Junior Habs, Toe Blake and Kenny Reardon dropped by to watch a game. Pollock hollered at his players—referees, too—nonstop. After one tantrum, an appalled Blake turned to Reardon and asked, "Tell me, do I look like that when I coach?"

Pollock remained a tough GM. When he ran Hull-Ottawa, with Scotty coaching, the Canadiens held a regular promotion—Pot of Gold

Night. Three contestants were brought onto the ice between periods and asked to guess how much was in the pot. An impossible task, really. And there was always a trick question if contestants did somehow manage to get the number right. One evening in Ottawa—the team alternated between the old Ottawa Auditorium and Hull Arena—a fan guessed the right total, several thousand dollars. Next came the skill-testing question: "Who is the leading scorer of the Hull-Ottawa Canadiens?" At the time, Ralph Backstrom was the team's big star and top goal scorer. Most fans would've guessed him. But he wasn't the right answer. Lesser-known Bobby Boucher had a lot of assists. Miraculously, one fan, a factory worker from LeBreton Flats, guessed both the correct pot and point-getter. What do you know, a winner! Everyone cheered. Smiling Scotty helped the guy shovel his winnings into burlap bags, slapping him on the back in congratulation. Afterwards, Pollock gave his coach nothing but grief.

Cripes, that guy took home more money tonight than we did, you know that?

Aw c'mon, Sam. It's a contest.

So is making a living running a hockey team.

Sam mellowed. Coaching made him crazy—turned a highly intelligent, religious, civilized man into a raging churl. That was why Pollock preferred the executive suite, where there was more time for contemplative thinking and almost no chance of destroying your wristwatch. Besides, Sam was always better at the sweet con—reading people and reacting to situations. In the spring of 1966, he sidled up to Big Jean Béliveau after the Habs dropped the first two Stanley Cup final games at home to redhot Roger Crozier and the Detroit Red Wings. "The boys look tight, Jean," Pollock told Béliveau. "Here's $500; take them out to dinner in Detroit. If you have to spend any more, get back to me, I'll reimburse you." The Habs took the next four games, winning yet another Cup.

Pollock and the Canadiens had problems negotiating the violent turn that saw the '60s become the '70s. After Toe Blake quit in 1968, the Canadiens won Stanley Cups in 1969 and 1971. But they spit out two coaches along the way. Claude Ruel quit in late 1970—pressure. Al

MacNeil took the Habs to a Cup in 1971, but endured a public fight with Henri Richard, who accused him of favouring English players over French. At the time, there were threats against MacNeil's life. While all of this was going on, Scotty Bowman was fired by the St. Louis Blues. He was GM at the time and the Blues' new boss, Sidney Salomon III, had come to hate him. Scotty dropped in on Sam to say hi when he was back in Montreal. Bowman had coaching offers from the West Coast in his pocket—the Kings and the Seals both wanted him—but he probably thought that'd be like being in Omaha, only worse, surrounded by even more people who didn't care about hockey.

"I may have something for you here," Sam said.

Such was Pollock's genius that, in the summer of 1971, Montreal somehow ended the 1970-71 season with both the Stanley Cup and the first-overall draft pick. Those headlines gave Sam some time, but what was he going to do with his coaching mess? And what about the suddenly rebellious Henri Richard and the latest French–English snowball fight? He didn't want to lose anybody, especially fans, but it seemed as if Sam was cornered. MacNeil wanted back and deserved to be coach; he had just won the Cup, after all. But the perception was that he had insulted a Richard, and the public all felt the time had come for a French coach. Then there was the problem of whom to make captain. Béliveau was retiring. What was Sam to do?

More genius: he made MacNeil GM of the team's Halifax affiliate, hinting he'd be next in line for Sam's job. The master stroke, though, was making Henri captain so that the public might accept, maybe not a French coach, but a Verdun native who could at least speak the language of Quebec's majority. William Scott Bowman finally had the job he always wanted—Toe Blake's. And like Blake himself, who was made coach just in time to enjoy the fruits of Frank Selke's labour, Scotty was fortunate to be taking over the Canadiens when he did.

Once, when coaching the Blues, Bowman confronted his overachieving team during a losing streak, saying, "I suppose you all have a better way to shuffle this deck and come up with a winning hand." After which

Scotty sneered, "But let me tell you this, gentlemen, you can't shuffle deuces and threes."

That wouldn't be his problem in Montreal. Thanks to Sam Pollock, Scotty Bowman would be dealing from a stacked deck—among the 50 players he coached during his eight-year reign in Montreal, 12 became Hall of Famers.

HABS TO
THE RESCUE

Montreal Canadiens vs. Philadelphia Flyers, May 9–16, 1976

For once, the Montreal Canadiens were in the Forum watching someone else work: veteran comedian Bob Hope was booked into the
hockey arena in mid-April, taping his latest NBC-TV special, *The Road
to the Montreal Olympics*, with guests Bing Crosby, Shirley Jones (Broadway
singer and keyboard player for TV's *The Partridge Family*), Freddie
Prinze and Quebec teen sensation René Simard. Ever topical, Bob joked
about labour difficulties threatening the upcoming 1976 Summer Games:
"I'm here in Montreal, where the women are really built and the Olympics
are half-built." With the Canadiens in attendance, seated front and
centre, the comedian had hockey gags, too. Why not? There was plenty
of material: this past January, the Broad Street Bullies had made front-
page news, hounding the Soviet Red Army off the ice in Philadelphia.
And days prior to Hope's Montreal appearance, Toronto police arrested

three Philadelphia Flyers for exhibiting too much of the old ultraviolence during a playoff game at Maple Leaf Gardens. Leaning on his familiar stage prop, a golf driver, Old Ski-Jump Nose began riffing on Canada's troubled winter pastime.

"With a national sport like hockey, no wonder you have social medicine. Speaking of hockey, I heard of a player who had a concussion and three fractures and lost four front teeth . . . and he was still in the dressing room. I want to tell you, though, hockey is an easy game to understand. It starts with a faceoff, and after that, it's arms off and heads off . . ."

Noting that the Canadiens weren't exactly rolling in the aisles, Bob tossed the players a nervous aside: "Look, I watched you last night and you weren't that funny, either."

No, the Canadiens weren't laughing. Hockey's most storied team took the game very seriously. *"Nos bras meurtris vous tendent le flambeau, à vous toujours de le porter bien haut!"* In 1952, Habs coach Dick Irvin had that passage, a translated quote from John McRae's World War I anthem "In Flanders Fields," inscribed on Forum walls. "To you from failing hands we throw the torch; be yours to hold it high."

Right now—up in the clouds, presumably—Howie Morenz and Newsy Lalonde had *Hockey Night in Heaven* on, awaiting the first game of the 1976 Stanley Cup finals, the long-anticipated clash between the Canadiens and the Flyers. Aurèle Joliat was still alive, living in Ottawa, most likely watching the game at his local, the Prescott Hotel on Preston Street. As for the Rocket, he'd be in the Forum. As was Prime Minister Trudeau, seated in the first row behind the Canadiens bench, dressed in a caramel leather jacket, with five-year-old Justin squirming in his lap. Like Morenz, Joliat and the others, Pierre *et famille* wanted the Canadiens to win. Quebec, most of Canada and the U.S. hockey establishment were all pulling for the Habs, too, in what would be the most eagerly awaited Cup final since Rocket Richard's Canadiens battled Gordie Howe's Red Wings for the Cup in the mid-'50s.

What a matchup: hockey's greatest team, *Les Glorieux,* vs. the defending Stanley Cup champions, Freddy Shero's rough-and-ready Philadelphia

A ubiquitous party crasher on the Canadian sports scene throughout the 1970s, Prime Minister Pierre Elliot Trudeau showed up regularly at Grey Cup and Stanley Cup games. His adored father, Charles Trudeau, was a wealthy businessman/sportsman who sat on the board of directors of the Montreal Royals baseball team. Charles Trudeau died when son Pierre was in his adolescence, and biographers have speculated that his early departure robbed Trudeau of an authority figure to defy. Hence, PET's rebellious streak—sliding down banisters in public and telling opposition members to "fuddle duddle." In any case, the prime minister embraced the sporting life in public, sometimes showing up to winter games in his father's college raccoon coat.

Flyers. At last, a fair fight between good and evil! Vegas had the Canadiens winning it all, but Ted Burke at the Montreal *Gazette* liked evil—the Flyers in six.

That was the storyline, anyway. The Flyers were hockey with ketchup on it—blood everywhere. History required that *Les Canadiens,* dressed in their save-the-day RCMP scarlet tunics, rescue the sport that they had made great.

It could be argued the standard narrative of the '76 finals was a disservice to the Philadelphia Flyers, who were not always what they seemed.

After the Flyers bludgeoned the Leafs, playing at times disgraceful hockey, losing their poise and discipline (not to mention three games to a .500 club), Shero's team played an efficient, errorless series against the Boston Bruins, who'd finished in third place overall, with 113 points. Philly brushed the Bruins aside in five games. And did so with a minimum of rough stuff—four penalties in games three and five; in the fourth, only Reggie Leach and Hound Kelly were penalized, and even then for minor infractions. "We were ready for lots of fights, penalties, using our power play and penalty killers, and they totally surprised us," lamented Bruins leader Don Cherry, NHL coach of the year. "Fred Shero is the best coach in hockey."

And if Shero was the sport's top coach, Bobby Clarke had to be its best on-ice leader. One story from this season demonstrated Bobby's ability to make every Flyer feel a part of the team. Injuries forced Philly to bring up defenceman Terry Murray from Richmond. Clarke saw that the kid was unsure of his place on the team. "Hey, Terry, you got no wheels? Here are the keys to my Mercedes," Clarke said. "I prefer to drive my Jeep anyways."

While the Flyers weren't always thugs, neither were the Habs faultless good guys, angels playing hockey instead of harps. Midway through the 1975–76 preseason, Philadelphia and Montreal played back-to-back games. In Quebec on Saturday night, Scotty Bowman started bruisers Pierre Bouchard and Rick Chartraw at forward, a clear signal for the Flyers to put up their dukes. Minutes in, Dave Schultz cross-checked Habs captain Yvan Cournoyer. A split-second later, Dougie Risebrough hopped onto Schultz's back, clawing and snarling—a mountain lion fighting a grizzly.

But it was in Philadelphia where Montreal really let the Flyers have it. Poor referee Bruce Hood—380 penalty minutes, 11 fights. All that in a game that failed to go the distance. With two minutes left and Montreal up 6–2, Bowman threw out a power play with Larry Robinson at centre, flanked by big, tough minor leaguers Sean Shanahan and Glenn Goldup. Hulks Bouchard and Chartraw were on defence. It was a lineup calculated to raise welts, not score goals. Scotty was challenging the Flyers to a showdown. Philly never had to be asked twice. Before the puck was dropped, the benches emptied. Mel Bridgman grabbed Guy Lafleur. Mario Tremblay asked to cut in—"Come round here, you'll see I'm no Lafleur." They went at it. As did Risebrough and Clarke. In fact Risebrough started the whole ruckus.

"See you next game," Clarke said after taking a shot.

"Why wait?" Risebrough responded.

Soon everyone had paired off, cursing and yanking each other's sweaters, except for goalies Ken Dryden and Bernie Parent. "I just had my teeth capped," Bernie explained after the game, which Hood called off with a few minutes to go. The Canadiens more than held their own through all the rough stuff. Risebrough gave Clarke a shiner. And Bouchard got in the best insult.

"I'll remember you," Flyer Jack McIlhargey screamed.

"I'm not worried—you'll be in the minors," Pierre laughed.

Shero kept the Flyers dressing room closed for 15 minutes after the fight-shortened game, Réjean Tremblay would report in *La Presse*. Once the doors opened, Shero's boys laughed off the loss of a game and a few fights. "Don't know what happened," Clarke said, referring to his purple swollen eye. "I think Mahovlich got hold of my arms and Risebrough gave me a shot. Ah, it's only a cut, but I earned my 60 bucks tonight." (At the time, NHLers received $60 for exhibition games.) On the plane to Montreal, Canadiens players seemed happier than they'd been in years, Tremblay wrote. Mario and Gainey told him the fights were good for the team. They now knew they could play Philadelphia hockey and win. The reporter then found Bowman, telling him, "The boys say the fights are a big boost for the season." Scotty gave Tremblay a little wink, and then looked away when players lost a 26er of Tia Maria into their coffees.

Montreal's coach couldn't be happier. He knew the Flyers were the team to beat this season, and so he wanted to start preparing for them early. Throughout the year, he would keep reminding players of their chief rival.

"You've got to move the puck around like Philadelphia," he would yell at practice. Or "If you're going to forecheck, you're going to have to do like Philadelphia." Bowman's steady praise of the Flyers upset his players, as intended. In his book, *Robinson for the Defence*, co-written with Chrys Goyens, Larry Robinson remembered Guy Lapointe storming into the dressing room after one workout, grumbling, "Remember boys, you have to play like Philadelphia, because they're so good and we suck. Even though we're 15 points ahead of them in the standings and they couldn't catch us if the season lasted until August."

Montreal did finish first, probably because they gave up the fewest goals in the league, nine fewer than Philadelphia. "Win the Vézina and you'll be there," Toe Blake always said. That was Scotty's mantra, too. It helped to have Dryden in nets, but Bowman deserved credit for turning the goalie into a better teammate. Years earlier, the coach noticed Dryden was sometimes a little distant in the dressing room, reluctant to mix with co-workers. *Think you're better than others?* Bowman asked Dryden one day, point blank. The goalie became furious. *Going to Cornell didn't make me a snob.* But upon returning to Montreal after a prolonged contract dispute that saw him article at a Toronto law firm for a year, Dryden figured that, yes, maybe he could work harder at being one of the guys. A new-and-improved, easier-to-get-along-with Dryden returned to Montreal in the fall of 1974, making the Habs a better team.

So did Sam Pollock's recycling program, of course. What a deal-maker! In 1964, he traded Billy Hicke for Dick Duff, who helped the team win four Stanley Cups, and then swapped Duff to the Los Angeles Kings for a draft pick who turned into Larry Robinson. (Nine Stanley Cups for Billy Hicke!) In addition to Big Bird, *La Kid Line*—Risebrough, Mario Tremblay and Yvon Lambert—were coming on. As old now as his sweater number, 22, Steve Shutt was suddenly the premier left winger in hockey. And Gainey turned out even better than Claude Ruel imagined. Montreal's checking line—Gainey, Doug Jarvis and old pro Jim Roberts—held the Islanders' top line of Bryan Trottier, Clark Gillies and Billy Harris to a single goal in the '76 semifinals.

New York Rangers star Rod Gilbert summed up what it was like playing against hockey's first (and only ever) superstar defensive forward: "If I got a headache, Gainey would check the Aspirin off me."

But if there was one player who made Montreal great, inspiring players and fans alike, it was Guy Lafleur. Becoming a star didn't happen right away, mind you. Before exciting teammates, Guy first had to learn to turn himself on. And in the beginning, Montreal was too much for the NHL rookie. After games, he floated up Autoroute 40 to Quebec City in his new Cadillac Eldorado. Once, after a Sunday afternoon contest at the Forum, he raced to catch the end of the Quebec peewee tournament. Like Beatle Paul, Guy believed in yesterday. In Montreal, he seldom went out. Stood alone in the beautiful Longueuil apartment Jean Béliveau's wife, Elise, had found for him, staring out his 14th-floor picture window. Across the St. Lawrence were ghostly reminders of Expo 67—La Ronde, the Ferris wheel. Maybe empty carnival rides got him thinking about his lost youth. He played Barbra Streisand and Mireille Mathieu albums and moped. Sometimes it got so bad he wrote poetry.

The Canadiens weren't happy, either. Forget Baudelaire; they expected another Béliveau. For three seasons, Guy scored fewer than 30 goals. Seemed to be getting worse, too—29 goals as a rookie, then 25 and . . . 21. Alarmed, Pollock told Ruel, "Use whatever method you want; prod him or pamper him, whatever it takes to get him going."

At first, Claude wondered if the problem was Guy's roommate, Frank Mahovlich. The Big M was too gloomy, Ruel told Bowman. So the Canadiens made effervescent Steve Shutt Guy's road companion. Bowman tried him at centre with Reggie Houle and Marc Tardif; auditioned him on Lemaire's wing. Nothing worked, not even Cupid's arrow. There was this girl in Lafleur's apartment building, an airline hostess, Lise Barré—beautiful, worldly. Guy felt complete around her. They moved in—but didn't sleep—together. There was another woman, a second flight attendant, Collette. It was she whom Guy took to a 1972 Habs Christmas function. Who knew why? Lafleur didn't want to settle down yet, maybe. What did Baudelaire say? "A sweetheart is a bottle of wine; a wife is a wine bottle."

When Guy returned home from the party, Lise was gone, clothes and everything. Panicking, Lafleur phoned her parents in Quebec City in the middle of the night. Lise's grumpy dad told him off. Lafleur showed up 90 minutes later, eyes wild with panic. How often does a story like this end badly? Some guy goes to a Christmas work party, has too much to drink, there is some incident, and he tears off in a car, going 140 miles an hour on winter highways. That didn't happen tonight, though. Not with this Guy.

"What do you want?" Lise asked, bursting into tears when she found Lafleur at her door.

"Do you have any cognac?" After that, a confession: "I can't live without you."

"I don't want to be your servant."

"Then be my wife."

Though happy, Guy remained a mess at work. During practice, Bowman would call out drills: "I want the forwards to skate to centre ice, turn behind a defenceman, look for the puck and then make a pass up the left wing." Guy inevitably flubbed the play. On and off the ice, he was driving Pollock nuts. The kid couldn't score, and with a million Montreal girls to fall in love with, why oh why did he pick Roger Barré's daughter? The wealthy car dealer was part owner of the World Hockey Association's Quebec Nordiques. "From now on, we consider Guy Lafleur to be an ordinary player," Sam told reporters. "If he has some good moments, so much the better. But we aren't expecting anything from him."

Left alone, finally something clicked. In the summer of 1974, Guy advised Lise he felt like playing hockey again. He would arrive at the Forum early during training camp, skating alone before everyone else arrived. Never mind Bowman's plays; Guy began choreographing his own moves again, like back in Thurso on those weekend mornings before Ti-Paul showed up at the Singer Arena. In the team's second practice that autumn, he forgot his helmet in the dressing room. Seemingly liberated, he played better. Fans noticed the difference, screaming for him again during exhibition games. Could it be the helmet? Was this like in an old Hollywood movie where the shy ingénue finally lets her hair down, becoming instantly beautiful? No, Lafleur had tried removing his helmet before, in a March 1972 game against Pittsburgh. Nothing happened. No, it was something else. Guy had cut down on smoking. Thinking of Brother Leo, or maybe his recently deceased *grand-père* Damien, Lafleur now said a few prayers before games—*Je vous salue, Marie, pleine de grace . . . Hail Mary, full of grace . . .*

The prayers didn't work, not at first. Guy scored one goal in the first ten games of the '74–75 season. Still, everyone agreed he looked better helmetless, his hair a rippling flag in the breeze. "He looks faster," Buffalo's Jerry Korab commented. Then it happened: the Flower finally blossomed. Guy fired two past Tony Esposito on Saturday, October 30, a 3–3 tie against Chicago. With that, he was off—13 goals in November. For the next six seasons, he would be the best hockey player in the world.

No one was happier than Bowman. Guy had the perfect anatomy for hockey, it turned out. At rest, his heart beat less than 40 times a minute, the same as Belgian cycling champion Eddy Merckx. And Lafleur had unusual recuperative powers. What hockey coach wouldn't like to tweak and improve his second and third lines? Add more speed and the league's best scorer to the mix. Lafleur gave Bowman that option. He could be double- and triple-shifted—play with Pete Mahovlich and Steve Shutt, and then pop up alongside Lemaire two shifts later. If Mario Tremblay was out of bionic blueberries, Scotty placed Guy alongside Doug Risebrough and Yvon Lambert. Sometimes he was a centre, with Bouchard and Chartraw on his flanks.

With Guy, Scotty worked on his communication skills. Lafleur finished the '75–76 season on a Sunday afternoon, leading the NHL in scoring, a couple points up on Bobby Clarke. The Flyers played that evening, however. Not that Guy was paying attention to their game. Someone else was, though. Late that night, Guy received a call in his Washington hotel room.

"Guy Lafleur there?"

"He's not here," Lafleur said. Why admit who he was? Could be a fan . . . or worse still, a reporter.

"It's Scotty. The scoring record looks pretty safe. Rangers are leading [Philadelphia] 2–0. Clarke's not going to come up with five points in a minute."

That Scotty was suddenly so chummy with a player didn't make him a front-runner or hypocrite. Lafleur was just one of those players who turned everyone, even coaches and rival players, into fans. Bowman was also paying rightful homage to the first Canadien to win a scoring championship since Boom Boom Geoffrion in 1961. Otherwise, Scotty was Mean Mr. Mustard with players, even though the team was winning . . . maybe we should say *because* they were winning. He was funny that way. When the Habs lost, Bowman pretty well left players alone. When they won, he was sometimes impossible.

On one successful road trip, Pete Mahovlich showed up at the team's hotel hours after curfew. Bowman charged him from across the lobby. "You're late for curfew," he said, getting in Pete's face. "You know how long I've been waiting? I've been waiting here two hours, and that will cost you $200."

A strong-willed bunch, Montreal players banded together against their coach. On off days, he was the other team! The night Scotty jumped on Mahovlich, Big Pete just gave him a bleary Seagram smile. "I'm going to help you get your beauty sleep tomorrow night, Scotty," Mahovlich said, handing him a pile of crumpled bills. "Here's the money for tomorrow night, too." One morning on the road, Scotty called an early practice. Players were to meet in front of the hotel right after breakfast. They did. Everyone was eventually there. Except where was their ride?

C'mon Scotty, where's the bus? Morning's wasting away here.

Osti, what are we doing standing around? Me, I feel like a good practice.

Bowman paced angrily, checking his watch. Finally, he stormed inside the hotel. "Where's my bus?" he demanded. "Why, it's been cancelled, sir. Someone with a French accent called," he was told. Outside, Serge Savard and Guy Lapointe tried not to laugh.

Sometimes, you'd swear the Canadiens were a last-place team. Most coaches sat at the front of the team bus and buried their heads in a newspaper, oblivious to the clowning players behind them. Not Bowman: he positioned himself at the back, glaring. Minutes before departure time, there'd always one seat empty. Scotty would squirm, checking his watch. Then, at 9:01, Pete Mahovlich inevitably bounced onto the bus, coffee in hand. "Morning, everyone." Then he would tell the driver, "We're all here now." With that, his teammates would all let out a whoop.

"Fuck off, Mahovlich," Scotty yelled from back of the bus.

"Fuck me?" the player said, feigning astonishment. "Fuck you."

How much of this was role-playing is debatable. Scotty could be a tyrant and was seemingly indifferent to suffering. Henri Richard discovered he wasn't playing the first game of the 1974–75 season by reading a blackboard lineup. Didn't matter if you were captain, a Richard—couple of bad shifts, you were on the bench. Even there, you weren't safe. Once, Scotty barked at Rick Chartraw and Pierre Bouchard during an intermission. Pierre looked up. Neither he nor Rick had played the period previous. "You guys aren't cheering loud enough," Scotty said.

Montreal's coach wanted inside players' heads. "He loved to take charge of human beings called hockey players," Canadiens scout Ron Caron would later comment. "I think Scotty dreamt of being a detective." Whatever, by the time Robinson, Shutt and Lafleur rounded into shape, Inspector Bowman had developed an uncanny sense of how to goad his team into playing their best, even if that meant they frequently despised him.

On the morning of Saturday, May 8, 1976, Scotty put the Canadiens through a furious scrimmage. The Flyers were in the next day—first game of the Cup finals. At last, the epic showdown—the Habs vs. the Hab-nots, those villainous bullies from Philly. Canadiens scrimmages were great entertainment—Gainey checked Lafleur. There were also side bets—who came closest to hitting Bowman, out there on the ice, with a cock-high clearing shot? An hour into the session, Lapointe made one of his patented rushes, hoping to resolve a tie game. He was yelling as he went, drawing jeers from fellow players. Pointu deked around a falling check and was closing in on net when he heard a whistle.

"Offside," Bowman yelled.

Lapointe pretended to be furious and let out a curse, throwing off a glove and kicking it into a high arc towards the net, as if attempting a football field goal. The Canadiens howled. Perhaps remembering what Dick Irvin said about it being a good omen when a team laughed before a big game, Scotty called practice right there.

"OK boys, that's it," Scotty said. He'd been preparing the Canadiens for this series against Philadelphia since training camp. *Les Glorieux* finally seemed ready.

But were they? We were still in the '70s, remember—an era when violence and disorder seeped from the front pages of newspapers into the sport section. What was it this time? Another natural disaster? Well, yes, floods had hit Montreal hard this spring; the Ottawa River acted up, swamping the north shore. But that wasn't it. Civil unrest? For sure, this was perpetually aggrieved Quebec. The province's teachers were on strike. Liquor stores were threatening a walkout; drinkers might have to give up gin for Lent. The National Association of Broadcast Employees (NABET) threatened to shut down broadcasts of the finals. But, no, labour problems weren't the issue, either.

Give up? It was a bank robbery. On March 31, a Brink's truck stopped outside a Royal Bank of Canada on St. James Street. Jumping from the truck, the driver heard scurrying feet. Turning, he found himself staring into the business end of a WWII anti-aircraft gun. The weapon had sprung from the doors of a parked van in front of him. In 24 minutes, five thieves grabbed between 50 and 75 bags of loot. Close to $3 million. And then took off on foot, disappearing.

Montreal loved a good bank robbery the way Londoners enjoyed a proper murder. For weeks, the papers—especially *Allo Police*, Quebec's racy crime tabloid—dissected the case. Cops rounded up the usual suspects and heard something: one group of robbers, perhaps the guys responsible for the Brink's heist, planned to kidnap Guy Lafleur, hoping for a million-dollar payoff from the Canadiens. The police informed Montreal management. Soon, Lise and the Lafleurs' baby, Martin, were hiding out in the Hotel Bonaventure. Two armed cops moved in with Guy. Mornings, they drove behind him in an unmarked car to the Forum. If something went wrong, Lafleur was wearing a transmitter. After playing well in a low-scoring, four-game series sweep of Chicago, scoring three goals and chipping in two assists, Guy looked off against the Islanders—two goals in five games. "What's wrong with Lafleur?" Isles goalie Chico Resch asked Montreal reporters. It was like he suddenly didn't want the puck.

Guy wasn't sleeping, couldn't eat. Day after day, he became further withdrawn. The Canadiens must've wondered how they'd be without their top performer at 100 per cent. They'd find out soon enough. There he was, on the ice, with millions watching—including his would-be kidnappers, no doubt—as Roger Doucet, the silver-haired tenor who turned "O Canada" into vivid, thrilling opera, belted out the Canadian national anthem, minutes before the Philadelphia–Montreal Cup finals.

O Canada! Terre de nos aïeux . . .

Uh-oh, before everyone could take their seats, Philly was up 1–0. Bowman changed lines at 19 seconds. In the two-second gap between Murray Wilson going off and Bob Gainey finding his man, Bobby Clarke dropped a pass to a wide-open Reggie Leach and it was over Ken Dryden's left shoulder. The crowd made a grumbling sound. *Maybe the Flyers are too good.* Two Cups in a row, and three months earlier Shero's bunch easily dispensed with Red Army, 4–1. Yeah, the Canadiens were great—just three home losses all year. Then again, the Flyers were only beaten twice at the Spectrum. *Le bleu-blanc-rouge* could score—337 this season. Philadelphia counted 348 goals. Montreal had hockey's best right winger: Lafleur, 56 goals. Flyers had Leach, with 61. And Reggie was hotter than July—16 goals in 10 playoff games. Oops, Robinson made a bad clearing pass, old pro Ross Lonsberry scored, and it was 2–0 Philly at the end of the first period.

Fred Shero wasn't working with a full deck, either. Bernie Parent was out—bad back. And the team's best scorer from their Cup wins, speedy, swooping Rick MacLeish, was gone, victim of a Harold Snepsts late-season check. Freddy was therefore more conservative than usual. One guy in on the forecheck; clog the middle, no penalties. In the dressing room between periods, Canadiens loosened skates and shouted out a decades-old mantra: "Let's start skating, boys." Lafleur hid his cigarette when Bowman popped in to say they had just outshot Flyers 11–4. *Keep skating, boys.* The trailer was often open, he likely pointed out. With MacLeish gone, Clarke was playing too much. Their centres weren't back fast enough. Scotty wanted his defence jumping to the attack at every chance. More pressure.

The second period was all Montreal: 16–8 in shots. The checking line scored first—Gainey set up workhorse Jimmy Roberts. And then Robinson, pinching in, backhanded the tying goal past Flyers goalie Wayne Stephenson. This was the way to beat Philly, Scotty figured: roll four lines, attack Clarke with short-shifted centres and lean on the Big Three. In the first two periods, Montreal's defencemen would outshoot the entire Philadelphia team, 14–12. The Flyers scored on a power play to open the third, but Montreal staged an overwhelming counterattack. Lemaire tied it, and then, on his tenth shot on goal that afternoon, defenceman Lapointe pinged one in off the far post with 90 seconds left.

Good triumphed! After defeating the Flyers 4–3, the Habs players returned to their families for Sunday night dinner. Not Guy Lafleur, though. He ended Mother's Day back at home with cops in Verchères. Not even next-door neighbour Pierre Bouchard knew about the kidnap threat. Guy didn't play cards, so maybe he and the boys in blue watched the second half of the Expos' Sunday doubleheader on Radio-Canada. Steve Rogers pitched a shutout, 8–0 over San Francisco. Or maybe they took in *Kojak* ("Who loves ya, baby?") reruns on American TV. Whatever the case, Guy was in in a bitter mood that evening.

"I can't help having, somewhere inside of me, a certain sympathy with those guys," Guy said to police. "They think I'm worth ten times more than the Canadiens do."

Oh boy, Flower was complaining about his contract again. Pollock had given him a one-day, take-it-or-leave-it option on a five-year, half-million-dollar deal earlier in the season. Guy couldn't get in touch with his father-in-law to see what the Nordiques might offer. He re-signed with Montreal, only to discover Quebec would have offered him a million over five years.

Lafleur's playoff slump ended in game two of the finals, a Tuesday night home affair. It was scoreless in the second period. Shero was now responding to pressure from the Big Three by using two fore-checkers in deep and bringing his defence up. Bowman decided to mix things up. On a second-period power play, Scotty's starting five was Lambert, Lemaire and Mahovlich up front, with Lapointe and Lafleur on the points. After that, he went with Robinson, Lafleur at centre and Cournoyer on right wing. The changes finally threw a charge into Guy, who set Lambert up with what looked like a sure goal. But Yvon whiffed. Guy also made a few nice plays on defence, getting the crowd back on his side.

Suddenly, Montreal was all over the Flyers, stealing the puck, hitting. When Lapointe drew a penalty, Bowman kept the pressure on, using Lemaire instead of Risebrough or Jarvis at centre. Jacques knocked the puck loose off Larry Goodenough and walked in alone, beating Stephenson with a low skimmer to the stick side. Early in the third, Flower poke-checked Tom Bladon and then raced in, cutting right and shooting left simultaneously, using Joe Watson as a screen, catching the goalie moving the wrong way. Gorgeous move. Two–nothing, Habs.

Canadiens put an exclamation point on their second-game win minutes later when Robinson caught Gary Dornhoefer with a murderous hip check, leaving an impression of the Flyers forward on the boards. Maintenance workers needed ten minutes to repair the damage. Dornhoefer would take longer to fix. He'd be coughing blood two weeks later. The Canadiens were now up two games, and unless kidnappers got him, Lafleur seemed to be back for good.

On to Philadelphia!

Flyers fans welcomed their heroes back with a resounding ovation. No panic yet—Kate Smith wasn't around. Sign Guy Dave Leonardi lofted a placard reading WELCOME BACK to cameras—a play on the hit TV series of the day, *Welcome Back, Kotter*. (Truth be told, with his sweater vest and pornstache, Dave looked a lot like series star Gabe Kaplan.) Soon, the old Flyers *were* definitely back, hitting everything that moved. Early on, Barber threw an elbow at Cournoyer, but ended up knocking out teammate Jack McIlhargey. Shutt scored on the ensuing power play, a fluttering 90-foot knuckleball—the Expos' French announcer, Claude Raymond, would have called it *"une balle papillon"*—that somehow squeezed under Stephenson's armpit. Discouraged not a whit, Flyers resumed their hitting. Reggie Leach, Dryden's kryptonite, managed two slapshots on net, scoring both times. Including the five goals he scored against Boston in the last game of the semifinals, he'd now totalled eight goals on his last 12 shots. Incredible. Flyers fans gave him a standing O after the second goal. With the Flyers up 2–1, Leonardi materialized on camera with a new slogan: ONLY THE BEGINNING, a reference to the rock group Chicago's easy-listening hit "Beginnings."

> *Only the beginning*
> *Of what I want to feel forever . . .*

The period ended with fans still up and cheering and the Flyers in an ugly mood, playing great. After missing on a breakaway, Barber bowled over Dryden behind the net. Before the period ended, Moose Dupont poked Murray Wilson as Dornhoefer combed Risebrough's face with an elbow. One second left now: on the faceoff, Orest Kindrachuk speared Risebrough in the leg. A penalty. The Canadien retaliated. Benches cleared.

While the Flyers were back, so, unfortunately for them, was Montreal's power play. Shutt's first-period goal would be their first with a man advantage this series. Lafleur was at the point as the power-play unit began the second period. It was a way for Bowman to give Guy room to manoeuvre. That he did. Grabbing the puck from Lemaire in Montreal's end, Lafleur evaded Clarke, slipping a blind sideways pass to Lapointe, darting up the left boards. Pointu hit Shutt crossing the Flyers line on the far boards. He made a nice drop pass to Mahovlich, who circled in the middle, drawing three defenders, before leaving the puck for Lafleur. With the Flyers spinning, growing dizzy, Guy instantly redirected the puck to Shutt, alone at the crease. Stephenson made a fine save, but Shutt knocked Dupont's clearing effort out of the air—a brilliant bit of hand-eye coordination—tying the game.

Six perfect passes in three zones inside a dozen seconds: vintage Canadiens! The crowd—the Flyers too—seemed momentarily dispirited. Sensing a suddenly vulnerable foe, the Habs went to the body, like a boxer setting up a tired opponent for a knockout punch. Perhaps because he was in a bad mood, having allowed Leach off-leash for two goals, Gainey was a one-man wrecking crew. First, he flattened Hound Kelly, then Terry Murray and Clarke. Robinson and Mahovlich put the body to the Flyers captain as well. Bouchard rubbed Leach out along the boards. Chartraw, too, was a hitting machine. But the knockout punch didn't come in the second period, despite breakaways by Cournoyer and Wilson. Stephenson also made a fine in-close save on Gainey.

It was a tie game going into the third period of a match the great Stanley Cup champion Philadelphia Flyers knew they couldn't afford to lose. For three seasons now, the Flyers had never encountered a challenge Fred Shero couldn't solve—the Big Bad Bruins, the French Connection, the Red Army—the Flyers had beaten them all. Against the Canadiens, Freddy tried everything—the neutral zone trap; two men in forechecking; bumper-car hockey. Tonight, early in the final period, he even broke up the Clarke-Leach-Barber line—nothing worked. The Canadiens were too good. It was like trying to make a bed with a too-small sheet. You tucked in one corner, and another side popped open. Bowman, meanwhile, seemed to be pushing all the right buttons. For this game, he sat Lambert and Mario Tremblay to play Chartraw and Wilson, and replaced Nyrop with Bouchard. Controversial moves, given how well the suddenly benched players had performed in Montreal. Lo and behold, midway through the third period, the Habs' carousel was once again underway. And guess who was on board? Wilson made a nice drop pass to Lemaire flying up the left side. His slapshot missed the net. Chartraw beat Joe Watson and Schultz to the puck. Wilson was there again to relay the puck to Bouchard. The defenceman hurried a snapshot that wobbled past Saleski's stick through Tom Bladon, Chartraw, and, finally, Wayne Stephenson's legs.

Now it was 3–2, Montreal. Chartraw and Wilson engulfed goal scorer Bouchard. Drinks would be on the house at Pierre's dad's restaurant, Chez Butch, tonight. Flyers were a game away from elimination.

What was Kate Smith doing Sunday afternoon?

That Saturday night, the Canadiens were in Jersey, lodged at the Cherry Hill Inn. Nobody could sleep, so they played pool, nursing beers, joking. There was little talk of hockey, though maybe they hit the Flyer-orange 5 and 13 balls a little harder. Sunday morning, the horseplay stopped on the spearmint-green Walt Whitman Bridge over to the Spectrum. This sky-high, 3,000-metre concrete-and-steel stretch was where other teams typically succumbed to Flyers flu. Not the Canadiens. Though quiet, they could hardly wait. One player was particularly relieved to be on his way to battle. That morning, Lafleur had received news that his bank robber/kidnappers had been arrested in Ottawa. No more TV dinners at home with flatfoots. No more scratchy transmitters under his shirt.

If the Habs weren't intimidated busing to the Spectrum, they did go a little bit weak in the knees right before the game as the arena turned dark and Kate Smith promenaded down a red carpet into a diamond-blue spotlight, passing Springfield union electrician and part-time organist John H. Hoffman. The noise in the Spectrum was incredible when she finally reached the on-ice microphone, blowing kisses everywhere.

God bless America, land that I love . . .

The second time through the only verse she ever sang, Kate reached out to the crowd: "All right, everybody, let's sing it!" And 17,077 fans joined in:

From the mountains, to the prairies,
To the oceans, white with foam,
God bless America, My home sweet home.
GOD BLESS AMERICA, MY HOME SWEEEET HOOOOOOME!

The sing-a-long shook the Spectrum. Shook the Canadiens, too. "That was the one time with the Canadiens I ever played a game where, forgive me, I thought we would lose," Yvon Lambert would remember years later. "Only for a second, because just as the song was ending, Yvan Cournoyer skated behind us and gave us all a whack on the pants. 'C'mon boys, we can do it.' I always remember that. What leadership!"

Nevertheless, Flyers struck first. A frighteningly amped-up Dave Schultz attacked Serge Savard along the boards. Both were tossed by referee Lloyd Gilmour, with Schultz getting an extra two. Shero won what would be an ongoing chess match with Bowman, as Leach and Clarke faced Lemaire and Lafleur. No Gainey. Forty seconds in, Reggie drilled his 19th playoff goal—another slapshot that had Dryden looking like he was waking startled from a nap.

When the Canadiens finally went on the power play, though, it was another game: Mahovlich, Lafleur and the Big Three flew effortlessly around and past Flyers forecheckers. It was pinball in the Flyers end, with Shutt finally scoring on a lovely pass from Cournoyer. Later, Bouchard with a wrister from the point, a shot his dad might've employed 30 years before, surprised Stephenson on the tail end of another power play—2–1 Montreal. The Flyers responded by heaving their weight around and attacking Dryden. Bladon fired a puck that caromed of Barber's hip into the net. The Flyers forward celebrated by doing a chin-up on the crossbar, his legs draped over the fallen, angry Montreal goalie.

The period ended as it began, with the crowd cheering a tie game that, in a single period, saw Bowman employ 16 line combinations (Lafleur played right wing, centre and defence on the power play), while Shero went with 14 different units.

The second period was more of the same: coaches scheming, and furious skating supplemented by corner swordfights and pileups in the goal crease. Shero's team enjoyed a slight edge in play and finally parlayed a power play into a Dupont goal. *The lead at last!* After popping in a goalmouth rebound, the Moose broke into his signature victory dance—knees high in the air like he was stomping out a fire. The crowd loved it: "Mooooooooose!"

Five minutes after that, Lemaire chased Barber. Jacques got his stick up. The Flyers forward grabbed it and then inexplicably lost control. Up went Referee Gilmour's arm. Two minutes. At the bench, several Canadiens put their hands together as if in prayer, simulating a pool plunge. "It's a dive!" Bowman and players shouted. Montreal would survive the ensuing power play, maybe because a half minute later, Jarvis collapsed when Dornhoefer gave him a tickle with his stick. Gilmour's hand was up again. A makeup call, obviously. The crowd was furious, venting their displeasure when the penalty was called, and again with 11 seconds left in the period, as Cournoyer banged in yet another power-play goal after a heroic (unacknowledged) effort by Lambert.

Though he was not credited with an assist, replays showed Lambert bulled past Clarke to tip Robinson's pass into Stephenson's pads. Cournoyer grabbed the rebound, dribbling a low backhand that rippled the fallen goalie's jersey, crawling into the net.

Temperatures reached into the 80s in Philly that afternoon. The Spectrum ice was wet by the third period. Raining sweat, the Shirley Temple curl gone from his hair, Clarke looked exhausted. Kindrachuk's line was slowing down. Schultz had lost the mad, Rasputin-like glint in his eye. And he and Saleski were covering Lafleur and Shutt. This was the Flyers' 16th game this postseason—three more than Montreal, who had a longer bench. Murray Wilson, who played so well game three, wasn't even dressed for game four. Lambert was back in and working like hell to impress/punish Bowman. The writing was literally on the wall for Philadelphia. A sign hanging from the rafters read:

WIN OR LOSE, YOU'VE GIVEN PHILLY A LOT TO BE PROUD OF. NO MATTER WHAT HAPPENS YOU'LL ALWAYS BE #1.

Though still on their skates, the champions were wobbling, awaiting the final blows. They occurred in rapid succession late in the third period. But first the Flyers enjoyed one last chance. With Gainey in the box, Dornhoefer grabbed a fat rebound, firing one past Dryden. Flyers lifted their sticks. Fans jumped. Jubila—no, it hit the post, wobbling like a fallen coin in the crease until a falling, seemingly out-of-the-play Dryden extended his long arm and trapper (an 11-foot reach!), smothering the loose puck. Next shift, Bouchard pushed Saleski off the puck in the Montreal end. And here came the executioner—Lafleur snatched a loose puck, one-on-three. He turned and dawdled at the Philly blue line, waiting for help. Saleski and Jim Watson attacked. Having drawn two defenders, Guy slipped the puck to a speeding Shutt who—*presto*—now enjoyed a two-on-one with Mahovlich close by. Shutt shot—it's what he did—banging the puck off Joe Watson's shin. Mahovlich turned away from the net with the puck, circling the boards, firing an awkward, across-the-body diagonal pass. Lafleur, on his off wing, was in midshot when the puck arrived. It was in the Philly net, high on the stick side, before Stephenson could move. Four–three, Montreal.

The Canadiens were all off the bench, celebrating the moment. Not Bowman. Scotty was plotting his next move. He knew Shero would respond with the Clarke line. The Habs coach moved back and forth behind his players. For the first time this game, he put Gainey, Risebrough and Cournoyer together. Three players from different lines, and Cournoyer was an offensive forward. But Scotty knew the Roadrunner had that tailwind working tonight. Ten seconds later, Cournoyer made his coach look good, speeding past the Flyers' fastest player, Jimmy Watson, to nullify an icing call. Instead of a faceoff in Montreal's end, the Flyers had to lug it out again. Twenty seconds down the drain. A rushing Bladon finally slapped it in from the blue line. Dryden kicked the puck into the crowd.

Now, the Flyers had the faceoff they were looking for. It was either Jarvis or Lemaire's turn. But Bowman threw the Lafleur line out again, even though they had just got off the ice 40 seconds earlier. Up a goal, you'd figure Montreal might play it safe. But Scotty wanted Shero to send out Kindrachuk-Schultz-Saleski. They weren't going to score. And there was no way the Hammer could keep up with the perpetually fresh Lafleur. Saleski won the faceoff, but Mahovlich was on the point man, Goodenough, quickly. A deflected puck ended up on Shutt's stick. He quickly relayed it to Lafleur, who, having left Schultz far behind, cruised into the Flyers end.

"Guy, Guy," a trailing Shutt hollered. Guy put a blind backhand on the tape of his stick. Shutt moved to the slot, but was bowled over by (give him credit) a hustling Schultz. The puck dribbled into the left corner where Lafleur, again out of position—he was everywhere!— grabbed it, sending another no-look pass into the slot. Mahovlich backhanded that gift into the net.

Five–three Montreal.

Bowman continued to plot and scheme. He'd throw together another new combination—Lemaire, Lambert and Roberts—and follow that up with the Lafleur line again. But everyone knew the game, series and season were over. With three minutes left, the Flyers fans (give them credit) stood to cheer on the team that had put Philadelphia back on the sports map, rightfully acknowledging a group that, for three seasons, outworked, outsmarted and, yes, outslugged everyone in its path. With a minute left, the crowd was still on its feet, cheering. And let it be said that both teams went all out right to the end of the 1975–76 campaign. After pulling Stephenson, Shero threw Dornhoefer on with the Clarke line. Bowman would use three different centres against Clarke in the final 70 seconds. The season ended with Barber throwing a vicious elbow Gainey's way.

When the siren sounded, however, everyone reverted to being nice-guy Canadians again, shaking hands. Philly fans graciously applauded as Captain Cournoyer circled the Spectrum ice with a Stanley Cup that had been pulled from the trunk of Hockey Hall of Fame curator Lefty Reid's car in an underground parking lot. In the Flyers dressing room, Bobby Clarke was generous. "I never thought anyone could sweep us," he told reporters. "Canadiens are just the best club I've seen since I came to the NHL [in 1969]." Madness prevailed in the visitors' chambers. Players sang "God Bless America" and sprayed each other with champagne. Minutes later, a sad little boy in a Flyers bomber jacket entered, asking for Mr. Bowman. The Montreal coach was summoned.

"My dad says this is for you," 13-year-old Ray Shero said, handing Bowman a piece of folded paper. It read simply, "Congratulations on such a fantastic season. You're truly champions—not only of the league, but the world. Fred."

Reporters looked for hero Lafleur, the star performer who had shaken off kidnappers, Quebec police and Dave Schultz to score the game-winning goal. But Guy wasn't in the dressing room or shower. Mahovlich, Jimmy Roberts, trainer Eddy Palchak and Claude Larochelle, a reporter from the Quebec City newspaper *Le Soleil*, formed a search party. It was just like at Le Colisée decades earlier, during the Quebec peewee tournament. *Where's Guy?* Minutes later, they found Lafleur in a utility room at the far end of the Spectrum, smoking, slowly draining a Coke. He looked glum, as if he might cry. Mahovlich tried to cheer him up.

Come on, Guy, you're missing all the fun. Geez, what's wrong?

For some reason, who knows why, Lafleur was depressed. Sensing something was wrong, Palchak grabbed big, blundering Mahovlich, taking him away. The Canadiens trooped off to dinner without their superstar, who went to a restaurant with reporter Larochelle. Guy was fine a bottle of wine later. Tomorrow, he'd be in great shape for the Stanley Cup parade, laughing along with everyone else when Guy Lapointe arrived at the Forum in a Flyers jersey, again belting out "God Bless America." Tonight, though, he wanted to be alone with his past, chatting and drinking with someone from Quebec City.

Probably, Guy told the reporter about the kidnappers. Larochelle undoubtedly advised Guy of what had happened that morning in Montreal: they got one of the Brink's truck robbers. It'd be all over the papers tomorrow: in the middle of the night, police surrounded a west-side apartment building belonging to suspect John Slawvey.

"Police. Don't move," one officer, André Savard, barked out. The officer was carrying an M1 rifle.

"OK, OK," Slawvey responded, ducking to grab the .38 strapped above his shoe. At which point, four other cops stepped out of the darkness, lighting the garage with gunfire, sawing Slawvey in half.

It turned out Slawvey wasn't involved in the Brinks job, though. Forty years later, the biggest heist in North American banking history remains an unsolved mystery. As does Guy Lafleur, come to think of it.

DO IT AGAIN

Montreal Canadiens vs. Boston Boston, May 7–14, 1977

They kept winning. Montreal began the 1976–77 season with a 10–1
opening night drubbing of Pittsburgh. Guy Lafleur and Steve Shutt
collected two goals apiece. The following Saturday, in a graveyard-quiet
Spectrum, they beat up Philadelphia, 7–1. "We never had a chance,"
Bobby Clarke whispered in the dressing room afterwards. They kept on
keeping on. *Les Glorieux* lost but a single home contest all season, outscoring opponents 387–171 over the course of 80 games. Lafleur would
be named MVP. Shutt scored a league-high 60 goals. Ken Dryden and
Bunny Larocque won the Vézina. Larry Robinson was best defenceman;
Scotty Bowman, top coach.

Nevertheless, Scotty would be impossible. That first game in Montreal,
he benched Dryden, hero of so many Habs playoffs. The goalie, who
always hated practice, had had a mediocre training camp. Yvon Lambert
didn't dress, either. Reggie Houle—Peanut—back from the WHA, took

his place. First Claude Ruel, then Guy Lapointe and Serge Savard knocked on Bowman's door, arguing on behalf of Yvon. Lambert is a glue guy in the dressing room, Ruel told Bowman. "You can't do this," Guy and Serge pleaded on behalf of their teammate.

The WHA, Part Three

It's been said that WHA should have stood for "When Hull Arrived." Chicago Blackhawk star Bobby Hull agreed to a contract with the new league in 1972, giving it instant legitimacy. In time, he was the star and centrepiece of the league's best team, a squad that easily handled two NHL clubs (St. Louis and Pittsburgh) in 1976 exhibition games. Two years later, the Jets beat the Soviet national team, 5–3. These Jets were hockey's first North American–European hybrid, employing nine Swedes and Finns. The Jets' doctor, Gerry Wilson, discovered the team's most famous imports, Ulf Nilsson and Anders Hedberg, while on a Scandinavian sabbatical. When they arrived for their first workout at the University of Manitoba, Jets coach Rudy Pilous saw the kids skate and called out, "Bobby, you go with the Swedes." "The Hot Line" scored on its first shift together that practice . . . and never stopped. "The best I ever played with," Hull would always maintain. (Against the Soviets, Hull scored three goals, Nilsson two.) Edmonton Oiler player/coach Glen Sather was so impressed by the speedy, swirling, international Jet-setters that he would later model his Edmonton Oiler teams after them.

"Yes, I can," Scotty replied. Minutes later, he would stride into the dressing room, jaw upturned. "Guys, I have to talk to you," he said. "We have a big problem. Instead of dressing 18 players tonight, we're only allowed to dress 17. It's a league decision. One of you will have to sit out. Do I have any volunteers?"

Complete silence. Scotty figured the players got the message: everyone wanted to be out there; somebody had to make hard decisions, and that somebody was him! Probably, the players figured the clearly made-up story about league rules was just Bowman talking crazy again. On TV after games, Scotty was thoughtful if a little bland, slowing down to think. Off-camera, though—just him and the guys—he talked in scattershot bursts, routinely wandering off topic. "It's as if his mind is so fertile and alive that each thought acts like a probe, striking new parts of his brain, spilling out thoughts he is helpless to control," was how Dryden explained his coach's habit of stockpiling non sequiturs. Years later, Al Strachan would perform a wicked impersonation of Bowman in his book *Go to the Net*:

"What about the road trip [Scotty]?"

"West coast, eh? December. Sam doesn't like home games, eh? Can't sell tickets, eh? Too close to Christmas. The Kings, eh? They're tough. Good team. Bob Berry. TMR, eh? [The Town of Mount Royal, a Montreal suburb.] Vancouver. Always raining. You get up there and it's noon everywhere else. Oakland. Ever try that restaurant in our hotel? Duck specialty, eh? Great duck. They cook it for three days. No grease. After three days, the grease is all gone, eh?"

The Canadiens didn't get their coach, were bewildered by his mood swings—how he was Rain Man one minute, Captain Bligh the next. "Bowman can tell you how many tiles there are in every arena bathroom in the league," an NHL player would one day tell the *Toronto Star*. "But he can't carry on a 30-second conversation."

Still, Montreal's coach got results. Houle was one of the three stars on opening night. Making his season debut the following evening, Dryden shut out Vancouver 3–0. Collateral damage: Lambert was humiliated, inconsolable. "I don't want to talk about it," he told reporters. "I haven't even spoke to my wife for two days."

History tells us that this was the greatest hockey team ever built. The season is longer now. We have overtime wins. Still, no club has ever recorded more regular-season points than this edition of the Canadiens— 132. Credit Sam Pollock, the sport's greatest architect. Bowman, too—he knew where to hammer nails. And then there were the players, all just entering or still in their prime. Robinson, Lapointe and Savard were 25, 28 and 31. Bob Gainey was 23; Shutt, 24; Lafleur, 25. The team's top centres, Peter Mahovlich and Jacques Lemaire, were 30 and 31. Dryden, 29.

But there were two other factors that might—just might—have had something to do with the Canadiens' greatest team.

Montreal's '76–77 season coincided with the Parti Québécois' ascent to power. The province was a jittery, high-spirited mess going into the November 15 election. Unemployment was a record 10.1 per cent. Every week brought another public-sector strike, it seemed. Liberal premier Robert Bourassa's 1974 introduction of Bill 22, making French the *sole* official language of Quebec, was viewed as a betrayal by anglophones, who would vote in unprecedented numbers for the once-loathed Union Nationale. As the election neared, the Liberals fought back, warning of a ruined dollar. Expos owner Charles Bronfman told an audience, "If we turn our back on the Liberals, it's suicide. The moment [the PQ] get in, folks, it's over, done. They're a bunch of bastards trying to kill us." Although polls suggested the separatists would win, René Lévesque wasn't so sure. In 1970, the PQ took 23 per cent of the vote and ended up with seven of 108 seats. In 1973, they received 30 per cent and produced six members. What would a 40 per cent separatist vote mean?

The Canadiens were playing St. Louis at the Forum on election night. Watching the game at home, the telecast seemed off. Sometimes fans cheered when St. Louis had the puck. *Have the PQ won another seat?* Habs trooped to the dressing room between periods as news of the election raced around the Forum. Inside, some joker finally broke the ice, acknowledging Lévesque's majority.

"'Well, Kenny, thanks for everything.' 'It's all yours, Bunny.'"

"Jean-Pierre Mahovlich, I'd like you to meet Jacques Roberts."

While there was laughter in the dressing room, outside, teenagers danced in the streets. French youngsters waved blue *fleurdelisés* and chanted, "*On les a eus*" (We got them). There was more singing—crying, too—at the Paul Sauvé Arena, where Premier Lévesque, holding an unlit cigarette, eyes brimming with tears, told supporters, "I have never been as proud to be a Quebecer as tonight." *Pour un instant . . .* for a moment, everything had changed. The lyrics of the Montreal folk-rock band Harmonium's* mid-'70s hit "Pour un instant" now seemed a prophesy:

> *Des inconnus vivent en roi chez moi*
> *Moi qui accepte leurs lois*

"The strangers live in my home like kings / And I had accepted their rule . . ." No longer. Quebec and Canada now slept in separate bedrooms, as Lévesque liked to say.

Quebec in the 1970s was a time for valour. French hockey players performed with a heroic resolve. So did English players on the Habs, mind you. Both federalists and Péquistes found validation in the team's success. "The spiritual necessity of the Montreal Canadiens," as Mordecai Richler put it, had never been stronger. Montreal Expos reliever Mike Marshall called Quebec's preoccupation with hockey "sick." Oh, but what a glorious illness! *Les Habitants* won six Stanley Cups that decade. The team's best season occurred when nationalism was at its most pronounced. And it wasn't just the Canadiens. Seven French Canadians made the NHL's All-Star teams this season. Never had there been that many before, or since. Lafleur and Marcel Dionne were on the first team.

---

* Quebec folk heroes Harmonium were everywhere on the airwaves in the mid-'70s. It was impossible at the time to get a haircut in any fashionable, youth-oriented salon in Montreal or Ottawa without hearing "Pour un instant" or "100,000 Raisons" on CHOM-FM radio.

Rogie Vachon, Denis Potvin, Lapointe, Gilbert Perreault and Richard Martin were all on the second unit.

Of course, the Canadiens weren't a French team. They were half-and-half. And the English half presided in the dressing room. Although it was interesting to note that Larry Robinson swore in working-class French: *câlisse. Tabernac.* In fact, the whole team enjoyed playing at being working stiffs. Dryden's flavourful memoir of life with the Canadiens, *The Game,* suggested that the wealthiest labourers in Quebec complained like factory workers. And about the same things!

"*Câlisse,* you see the paper?" Houle cried at one point in Dryden's book. "Beer's goin' up sixty-five cents a case. *Sixty-five cents!*"

"Shit yeah, the only thing that should go up is what they pay 15-goal scorers, eh Reggie?"

"That's it, that's it," Lapointe wailed. "No more drinkin'."

"Hey Pointu, you just got to drink on the road," Shutt offered.

Someone else complained about the government, again about beer and cigarette taxes, punishments that hit a working Josèphe where he lived: "The government, who gives a shit about the government?" another growled. "We win Cups with the Liberals, we win 'em with the PQ. What the fuck's the difference?"

That was how the Habs skated around every political controversy. Don't ask us; we just work here. Having Bowman as your boss helped; you got to act like a downtrodden wage slave even if, like Shutt, you drove a mauve Bentley, or, like Robinson, owned a string of polo ponies. Canadiens players ignored the French–English question. They knew they needed each other to win. Take the election night 4–2 victory over St. Louis: Tremblay and Cournoyer scored early, Shutt and Risebrough tallied late. Assists on French goals went to English players—Robinson, Mahovlich, Murray Wilson and Risebrough. Assists on the English goals went to French teammates—Lambert, Bouchard, Houle and Savard.

And so, all through the troubling winter of 1976–77, these would-be factory hands showed up for work, hair still wet from the shower at

10:55 in the morning. Grabbing a coffee and a May West* at the Texas
Restaurant on Atwater, they signed autographs before ducking into the
Forum. Bowman liked 12 o'clock scrimmages. Everyone except Lafleur
drifted in around 11 o'clock. By then, Guy was already on the ice—
another solo concert, swinging around the boards, dreaming. At high
noon, the whistle blew for work—a spirited game of shinny, though not
exactly sticks-in; let's divvy up teams. Bowman handpicked the squads:
Lafleur against Gainey's line. Scotty was out there, too, feeling the wind
as players rushed past. For an hour, they'd just go, racing for the puck . . .
trying to score, to impress each other as much as Bowman. Ruel stayed
on the ice afterwards to work with pet projects. Larocque wanted more
shots. Avis had to try harder. Day after day, it was the same, except
every two and a half weeks, the Canadiens collected their cheques.
Trainer Eddy Palchak waddled into the dressing room after practice and
played Santa.

"How come my contract says I'm so rich and this cheque says I'm
not?" Houle once asked, ripping open his envelope.

"*Câlisse de tabernac,* taxes!" Mario snarled, heading to the shower.
Shutt peed into a plastic cup and then grabbed a nearby Coke, splashing
it into his own offering for colour. When the mixture was judged to be
just the right hue, he set the drink aside and hurried to the shower. When
Tremblay returned, dripping wet, he saw the abandoned cocktail in
Shutt's cubicle. Grinning, he winked at teammates, then grabbed what
he thought was a soft drink. Other players winked right back and then
began to roar. Right about then, Lambert, naked, his hair swept into an

---

*   Chocolate-covered pastries filled with squirting vanilla, Mae Wests were
created by a Quebec City baker, René Brousseau, during World War II. It was
widely assumed that the snack, found in every Quebec corner store in the '70s,
was named after the pillowy screen actress of the same name. But Brousseau's son,
Jacques, claimed it was in fact named after puffy war-era life preservers, nicknamed "Mae Wests." *La même chose.* When actress Mae West died in 1980, the
name of the Vachon pastry was changed to May West to avoid lawsuits.

elaborate pompadour, turned up the radio—some rock song—and went into "Land of 1,000 Dances." Doing the pony, like Bony Maronie.

"Aw-right, Lambert!"

Like the Bruins and Flyers, the two other NHL '70s champions, the Canadiens enjoyed a wonderful esprit de corps. Work and play blurred together. When the season ended, they played on a celebrity softball team. They were Montreal Canadiens year-long. But even by Montreal standards, these guys were special. At the conclusion of *Les Glorieux*'s 1976 Stanley Cup sweep of Philadelphia, *Hockey Night in Canada*'s Danny Gallivan commented, "Never have I witnessed such camaraderie, such goodwill, such great spirit among the players as this year." Danny began work with Montreal in 1952 and so had seen a lot of happy winners. Still, he couldn't help but notice how Bowman's bunch had kicked it up a gear. It was more than esprit de corps, though. These Canadiens were almost rabidly competitive.

Another incident from Dryden's book *The Game*: the author stared out from a Boston hotel lobby, waiting for the team bus. What was this? A side window revealed teammates outside, horsing around. Stepping out into the parking lot, Ken found players lost in a game of "curbsies." Contestants stepped out of a jeering crowd to flick quarters in arcing parabolas they hoped would land where curb and sidewalk met. Or at least closer than Shutt and Lapointe's quarters. They were winning so far. Still, there were two shooters left—Lemaire and Cam Connor, who couldn't get his shot off because Lapointe kept pretending to accidentally wander in front of him. After Pointu quit clowning, Connor tried and missed. The bus arrived. Now it was Lemaire's turn—last shot. Onlookers pushed and shouted, but Coco was suddenly slow and deliberate, like all of a sudden he was on the 18th hole at Augusta. Lemaire coiled and performed a balletic hop, lofting his coin, which settled right next to the curb. *A winner!* He pumped his right arm in the air. Lemaire and Shutt feigned outrage, lodged protests. The crowd jeered and shuffled to the bus, waiting for Coco to pick up his loot, maybe five bucks in change.

Nowhere was the team's crazy, competitive zeal more evident than in scrimmages. Hardly any NHL teams had them anymore—too many regular-season games. The Canadiens almost always found time. One workout that season almost didn't happen. Bunny Larocque's wife went into labour, and the players figured that scrimmage was cancelled, that they'd practise instead. No way. When the team showed up at the St-Laurent Arena, Trainer Palchak canvassed recreation teams leaving the ice. "Hey, wanna play goal for the Canadiens?" he asked Marc Doré, a postal worker.

"Sure, and I also want to play quarterback for the Alouettes and first base for Expos."

Palchak peeled off $25. *Game on!* Doré's pals hung around to watch. A front-page report in the Montreal *Gazette* suggested the scrimmage was great fun—furious action, lots of screaming, especially when Doré foiled a Mahovlich breakaway. Scotty would be delighted. "Hey, he really wasn't too bad, eh?" he said of the postie between the posts. "Really had the guys working for him, eh?" The guys were always working, though. It was never *just* practice. During the '77 Cup run, the club had a parallel internal playoff, with a trophy and prize money. Dryden's team, starring Robinson and Lafleur-Mahovlich-Shutt, went best-four-of-seven against Bunny's boys, with Savard, Gainey and Lemaire. Dryden's team won. There was a big party in the dressing room afterwards. Winners let a fat poker pot spill through their hands like pirate treasure—25 bucks apiece.

Bowman knew these wild, up-tempo scrimmages were worth it. Following a tough workout against Gainey, everything felt easier for Lafleur next game. It was the same for the whole team, really. After wrestling with each other for a hard, rampaging scrimmage, the Canadiens walloped slower, unprepared opponents. Subsequent to a spirited noon workout, they overwhelmed Washington 11–0 on the final weekend of the schedule. But it was the next game, the last game of the season, that demonstrated what pros these guys were. With first place in the bag and the team's stars taking fewer shifts, the Habs eked out a difficult 2–1 road win in Washington. And then not only celebrated, but took time to shake hands with the Capitals. Given how far ahead they were in the standings, *Hockey Night in Canada*'s Dick Irvin was surprised by how much importance the Canadiens placed on the game. Years later, he said as much to Scotty when they happened to be sharing a cab.

"That was an important game for us," Scotty replied.

"Important?"

"We were going for our 60th win!"

The handshakes were because Montreal appreciated the Caps' putting up a good effort after an 11–0 drubbing. Historic wins, not cheating the game—these concepts were often lost on players weathering 100-game seasons. Not in Montreal. There were a dozen future coaches and GMs in this lineup. Robinson and Lemaire eventually won Stanley Cups as coaches; Risebrough as an assistant; Gainey and Serge Savard as GMs. These guys got the big picture. And they were unflappable. When there was an attempt to create a Team Quebec for the 1976 Canada Cup, Savard and Lapointe quietly killed the plan. Sorry, previous engagement—Team Canada. Needy fans? Flower had that one covered. Guy went through 20 sticks a week; most would end up as souvenirs. One season, he used 780 sticks.

The team's biggest challenge, though, was always the same: Scotty Bowman.

The man who humiliated them, replayed their mistakes on game films for all to see, called them out in the paper. Every other game, he ragged Mahovlich. The year before, it was Lemaire. At the end of the season, Bowman benched Tremblay. Mario redecorated the dressing room—sticks and skates everywhere.

All that grief, even as they won.

And won and won. The team suffered one loss in the last three months of the season. Blew past St. Louis in the quarter-final round of the '77 playoffs—four straight wins. Guy gave notice he was ready—three goals and as many assists in the first game. Next up, they took care of the upstart Islanders in six. Good, hard series. For the first time since January, Lafleur failed to pick up a point, but Gainey scored both goals and

Dryden was superb in the 2–1 road victory in Uniondale that sent them into the Cup finals against the Boston Bruins.

Boston again. Scotty was worried sick about the Bruins and anxious for the illness to spread. Don Cherry's team had won the season series with Montreal, taking the first three games 5–3, 4–3 and 7–3. Forget that the Habs came back with convincing 8–3 and 5–1 victories. Scotty remembered the sting of those early defeats: a late collapse in Boston—three straight goals; Cheevers stoning them in Montreal; a 7–3 beating in January, Serge and Larry on for five, mistakes everywhere.

In particular, Scotty remembered Cherry standing on the bench in Montreal, hollering and carrying on. Wearing a three-piece banker's suit, high collar, stick pin, gold watch fob. A vest—the guy wore a vest! In hockey, you were only supposed to wear vests in the fall, duck hunting. Bowman didn't like Cherry much. His Boston rival was a players' coach—drank with his team sometimes. And he palled with media. In other words, he was the anti-Scotty. According to *La Presse*, just prior to game one of the finals, Bowman had a "stern reminder" for his guys about how Cherry's Bruins had beaten up the Canadiens this season. We can only imagine:

Boston'll kill us, guys. They're like Philly, eh? Get you mad, frustrated like; that's what they do. Terry O'Reilly—improved player—glove always in your face. Larry, let's keep our cool out there, eh? Make them skate—Ratelle, he's no spring chicken. And the defence is getting there. Park's knees are shot. Get on 'em. And no bad penalties, eh? Schmautz on the power play, he's hot, boys; gets it away fast. McNab, can we get somebody on him? Scored two in Boston, January—Serge, Larry, that was you, five goals. Cripes, McNab killed us. Let's put him on his ass, can we? Murray Wilson . . . January, you and McNab were out there, shooting the breeze, yakety-yak. What were you doin' . . . pickin' out drapes; maybe you're going to get married or somethin'. What? Why you laughing? Geez, we gotta pay attention here, guys, these Bruins, they just beat us three straight . . . one more, we're handing them the Cup. Guys, one more thing: no blind passes, always tell ya, stupidest play in hockey. One more thing . . .

But it was never just one more thing. Sometimes, Scotty went on forever. Players bit their lips, hid under towels. And when they couldn't help it, broke out laughing. Scotty stared back, confused. *What?* Once, years earlier, Bowman got lost in a pre-game speech; his speeding mouth couldn't find a place to land. Finally, Frank Mahovlich had had enough: "Scotty, you been talking for a half hour now and nobody can understand a fuckin' word you're saying."

After Scotty quit the dressing room, players would dissect his sermon. "I thought Scott was good tonight," Shutt might say. More laughter. Before long, though, they had extracted what wisdom there was in Bowman's remarks: stay disciplined. Skate. Watch Schmautz. Skate. Someone might suggest the movie *Rocky* was still on, playing at the Laval, should Murray Wilson and Peter McNab want to catch a flick after the game. As the first game of the '77 finals drew close, however, the Canadiens would begin winding each other up. Robinson grew stern. Pointu stopped joking. Cournoyer was out—bad back. Savard was acting captain, but the Canadiens had no one commander. There were multiple team leaders: the Big Three, Gainey, Risebrough, Lambert, Tremblay. Minutes before the game, everyone would be shouting. Banging sticks.

First goal, guys. First goal.

Gotta skate.

Have it now.

First goal . . .

Sure enough, they scored the first two goals of the Saturday, May 7 Stanley Cup finals opener at the Forum—Risebrough and Lambert. Mario made it 3–1 to end the first. The Big Three were in on every goal. The Bruins rallied, but Montreal blew them away in the third—Chartraw, then Mario and Lambert scored again, stoking a delirious, joyously singing Habs crowd. The next two matches were the team's best all year. Boston was ready, but Montreal was flying. Dryden recorded a 3–0 shutout in Montreal and then, in an ever-quietening Boston Garden, Flower put on a show, scoring and setting up two goals in the first—all power-play efforts—before finishing the Bruins off with a dazzling third-period score. "Guy Lafleur is the best hockey player in the world," Cherry said after the game.

One more to go.

Midway through first period of game four, the best hockey player in the world committed what was, according to his coach, the sport's unpardonable sin. Al Sims was about to smear Guy Lafleur into the boards, deep in Montreal's end, when Guy, face pressed to the glass, zipped a gorgeous blind, backhand pass up the middle of the ice, catching Shutt in full stride. What a play! Oh well, as Scotty himself sometimes allowed, you have to have different rules for .200 hitters than you do for .300 hitters.

Because the Canadiens were weakened by injuries—Risebrough and Cournoyer were out—Scotty used Flower everywhere. With Lemaire and Shutt mostly, but also centring his own line with Lambert and Mario. Guy sometimes played with Gainey as well. For once, Boston scored first—typical Bruins blue-collar goal. Schmautz stormed the crease, ripping Dryden's mask off. Later, the little winger fired a slapshot that glanced off Ratelle's leg, deflecting past a barefaced Dryden. Flower's line soon got that one back. They were so fast; it was like watching a young Muhammad Ali take on a plodding, late-in-his-career Archie Moore. Three times, the Bruins had a chance to clear the puck—Peter McNab, O'Reilly and Stan Jonathan. But a speeding Hab always got a stick or body in the way. Lafleur, on his off wing, set up Robinson in the middle. Cheevers made the save. Seconds later, from the right-wing corner this time, Guy feathered a backhand pass into the slot. Lemaire snapped it just under the crossbar.

Tie game.

Seconds later, Wilson flew past Park with the puck, one of two unsuccessful breakaways in the second period by the Habs' number 17. Again and again, the spring-loaded Habs barged past opponents. Shutt, Lemaire, Lafleur and Chartraw lapped various Bruins defenders to nullify icings. For the last half of the game, the battle came down to Flower vs. Cheevers. Lafleur had five good chances. Cheesy skated out with the puck after another glove save, only to be swallowed up by checkers—Lafleur, Lambert or Lemaire. The Bruins started out hitting, but were now just hanging on. On *Hockey Night in Canada*, Danny Gallivan couldn't help but notice how tame the deflated Big Bad Bruins now seemed.

"This game has been well handled. Not too many decisions have been disputatiously construed by the players. No bickering, no arguing to speak of. *Now Bouchard shoots it!* Knocked down by Sims. *Another shot by Lapointe!* Gainey getting ready to centre it . . ."

It went to overtime. Canadiens were standing on the bench, ready to end this. "They want the kill quickly," Gallivan said. Shutt and Lafleur bewildered Park on a two-on-one. Guy hit the post. Robinson sharked in for the rebound, banging a shot off the side of the net. Seconds later, the puck was in the corner. An exhausted Sims tried to freeze it, as Lafleur and Shutt stared at him. "Move it!" referee Bruce Hood yelled. Fearful of picking up a penalty, Sims kicked the puck along the boards. Guy then picked it up, moving behind the net—no, he decided to pass it out at the last second, just as he disappeared behind the net—another sin, another blind pass. Lemaire scored before Cheevers could turn around.

"And the Canadiens win the Stanley Cup!" Gallivan shouted.

Minutes later, in the visitors' dressing room, champagne corks flew. Dryden yelled out, "Just 120 days till training camp," earning a derisive cheer. French players sang "La vie est belle" before passing through a champagne shower, courtesy of Robinson and Pointu, on their way to join Radio-Canada's devilishly handsome Richard Garneau, who had set up his post outside the Canadiens dressing room. Conn Smythe Trophy winner Guy Lafleur advised Garneau that he was heading to the south of France after the Cup parties were over—Saint-Tropez. Serge told the broadcaster he'd met French-Canadian migrants from all over New England in Boston the past week. Lapointe, Bouchard and Lemaire all collected congratulations. So what was new? Montreal had won another championship. Another Cup. Everyone was happy on Radio-Canada.

But maybe something *was* different. Here was coach Scotty Bowman with Garneau, speaking easily in French. Next, Ken Dryden appeared, advising Radio-Canada's audience that "*les Bruins jouent très, très bien.*" Yes, 1977 was different. *Mon dieu,* Englishers were making an effort to speak the language of Quebec's majority.

Some things remained the same, however. Just before the Canadiens climbed aboard the bus to the airport, beer cans in their pockets ready to be hissed open, Mayor Jean Drapeau of Montreal issued a press release. "The Stanley Cup parade will follow the usual route."

Hockey's great lyricist, Danny Gallivan, was the English voice of the Montreal Canadiens on *Hockey Night in Canada* from 1952 through 1984. Verbs and nouns in hockey have never been the same. Below, 18 Gallivanisms, one for each time the Canadiens won the Cup under his watch.

Oh, and Dryden kicks his pad out in rapier-like fashion.
And the Flyers have wasted a *glorious* scoring opportunity.
Mahovlich dipsy-doodles over the blue line. What's he going to do?
Lapointe steps gingerly through centre ice.
With Lemaire's goal, Boston now face a Herculean task.
The puck is lost in Cheevers' paraphernalia. Where is it?
Montreal fans campaign for a penalty against Philadelphia.
And now Tremblay makes a visitation to the penalty box.
Napier is on the prowl.
Gainey manoeuvring at centre.
A cannonading drive by Shutt.
And a larcenous save by Gilles Gilbert.
Jarvis turns, wasting valuable seconds.
Savard avoids Cashman with a deft spinorama move.
Dryden stymies Clarke with a scintillating save.
Oh, and an *enormous* save by Larocque.
A classic Robinsonian effort has tied the game.
Now Guy Lafleur gobbles up the puck. Away he goes!

TOO MANY MEN ON THE ICE

Boston Bruins vs. Montreal Canadiens,
April 26–May 10, 1979

Something was wrong with the Montreal Canadiens. After finishing first and taking the Cup three straight seasons, the once-superb club was merely excellent in the 1978–79 campaign. The New York Islanders finished on top. Captain Bryan Trottier was judged the league's best player; teammate Denis Potvin, the NHL's best defender. Well, good for the Isles. But everyone in Montreal understood that the Habs had made the mistake, and it was a whopper, that allowed New York to come on. And the thing was, they should've known better.

In 1975, Scotty Bowman received a midnight phone call. *Who the hell . . .* It was Claude Ruel, drunk with excitement. "Scotty, I just saw a junior player who lift me out of my seat, first one since Guy Lafleur—Michel Bossy." Alas, the Habs passed on Bossy, a francophone Montrealer, choosing Mark Napier in the 1977 draft. Napier was faster, a very good player. Bossy, though, was *un original*. Had magic in his hands. Michel scored 69 goals for the Isles in 1978–79, putting him 17 up on Guy and—no getting around it—58 ahead of Napier, another right winger.

More trouble signs: GM Sam Pollock retired before the '78–79 season. No explanation. Over the course of the year, Ken Dryden and Jacques Lemaire indicated that they too would be leaving. Ken had just turned 32; Coco, 33. At 52, Pollock was still young for an executive. Why the premature exodus? Steve Shutt had the answer: "It's like a piano wire. If you just keep tightening it and tightening it, it'll snap." The tightening piano wire was the pressure of playing in Montreal. For all Quebec. Making sure the legacy continued—one more banner for the Forum rafters. Winning, then winning again.

Even the piano tuner was weary. In Boston one morning that season, the team met for breakfast. That, and to figure what was wrong with their coach. Guy Lapointe got the puck rolling: "*Tabernac,* did you hear [Scotty] last night? 'Pretty good effort, gang.' Pretty good effort! We were horseshit."

"Those two goals they got near the end," Larry Robinson moaned. "*Câlisse,* that used to drive him crazy."

"How the hell we gonna win this way?" Pointu asked. "He's gotta start givin' us some shit out there."

"Hell, in practice other day, I'm skatin' around, he calls me over," Shutt shuddered. "'How you feelin' Steve?' What kinda question's that? I tell ya, he's losing his marbles."

No, just his enthusiasm. Scotty Bowman coveted Pollock's job; wanted his mentor to validate all that he had achieved by crowning him successor. Instead, Sam chose assistant Irving Grundman, who got his start running a string of Montreal bowling alleys. Scotty had been beaten out of his dream job by a guy named Irving. Depressed, he was turning into a mopey nice guy. God help the Canadiens.

Hockey itself was changing. How much, nobody knew just yet. The European-flavoured WHA was about to fold, with four teams joining the NHL in 1980—Hartford, Edmonton, Winnipeg and Quebec City. Swedes and Finns, Czechs and Russians too, were on the way to the NHL. There would be more significant departures: on January 9, 1979, Bobby Orr retired at age 31. His knees were shot; he could no longer skate. Five months later, Bernie Parent quit after getting a stick in the eye. Doctor's orders. Fred Shero left Philadelphia for his first love, the New York Rangers, taking that team to the Cup finals, his fourth of the decade, before leaving the NHL entirely in 1980. Paul Henderson, Stan Mikita, Bobby Hull, Gordie Howe, Yvan Cournoyer, Gerry Cheevers and Dave Schultz would retire in 1980. Peter Mahovlich tumbled to the minors. Russian great Valeri Kharlamov died in 1981 in a car accident.

On April 11, 1980, the Habs finished off the Hartford Whalers in the first round of the playoffs. Lafleur was hurt in that game. Pat Boutette took out his knee as Flower swung around the boards, leading a power-play rush.

Flower never really recovered. His firing pin was damaged. The breakaway speed would no longer be there. With it went Lafleur's confidence. He'd play for a few more years, but . . .

And yes, Bowman left Montreal at the end of the '78–79 season. At the same time, his Boston coaching nemesis, Don Cherry, was "released from his contract." He'd had enough of GM Harry Sinden . . . and vice versa. He would leave the NHL following season, done with coaching at 46. Even Scotty was shocked when the Bruins let Grapes walk. "I'll bet you [Cherry] averaged 45 wins a year," Rain Man told a reporter. Pretty close. Cherry led the Bruins to 231 wins in five seasons, an average of just over 46 victories.

Nineteen eighty wasn't an artificial dividing point—1979 would be the last year of a historic run. Between 1953 and 1979, the Montreal Canadiens collected championships in sprees—two, four and five at a time. Never again. But it was more than just the end of Montreal's dynasty. Viewed in retrospect, '70s hockey can be seen as a self-contained chapter. So many players, coaches and teams that defined the sport in this decade failed to cross or get much past the 1980 finish line. Let's go over those names again—Orr, Parent, Dryden, Lafleur, Lemaire, Mahovlich, Cournoyer, Henderson, Cheevers, Schultz, Kharlamov, Shero and Cherry . . . all of them gone or on their way out the door inside a single season.

That's all in hindsight, of course. At the time, no one stared in regret out the back window at the disappearing highway. There was so much to look forward to. Wayne Gretzky and Mark Messier began their NHL careers in Edmonton in the fall of 1979. What with WHA franchises joining the fold and the Atlanta Flames moving to Calgary, the NHL was suddenly alive in four new Canadian cities. Edmonton–Calgary and Montreal–Quebec City resumed and escalated historic civic rivalries.

Elsewhere in sports, basketball reached the modern age with the arrival of Magic Johnson and Larry Bird in 1979. Baseball's Toronto Blue Jays started up shop in 1977, though without their first choice as GM, Sam Pollock.*

A new *Star Wars* had commenced.

But oh, how the last era ended. The climax of '70s hockey was a game for the ages. The combatants were appropriate—Montreal vs. Boston. These teams battled it out in the 1968, 1969 and 1971 playoffs, with Montreal emerging victorious every time, winning when they should have . . . when they shouldn't have, too. The Bruins took the Cup in 1970 and '72. And then Boston and Montreal fought it out again in the '77 and '78 Cup finals. If you accept that the Habs–Bruins playoffs in 1971 and 1979 were de facto finals, the best teams playing in preliminary rounds, the Bruins made it to the final dance seven times that decade; Montreal, six. Ensuring that the '79 Stanley Cup playoffs were an all-the-more-fitting resolution of the decade, Shero's Rangers—starring Phil Esposito, no less—upset the New York Islanders in the other

---

* An April, 18, 1977, issue of *Sports Illustrated* reported that the Blue Jays "sounded out" Pollock for the GM job. Sam turned them down, but "allows that he might have welcomed such a challenge 10 years ago." Or ten years later— Pollock served as CEO and chair of the Blue Jays from 1995 to 2000.

semifinal. The gang that defined hockey in the '70s was pretty well all there, except for Bobbys Orr and Clarke.

Making the playoffs more dramatic still, the Bruins–Canadiens series would go to a sudden-death, seventh-game overtime.

For the Canadiens, nothing was easy anymore. Fatigue would be a factor. What with international matches and NHL work, including full playoff runs, the Big Three, along with Bob Gainey, Guy Lafleur and Steve Shutt, put in 110-game seasons year after year. Larry Robinson, Guy Lapointe and Shutt were injured for large chunks of the 1978–79 schedule. Cournoyer was out four months. Lemaire, Reggie Houle, Doug Risebrough and Mark Napier missed significant time. Pete Mahovlich was gone, traded to Pittsburgh. Pete showed up at the Forum with the Penguins in November, collected a Stanley Cup ring and then shuffled back to the visitors' quarters, his face streaming with tears.

Dryden was sore, too. His catching hand didn't work as well as it once did—too many slapshots. He would adapt, using his pads and stick to ward off more shots.

Everyone was exhausted and beat up, except—for a little while longer—the perennial Flower. Guy played every game, scored 52 goals, while working as a full-time pitchman—General Motors, Yoplait, Bauer, Koho skates. There was a Lafleur cologne, Number 10 ("a mixture of exotic woods with a hint of musk for the real man"). The Canadiens star never stopped. He had a CKVL radio show, *Le monde des champions*. There was also a disco album—fitness tips with a throbbing nightclub pulse. "Stand straight," Guy murmured, doing his best Barry White. "Now bend your knees, just your knees." That Lafleur had a fitness record out was rich, because outside of practice, he didn't work out . . . like, ever. And he smoked a pack a day—it was almost as if Guy was determined to bring the billowing chimneys of Thurso with him everywhere. He was also out most nights, all night, partying at Montreal clubs—Thursdays, Gatsby and 1234, a Rue Crescent funeral parlour turned disco. He drank too much. Good scotch, champagne, wine. Biographer Georges-Hébert Germain intimated that the superstar enjoyed an occasional Baudelairean bottle of wine on the road . . . while having a wine bottle at home. Hockey's greatest star would buy roses for women in restaurants, champagne for the house. Still, he was a solitary man. On the road, he sometimes wandered off to saloons by himself, like Shero. There was a bar in Dorval, not far from the airport, where he could be found some nights.

Alone even in a crowd, he sometimes grew restless. One night, he got in a car and flew to Quebec City, making the 142-mile journey in an hour flat.

Still, he was a good teammate. Once a season, he would give his fellow players a wink. "Tell your wives and girlfriends we're having a union meeting," he said. With that, Flower booked two rooms at the Ritz, Montreal's best hotel, where the Queen stayed when she and Prince Philip were in town. There, he hosted a team party—room-service steaks for all the guys, free bar, of course. "My way of saying thanks," he said. The Canadiens loved him; they were fans, too. And they joined together as a support group when the Flower occasionally wilted. It happened at the end of the season sometimes. After the Canadiens beat Boston in '77, Flower fell apart again, crying in the dressing room.

"Want us to get a masseur?" Houle asked.

"You been constantly on the go nine months," Robinson said. "You're tired, that's all."

"You need a break," Shutt offered. "Guy, for your own sake, give yourself a break."

But there were no intermissions, no off-seasons for Lafleur. Being a Quebec folk hero, pleasing everyone, was a full-time job.

Then you had the Montreal Canadien whose job it was to please no one. "The key guy on our team was Scotty," Shutt would later tell Al Strachan. "He realized that the only team that could beat us was ourselves. We had such a good team that petty little grievances could develop that might bring the team down. So what Scotty did, he made himself the focal point. The only thing that everyone had in common was that they hated Scotty."

Like Lafleur, Bowman was a full-time Canadien. In 1975, he spent an off night driving from his farm in Acton Vale, 60 miles outside Montreal, to Ville-Émard in the city's west end. He wanted to see the ten-year-old hockey player everyone was talking about—Mario Lemieux. Earlier that summer, he worked at a hockey clinic in Winnipeg, where he complimented junior coach Roger Neilson on the work of one of his graduates, Buffalo's defensive forward Craig Ramsay. "My last guy is even better than Ramsay," Neilson boasted. "Who's that?" Scotty said. "Doug Jarvis," Neilson replied. Bowman was on the phone right away to Pollock, who immediately traded for Jarvis, stealing him from the Leafs.

Now, though, Scotty was barely present. The cross every Canadien was forced to bear, uniting them in suffering, had one skate out the Forum door. As a result, the team was pulling apart at the seams. What did Mario Tremblay, an avowed separatist, and Shutt, who caused a stink in French dailies by complaining about Quebec language laws, have in common outside the rink? Complaining, telling Scotty stories, was a comforting daily ritual—something that made every Canadien a brother.

"How come you don't play me?" Mario asked Bowman early in his career.

"Because I don't like your face," the coach replied.

During a practice once, Shutt accidentally nailed Scotty with a shot in the ankle. "That didn't hurt," Bowman sneered, eyes watering. "I thought you had a good shot."

"That was a pass," Steve replied. "Wait till I hit you with a good shot."

Oh, how the Canadiens enjoyed that last story.

Fortunately for Montreal, Scotty got his mojo back in the playoffs. The postseason energized a coach who had named his first son Stanley, after the Cup. It helped that he disliked his counterpart in the semifinals, Cherry, engaging in a public feud so nasty that new NHL president John Ziegler would have to intervene, like a teacher forced to break up a recess scrap. Hockey in the '70s was punctuated and defined by volcanic disturbances, on-ice disputes that spilled into swelling mobs—the (near-)public execution of Pat Quinn by Bruins fans in the 1969 playoffs; a Rangers fan

lunging from the crowd to knife Turk Sanderson during the 1972 playoffs; anti-Soviet hockey riots in Prague; the Lafleur–Dionne civil war
in Quebec City; Ontario Attorney General Roy McMurtry busting the
Flyers in 1976. But there had never been a dispute quite like the Bowman–
Cherry contretemps. Hockey's first public relations war took place on
two fronts. Grapes lobbied for his team in the press, while Bowman
ignored reporters, conducting guerilla theatre events on the ice.

Yes, the 1980s, a decade that would see corporate PR turned into a
profitable art, were right around the corner.

The coaches got started early in the semifinal opener, at the Forum
on Thursday, April 26. Lemaire beat Cheevers on a setup from Lafleur.
Bowman quickly sent his entire team out to celebrate. It was something
Habs did in the playoffs—a demonstration of pageantry meant to humble
lesser opponents. This time, Cherry was ready. In a premeditated move,
he ordered his bench over the boards to console Cheevers. That had
never been done before. At first, Gilles Gilbert was reluctant. "Get out
there," Cherry said, grabbing his substitute goalie. Referee Dave Newell
skated to the almost-empty Boston bench.

"You can't do that."

"Well, stop them. Or else after every goal, we're coming out."

Canadiens won the first two in Montreal, coming from behind both
times. The Bruins suffered from bad luck . . . and worse goaltending.
First game, they had a goal by Middleton called back. Montreal scored
the winner on a mysterious non-call. Savard took a puck in the face and
crumpled, spitting out teeth. "Injury, injury," Dryden yelled, beaver-
slapping the ice with his stick. In the confusion, Pierre Larouche raced
down and scored at the other end. In the second game, a Saturday evening affair, Boston jumped to a two–nothing lead, but Cheevers had a
bad night, allowing three goals on consecutive shots within 86 seconds
late in the first period.

One of the Canadiens goals was clearly offside.

The Habs were up two games. They'd already bested Boston in two
straight playoff series. It was worse than that when you stopped to think

about it (and Boston papers were in a reflective mode these days): the last time the Bruins had knocked the Canadiens out of the playoffs, Roosevelt and Mackenzie King were in office, way back in 1943. Since then, the Habs had won 11 straight series. And it wasn't very close: Montreal had 48 wins, Boston 15.

After the second game, Montreal fans laughed at the Bruins outside the visitors' dressing room. "See you next year," they jeered. Growing hot under his Edwardian shirt collar, Cherry began talking—loudly—in sound bites. "We'll be back here next Saturday," he assured reporters. "I've already ordered the steaks. These [Canadiens] can be had. We know it and you guys know it, too." Buddying up to Al Strachan, he asked the Montreal *Gazette* reporter about Gainey's first-period goal, which replays suggested was offside. "What did you think?"

"[It was offside] by a foot."

"You're being kind."

Now Grapes pretended confusion, asking scribes to help him solve a nagging mystery, something that had been bugging him for years. "Doesn't it seem strange, all the calls go against us [in Montreal]?" he asked, slowing to reflect upon his club's experiences in the Forum. "Oh well, maybe we'll get all the breaks in Boston." This thought was followed by a phony Santa Claus laugh: "Ho, ho, ho." *Like that'll happen.* No, everyone knew the referees had it in for Boston, he continued. "It makes you laugh," Cherry said, though he was far from mirth. "It's like they're the Peggy Flemings of hockey and we're the blacksmiths."

Grapes was having quite a day. After that morning's practice, he made like a tavern bouncer, tossing a heckler from a press scrum. "Why don't you play Gilles Gilbert in nets?" a stranger asked. "Cheevers is killing you."

"And what are your qualifications as a coach?" Cherry barked. "Who the hell are you anyway? What paper are you with?"

"North Andover," the guy said. In fact, he was a civilian, an irate Bruins fan from Grapes's own neighbourhood. Cheevers also lived in the Boston suburb.

"Get the hell out of here," Grapes said. "Security!" When cops failed to show, Cherry waded through reporters to grab his tormentor, giving him the bum's rush. "Gee, that felt great," he said. "Wish he'd taken a swing at me. North Andover, indeed. I'll get Blue after him."

Back in Boston, Cherry really put on a show. In the past month, he'd been profiled in *Sports Illustrated* and the *Boston Globe*—stories that focused on Don and his best friend. Aside from Charlie Brown's Snoopy, Grapes's dog, Blue, a seven-year-old bull terrier with a history of kidney stones, was probably the most famous dog in America these days. Channel 38 in Boston ran a promo clip of Don and Blue before Bruins games. When the North American press converged on the old Boston Garden, Grapes welcomed reporters into his office. Aside from a jock strap labelled GRAPES pinned to a bulletin board, the room was crowded with dog memorabilia. An Australian newspaper clipping told the story of a bull terrier that saved his master from a giant kangaroo. Day after day, Grapes read reporters beddy-bye stories from a handy dog encyclopedia: "The bull terrier has his beginning in the bloody sport of baiting the bull . . ."

Eventually, the coach veered off script. "[Bull terriers] are not dogs you can let run free, eh? They'll want to play with other dogs; of course, if the other dogs want to fight . . . game over." There was a lesson here: the Bruins were Cherry's dog soldiers. "Look at Stanley Jonathan, John Wensik, Terry O'Reilly, Rick Middleton, Bobby Miller, Bobby Schmautz, the whole bunch of them," Grapes continued. "They have to have a little bull terrier in them." The Bruins coach invited a reporter to his place in North Andover. Grabbing a tennis racquet and ball, Cherry brought the visitor outside. Blue was now bouncing up and down. "Watch, I'll show you Terry O'Reilly going into a corner," Grapes said, serving a ball towards a distant wall. A growling Blue raced off at full speed, stopping with a mouthful of tennis ball just short of the fence. "Flat out, eh, no second gear!" the coach commented, smiling.

Not everyone liked Grapes and Blue, mind you; when the Bruins were last in Madison Square Garden, ever-gracious Rangers fans chanted, "Fuck Blue! Fuck Blue!" during stoppages in play.

In Boston, though, Cherry had it made. Fans gobbled up his story—career minor leaguer who played in Hershey, Springfield, Trois-Rivières, Spokane, Kitchener, Rochester. Rode the buses for 20 years—eight-hour trips some nights, no washrooms. The Hershey Bears had piss patrols at two in the morning. Guys stumbled out of the bus, four hours from Springfield, and wrote their names in the snow, squinting up at the treeline, on guard for hungry, swooping owls. Grapes even had a trick to help him sleep: "Kept a pilla with me, eh? I'd hang the pilla case out the window, keep it nice and fresh."

He worked a jackhammer in the off-season—after he retired, too. Painted houses, tried selling Cadillacs. Then he took over the Rochester Amerks, won the AHL coach-of-the-year award. Harry Sinden—like Cherry a naval warfare buff—hired him to coach the Bruins. The big league at last. The job was a perfect fit. Grapes was a Boston, drink-beer-from-the-bottle kind of guy. Bobby *Oah* liked him. That was good enough for working-class Hub fans, who saw Grapes as the boss they always wished they had.

Though a great players' coach, Grapes was prone to paranoia. The minor leaguer who figured he had never got a break was always present. "If it goes to a seventh game, we'll get screwed, because [the NHL] want Montreal and New York in the next round, not the Boston Bruins, a bunch of scum," he told reporters this series. *A bunch of scum?* In Montreal, in the second game of the semifinals, Stan Jonathan manhandled Doug Risebrough. Cherry watched a taped replay of the game on TV later and noticed there was no replay of the altercation. Suspicious, he called *Hockey Night in Canada* producer Ralph Mellanby. "That because we won the fight?" Grapes fumed.

"No, we don't replay fights," the producer said.

During game three in Boston, Mario Tremblay and Bruin Rick Smith got into a tussle. Tremblay won this one. Mellanby's cameras revealed that Grapes was suddenly gone from the Bruins bench. The producer asked someone to check into it—could be a story. Never mind: just then, Grapes burst into the control room, all upset. "You better not show that on replay," he told Mellanby before high-tailing it back to the bench.

The Bowman–Cherry feud worsened before game three. Visiting teams usually came out onto the ice first—to accept boos and stand there fidgeting when, minutes later, fans whooped and cheered for the home side. Not tonight. Always tricky, Bowman tried pulling a *slow* one. Scotty dawdled, wouldn't send his team out first. Neither would Grapes, of course. He wanted the Habs on the ice, listening to Garden fans roar their approval of his guys. Finally, referee Andy Van Hellemond began yelling at the coaches, who refused to budge.

We're not going first. They're supposta.

Ladies first . . .

The Bruins scored early—Jonathan from Brad Park. Montreal's Robinson tied it late in the third, banging a rebound past surprise Bruins starter Gilles Gilbert. Habs celebrated. But what was this? Instead of lapsing into doomed silence, Bruins fans stood up and gave their French-Canadian goalie what he later called "a stand-up ovation." The Garden had picked up on Grapes's screw-you tactic when Montreal scored. They were up on their feet roaring again a minute later, when Park surprised Dryden with a sudden wrist shot on a two-on-one.

What do you know, Boston won!

And won again in game four when another old pro, Jean Ratelle, beat Dryden in overtime on another two-on-one. *Tabernac,* what was wrong with Montreal? All these defensive mistakes. According to Scotty, nothing, nothing at all; it was the referee's fault. Habs received five penalties in game three to Boston's four—three if you didn't include a call for too many men on the ice. In game four, Boston was penalized twice—*twice!* It was incredible, Bowman complained. Here you had the Big Bad Bruins—well, they were Terrible really, with Jonathan, O'Reilly, Wensink et al., ruffians every one of them—and a mere six penalties in two games. Scotty revisited game films, splicing together uncalled Bruins transgressions, and then invited all the Stanley Cup media in for a press screening of his first feature film, *Gone with the Whistle.*

After that, Bowman took the fight into enemy camp. Referees had a regular morning skate at 8:00. Scotty was there at 7:30, standing along-side the boards, getting his pipes ready.

"You won't call anything against Boston," Bowman screamed at offi-cials. "You don't have the guts to call anything against Boston."

One reason why Bowman was so cranky had to be all the valentines Cherry was collecting in the press—some from Montreal Canadiens! Scotty couldn't stand the *Montreal Star's* Red Fisher. That Red had told him to "go and fuck yourself" one day didn't help.* Now, even read-ing the Montreal *Gazette* was dangerous to Scotty's health. He opened Montreal's English-language morning paper one day to read Guy Lapointe saying, "Cherry has done a super job with the defence he has. Milbury is playing pretty steady for them . . . I had a chance to be with Cherry during the 1976 Team Canada. You can see that he is very human. It's easy to have respect for a guy like that."

---

* Bowman was feuding with Red Fisher at the time, sometimes not inviting the *Montreal Star* to press conferences. One morning, Fisher asked Montreal's coach what was wrong with Lemaire; he seemed to be favouring a shoulder. "Upset stomach," Bowman said. Later, a player advised the reporter that Coco had a slightly separated shoulder. Hurrying back to the office, Fisher began his lede for that afternoon's paper with "Jacques Lemaire is doubtful for tonight's game with what Canadiens coach Scotty Bowman describes as an upset stomach. The pain, however, has gone all the way up to his slightly separated shoulder." Lemaire would play that night. In the dressing room afterwards, Scotty got in Fisher's grille.

"Lemaire played, eh, eh?"

"Excuse me?"

"You wrote he wasn't playing. He played."

"I wrote that his status was doubtful because of what you called an upset stomach. He has a separated shoulder."

"He played, eh?"

"He played and you said he had a bad stomach."

"He played."

"One more thing."

"Yeah?"

"Go and fuck yourself."

Very human! As opposed to Scotty, presumably.

Flower was asked if he worried at all about Bruins' tough guy Wensink taking him out. "I know Don Cherry as a coach," Lafleur told the *Gazette.* "He won't let it happen."

Yes, Grapes was having the time of his life. His team was back in the series and everybody loved him, including the opposition. And in going with Gilbert, he had won the coaching gamble of his career. Hell, in the kid's last playoff start, back in 1976, he'd given up five goals to the Flyers' Reggie Leach. Gilbert was so nervous he didn't even tell his girlfriend he was going to start until hours before game three. He was also fighting off chicken pox. "Cheesy, do I look all right?" he asked Cheevers before walking into the barrel with Boston's season on the line. Cheevers gave him a big wink. Grapes loved Cheevers, a former teammate back in Rochester in 1964. Steady, unflappable, Gerry was a pro's pro. Still, Cheevers had never had much luck with Montreal. So Grapes rolled the dice with Gilbert, a talented goalie born in Montreal. He knew the kid would like to show everyone back home.

The gamble paid off. Gilbert was brilliant this series. And Grapes's players were playing just as well, allowing Montreal a paltry 18 shots in game three. Cherry had an optional practice the next morning. Even he didn't get on the ice—bad cold. Ratelle ran the scrimmage. Why'd the coach even bother coming to the rink? "I had to give you guys something," the Boston coach laughed, sitting in his office, surrounded by reporters. "I know Scotty's not going to do it. Somebody's got to carry the papers." Right then, Peter McNab walked by the doorway on the way to the dressing room. "Hey, sorry there," Grapes called out in apology.

"Tell it to my wife," McNab laughed. "She's the one who was embarrassed."

Reporters pressed for an explanation. We're outworking Montreal, Grapes told them. Only problem is we're trying too hard, eh? McNab, he jumped on the ice too early during a line change last night. Holy geez, we got too many men on the ice.

"Get in the box, you dummy—you caused it!" Grapes told McNab once play was called. He got away with *dummy* because, before turning pro, McNab had attended the University of Denver on a baseball scholarship. It was like calling a big guy Tiny. The morning after the fourth-game mistake, Grapes and McNab could laugh about a harmless lapse of judgment. The Bruins were happy. A tied series, two wins in a row. And they knew the Canadiens weren't quite as good as they once were.

That they could be had.

There was only one cloud on the horizon, and it was as black as the team's away jerseys. Grapes had been feuding with GM Harry Sinden all season. By now, they were not even talking. They passed notes through intermediaries. Later, Grapes would tell *Sports Illustrated* that the falling-out was 90 per cent his fault. At this point, though, he couldn't help himself. It was always him and his guys against the world. He didn't like Harry offering suggestions. Didn't matter that Sinden was himself a Stanley Cup–winning coach and that he'd risked his neck trading Phil Esposito and Carol Vadnais for Park and Ratelle, an unpopular trade at the time; or that, a year later, he'd stolen Nifty Middleton from the Rangers, another bold move that worked out. This was Grapes's team—everyone else off the bus. Criticizing your boss in the newspaper was no way to get ahead. Maybe Grapes didn't know it yet, but he was painting himself into "Coach's Corner."

Game five and six were more of the same, with more hitting and vitriol. The home side won both times. In Montreal, referees called four penalties on Park, infuriating Grapes. *Bowman's got to them!* Lafleur scored twice on one shift, and two of the Big Three, Savard and Robinson, added singles in a 5–1 romp. The Bruins didn't have a chance. "We needed the Royal 22nd to fire howitzers at them and even then I'm not sure we could have done anything," Sinden sighed. Game six back in Boston was electric stuff—firewagon hockey the first period, a 2–2 tie. Habs continued to pour it on, but Gilbert was sensational, earning a series of ovations. Gradually, Boston's physical play and perseverance paid off. Cashman and then Jonathan, with two goals to give him a hat trick, polished Montreal off. Fans were standing, cheering in the Garden. Hell, they were even on their feet applauding across town in Fenway Park, where Boston sports fans brushed aside a 10–2 drubbing of the Red Sox by the California Angels to give the Bruins two parkwide standing ovations, first when the scoreboard registered that the Bruins were up 4–2, and then when a 5–2 win was signalled.

Not all Bruins players could even stand up after the game, however. Cashman went from the rink back to Massachusetts General, where he stayed overnight in a pelvic traction unit to settle a bad back. "What are you doing here?" Park asked Cash when he walked, stiff as Frankenstein, into the Bruins dressing room for practice the next morning.

"I'm playing."

"Listen, Cash, it's a hockey game. It's not that important."

Cashman stared at him. What could Park say? He was freezing a wonky knee before games. It was the same on the other side: in game five, Risebrough took on Terry O'Reilly. Bad move—the Bruin had three inches and 30 pounds on him. Risebrough got in some licks. O'Reilly left the ice bleeding, cut above the eye, but Risebrough's nose was now all over his face, broken in three places. Gone for the series, doctors said. Game seven, though, there he was—to hell with doctors— playing with a masked helmet. So was Brian Engblom. The defenceman had been knocked off planet Earth earlier in the series, again by O'Reilly. "Where's Billy?" he said on the bench at the time, before cursing Dave Hutchison. Big Serge, beside him, laughed. Maple Leafs defenceman Hutchison had hit Englom earlier in the playoffs. And "Billy" Nyrop was retired. Though concussed, Engblom was playing game seven, too.

Before the final encounter, league president John Ziegler met with Bowman and Cherry in Boston. He'd already blasted both coaches over the phone. After Grapes started in with the "NHL hates us" whining, Ziegler gave him a call. "I'll put up with you calling us stupid and every- thing, but I won't put up with you calling us dishonest," Ziegler com- plained. He had also contacted Bowman, decreeing that there should be no more military parades when Habs scored. *Leave your guys on the bench.* Now, in person, he informed both coaches he wanted them to stop yapping about refs. No more home movies, either. Or talk about who had the best dog. Stick to hockey. This was the Stanley Cup, not the Westminster Kennel Club Dog Show.

The dog comments arose because Scotty had complained, days earlier, that his dog wasn't getting enough ink. "I've got a dog, too, you know, Waldo," he told reporters, breaking what was pretty well a series-long boycott except to promote his anti-Bruins propaganda movie. The white German shepherd "has flown the team charter," Scotty said. "Blue ever done that?"

"His dog ever been in *Sports Illustrated*?" Cherry countered.

During their Boston meeting, Ziegler fined the coaches $1,000 each, promising a $10,000 penalty if the bitching and complaining got any worse. Grapes tried to keep his mouth clamped. He couldn't believe Ziegler was so upset that he and Bowman were generating publicity—what a hockey stick-in-the-mud. As Ziegler went on and on about league integrity, Cherry looked Bowman up and down, frowning when he came to his nemesis's Hush Puppies. Grapes couldn't help wondering, "How the hell can a guy wear brown shoes with a blue suit?"

Ziegler's talk had little impact on Cherry, apparently. When the Bruins passed through customs to Montreal for game seven, an official asked Boston's coach if he had anything to declare. "We're going to beat the fucking Canadiens and win the Stanley Cup," Don said, guaranteeing a delay. Happened all the time they went to Montreal. *Not my fault,* Grapes figured. *Geez, why do they keep asking me that stupid question?*

It was always the same challenge for visiting teams at the Forum—make it through the first 20 minutes alive. In Montreal's three home wins this series, they'd outscored Boston 7–2 in the first period. The Bruins did more than simply hang on this night—a warm, clear Tuesday in early May. The fans were sky high. It was game seven! *Les Canadiens sont là!* Scotty tried to rattle the Bruins by mixing lines. First shift, he had Lafleur with Jarvis and Gainey. Later, Guy centred Houle and Napier. (He also performed his regular shift alongside Lemaire and Shutt.)

On a successful power play, Bowman played Savard and Lapointe up front with Lemaire; Robinson and Lafleur manned the left and right points. First time he'd done that all season. And it worked, as Lemaire scored. Next power play, he switched Lafleur to the left point. Every shift there was a new look. And Montreal was flying. It was soon apparent they were trying to wear out Park. Lafleur, Gainey and Robinson took a run at the Bruins defenceman. Much of the action was in Boston's end. With the Canadiens defence pinching, there were wild scrambles in front of "Le Gros Gilles"—what Montreal French papers were now calling Gilbert. "It's bumptious out there!" Professor Gallivan advised fans on *Hockey Night in Canada*.

The Bruins handed out the most significant bumps. On a Boston power play, Cashman strolled through Dryden's crease, giving him a nudge, a move undetected by the local constabulary. The goalie spun awkwardly and was forced to dive, and so he missed Middleton's scoring shot. Later, Milbury clobbered Lambert, throwing him hard into the glass. Yvon tried to get up, but his legs weren't there anymore.

One–all, end of the first. Given the context, advantage Boston.

Seconds into the middle frame, a growingly confident Grapes bumped bellies with Bowman, throwing his top line—Ratelle, Cashman and Middleton—out against Montreal's best, Lemaire, Lafleur and Shutt. The faceoff was in Boston's end, and Cherry wanted Ratelle to take it. The veteran beat Lemaire. The Bruins dumped the puck into Montreal's end. Ratelle then rubbed Savard out along the boards, stripping him of the puck. Middleton spotted Cashman across from him, behind the Habs' net, and Phil Esposito's old linemate made a lovely move, going forehand-backhand, depositing the puck in the net before Dryden could cover the post. "Now the grinding Bruins have the lead," Gallivan intoned. "The lunch-pail brigade, as Don Cherry affectionately calls them [are out in front]."

Montreal rallied. Stayed long minutes, shift after shift, in their most forward gear. Shutt, Savard and Lambert (twice) were in alone. Gilbert jumped out time and again, foiling one and all—stick side was his weakness, allegedly, but his right leg would be a blur tonight. He had become the great equalizer—like Dryden in 1971, a wild card who made fools out of experts. A suddenly hot goalie in a short series could do that.

Late in the period, Boston counterattacked. The oldest lunch pail on the club did it again: Cashman, who played his first game for Boston in 1964 (two years before Orr!), brought the puck out from behind the Montreal net, whirled and surprised Dryden with a high shot. A goal! The Canadiens were a heavyweight champ sent to the canvas; all they wanted now was to hang on until the end of the round. Sensing the kill, Boston was all over them, but Montreal made it to the bell on their feet, down 3–1 with a period remaining.

For some reason, Scotty had been chewing gum this game. He'd do that sometimes in the playoffs—change his routine for luck. In the 1976 finals against Philly, he wore tinted aviator shades for some reason. Now, beginning what he knew might be his last period in Montreal, he switched back to gobbling ice, grabbing a handful every couple minutes. He had a lot to chew on. *Les Glorieux* were in a fix; this was the first time they'd faced elimination in their late-'70s championship run. In the player's lounge, where old Canadiens gathered, Doug Harvey complained to a reporter, "Last two and a half months, they haven't been the Canadiens." On TV, Gallivan suggested Lafleur must improve, while observing that Lemaire "has been very average" this series. That was a bit much. So far in six games and two periods this series, Coco had three goals and as many assists. Flower, meanwhile, led all scorers, with five goals and four assists. As Steve Shutt liked to say, "Montreal fans are behind you, win or tie." Yes, Canadiens fans had entitlement issues.

C'mon, Flower, save us. Right now.

And so he did. The greatest period of Guy Lafleur's career began with him racing everywhere, impossible to cover, feeding teammates with perfect no-look passes. First shift, Flower banged Rick Smith's stick away, stealing the puck and firing it to roommate Shutt. Kick save, Gilbert. On a late change, Bowman got him out with Gainey and Tremblay, thereby shaking Flower's perpetual shadow, Don Marcotte. Guy blew past Sims, circling the net with one hand on the stick. When

Gilbert pulled over to block a wraparound, Flower collected himself, slipping a pass through the crease. A suddenly *there* Napier had the whole net. Three–two. Next, Boston took a penalty. Dick Redmond hauled down Lemaire. It was a call made every time in the first period in the regular season, but not always late in a playoff game. Overture, curtain, lights. At the Bruins bench, Grapes was up, a smirk on his face, stealing a series of bows, a performance that would be part of the opening to his "Coach's Corner" segment on *Hockey Night in Canada* for decades.

Thank you, NHL. Thank you very much. Din't I tell you, game seven and everything, we're in Montreal, here it comes, the old shaftola! What'd I tell you— din't I call it?

With the Forum crowd screaming for more, Scotty threw out yet another power-play configuration—Lemaire, Savard and Gainey up front, Lafleur and Lapointe back. Flower and Lemaire soon swapped positions, further confusing the Bruins. And a minute into the penalty, Guy, in the corner, found Lapointe at the blue line. Park, Gainey, Savard and Milbury tangled and turned in front of Gilbert, who never saw the tying goal.

The teams continued slugging it out. Boston was going with four defenders, and Park, for one, was clearly exhausted—all those hits. Montreal continued to pile it on. They were pressing hard when disaster struck: Lapointe's leg buckled underneath him as he wrestled for the puck in the corner with Middleton. Out came the stretcher; down went the volume. The Forum was suddenly deathly quiet. In the awkward ceasefire, the Bruins gathered together at the bench. *It's time, boys.* Grapes threw out his top offensive unit—Cashman, Middleton and Ratelle. Scotty countered with Robinson, Savard and Gainey's line, his best defence. Boston worked the puck into Montreal's zone. Ratelle had it going into the corner. There was a scramble. Now Middleton grabbed the puck and swung around in the opposite direction behind the net. Dryden was momentarily lost, but got to the post in time. Didn't matter; Middleton demonstrated why he was nicknamed "Nifty," sending a bank shot off Dryden's blocker into the net. On the TV replay, you could see Dryden's head snap in anger.

Shit.

At that moment, "Savard let out a groan of curdled sadness," Dryden reported in *The Game*. It was now 4–3 Boston, with less than four minutes remaining. The next 90 seconds passed without incident. Boston was careful. Dumped the puck. Froze the play in corners. Hung back. Montreal had nothing left. And then came a moment of somersaulting confusion followed by a prolonged roar. At the end of a long double shift, Guy Lafleur coasted to a stop at his bench. Don Marcotte hopped off.

"Good shift, Donny," Cherry offered. And then he looked up.

What? No, Flower hadn't gone off. Seeing Lafleur—the player the Bruins feared above all others—uncovered, three Boston players volunteered for duty. McNab, Jonathan and O'Reilly jumped onto the ice— only O'Reilly belonged. The Bruins managed, after some angry stage whispers, to get McNab back, but Jonathan was beyond their command. The Bruins had picked the wrong rink to make this kind of mistake. In a few seconds, every one of the 17,453 referees in the stands was standing, yelling. How could this happen? At practice this morning, Grapes reminded everyone about too many men on the ice.

Happened in game three, guys. Don't let it happen again. Everybody got it? Now this.

Linesman John D'Amico saw it first. Waited and waited. *Get off, somebody get off.* No official wanted to make this call late in the third period of a seventh playoff game. But 20 seconds later, with the crowd and the Montreal bench going berserk, D'Amico had no choice but to blow his whistle. Referee Bob Myers approached him. D'Amico explained the situation. "You sure?" Myers asked. D'Amico grimaced.

For the Bruins, what happened next was like being in a car accident, skidding on a highway, watching—trapped, helpless—waiting for the inevitable collision. The Canadiens were turned away twice, but they remained unhurried, patient, almost as if they too knew what was about to happen. Curiously, Dryden never left the net for an extra attacker. Scotty was that confident in the players he had on the ice. With little more than a minute remaining, Lafleur gathered the puck behind his net. Marcotte was on top of him, so he circled back. *Let's try this again.* "Stepping gingerly," in TV announcer Gallivan's words, down the right boards, Flower spotted Lemaire dawdling at the Bruins blue line, hitting him with a long pass. Lemaire coasted in, weighing his options. A chugging Shutt hurried up the middle. No, the centreman felt Lafleur approaching from behind and so made a delicate drop pass. Marcotte was on his check, stick out. Too late—Flower was halfway through his shot when the puck reached him.

How many times had he done this before? Playing for Rockland at age ten, amazing everyone at the Quebec peewee tournament in 1964. The next winter, scoring from centre against Larry Robinson's team his first-ever game in Montreal. Six years later, a man now, he shattered goalie George Hulme's stick with a long shot for the winning goal in the first game of the 1971 war between Quebec City and St. Catharines.

How many mornings had he been out on the ice alone, an hour before anyone else, perfecting a task that he now performed without thought or conspicuous effort, bending his stick through a puck from the lip of the faceoff circle, sending a blurred missile low off the inside of the far goalpost 45 feet away? Same place every time.

The answer: so many times that the extraordinary was now routine.

What always surprised opponents—fans too, for that matter—was how quickly these historic strikes took place. *Hockey Night in Canada* cameras failed even to pick up Guy Lafleur's short, sharp shot. It was past Gilbert and in the net before Danny Gallivan could cry, "He shoots, he scores."

The Forum exploded. Tie game, four–all.

Gallivan's sidekick, colour man Dick Irvin, didn't see the goal either. Not live, anyway. Sensing a Bruins win, he left the TV booth upstairs and was entering an ice-level studio, preparing for an interview with Bruins hero Cashman, when he heard public address announcer Claude Mouton's voice. "I guess there's a penalty," he said to D. Leo Monahan, a reporter for the *Boston Herald American* who wanted to be there for the Cashman interview.

For Irvin, the son of former Habs coach Dick Irvin Sr., watching a replay of Lafleur's goal from a soundproof studio gave him an eerie sense of déjà vu. "The greatest goal I ever saw, I tell this to everyone, was The Rocket returning from an injury* and going through the entire Boston team late in the third period to tie up a seventh game semifinal, beating Sugar Jim Henry," Irvin would tell me, going on to explain that Richard's goal seemed, in retrospect, dramatic foreshadowing. "All this happens in 1952. Well, here we are, what, 27 years later. Montreal is again down a goal late in the third period of a semifinal seventh game against Boston. And once again, you have a Montreal right winger, the greatest goal scorer of his time, racing into the south end of the Forum to score the tying goal.

"Amazing."

What happened next was pure Flower. The two best players of their era, Lafleur and Orr, were drawn together by fate in the 1976 Canada Cup. Being roommates, they were given time to contemplate the nature of their gifts. Why this move? That shot? Somehow, they both just knew instinctively what to do at hero time. Shortly after scoring the greatest goal of his career, Guy Lafleur grabbed a pass from Robinson outside the Montreal blue line. A minute earlier, he beat Gilbert with a blazing shot to his stick side—his alleged weakness. Gilbert's jackknifing right pad caught a piece of the puck as it skipped into the net. Perfect shot. Two inches lower, he would've had it. After the goal, Gilbert collapsed as if shot; he took a full minute to climb back to his feet.

Was the kid still tired? Would he now favour his stick side? Flying up the middle of the Forum ice, Flower unexpectedly let a slapshot go just

---

* The Rocket was knocked out, suffering from a concussion through most of the seventh game of the 1952 playoff series against Boston. He sat in the dressing room with a towel over his head. With minutes remaining, as if responding to the desperate crowd's urging, he joined teammates on the bench, receiving a hero's welcome. Jumping to the ice, he raced through the entire Boston team, scoring the tying goal. After Montreal won in overtime, on a goal by Paul Masnick, the Rocket broke down and was immediately put under heavy sedation and taken to a hospital.

as he crossed centre—something he probably hadn't done all season. A voice somewhere told him it was worth a try. Perfect play, it turned out, for he caught a tired Gilbert hanging back, leaning on the crossbar. The goalie did the splits, but he couldn't reach the puck, which missed the post on his glove side by no more than an inch. Watching on TV, you could see fans behind the net buckle and throw up their hands as the puck pounded the boards.

So close. Almost. Boston was still alive.

In the dressing room before overtime, Grapes repeated what he'd been telling his players all series: Go for it; don't back down. Boston responded with a final, prolonged attack. A minute into the extra session, McNab fed Marcotte in the slot. Dryden was down. The upper third of the cage was wide, wide open. If Marcotte had found the beckoning open net, the whole meaning of hockey in the 1970s would have changed dramatically. Probably, the Bruins would have gone on to beat the Rangers, getting their third Cup that decade. But even if the Rangers had won, that would mean Freddy Shero collecting his third championship. The era would end tied—five wins for rough-and-tumble hockey (Boston and Philly), *cinq pour Les Glorieux*.

Marotte's shot hit Dryden high in the left shoulder, however. Seconds later, O'Reilly took a big slapshot just inside the line. Dryden smartly kicked that away.

Scotty Bowman was called hockey's best coach because he so often seemed clairvoyant, anticipating his team's needs. In the lost sixth game in Boston, Scotty barely played Robinson, Savard and Lafleur in the third period, saving them. He needed them now. With Lapointe out, Bowman utilized Savard and Robinson in all but two short shifts, close to 14 of the game's last 15 minutes. Lapointe was in Montreal General at this point, waiting for a doctor—although what he really needed, he would tell everyone, was a radio. "Look, I'll get you a signed sweater, get me something so I can hear the game," the fallen defenceman pleaded to nurses. Minutes later, Pointu was listening on radio, in double agony—his leg, of course, and, like everyone else back at the Forum, he was worried sick about the team and game he'd left behind.

The name Lapointe heard most often on the radio was Lafleur. Good thing Scotty had rested him late in game six, too, because he played over 33 minutes this night. Now in overtime, Bowman was triple-shifting the game's best player. All of Lafleur, Shutt and Lemaire enjoyed a scoring chance on one extra-long shift early in overtime. Gilbert remained steady. At the other end, Marotte just missed a dangerous passout. The play then swung the other way. Gilbert smothered a tip-in from Lambert. At nine minutes, Middleton, who had been terrific, broke in on Savard, giving him a little head feint, hoping to slip past. Instead, big Serge stole the puck, firing a quick pass to Houle at centre, coming back to check. Reggie quickly tipped the puck to Mario, already in forward motion. He would charge hard outside and around Sims at the Boston blue line. Tremblay had time and space . . . saw Lambert charging. Park was with him. But the Canadiens had been hitting Brad all night. Now they reaped their reward. The Bruins great was dead tired. Maybe the freezing on his knee was wearing out. He was skating now in a bad dream, legs moving, getting nowhere. Lambert tipped a perfect pass from Mario past a diving Gilbert into the open net.

Is it possible to parse a crowd's joy? Would it be fair or accurate to say that, where Forum audiences once experienced an almost haughty exhilaration in beating the Bruins in the playoffs, they here experienced grateful relief? Ultimately, it didn't matter. Montreal had beaten the Bruins in the postseason. Again!

It was awful in the Bruins dressing room afterwards. Jonathan, the seventh guy out on the ice late in the third period, was sobbing. "Hell of a game," Cashman said, staring off. Reporters tried not to intrude, but got everything down nevertheless, all the suffering. "Go away," Park said, sobbing. "Go away, I'm too upset—please." Only Grapes still had his voice. As expected, he went down with his ship.

"That was my fault," he said of the too-many-men penalty. "I feel like crying for them, I really do. Not for me, for them. I'm so proud of them. When you see players sneaking into the backroom to get things frozen, guys playing with a harness on their knee or shoulder, you know you've got a team with heart."

"Who do you want to win in the finals?" somebody asked Grapes.

"That's like asking me to choose between syphilis and gonorrhea," hockey's most quotable coach groaned. Before the HMS *Boston Bruins* sank entirely, its captain got off one final round. "Just remember who has talked to you for seven games," Grapes told the scribes before quitting the Forum for the Queen Elizabeth Hotel and what would be a night of serious drinking for the Bruins—a real Irish, South Boston wake.

Certainly there was more relief than joy in the winning dressing room. Scotty answered a few questions, then left. The players, every one a professional, said all the right things about the Bruins. Most praised first star of the game, Gilbert.* Cashman, Ratelle, Middleton, Park and Milbury were toasted. Dryden summed up Lafleur's heroic third period: "He's the ultimate Canadiens superstar," the goalie said. "He reacts and performs to the mystique of the Forum more than anyone I've ever seen."

There was also a wild scene in the corridor outside the dressing rooms as Harry Sinden laid into the officials. "I've talked to a lot of people and nobody can remember a call like that in a big game," Harry said, livid. The screaming stopped when a passing Bruin advised his GM they had an extra player out there for 20 seconds. Sinden shook his head. What a way to lose—trying too hard. Although it could be argued that it was fitting that the last great game of a fractious hockey decade should be decided by a crazy, unexpected penalty, nobody would've wanted to advance that theory to Harry just now.

Grapes still couldn't find sleep the next night, home in North Andover. He and Blue went out on the porch at midnight, staring into the ocean-deep heavens. So close, they'd come so close and lost—all because of a technical blunder. His team so it was his fault. How could Grapes know at the time that history would reward the Bruins for coming so

---

* Guy Lafleur was second star of the game. Lambert was the third.

close? That in time, David's heroism would be as valued as Goliath's cold-blooded professionalism. Luckily for Grapes, *almost* counted in Boston, where for decades local teams played Don Quixote, tilting at bigger, better-run dynasties, New York Yankees in baseball and Montreal Canadiens in hockey. Today, the Bruins' heroic 1979 playoff stand against the Canadiens is ranked a noble accomplishment in New England, as treasured as the Red Sox' valiant seven-game World Series loss to the Big Red Machine Cincinnati Reds in 1975. In Canada, too, Grapes would become famous (and rich) for *almost* doing the impossible, knocking off hockey's best ever team. These days, any time Cherry bumps into Yvon Lambert, the Canadien who broke the Bruins' heart in overtime that seventh game, he breaks into a big smile, shouting, "There's the guy who made me a millionaire, put it there Ee-von." Two days after losing to Montreal, however, Grapes was still grieving. They'd lost. And he was probably out of a job. What next?

A little over a week later, Cherry and Sinden met at a Holiday Inn outside Boston to sort things out. It would be disco night at the motel, however—Gloria Gaynor bleeding through the walls. *I will survive!* The old friends decided to go to a Chinese restaurant; no one would recognize them there.

"Mister Don Cherry," the waiter said bringing them menus.[†]

That same day, Montreal returned home after putting a lock on their Stanley Cup final series with the Rangers, winning 4–3 in overtime on a Savard goal. They took the series in five games, winning at home on a Monday night. Lemaire, playing his last NHL game, scored two goals, one on a slapshot from outside the blue line. Gainey also connected

---

† Sinden and Cherry mostly patched things up. The Bruins were willing to talk about a contract extension if Grapes was willing to stop talking to the press. That was like asking Niagara Falls to stop spraying so much water. Colorado and Toronto offered him coaching jobs. Leafs owner Harold Ballard wanted Bowman as GM and Cherry as coach. He would get neither. Grapes lasted a season in Denver before joining *Hockey Night in Canada*.

before picking up the Conn Smythe Trophy as (unanimous) playoff MVP. Despite Ziegler's warnings, the Habs broke a league edict by coming off the bench after every goal to show their colours.

After the game, Dick Irvin did his regular postgame interview with Bowman. "You know, it was funny," Irvin would remember. "I walked into the room and Scotty was kinda down. And I remember saying to myself, 'Geez, looking at him now, you would've thought he'd just lost.' Of course, this was his last game with the Canadiens, he knew that. An era was over."

Outside, in the dressing room, the Habs screamed and laughed, gargling champagne and beer. The biggest roar came when an old friend, Prime Minister Trudeau, entered the dressing room. Lambert gave him a big hug and then handed the PM a bottle of champagne, which Pierre tipped back. Trudeau was single now, separated from wife Margaret. In two weeks, he'd be booted out of office.* Yes, the '70s were rough on a lot of people.

Not the Canadiens, though. When Trudeau left, the guys started doing the math. This was Cournoyer's tenth Stanley Cup. Savard and Lemaire's eighth. Dryden had six. Lafleur, five. Everyone was happy and tired. But they couldn't be too tired. There was a Stanley Cup parade the next day. Not to mention the annual post-championship visit to Henri Richard's tavern. But first, let's have another drink.

Here's to Scotty and Sam, to Flower, La Kid Line, Pointu, Dryden, Gainey, Robinson and all the others. The battle for the '70s was officially over. Philadelphia and Boston had given it a good shot, but everyone now knew who won hockey's most tumultuous decade: the Montreal Canadiens—*Les Glorieux*.

---

* Pierre Trudeau's Liberals went down to defeat on May 22, 1979. Seven months later, Joe Clark's Conservatives failed to survive a non-confidence motion—too few (Conservatives) in the House of Commons—and Trudeau returned to power on February 18, 1980. He would continue to govern until his retirement in the summer of 1984.

THE MAN THAT GOT AWAY

In the summer of 1978, *Hockey Night in Canada* regular and CFCF-TV sports director Dick Irvin got a surprise call at work. "Hi Dick, it's Sam Pollock. Just phoning to say I'm retiring from Canadiens. I wanted to phone you to let you know. I remember your father [former coach of the Canadiens]. I use to watch him run practices. He was so kind and helpful."

Irvin was caught off guard because Pollock seldom acknowledged him when they passed at the Forum. Always had his head down. "He was a hard guy to know," Irvin told me. "Nobody understood why he retired. Or why he hired a non-hockey guy, Irving Grundman, instead of Scotty as his replacement." Jean Béliveau would eventually solve that mystery in his memoir, *My Life in Hockey*, written with Chrys Goyens and Allan Turowetz.

Whatever his personal quirks, Scotty had proved himself behind the bench. The trouble was, he'd "proved" himself behind the scenes as well . . . Whenever

Scotty took issue with a player for any reason at all, he'd run upstairs to Sam's office and demand an instant trade. Bringing all his experience and knowledge to bear, Sam would calm him down. Sam knew that no one was about to turn in 80 perfect games. Sometimes Scotty would barge in while I was meeting with Sam, whereupon I'd personally witness these unfortunate harangues. I made up my mind up that if this guy was ever in the running for general manager, or for any position within the organization in which he'd have the final say on personnel matters, the Canadiens were going to be in trouble.

When Pollock retired, both he and Béliveau, a team executive at the time, opted for Grundman as GM. He would last five seasons.

For the record, Bowman went down feuding in Montreal. He gave the scoop of his retirement to Réjean Tremblay of *La Presse* weeks after winning the 1979 Stanley Cup. "I have no respect for [Grundman] as a hockey man. . . . There were all sorts of things I couldn't endure anymore," he told Tremblay. "I couldn't take Red Fisher of the *Star* anymore." An hour later, before Tremblay's story went to print, Scotty passed Fisher in the hallway at the NHL meetings in the Queen Elizabeth.

"Hi, how's everything?" Bowman chirped, smiling.

"Fine. You? Anything happening?"

"Nothing much," Scotty said with a grin. *Screw you.*

Another, bigger, still unresolved mystery: How could so many wary, reclusive, gentleman-farmer types—Pollock owned Jersey cattle, Bowman lived on a farm outside Montreal—have breathed fire and life into in hockey's most thrilling dynasty? Here's GM Frank Selke, talking about his relationship with coach Dick Irvin in his 1962 autobiography, *Behind the Cheering*.

I am sure that some of my best days were those spent with Dick [Irvin] and the fancy chickens and pigeons we used to keep out at Gordon Green's farm near Sainte-Thérèse. Since 1956, I have had a lovely farm of my own near Rigaud; and as I putter about the assortment of good birds I keep there, I cannot help but think of how wonderful it would be if Dick could just come by . . .

A characteristic that all Canadiens leaders shared was love of hard work. Maybe that's why so many gravitated to farms, where labour never ended. Pollock was so good at his job that his efforts continued to bear fruit long after he was gone. Sam believed in the future: he made the Canadiens into champions by trading yesterday for tomorrow and keeping his fingers crossed.

In the off-season of 1976, Sam made what might have been his best trade. Yes, better even than the swap of Ralph Backstrom that eventually brought Guy Lafleur. Shortly before the Canadiens began defence of their '76 Stanley Cup win over Philadelphia, Pollock sent Ron Andruff, Sean Shanahan and the 19th-overall pick to the Colorado Rockies for Colorado's first pick in 1980.

As it happens, the best graduating junior of that year would have been Wayne Gretzky, had the cradle-robbing WHA never arrived, or had it collapsed without any surviving members.

Just think: Gretzky on the Canadiens alongside a revitalized Lafleur. Seventies hockey and the Montreal dynasty might've gone on clear through to 1990.

EPILOGUE: RUST NEVER SLEEPS

Good news: most major players in hockey's stormiest decade ended up doing better than one might have expected or feared. Freddy Shero left us too quickly—gone in 1990. He returned to the Flyers as a special assistant shortly before passing away, however. And Freddy's son, Ray, the kid who handed Scotty Bowman a note at the end of the 1976 finals, ended up GM of the Pittsburgh Penguins,* winning a third championship for the Shero clan in 2009. Ray was also there for his father's induction into the Hockey Hall of Fame in 2013. Fifteen of Freddy's players, including Bobby Clarke, Bernie Parent, Reggie Leach, Gary Dornhoefer, Terry Crisp, and the Watson boys, along with a Moose, a Hound and a Big Bird, travelled to Toronto for the ceremony.

---

*　In the summer of 2015, Ray Shero was named General Manager of the New Jersey Devils and so returned home. Forty years earlier, the Sheros lived in Jersey while Freddy Shero coached the Flyers.

Shero's Flyers would indeed walk together forever.

They no longer drink together, however. Leach and Parent have been sober for 30 years. A self-help author/guru (*Journey Through Risk and Fear*), Bernie still lives outside Philly on a 45-foot houseboat, the *French Connection*. Leach and son Jamie, who also played in the NHL, run hockey camps and are active in the First Nations community. Daughter Brandie is a doctor in Texas.

Clarke enjoyed a long, tempestuous career as an NHL GM/executive, taking Minnesota (once) and Philadelphia (three times) to the Stanley Cup Finals. Predictably, he made a few enemies along the way—no surprise from a guy who once kept fans from climbing aboard his Stanley Cup parade car by tattooing their arms with a lit cigarette. Bobby once dismissed a coach battling cancer, Roger Neilson, complaining he'd turned "goofy." Frequently injured captain Eric Lindros also failed to pass Bobby's toughness test. Clarke heard it for some of his moves, but didn't seem to care. Maybe bibliophile Shero had shared with him what Chekov always said about critics—that they're flies bothering field horses as they work.

Owner Ed Snider would end up rich as Croesus, owner of a regional cable network (Comcast Sports) in addition to the Flyers. He'd be wealthier still if he hadn't served as executive producer of the 2011 Ayn Rand film flop, *Atlas Shrugged: Part 1*.

On to the Bruins: connoisseurs of frontier justice savoured the resolution of hockey's Cain-vs.-Abel showdown, the windup of the Bobby Orr–Alan Eagleson affair. Hockey players often take their time settling grudges. It's how the game works. In 1957, Maple Leafs rookie Bobby Baun caught Detroit's Gordie Howe with his head down, laying him out with a murderous check. A thousand games later, in 1968, Old Man Winter was playing Baun's California Golden Seals. Howe swooped down his wing. Just as he was about to shoot, defenceman Baun dropped to his knees. After releasing the puck, Howe let his stick follow through high, stabbing his opponent in the throat. As Baun knelt, struggling for breath, choking, Howe skated past, bent at the waist.

"Now we're even," he said.

And so it was with Bobby and the agent/older brother who left him stranded in the desert without a horse or canteen. Broke at retirement, Bobby slowly put his life back together, first as a corporate spokesman, then as a successful hockey agent. The 27-year-old had always been terrific with kids, working hospital wards, taking forever to shake hands and muss the hair of patients. Eventually, he learned to relax and be himself in front of a camera, selling everything—cars, shoes, credit cards, peanuts, booze, boats, soft drinks and breakfast cereal. Shocking many who once knew him, he would become an animated, hands-on agent. That's his current job. He likes to "work the living room," it's said, coming alive for players and parents in their homes. But the fighter still remains. He never forgot the older brother who left him for dead, and worked with an old reporter friend, Russ Conway, author of a five-part, Pulitzer Prize–nominated series in 1992, "Cracking the Ice," that exposed how the Eagle embezzled player funds and siphoned off player disability payments. Eventually, in 1994, the FBI charged Eagleson with 34 counts of racketeering, embezzlement and fraud. In 1998, he was extradited to Boston, where he pleaded guilty to mail fraud, paying a million-dollar fine. In Canada, the RCMP wanted him too. Finally, he was sentenced to 18 months in a Toronto jail.

Orr showed up in the back of the Boston court. He said nothing, but everyone knew what Bobby was thinking when the gavel came down on Eagleson.

Now we're even.

Otherwise, our hockey hero's public life appears to be free of pain and vengeance. Replacement knees make walking tolerable, allowing God to go about his other job—helping others. He still visits hospitals and ailing kids, although as a *former* star, he has to introduce himself now. He would also continue to look after teammates. When Boston trainer Frosty Forristall succumbed to cancer, Bobby turned his home into a hospice for his old roommate. After former Bruin Ace Bailey died aboard the hijacked airliner that struck the World Trade Center in 2001, Bobby turned up the next morning at the door of Ace's widow, Katherine.

The good guy stories would go on and on . . . a Catholic kid, Boston-born Jim Craig, chose James "Bobby Orr" Craig as his honorary confirmation name. Jim grew up to star for the American team that in 1980 pulled off the "Miracle on Ice," defeating the Soviets en route to winning Olympic gold. The goalie's pro career never took off, however, and in 1988 he hit a rough patch when his dad died. Hearing of his plight, Bobby showed up at Jim's home to help out. The former hockey star would be there in good times, too. Noel Picard, the St. Louis defender who trip-launched Orr into the air after Bobby's 1970 Cup-winning goal, has a picture of the epic encounter on the wall of his Montreal home. Orr signed it, "Pic, thanks for the trip. Maybe I can return the favour . . ." And so he did. Picard's daughter went away to school, attending a Boston conservatory. "[Bobby] really take care of her very good, find her an apartment," Picard would tell a TV reporter.

What's striking about Orr today is his belated acceptance of fame. Early one morning in 1984, while salmon fishing in Gaspé, he bumped into an English CBC radio crew setting up for a live remote. "Hi, I'm Bobby Orr. How ya doin'?" he told a crew member. Sure, he'd be happy to go on air. "He was just so wonderful and friendly," remembered former CBC host Jennifer Fry.

Yes, Peter Puck grew up.

Orr's most famous kindness involved teammate Derek Sanderson. After hitting rock bottom, living for a while on a New York park bench, Derek returned to Boston. Bobby paid to have him enter rehab—twice—and then invested in his sports management group. Derek, too, recovered. He found a second career doing what he had always done best—talking. He would become a Bruins TV announcer for a decade and later vice-president of Baystate Wealth Management in Boston, advising athletes on what (and what not) to do with their fortunes. As mentioned, he would also write a best-selling book, *Crossing the Line*, and he continues to make appearances at schools, advising kids not to do what he has done. Oh, don't worry; he's still a know-it-all. Promoting his book, he let the *National Post*'s Sean Fitz-Gerald in on the best way to sleep on a park bench: "Put the newspaper on the bottom side, too. Stay dry on both sides."

Derek's still Derek, but no longer Turk. He has given up drinking and skating close to the edge. And it's wonderful to think, given all they've been through, that Derek and Bobby are still together 40 years later, playing weekly golf games in Cape Cod, enjoying each other and the warm-as-a-hand feel of the sun on their backs.

Big Bad Bruins stories tend to sound like they've been polished by sympathetic sports reporters. Take the incident that helped turn Boston into Don Cherry's lunch-pail brigade: In late 1975, GM Harry Sinden traded Phil Esposito and Carol Vadnais to New York. Sinden couldn't bear to break the news to Esposito, leaving that to Don Cherry. First thing next morning, Grapes woke Phil up over a hotel phone, inviting him to his room. Espo was crazy with worry . . . knew something was up. Cherry too was a wreck, so asked Bobby Orr to join him. Bobby was by the window when Phil barged in.

"Grapes, if you tell me I've been traded I'm going to jump out that window!" Esposito moaned.

"Bobby, get out of the way," Cherry shot back.

Perfect comeback. And sometimes Orr-Esposito era yarns, all the skyscraper-tall tales—lost chimps in Garden rafters and small-town Canadian Bruins rampaging big American cities—seem too good to be true. Then again, when the Boston Garden fell under the wrecking ball in May of 1998, the *Associated Press* duly reported, "Monkey's remains found in Boston Garden demolition."

Yes, the old Boston Garden and Big Bad Bruins were something else.

As for the Montreal Canadiens, they stopped winning championships in gaudy clusters and the Forum was turned into a big movie house, but still somehow the team remains, indisputably, *Les Glorieux*. Fans everywhere agree the new Bell Centre is the best place in the world to be on a winter night. And Canadiens fans are indeed everywhere. Viggo Mortensen, a Guy Lafleur loyalist, would wear Flower's jersey under his costume while playing Aragon in the *Lord of the Rings* trilogy—helped the method actor feel like a hero, apparently. When Serge Savard took over as GM of the Canadiens in the 1980s, he made a goodwill pilgrimage to Europe, stopping in Moscow. There, he was sought out by an ancient member of the politburo. "What is happening with our Canadiens?" the stranger asked.

Our Canadiens?

"We in the Old Guard have been Canadiens fans for many, many years," the Russian advised GM Savard. "I have long been a supporter of your illustrious team and great hockey players like Maurice Richard, Jean Béliveau . . ."

As Michael Farber once noted, "only two organizations in Western civilization truly get ceremony: the House of Windsor and the Montreal Canadiens." Who could forget the moment of pristine silence that attended Jean Béliveau's 2014 Bell Centre wake? Or the closing of the Forum in 1996, when the Rocket was reduced to grateful tears by a relentless ovation? Faber was right: no team can stage an event like the Canadiens. The players have always helped, of course. Returning to hockey (after a three-year retirement) in 1988, New York Ranger Guy Lafleur scored two goals in his first visit home, torturing and thrilling the Forum crowd. Or how about that game in 1984 when the Habs introduced their dream team—coach Toe Blake; Jacques Plante in net; Doug Harvey and Larry Robinson on defence; Dickie Moore, Béliveau and the Rocket up front. The Canadiens being the Canadiens, the club threw in *un surprise,* introducing the oldest Canadien, an athlete who'd played and partied with Howie Morenz.

> *He weigh one hunert fifty pound*
> *If he were sex feet tall*
> *He'd score one hunert goal so quick*
> *Dere'd be no game at all.*

Out bounded Aurèle Joliat, 45 seasons removed from Forum ice. Rust never sleeps: Joliat's left and right skates disagreed on which would go first. Down the 83-year-old went. A Buffalo Sabre helped Joliat to his skates. Getting mad, Aurèle threw down the puck. *Where's the bloody net?* Racing towards Plante, he failed to see the red strip of carpet at centre. And so went for another swim. He'd be up right away, though. Harvey found the puck and pushed him a soft pass. Joliat continued his wobbly journey, skimming the puck past Plante into the net. *His first goal since 1938!* Aurèle slammed his stick and doffed the black cap he wore even as a young man (to hide a spreading bald spot). Chopping his way back to the dream team gathered at centre, he'd be swallowed up by Toe, Doug, Larry and the boys.

Announcer Claude Mouton was about to get back to business. But what was this? Aurèle decided to steal another bow. The octogenarian dashed around the rink again. *Thank you, thank you.* Mesdames et messieurs, here was a Montreal Canadien—good to the last drop of the puck! The crowd jumped to its feet, giving Aurèle Joliat a prolonged ovation meant to last him the rest of his days.

Ah yes, the crowd. What does it say again on Quebec licence plates? *Je me souviens.* Maybe Montreal hockey fans remember better than anyone else. Take that last night at the Forum, March 11, 1996. The crowd had been cheering a half hour when the Rocket finally appeared. Scotty, Sam, Pointu, Shutt, Gainey, Lafleur, Laperrière, Savard, Lemaire, Dryden, the Big M, Cournoyer, Gump Worsley, the Pocket Rocket, Moore, Elmer Lach, Béliveau and Butch Bouchard had all been introduced. And then Number Nine arrived. The ovation was immediate, and grew louder. After two minutes, Maurice was overcome. Lach and Bouchard joined him for an instant. His eyes brimming with tears, Rocket waved everyone to sit down. It was no use. At the four-minute mark, *Hockey Night in Canada* cameras captured fans in an upper balcony clasping hands, holding them high. *We are Maurice Richard.* This was blood memory. The Rocket had last played in the Forum in 1960. Few there that evening would actually have seen him perform live. Still, they applauded the *idea* of Rocket Richard . . . history, the continuum, their ancestors, themselves. Five and a half minutes into the ovation, Claude

Mouton attempted to intercede, but thought better of it. The applause grew louder. Chants broke out: "Mau-rice! Mau-rice!" . . . "Go Habs go! Go Habs go . . ."

We watched a smiling Lafleur look on, experiencing the Rocket's last magic moment. Ah, Guy—the Flower! He and wife Lise had two boys. The second, Mark Lafleur, would have issues . . . would prove vulnerable to violent outbreaks; would sometimes threaten to kill his parents. Mark attacked his girlfriend in 2008. Guy unwisely brought them together, contravening a court order. He would be charged, convicted and later acquitted of any wrongdoing. Explaining his actions, Guy told writer Roy MacGregor, "*Ton enfant, reste ton enfant.*" Once your son, always your son.

HAIR TODAY, GONE TOMORROW

The Montreal Canadiens would be the last bare-headed NHL dynasty. A new league rule prevented players who had arrived in the league after 1979 from playing without a helmet. Hopelessly addicted to the superhero feel of hair blowing in the wind, young players got around that edict by fertilizing their noggins with grooming products, growing their hair extra-long at the back. Hockey mullets, they would be called, but not until the mid–'90s, when the Beastie Boys coined the phrase in the song "Mullet Head" ("Cut the sides, don't touch the back").

Though continuously beset by controversy, Guy remains essentially the same. The player who hid from the world at a Quebec peewee tournament by climbing to the top of Le Colisée still likes to be above the fray—an eagle hunting from on high. Today, he operates a Montreal helicopter rental company and is honorary colonel of a Quebec air force unit. And though he was fired from the Canadiens for grumbling about his salary, he would be rehired as goodwill ambassador in 1996. Everywhere he now goes in Quebec, the Last Great Canadien is greeted as a hero.

Ton enfant, reste ton enfant.

———

Returning to our still unanswered question: Who killed Lady Byng? What do we ultimately make of Clarence Campbell's assertion that the worst of hockey in the '70s—the riots, gang fights and police busts—was society's fault? The NHL president would cling to that narrative . . . and for good reason. In 1977, Campbell was convicted of bribing a Quebec senator to maintain a lucrative duty-free concession at Montreal's Dorval Airport. The league paid his fines and helped secure a get-out-of-jail-free card. Clarence would go to his grave believing the world was out to get you.

Still, there was no getting around it. Hockey was different—rougher, more prone to larceny—in the 1970s. And part of it was indeed the world's fault. For decades, the NHL was a six-team, northeastern family compact. Then, suddenly, there were 20-some NHL and WHA clubs, many hemorrhaging cash. Russians and Czechs would soon be smuggled out of Eastern Europe, providing a cloak-and-dagger storyline. Hockey in the '70s was a wide-open frontier industry operating at a time of—let's give Clarence this much—dissolving social mores. What other hockey decade could feature: a) two wigged goalies on the same team; and b) a netminder who cheated by hanging fish net beneath his crotch down to his knees?*

Expansion in 1967 coincided with the emergence of a generation brought up on Steve McQueen and the Rolling Stones. The first Baby Boomers to make an impact in the NHL were Bobby Orr (born in 1948), Derek Sanderson (1946), Serge Savard (1946), Brad Park (1948) and Bobby Clarke (1949), all of whom arrived between 1966 and 1969.

All of whom, aside from Serge maybe, hit the ice like a crossfire hurricane.

Maybe the most useful way to look at hockey in the 1970s (in the Roaring '80s, too) is to understand that this was the sport's thrilling,

---

* The toupée-wearing goalies would be Billy Smith and Chico Resch, both of the New York Islanders. Chicago netminder Tony Esposito had an elastic mesh sewn between the thighs of his pants. Pucks would catapult off his extended spider web crotch . . . until the NHL outlawed the accessory.

wayward adolescence—the teenage interlude between the Original Six era—hockey's placid, overlong childhood—and its current adult state: the stable, sensible, dead puck era that arrived with Commissioner Gary Bettman in the early '90s.

There's hardly any fighting these days, certainly no riots, just an occasional labour disturbance resolved by intemperate lawyers. Goons are gone . . . dynasties, too. Boston, Montreal and Philadelphia won all ten Stanley Cups in the 1970s. Two teams—the New York Islanders and Edmonton Oilers—combined to take eight championships in the '80s. After that, parity: eight different clubs emerged victorious in the '90s; seven teams took turns winning nine Cups in the 2000s. There is more protective headgear in hockey now—helmets and salary caps—making the game safer for players and owners alike. There are more countries, too. Whereas the '70s Flyers, Bruins and Canadiens were almost entirely Canadian-born, championship clubs today are North American, with a sprinkling of Europeans. The Los Angeles Kings won the Stanley Cup in 2014 with six American and 13 Canadian-born players, along with skaters from Slovenia (Anze Kopitar), Slovakia (Marian Gaborik) and Indonesia (Robyn Regher, who moved to Canada at age seven).

The game is faster, better coached and better played today. Everyone can shoot. The *Call of Duty* weaponry has something to do with that—400-gram carbon-fibre hockey sticks with names out of a Halliburton arms brochure: *Warrior Covert DX1 . . . Bauer Vapor APX2 . . .*

Still, if a stranger to hockey were to ask me to recommend an entrée into the sport, a single match that might reveal all the flavours of the game, I would, without hesitation, suggest a Montreal Canadiens–Boston Bruins playoff encounter. In either the Bell Centre or the TD Garden in Boston. And both of those teams, when they meet each other anyway, revert to their primitive teenage selves, playing lusty, dangerously passionate 1970s hockey. Why, the game even sounds the way it used to in Montreal and Boston, maybe because the Canadiens and Bruins are the only Original Six teams that thought to bring their old, pre–World War II sirens with them to their new buildings.

As in Montreal, Bruins fans remember. How could you forget Bobby Orr?

The '70s were a long time ago. Bernie Parent was recently at a New York card show. A young woman, spying his monogrammed Cup ring, exclaimed, "That's great, they made ones for parents, too." An easy mistake: Bernie's now crowding 70. Only a handful of NHL players from the '70s are still active in the league, working as assistant coaches (Bryan Trottier and Doug Jarvis) or in management—Bobby Clarke, John Davidson, Doug Wilson, Bob Murray, Glen Sather and Larry Robinson. Phil Esposito is in the broadcast booth (whining about referees on behalf of the Tampa Bay Lightning). One old coach remains standing: after leaving Montreal, Scotty Bowman won four more Cups—one with Pittsburgh, coaching Mario Lemieux, and another three in Detroit, presiding over a galaxy of stars. In 2008, Scotty became senior advisor to son Stanley Bowman, GM of the Chicago Blackhawks, who netted championships in 2010, 2012 and 2015. (Scotty won another Cup as director of player personnel in Pittsburgh in 1991.)

Fourteen championships! Two more than mentor Sam Pollock. And if you think Scotty didn't notice or wasn't counting, you don't know Scotty Bowman.

I bumped into Scotty once. I was in Florida in April 1988, walking along the beach early in the morning, when gulls outnumber humans. There were only two other people within sight. As they drew nearer, the tall guy wearing glasses looked familiar. Was that Al Arbour, former coach of the New York Islanders? Then I noticed the shorter guy in the billowing Bermuda shirt. Wow—Scotty Bowman!

"Hey, Al Arbour and Scotty Bowman," I half-shouted. "What're you guys doing here?"

"Holidays," Arbour replied, asking where I was from. We—that is to say, Al and I—exchanged small talk. Scotty looked pained, as if he and Al were now going to be late for something. "So hey, who's going to win tonight—Edmonton and Calgary?" I asked. The playoff Battle of Alberta was just underway. "Going to be a good series," Arbour replied, then offered, "Oh well, if you can't be in the playoffs, may as well be in Florida, eh—beautiful morning." Perfect segue. He was turning to leave when Bowman finally spoke: "Edmonton." He was looking out at the water when he said it.

"There you go," Arbour laughed.

"Because of [goalie Grant] Fuhr," Scotty continued, still looking away.

That night, Wayne Gretzky scored a big goal in overtime and Edmonton went on to sweep the pre-series favourite Calgary Flames, surprising many hockey fans. But not the Rain Man evidently.

Another personal story: When the Rocket died on May 27, 2000, over 115,000 Quebecers filed past his open coffin in the Bell Centre. Fans throughout the province wore Richard jerseys that day. More than when he played the game. Rocket's funeral was covered live on Canadian national and Quebec TV networks. Prime Minister Jean Chretien, a slew of Quebec premiers, NHL Commissioner Bettman, former players and coaches, including Gordie Howe, Scotty Bowman and Don Cherry, along with 2,700 mourners crammed Montreal's Notre-Dame Basilica. Thousands more watched the ceremony on a giant screen set up outside the church. MAURICE RICHARD'S FUNERAL BRINGS CANADA TO A STAND-STILL, reported a *New York Times* story.

"Is Richard, like, the first hockey player who ever died?" a non-hockey friend of mine snorted.

"Hey, all hockey players are family in Canada—guys from the neigh-bourhood who make good," I replied. A throwaway line. Now, though, I wonder. Over the years, I've bumped into so many of the characters in this book. On sandy beaches, in bars . . . crossing the street. And I always feel it my duty to say hello. Like we're neighbours. When I was in col-lege, Aurèle Joliat regularly showed up (after bowling) at my local, the Prescott Hotel on Preston Street in Ottawa. Years later, I encountered goalie Eddie Johnston in a Boston bar. I talked to Hot Rod Gilbert at Mickey Mantle's Central Park South restaurant in New York. Alan Eagleson, Phil Esposito, Paul Henderson and Team Canada '72 defence pairing Bill White and Pat Stapleton, I spied at a Toronto hockey game, bar, bank queue and sports museum. Skinny, spitting Bobby Clarke, I once ran into on Bank Street in Ottawa when I was in high school. I smiled. *Hey.* Bobby winked back. The guy marching beside him—a Watson, I believe—shouted, "How ya' doin' there?"

Like I said—neighbours.

I once had a drink with René Lévesque at a Vancouver publishing event. He was sitting alone, noticed by everyone, but undisturbed. I introduced myself as a "fellow Quebecer," whereupon the former premier began speaking French. I made it through a single sentence before he let me off the hook, turning to English.

When Lévesque asked where I was from, I soon broke into my everready, what-Quebec-was-like-in-1963 recital—how Rocket Richard shook hands and handed out trophies at my first hockey banquet. This was in my neighbourhood, Lakeview Terrace. He was to land in a helicopter at the nearby "Protestant school." *A helicopter!* Everyone in the French village of Deschênes poured upstream along Rue Vanier to an Anglo institution few had visited. Hundreds, maybe thousands of kids, adults, grandparents—a murmuring, slow-moving tide—swallowed up the asphalt road, spilling into ditches, making car travel impossible. Most were squinting, their heads turned to heaven, searching for the Rocket ship. The schoolground landing spot, the outfield where I played Deschênes-Aylmer-South Hull (DASH) Little League, was soon overcrowded with worshippers, forcing the Rocket to land elsewhere. But he made the banquet . . . softly shook everyone's hand, smiling warmly. When I left the banquet with my dad, there were still maybe 100 nervous Deschênes visitors outside, windbreakered youngsters mostly, hoping for another glimpse of Quebec's national hero.

"Maurice!"

"Rocket . . . Rocket *ici*."

Growing up in Deschênes, there were three seasons—hockey, baseball and football. Hockey trumped the other two, maybe because no one we knew played pro baseball or football. Hockey seemed within our grasp. Indeed, I learned about the Rocket's eventual heir tying up my skates before a tyke game. Some older kids in the (unheated) change shack were talking about a player from a nearby town—best from around here, fast, and oh boy, what a shot. He could score from centre, like.

Eleven-year-old Guy Lafleur!

I was astonished to learn recently that two actual Lakeview Drive neighbours of mine figured in this story. As a kid, my dad would bring me to Hull-Ottawa Canadiens games at the smoke-filled Hull Auditorium, sometimes to exhibition matches between Montreal's farm team and pro clubs like the Detroit Red Wings and Boston Bruins. (A souvenir program suggests I watched Don Cherry play for Montreal's farm team *against* the Bruins! Although I have no memory of him playing.) I remember my father saying that the tickets we had for a Detroit game were probably pretty good because he got them from Jack Kinsella, who lived a couple houses down. Mr. Kinsella I knew to be an *Ottawa Citizen* sports reporter. Rereading Sam Pollock's 2007 obituary, I learned that Jack Kinsella was also Sam's brother-in-law. Kay Kinsella, whom my mom played bridge with, was born Kay Pollock. Way back then, Sam was still GM of the Hull-Ottawa Canadiens. Scotty Bowman, the coach. How about that? The tickets I was using to see my first NHL team undoubtedly came from Sam.

A final '70s hockey story: while working in publishing in the '80s, I came to know Paul King, who ran Food for Thought, a really good, now-gone Ottawa bookstore. We became friendly upon discovering that Paul lived a few houses away from my childhood home, on Lakeview Drive. Though a big Bruins fan, Paul would say, "Tell him about the Rocket story," upon introducing me to someone from the old neighbourhood. In 2009, Paul passed away. I had written him a letter shortly before he died, sharing a few more hockey stories about a place I know he loved. I kept in touch with his progress through a mutual friend, Ken Rockburn. It was Ken who told me about one of Paul's last great moments.

He was near the end. The phone rang. His wife, Sue, answered. She was silent for a while, and then said, "Wait a moment, I'll get him."

"Paul," she said, entering the bedroom in which her husband was resting, "phone call for you."

Another neighbour calling?

"I really don't feel like talking to anyone."

"I think you'll want to take this one."

"OK."

She handed him the receiver.

"Hello."

"Is this Paul King?"

"Yes."

Indeed, it was someone Paul knew well—admired, in fact.

"Hi Paul, this is Bobby Orr. Roy MacGregor told me you were a big Bruins fan, so I wanted to give you a call . . ."

More proof, if any was needed, that 1970s hockey, despite the occasional misconduct, was a pretty good place to come from.

ACKNOWLEDGEMENTS

This project has been a pleasure from start to finish and I feel fortunate to have worked on it with so many talented, cherished comrades. In late 2013, Scott Sellers, Penguin Random House's Vice President of Marketing Strategy, but also a rock and roll friend, took me out for a drink, trying to sell me on the idea of doing a '70s hockey book—disco balls, Stanley Cups, long hair and short tempers . . . the whole slap shooting match. Was I interested? *Was I ever!* Weeks later my invaluable, long-time agent-friend Dean Cooke secured a generous contract that allowed me to undertake *Hockey Night Fever*. Bradley Martin, CEO Penguin Random House, not to mention a pal I first played hockey with and befriended at (OK near) Maple Leaf Gardens back in the actual '70s, signed off on the contract, advising me with a sunny smile, "Have fun."

I did, Brad. I did.

But not without the help of editor, Tim Rostron, who as Arts Editor of the *National Post* once hired me to write about movies, keeping me laughing and employed for several happy seasons. (When advertisers grumbled, Tim advised, "How about we don't tell anyone and you rate films out of 100; that way you'll have no problem giving their dreadful movies three stars.") I can't thank Tim enough for his help on this book. He talked me out of several bad ideas, made countless valuable editorial suggestions and came up with the book's title, which I now love.

I was also fortunate to work with hockey's best researcher, Paul Patskou, an invaluable linemate and corner digger who has been setting me up for five books now. Copyeditor Lloyd Davis was also a great help, checking me closer than Bobby Clarke (or if you prefer, Lloyd, Bob Gainey). I'd also like to thank Melanie Tutino, a young woman from Montreal who came onto the project late but did wonders, finding and securing photos for this book. Melanie, you're Topps in my book.

Again to Scott, Dean, Brad, Tim, Paul, Lloyd and Melanie, thanks for everything.

I'd also like to thank my Godson, Ellis Rockburn, for occasional help with French-English translation, as well as lifelong teammates, my wife, Jacquie and our kids, Harry and Lewis, and also my parents, Frank and Frances, and brothers, Rob and Bill and their families—long may we skate.

SOURCES

Son of a Gun: Much of the dialogue here comes from Derek Sanderson's engaging autobiography (co-written with Kevin Shea), *Crossing the Line*, along with his early memoir (co-written with Stan Fischler), *I've Got to Be Me.* I also interviewed Fischler. Video of Bob Falkenberg-Sanderson 1965 fight; Sanderson's 1968 interview with *Hockey Night in Canada*'s Ward Cornell; and Sanderson's 1980s interview with Global-TV's Mike Anscombe, courtesy of Paul Patskou. Further references: Earl McRae's book, *The Victors and the Vanquished*, along with *Sports Illustrated*, *The Boston Globe* and *Edmonton Journal* articles.

Peter Puck: I interviewed referees Ron Wicks and Bruce Hood, broadcaster/author Stan Fischler and (in 1993) Harry Sinden. Books: *Number Four, Bobby Orr* (*Sports Illustrated*); *Searching for Bobby Orr*, by Stephen Brunt; *Orr: My Story*, by Bobby Orr; *The Rock, the Curse and the Hub*, edited by Randy Roberts; and *The Rangers, the Bruins, and the End of an Era*, by Jay Moran. Magazine articles: Trent Frayne and Peter Gzowski (*Maclean's*), along with Earl McRae (*Quest Magazine*). Further references: NESN documentary *Bobby Orr and the Big Bad Bruins*, along with Orr's interview on Don Cherry's late '70s CHCH-TV show, *Grapevine*. Further references: *Boston Globe* articles, 1966–75, *The New York Times*, *Toronto Star*, *The Globe and Mail* and *Montreal Star*.

Paint it Black: Interviews with Ron Wicks and Bruce Hood. Books: Phil Esposito's *Thunder and Lightning*, with Peter Golenbock; Stan Fischler's *Bobby Orr and the Big, Bad Bruins*; Tony and Phil Esposito's *The Brothers Esposito*, with Tim Moriarty; *Hockey in my Blood*, by Johnny Bucyk; *The Rangers, the Bruins, and the End of an Era*; and *Goaltender, Cheevers of the Bruins*, by Trent Frayne. Film: NESN documentary *Bobby Orr and the Big Bad Bruins*. Further references: Red Fisher stories from *Montreal Star* and *Montreal Gazette*; *The Boston Globe* articles, 1966–1975.

Get Quinn! Get Quinn!: Interviews with NHL officials Bruce Hood and linesman George Ashley. Ashley read his game report of the Forbes Kennedy riot to me over the phone. Game film of the April 2, 1969 Bruin–Maple Leaf game along with a Leafs TV documentary on Pat Quinn, courtesy of Paul Patskou. Various articles on game in question, by hockey historian Howard Berger. Further references: *Toronto Star*, *Toronto Telegram* and *The Boston Globe* articles from the period, along with later *Montreal Gazette* story by Dave Stubbs. Boston Bruins nicknames checklist by Bruin Rick Smith (courtesy of Paul Patskou).

Gangs of New York: Interviews with former New York Rangers coach Emile Francis and Stan Fischler. Books: *Play the Man*, by Brad Park (with Stan Fischler); *Straight Shooter: The Brad Park Story*, by Thom Sears; and *The Rangers, the Bruins, and the End of an Era*. Film: game film of May 11, 1972 Ranger–Bruin game courtesy of Paul Patskou; ESPN 30x30, 2014 documentary *Robbed*, the story of 1976 Ali–Ken Norton Fight at Yankee Stadium. Further references: *The New York Times*, *Montreal Star*, *New York Daily News* and *The Boston Globe* articles from the period.

Them Again: Books: *Goaltender, Cheevers of the Bruins*; *Lions in Winter*, by Chrys Goyens and Allan Turowetz; *The Habs* and *Tough Calls*, by Dick Irvin; *Black and White and Never Right*, by Vern Buffey; *Straight Shooter: The Brad Park Story*. Film: NESN footage of 1971 Montreal–Boston series, courtesy of Paul Patskou; the 1973 film, *The Friends of Eddie Coyle*.

Further references: story on Harry Sinden by Bob Duffy of *The Hamilton Spectator*; various articles by Red Fisher in *Montreal Star* and *Montreal Gazette*; a *Harvard Magazine* story: "The Abduction of Phil Esposito," along with period stories from *The Boston Globe*. *Globe* reporters I've quoted from in this and previous chapters include Harold Kaese, Tom Fitzgerald, Francis Rosa, Bud Collins, Kevin Walsh, John Ahern and Peter Gammons. I thank them one and all.

The Bruins Are Coming, The Bruins Are Coming: Interviews with *Hockey Night in Canada* producer Ralph Mellanby and CTV broadcaster Johnny Esaw from 2002. I also re-watched the 1972 series (on a DVD called *Canada's Team of the Century*, with hours of player commentary) in addition to producer Ross Greenburg's documentary, *Cold War on Ice*. Books: Jack Ludwig's *Hockey Night in Moscow*; Harry Sinden's *Hockey Showdown*; Lawrence Martin's *The Red Machine*. Magazines: Fred Shero references Soviet blood doping in the October 21, 1974 edition of *Sports Illustrated*. Particularly helpful were the website *1972SummitSeries.com* and a superb, well-assembled 2012 retrospective on the Canada-Russia series by *The Globe and Mail*'s Patrick White. Further references: David Staples, *Edmonton Journal*. While playing ball hockey with Russian refugees in a New York, Soho handball court in the early 1990s, I first heard a Russian utter the curse "Esposito!".

God's Last Game: Much of the colour and dialogue here comes from a very good 1998 *Globe and Mail* profile of Alan Eagleson by Sean Fine, as well as the 1982 *Quest Magazine* story on Orr by Earl McRae, along with the 2011 *Sports Illustrated* piece on Orr, "Forever Elusive," by S.L. Price. Books: *Thunder and Lightning*; *Overtime: The Legend of Guy Lafleur*, by Georges-Hébert Germain. I also re-watched the Canadian games in the 1976 Canada Cup.

99-Pound Weakling: Interview with Ron Wicks. Books: *The Great Philadelphia Fan Book*, by Glen Macnow; *Jerry Wolman: The World's Richest*

Man, by Jerry Wolman with Joseph and Richard Bockol; *Pouring Six Beers at a Time: And Other Stories from a Lifetime in Baseball*, by Bill Giles and Doug Myers; and *The Broad Street Bullies: The Incredible Story of the Philadelphia Flyers*, by Jack Chevalier. Further references: John Z. Klein, *The New York Times*; Martha Woodall, *Philadelphia Inquirer*; John Sonderegger, *St. Louis Post-Dispatch*; Joe Pelletier, *GreatestHockeyLegends. com*; and *TheEHL.blogspot.ca*.

Puck Finn: Interviews with referees Bruce Hood, Ron Wicks and Bryan Lewis. Books: *Flyer Lives* by Jakki Clarke (Bobby's daughter); *Bobby Clarke: Something to Prove*, by Nicole Mortillaro; *They Call Me Chief: Warriors on Ice*, by Don Marks and Phil Fontaine; and *Flin Flon: A Visual History, 1933-1983*, compiled by Stephanie Jarvis, Lois Burke and Joyce Henderson. Film: *They Call Me Chief*, by Don Marks; and *Bobby Clarke, Legends of Hockey* (2010). Magazines: *The Flyer From Flin Flon*, by Mark Mulvoy, *Sports Illustrated*, October 22, 1973. Further references: Dave Supleve, *Winnipeg Free Press*; Tim Panaccio, *Philadelphia Inquirer*; Jay Greenberg, *Philadelphia Bulletin* and *Philadelphia Daily News*; Jack Chevalier, *Philadelphia Bulletin*; Bob Verdi, *Chicago Tribune*; Dick Beddoes, *The Globe and Mail*; and *The Hockey News*.

Smoke on the Water: Interviews with Emile Francis and Ron Wicks. Books: *The Broad Street Bullies: The Incredible Story of the Philadelphia Flyers*. Film: 2010 HBO documentary *Broad Street Bullies*; *History of the Philadelphia Flyers, 40th anniversary edition* (2007); and Bobby Clarke, *Legends of Hockey* (2010). Further references: Steve Summers, *The Patriot-News*; Mark Herrmann, *Newsday*; Jack Chevalier, *Philadelphia Bulletin*; John Halligan, *The New York Times*; Patrick Kennedy, *Kingston Whig Standard*; and Patrick Kennedy, *The Philadelphia Daily News*.

Bernie, Bernie: Books: *Unmasked: Bernie Parent and the Broad Street Bullies*, by Bernie Parent and Stan Hochman; and *Glenn Hall: The Man They Call Mr. Goalie*, by Tom Adrahtas; along with *Philly Mag* profile of Parent by Richard Rhys (2007).

Stairway to Heaven: Books: *The Broad Street Bullies: The Incredible Story of the Philadelphia Flyers*; *Unmasked: Bernie Parent and the Broad Street Bullies*; and *Flyer Lives*. Magazines: *Newsweek*'s April 30, 1973 issue. Film: 2010 HBO documentary *Broad Street Bullies*; and *History of the Philadelphia Flyers, 40ᵗʰ anniversary edition* (2007). Film of the May 19, 1974 Philadelphia-Boston Stanley Cup game six final courtesy of Paul Patskou. Further references: Sam Carchidi, *Philadelphia Inquirer*, and Frank Seravalli, *Philadelphia Daily News*.

The Sack of Toronto: Film: 2010 HBO documentary, *Broad Street Bullies*; and *History of the Philadelphia Flyers, 40ᵗʰ anniversary edition* (2007). Game film of the April 15, 1976 Philadelphia-Toronto playoff game on both *Hockey Night in Canada* and WTFX-TV, Philadelphia, courtesy of Paul Patskou; and *The Simpsons*, "Halloween Treehouse of Horrors," 1993 episode. Magazines: December 23, 1974 and May 26, 1975 *Sports Illustrated* articles by Mark Mulvey. Toronto journalist Howard Berger's online piece "Study in Violence: Leafs vs. Flyers 1976" was particularly valuable. Further references: Frank Orr and Jim Proudfoot, *Toronto Star*, and Jack Chevalier, *Philadelphia Bulletin*.

"Tell It to the Czar": Film: 2010 HBO documentary, *Broad Street Bullies*; *History of the Philadelphia Flyers, 40ᵗʰ anniversary edition* (2007); the brilliant 2014 Gabe Polsky film, *Red Army*; and *Legend: Number 17*, a Russian biopic of Valery Kharlamov. *Hockey Night in Canada* game film of the January 11, 1976 Red Army-Philadelphia game courtesy of Paul Patskou. An Oct. 3, 2011 story on *TheHockeyGuys.net*, "Hockey's Coldest War, parts 1 and II," by Ed Gruyer, was particularly helpful. Books: *Tretiak, The Legend*, By Vladislav Tretiak. Further references: Tim Panaccio, *Philadelphia Inquirer*; Paul Patton, *The Globe and Mail*; June Callwood, *The Globe and Mail*; and James Ellingworth, *Moscow News*.

Ogie Ogilthorpe: Interviews with referees Ron Wicks and Bruce Hood. Books: *The Game*, by Ken Dryden; and *From Peanuts to the Press Box*, by

Eli Gold. Film: *Slap Shot*, the 1977 Paul Newman movie; *Hockey Night in Canada*'s game film of the Red Army-Philadelphia game courtesy of Paul Patskou. NBC's Bob Costas told his Goldie Goldthorpe story during the first intermission of the January 1, 2008 Winter Classic, a game featuring Buffalo and Pittsburgh. An extended interview with Ed Snider appeared on the C-Span 11 show *Book TV*. Further references: Alan Maki, *The Globe and Mail*; Ed Willes, *National Post*; Don Hammack, *The Biloxi Sun Herald*; Jim Proudfoot, *Toronto Star*; and Dick Beddoes, *The Globe and Mail*.

A Civil War: I lived in Quebec City for four months in 1973 as part of a student exchange program and attended several hockey games at Le Colisée. I interviewed Sam Pollock in 1993. Books: *Overtime: The Legend of Guy Lafleur*, the best book that will ever be written on Guy Lafleur, by Georges-Hébert Germain; *Lions in Winter*; *Triple Crown: The Marcel Dionne Story*, by Ted Mahovlich; *Duplessis*, by Conrad Black; and *Dick Beddoes' Greatest Hockey Stories*. Film: the 1971 feature, *Mon oncle Antoine*, by Claude Jutra; *Fire and Ice: The Rocket Richard Story*, a documentary by Brian McKenna; and a sixtieth anniversary reflection on the Richard Riot, by Stephen Brunt. I would also like to thank the very helpful ladies at the Ste. Catharines Public Library for splicing microfiche that allowed me to read Jack Gatecliff's account of the Ste. Catharines Blackhawks-Quebec Remparts 1971 series. Further references: Ronald King, *La Presse*; André Laurendeau, *Le Devoir*; and various Canadian Press articles in *Montreal Star*.

Harvest, Part One: Interview with Frank Selke Jr. in 2004. Books: *Lions in Winter*; *Overtime: The Legend of Guy Lafleur*; Trent Frayne's books, *Mad Men of Hockey*, *Famous Hockey Players* and *It's Easy: All You Have to Do Is Win*; and *Robinson for the Defence*, by Larry Robinson and Chrys Goyens. I was delighted to find the Joliat poem in super fan Dennis Kane's Habs-flavoured website, Dennis-Kane.com.

Harvest, Part Two: *Overtime: The Legend of Guy Lafleur.*

The Greatest Team Ever: Interview with Sam Pollock, 1993. Film: *Ken Dryden: The Legends of Hockey*; *Montreal Canadiens: 100 Years 100 Stars* (2009 CBC-TV special). Books: *Mario Tremblay: la bagarreur*, by Mathias Brunet; *Lions in Winter*; *The Habs*, by Dick Irvin. Further references: Red Fisher, *Montreal Gazette*; Paul Dupont, *The Boston Globe*; and Dan Shaughnessy, *The Boston Globe*.

Rain Man: Books: *Scotty Bowman: A Life in Hockey*, by Doug Hunter; *Go to the Net: Eight Goals That Changed the Game,* by Al Strachan. Further references: Mike Boone, *Montreal Gazette*; Bob Dubois, *Le Verdun Messager*; Jerry Sullivan, *Buffalo News*; Don Campbell, *Ottawa Citizen*; Al Strachan, *Montreal Gazette*; Gare Joyce, *The Globe and Mail*; and Jack Todd, *Montreal Gazette*.

Habs to the Rescue: Information on Bob Hope's *The Road to the Olympics*, from American Press (AP), Canadian Press (CP), *Montreal Star* and *TV Guide* stories. Film: *Hockey Night in Canada* game films of the Montreal-Philadelphia Stanley Cup finals courtesy of Paul Patskou; and *Il était une fois* (a 2009 documentary on Guy Lafleur). Books: *Overtime: The Legend of Guy Lafleur*; *The Habs*; *Robinson for the Defence*; *Who's Who in Hockey*, by Stan Fischler. Magazines: *Sports Illustrated*, May 24, 1976 cover story, "Montreal Stuns the Flyers." Brinks truck, Montreal robbery information, Steve Kowch, *Montreal Gazette*. Further references: Claude Larochelle, *Le Soleil*; Réjean Tremblay, *La Presse*; Gerald Eskenazi, *The New York Times*; Tim Burke, Dink Carroll, Al Strachan and Bob Morrissey, *Montreal Gazette*; Red Fisher and Wayne Parrish, *Montreal Star*. The website, *Flyershistory.com* was also very useful.

Do it Again: Film: Montreal-Boston *Hockey Night in Canada* and *Radio Canada* Stanley Cup final broadcasts courtesy of Paul Patskou; *Champions*, Donald Brittain's three-part documentary on the careers of political adversaries Pierre Elliott Trudeau and René Lévesque. Books: *Go to the Net: Eight Goals That Changed the Game*; and *The Game*. Music: The orange 1974 album, *Harmonium*, by Harmonium. Further references: Gare Joyce, *The Globe and Mail*; Tim Burke, Dink Carroll and Bob Morrissey, *Montreal Gazette*; Réjean Tremblay, *La Presse*; Red Fisher, *Montreal Star*; Kevin Paul Dupont, *The Boston Globe*.

Too Many Men on the Ice: Interviews with Dick Irvin, Ralph Mellanby and Don Cherry (the latter was done in 2002). Books: *Walking with Legends*, by Ralph Mellanby; *The Game*; *Overtime: The Legend of Guy Lafleur*; *Lions in Winter*; *The Habs*; and *Go to the Net: Eight Goals That Changed the Game*. Magazines: the wonderful May 9, 2014 *Sports Illustrated* story, "Too Many Men" by Michael Farber. Film: *Memorable Games in Canadien History* (Warner Bros. Home Video, 2008); and *Il était une fois*. Music: the 1979 disco album *Lafleur!* Further references: Tim Burke, Dink Carroll and Bob Morrissey, *Montreal Gazette*; Réjean Tremblay, *La Presse*; Red Fisher, *Montreal Star* and later, *Montreal Gazette*; William Houston, *The Globe and Mail*; Frank Orr, *Toronto Star*; Gerald Eskenazi, *The New York Times*; Kevin Paul Dupont, *Boston Globe*.

The Man That Got Away: Interview with Dick Irvin. Books: *My Life in Hockey*, by Jean Beliveau, with Chrys Goyens and Allan Turowetz; *Hockey, Heroes & Me*, by Red Fisher; *Behind the Cheering*, by Frank Selke. Further references: Rejean Tremblay, *La Presse*.

Rust Never Sleeps: Books: *Searching for Bobby Orr*; *Game Misconduct: Alan Eagleson and the Corruption of Hockey*, by Russ Conway; and *It Happened in Hockey*, by Brian McFarlane. Further references: Bob Hohler, *The Boston Globe*; Roy MacGregor, *The Globe and Mail*; and Russ Conway, *The Eagle-Tribune*. Thanks also to Ken Rockburn, Alison Gordon and Jennifer Fry.

IMAGE CREDITS

Part One: Two-Drink Minimum
Boston Bruins (1965–76)

    xviii–1. Zimmerman, John G. *Boston Bruins Bobby Orr*. 1970. *Sports Illustrated*. Courtesy of Getty Images, Sports Illustrated Collection.

Part Two: Clockwork Orange
Philadelphia Flyers (1969–76)

    132–133. *Montreal vs. Philadelphia*. 1974. Courtesy of the Associated Press.

Part Three: *Les Glorieux*
Montreal Canadiens (1932–79)

    228–229. Bennett, Bruce. *Montreal Canadiens* (Guy Lafleur). 1976. Courtesy of Getty Images.

Image Insert
1. *The Bobby Orr Story*. 1971–1972. The Topps Company, Inc. "The Bobby Orr Story" hockey booklet used courtesy of The Topps Company, Inc. For more information about The Topps Company, please see their website at www.topps.com.
2. Bettmann. *Bruins Celebrating on Ice*. 1970. Courtesy of Corbis Images, Bettmann Collection.
3 (top). *Flyers Luncheon*. 1976. Courtesy of the Philadelphia Flyers, L.P.
3 (middle). *Hamilton Workers Watch 1972 Canada-Russia Hockey Finale*. 1972. Courtesy of *The Hamilton Spectator*.
3 (bottom). TV stock image. © Bortn66 /Dreamstime.com.
3 (bottom, inset). Hanlon, John D. *1972 Summit Series—Game 3: Soviet Union v Canada*. 1972. *Sports Illustrated*. Courtesy of Getty Images, Sports Illustrated Collection.
4 (from top, left). *Bob Gainey*, 1975–76 (#278); *Brad Park*, 1971–72 (#40); *Juha Widing*, 1975–76 (#142); *Gary Unger*, 1974–75 (#237);

Henry Boucha, 1974–75 (#38); *Darryl Sittler*, 1973–74 (#132); *Rick Middleton*, 2001–02 (Archives series, #18); *Gary Smith*, 1974–75 (#22); *Wilf Paiement*, 1976–77 (#37). The Topps Company, Inc. Topps hockey cards used courtesy of The Topps Company, Inc. For more information about The Topps Company, please see their website at www.topps.com.

5 (top). Kluetmeier, Heinz. *Atlanta Flames vs Philadelphia Flyers*. 1974. *Sports Illustrated*. Courtesy of Getty Images, Sports Illustrated Collection.

5 (bottom). Fox, Robert L. *Philadelphia Flyers vs. Vancouver Canucks*. 1973. *Philadelphia Evening Bulletin*. Courtesy of Temple University Libraries, Special Collections Research Center, *Philadelphia Evening Bulletin* Collection, Philadelphia, PA.

6 (top). Raphael, Dick. *Boston Bruins vs Montreal Canadiens, 1977 NHL Stanley Cup Finals* (Scotty Bowman). 1977. *Sports Illustrated*. Courtesy of Getty Images, Sports Illustrated Collection.

6 (bottom). Brodeur, Denis. *Habs Win 1979 Stanley Cup*. 1979. Club de Hockey Canadiens, Inc. Courtesy of the Canadiens de Montréal.

7 (top). Brodeur, Denis. *Canada Cup: Canada v Czechoslovakia* (Bobby Orr). 1976. NHLI. Courtesy of Getty Images, NHLI Collection.

7 (bottom). *Lapointe and Lambert at 1976 Stanley Cup Parade*. 1976. Club de Hockey Canadiens, Inc. Courtesy of the Canadiens de Montréal.

7 (bottom, inset). *Wild and Crazy Guys*. c.1978. NBC Television/Handout. Courtesy of Getty Images, Archive Photos.

8 (top). O'Brien, Frank. *Derek Sanderson, Bobby Orr, Phil Esposito*. 1970. *The Boston Globe*. Courtesy of Getty Images, Boston Globe Collection.

8 (middle). Kennedy, Rusty. *Flyers Celebrate 1976*. 1976. Courtesy of the Associated Press.

8 (bottom). Ball, Doug. *Montreal Canadiens Guy Lafleur acknowledges a standing ovation after marking his 1,000th NHL point against the Winnipeg Jets, Montreal, Que., March 4, 1981*. 1981. Courtesy of the Canadian Press.

INDEX